Making Precious
Things Plain

A Book of Mormon Study Guide

Randal S. Chase, Ph.D.

Making Precious Things Plain

A Book of Mormon Study Guide

Volume 2
Alma 17–3 Nephi 7

Randal S. Chase, Ph.D.

CFI
Springville, Utah

ISBN 13: 978-1-59955-130-2

Published by CFI, an imprint of Cedar Fort, Inc., 2373 W. 700 S., Springville, UT, 84663
Distributed by Cedar Fort, Inc. www.cedarfort.com

LIBRARY OF CONGRESS CATALOGING-IN-PUBLICATION DATA

Chase, Randal S., 1949-
Making precious things plain : a book of mormon study guide
/ Randal S. Chase.
p. cm.
Includes bibliographical references and index.
ISBN 978-1-59955-130-2 (alk. paper)
1. Book of Mormon—Criticism, interpretation, etc. I. Title.

BX8627.C43 2007
289.3'22—dc22
                                        2007030428

Cover design by Nicole Williams
Cover design © 2008 by Lyle Mortimer
Edited and typeset by Lyndsee Simpson Cordes

Printed in the United States of America

10 9 8 7 6 5 4 3 2 1

Printed on acid-free paper

Table of Contents

"They Taught with Power and Authority of God"

ALMA 17–22

The Missions of the Sons of Mosiah

During the fourteen years between 91 and 77 BC, Alma served as chief judge. He resigned in order to devote more time to the ministry. During that same period of time, the sons of Mosiah went and taught the Lamanites (Mosiah 27:34–37). Their experiences provide some of the greatest examples of missionary service in the scriptures. The record tells how they became instruments in the hands of God in bringing the Lamanites to a knowledge of the truth (Mosiah 28:1–9).

Carlos E. Asay said,

> Not too long ago, I heard the testimony of a new convert—a young man obviously touched by the Spirit. Among other things, he indicated that it was his great desire to share the restored gospel with his family and friends. With tears in his eyes and a quiver in his voice, he said, "I want them to know what I know, I want them to feel what I feel, [and] I want them to do what I have done." There is a missionary spirit—a spirit which urges us to live outside ourselves and to be concerned for the welfare of others. And anyone who has ever served an honorable mission, assisted in the conversion of a friend, supported a son or daughter in the mission field, or enjoyed close associations with missionaries will testify of its reality.[1]

After the sons of Mosiah were converted, they felt a great desire to share the gospel with others. Once among the vilest of sinners, and having been brought back from the precipice of hell, it was unbearable for them to think of any soul tumbling over that edge into the abyss of darkness reserved for the damned. They asked themselves how they could help others avoid this fate. Their answer was to go and share the gospel with the Lamanites, their most feared and fierce enemies. The equivalent today would be for a American to request a mission to teach terrorists in the mountainous western borders of Pakistan, who are committed to his country's utter destruction. It was a stunning request, and there is little wonder that King Mosiah was reluctant to allow it.

Can we even imagine the concern of a parent who is sending his sons into the "belly of the beast"—their terrorizing and brutal enemies, the Lamanites? Mosiah was deeply troubled by it and sought reassurances from the Lord. And he received them. He was promised that they would be an instrument in the Lord's hands for great good, and that they would return safely (Mosiah 28:6–7). For many years thereafter, this promise sustained and reassured Mosiah's sons through life-threatening situations. And King Mosiah was sufficiently reassured that he never assumed that his sons were dead even when they didn't return for many years.

These converted young men knew from personal experience that even the vilest and most violent enemies of God can be saved, because they themselves had been so saved. They wanted the Lamanites to know what they knew, to feel what they felt, and to do what they themselves had done—repent and be redeemed.

A Mission to the Lamanites
(ALMA 17)

THEIR QUALIFICATIONS FOR MISSIONARY WORK

Alma 17:1–4 • As Alma travels to Manti, he meets the sons of King Mosiah, who are returning from their fourteen-year mission to the Lamanites. Alma rejoiced in his unexpected reunion with his friends because "they had waxed strong in the knowledge of the truth." This reunion of faithful friends reminds us of the joy that returned missionaries feel when they are reunited with their high school friends after they have all served faithful missions. They are men now—men of strength and maturity and testimony. There are few things in the world more satisfying than such reunions.

The sons of Mosiah were powerful and effective teachers. They had excellent qualifications to serve as missionaries, including all of the following:

▷ A great desire to serve. Those who have a desire to serve are called (D&C 4:3).
▷ Love for others. They "could not bear that any human soul should perish" (Mosiah 28:3) because they had personally experienced the pain of alienation from God.
▷ Strong testimonies of the gospel and of the truthfulness of the message they taught.
▷ The ability to teach with power and authority of God. To teach with power means to have the Holy Ghost bear record that your teachings are true. When this occurs, both the missionaries and those they teach feel the same powerful witness and their faith and testimonies are increased.
▷ Knowledge of the scriptures gained by searching diligently "that they might know the word of God" (Alma 17:2).
▷ A testimony of Jesus Christ ("the spirit of prophecy") obtained through much fasting and prayer (Alma 17:3).

Alma 17:5 • Like most missionaries, the sons of Mosiah leave for their mission with great enthusiasm, some anxiety, but plenty of confidence that God would give them great success. They did not know the level of pain, challenges, and difficulties that awaited them. But they wanted to serve and were convinced they could bring many Lamanite souls unto the Savior, who had so recently redeemed them and their friend Alma the Younger.

Alma 17:5–6 • The sons of Mosiah make many sacrifices they perform their missionary work. They left behind their comfortable home and the honors that both their father and the people wanted to confer upon them as successors on the throne (v. 6). In contrast to such honors and comforts, their missions were difficult in just about every imaginable way. They had to face and overcome "many afflictions . . . both in body and in mind, such as hunger, thirst and fatigue, and also much labor in the spirit" (v. 5). Just getting to the land of Nephi on foot would have tried their faith and devotion. And it didn't get easier once they got there. The Lord tested their will with adversity.

These circumstances remind me of a story told by J. Golden Kimball about missionaries who experience difficulty while serving: "That is what I am telling our elders, these young boys going on missions. I am trying, when I set them apart, to impress them that the Lord is their shepherd and they shall not want. One good mother stated that her son wrote her and said, 'I have only three dollars, and if you do not send me some money I will be licking the paste off the signboards.' And the mother came to me somewhat disturbed and said, 'Brother Kimball, what shall I do?' I said, 'Let him lick paste for a while. He will find the Lord. But he never will with his pockets full of money.'"[2]

Known as somewhat of a maverick, and often the central character of irreverent Latter-day Saint urban legends, J. Golden Kimball was also a deeply spiritual man who understood adversity, who loved the Lord, and who knew that he was loved:

> I acknowledge that I am imperfect, and no one is more sorry than I am. I have made mistakes, but I have faith in God, and I know God will forgive a man who repents. I have no fancied notions; I have gotten rid of tradition and of a few false ideas that rested upon me. I do not expect to become a god right away. No, it will take a long time; I am too ignorant. I have been surprised that I was chosen [as a General Authority], but there will come another time of choosing, and I don't know whether I will be among the number then or not. You don't know either. Now I am speaking of myself; I am not criticizing others; I am talking about principles. I stand before you a transgressor, but I am trying to be saved, and that is all God asks me to do. I am a man of weakness; I am a man full of faults; but God knows I have given him the best effort there was in me.[3]

Alma 17:9–12, 16 • Mosiah's sons' motivation for serving their missions is charity—pure love of the kind that Christ manifested. They were not serving out of a sense of cultural necessity or out of fear. They were serving out of pure love for the Lamanites and for God (v. 16; see also Mosiah 28:1–3).

The Prophet Joseph Smith said, "Love is one of the chief characteristics of Deity, and ought to be manifested by those who aspire to be the sons of God. A man filled with the love of God, is not content with blessing his family alone, but ranges through the whole world, anxious to bless the whole human race."[4]

Through all of their difficulties, the sons of Mosiah received comfort and counsel from the Lord. He visited and comforted them with his Spirit (v. 10). He counseled them to press forward despite their challenges and to "be patient in long-suffering and afflictions, that ye may show forth good examples unto them in me" (v. 11). He promised that if they would do this, "I will make an instrument of thee in my hands unto the salvation of many souls" (v. 11). Thus encouraged, they took courage to carry on.

One important side note of these verses is the statement that the "sons of Mosiah, and also those who were with them" took courage (v. 12). We thus know that there were other missionaries with them, though they remain nameless in the record.

MISSIONARY WORK AMONG THE LAMANITES WAS DIFFICULT

Alma 17:13–14 • The spiritual condition of the Lamanites. In earlier writings, Nephi said the Lamanites were "an idle people, full of mischief and subtlety" (2 Nephi 5:24). Enos said they were "a wild, and a ferocious, and a bloodthirsty people, full of idolatry and filthiness" (Enos 1:20).

And Jarom said they "loved murder and would drink the blood of beasts" (Jarom 1:6). Thus, it was no exaggeration when Mormon said concerning their missions that the work "was great, for they had undertaken to preach the word of God to a wild and a hardened and a ferocious people" (v. 14).

Mosiah 10:11–17 • Parental teaching can determine whether or not children will hear and understand the truth. King Zeniff, whose people once lived in the very area where the sons of Mosiah were coming to teach, said, "The Lamanites knew nothing concerning the Lord, nor the strength of the Lord, therefore they depended upon their own strength. Yet they were a strong people, as to the strength of men. They were a wild, and ferocious, and a blood-thirsty people, believing in the tradition of their fathers, which is this—Believing that they were driven out of the land of Jerusalem because of the iniquities of their fathers, and that they were wronged in the wilderness by their brethren, and they were also wronged while crossing the sea; And again, that they were wronged while in the land of their first inheritance" (vv. 11–13). Even though five hundred years had passed since the time of Laman and Lemuel, the Lamanites were still filled with their ancient parents' sense of anger and frustration.

For all of these reasons,

> his brethren were wroth with him because they understood not the dealings of the Lord; they were also wroth with him upon the waters because they hardened their hearts against the Lord.
> And again, they were wroth with him when they had arrived in the promised land, because they said that he had taken the ruling of the people out of their hands; and they sought to kill him.
> And again, they were wroth with him because he departed into the wilderness as the Lord had commanded him, and took the records which were engraven on the plates of brass, for they said that he robbed them. And thus they have taught their children that they should hate them, and that they should murder them, and that they should rob and plunder them, and do all they could to destroy them; therefore they have an eternal hatred towards the children of Nephi. (vv. 14–17)

From this we can also see why parents are accountable for the understanding their children receive (D&C 93:40–42). The effects of their attitudes and teachings can last for generations. A common saying among the Jews in the days of Lehi and Jeremiah expressed it this way: "The fathers have eaten a sour grape, and the children's teeth are set on edge" (Jeremiah 31:29). Little wonder that Nephi was anxious that his posterity know of Christ and his plan for them (2 Nephi 25:26). He knew it was their only hope for avoiding destruction in this world and obtaining salvation in the world to come.

The parallels between the circumstances of the Lamanites in the days of the sons of Mosiah and present-day Middle Eastern terrorists are very clear. Much of the hatred and violence exhibited toward the West today by Muslim terrorists goes back for centuries to the times of the Christian crusaders who invaded their homelands with the avowed purpose of wiping them out. For centuries, from one generation to another, their children and their children's children have been taught to hate and to seek to eradicate their enemies. Wars and weapons will never eradicate such traditions. Only a correct understanding of the plan of salvation, the eternal brotherhood of man, and the infinite atonement of Jesus Christ can bring peace.

David O. McKay observed, "No peace, even though temporarily obtained, will be permanent unless it is built upon the solid foundation of eternal principles. The first of these [is] . . . when we sincerely accept God as our Father and make Him the center of our being. . . . Of equal importance is the acceptance of the Son of God as the Savior of mankind. . . . Men may yearn for peace, cry for peace, and work for peace, but there will be no peace until they follow the path pointed out by the living Christ."[5]

When placed into this context, we can understand the immense value of the mission of the sons of Mosiah among the Lamanites. As we shall see, they did indeed eradicate hatred and establish peace for awhile. Knowing this, I have frequently reflected on the fact that our missionaries are the greatest ambassadors for world peace that live on this planet. No amount of diplomacy or warfare can turn swords into plowshares. Only faithful missionaries can do that—in our own time as well as in the Book of Mormon.

Ammon Teaches King Lamoni
(ALMA 17–18)

FIRST A SERVANT, THEN A TEACHER

A young woman from Seoul, Korea, who participated in the Young Women worldwide balloon lift in October of 1986, attached this message to a helium balloon: "Live so that those who know you but don't know Him, will want to know Him because they know you."[6] This is a beautiful way to summarize the missionary methods of Ammon.

Alma 17:17–19 • Once they arrive in the land of Nephi, the missionaries "separate . . . themselves one from another. They went forth among them [the Lamanites], every man alone, according to the word and power of God which was given unto him" (v. 17). Ammon was their leader, and prior to their departure he "blessed them according to their several stations" and "imparted the word of God unto them" (v. 18). Ammon himself "went to the land of Ishmael, the land being called after the sons of Ishmael, who also became Lamanites" (v. 19).

Alma 17:20–21 • Ammon is captured immediately by the Lamanites. "And Ammon entered the land of Ishmael, the Lamanites took him and abound him, as was their custom to bind all the Nephites who fell into their hands" (v. 20). According to their custom, such captives were taken before the king, who could choose according to his whim and pleasure whether to slay them or cast them out of their lands (v. 20). "And thus Ammon was carried before the king who was over the land of Ishmael; and his name was Lamoni; and he was a descendant of Ishmael" (v. 21).

Alma 17:22–25 • Alma wins his freedom through faith and willingness to serve others. The Lamanite king asked Ammon if he wanted to dwell in the land among the Lamanites (v. 22). Over the years, there had been many Nephite deserters who had rebelled against God and sought to join the Lamanites. Perhaps the king thought Ammon was one of these. "And Ammon said unto him: Yea, I desire to dwell among this people for a time; yea, and perhaps until the day I die" (v. 23). This pleased King Lamoni. He not only freed Ammon immediately but also wanted him to "take one of his daughters to wife" (v. 24).

The irony of this is interesting and reveals much about the character and personal motives of Ammon. Had he remained at home, he might even now have been crowned the new king of the Nephites. He was, after all, the rightful heir. Now he is being offered the opportunity to marry into the royal family of these Lamanites, perhaps ascending to their throne at some point. Wouldn't it have been nifty if he were crowned king of the Lamanites and then returned home to

Zarahemla to assume his rightful place as their king? Surely this would bring peace. Many such treaties of peace have been made and maintained in Europe over the centuries precisely through such marriages. But this was not Ammon's desire nor his chosen method. He said to the Lamanite king, "Nay, but I will be thy servant," and "he was set among other servants to watch the flocks of Lamoni" (v. 25).

In missionary work, it is a trite but true statement that "people don't care how much you know until they know how much you care." Ammon did not jump up on a rock and call upon the Lamanites to change their evil ways. Nor did he marry into the royal family and seek to establish the Church by royal decree. Instead he sought first to serve them—to win their love and their trust—so that eventually he might have the opportunity to teach and testify. This was the Lord's way, and Ammon was careful to do things in no other way.

Ezra Taft Benson said,

> It was while I was on my first mission that I discovered the constant need for dependence on the Lord. I learned through experience that I could not convince another soul to come unto Christ. I learned that one cannot convert another by just quoting scripture. Conversion comes when another is touched by the Spirit of the Lord and receives a witness, independent of the missionary, that what he or she is being taught is true.
>
> I learned that a missionary is only a vessel through whom the Lord can transmit His Spirit. To acquire that Spirit, a missionary must humble himself in prayer and ask our Heavenly Father to use him to touch the hearts of investigators. The first lesson of missionary work is to be dependent on the Lord for our success. We must develop an attitude that it doesn't matter where we serve, but how.[7]

Alma 17:26–39 • Ammon wins the hearts of his Lamanite guards by protecting the king's flocks from marauding thieves. It didn't take long for the Lord to create an opportunity for Ammon. "And after he had been in the service of the king three days, as he was with the Lamanitish servants going forth with their flocks to the place of water . . . behold, a certain number of the Lamanites . . . stood and scattered the flocks of Ammon and the servants of the king, and . . . they fled many ways" (vv. 26–27). This was a serious situation and the king's servants began to murmur and to weep, fearing the king would kill them for losing his flocks (vv. 28–29). He had done it before (Alma 18:6–7).

In contrast, Ammon was filled with joy over the opportunity that the situation presented to him. He knew that if he could solve this problem for them, they would both love and trust him and would therefore believe his teachings (vv. 29–30). He said to them, "My brethren, be of good cheer and let us go in search of the flocks, and we will gather them together and bring them back unto the place of water; and thus we will preserve the flocks unto the king and he will not slay us" (v. 31). They followed Ammon in immediately taking action to round up the scattered sheep and return them to the watering place (v. 32).

At this point the thieves returned, intending to again scatter the sheep (v. 33). Taking up his sword, Ammon instructed the king's servants to guard the sheep and stepped forward to contend with them, "and they were in number not a few" (v. 34). This was laughable to them, that one man should think he could defeat them, "for they supposed that one of their men could slay him according to their pleasure" (v. 35). But Ammon had been promised before departing for his mission that the Lord would protect his life and bring him home safely to his father. With absolute faith in this promise, he was fearless. He knew that God would make him equal to the task before him.

Reflecting on such faith, Neal A. Maxwell said, "God does not begin by asking us about our ability, but only about our availability, and if we then prove our dependability, he will increase our capability."[8]

Ammon "stood forth and began to cast stones at them with his sling; yea, with mighty power he did sling stones amongst them; and thus he slew a certain number of them insomuch that they began to be astonished at his power; nevertheless they were angry because of the slain of their brethren, and they were determined that he should fall; therefore, seeing that they could not hit him with their stones, they came forth with clubs to slay him" (v. 36).

As each man came forward with his club to kill Ammon, he "smote off their arms with his sword" (v. 37). Now completely astonished at his power over them, they began to flee. He had killed six of them with his sling and had killed their leader with his sword, and "he smote off as many of their arms as were lifted against him, and they were not a few" (v. 38). Returning to the watering place, he and the king's servants "watered their flocks and returned them to the pasture of the king" (v. 39). Ammon then returned and reported to the king, "bearing arms" so to speak, as he carried the arms of his wounded opponents "in unto the king for a testimony of the things which they had done" (v. 39).

Alma 18:1–5 • The king and his servants believe Ammon is "the Great Spirit." After hearing his servants' report of what Ammon had done, King Lamoni said, "Surely, this is more than a man. Behold, is not this the Great Spirit who doth send such great punishments upon this people, because of their murders?" (v. 2). Note that he knew full well that God was not pleased with his people. Traditions and myths notwithstanding, the light of Christ had certainly whispered to them that their bloodthirsty ways were evil.

The king's servants replied, "Whether he be the Great Spirit or a man, we know not; but this much we do know, that he cannot be slain by the enemies of the king; neither can they scatter the king's flocks when he is with us, because of his expertness and great strength" and "we do not believe that a man has such great power" (v. 3). They also observed that he was a friend to the king, who concludes from it all that "this is the Great Spirit of whom our fathers have spoken" (v. 4).

This tradition of a "Great Spirit" had been passed down to the king from his father. And even though "they believed in a Great Spirit, they supposed that whatsoever they did was right; nevertheless, Lamoni began to fear exceedingly, with fear lest he had done wrong in slaying his servants" (v. 5). This is the same guilty conscience he manifested in verse 2.

Alma 18:8–11 • Ammon keeps humbly serving rather than basking in his success. Having delivered the pile of arms to the king, Ammon did not remain there but went immediately to water the king's horses (v. 8). They king had previously commanded (prior to the incident with the flocks) for his servants to prepare his horses for a journey he would be taking to a great feast being thrown by his father, who was the king of all the Lamanites (v. 9). Ammon had not forgotten this command, and he dutifully turned to the task immediately upon his return. This king marveled at his faithfulness, saying, "Surely there has not been any servant among all my servants that has been so faithful as this man; for even he doth remember all my commandments to execute them" (v. 10). He wanted to call Ammon unto him but feared giving him any commandments because he believed he was the Great Spirit (v. 11).

Daniel H. Ludlow notes that critics of the Book of Mormon used to claim that the mention of horses and wheels in verse 9 proved the book to be false. "These critics have maintained: (1) no horses existed on the American continents before the time of Columbus, and (2) the people who lived on the American continents did not know the principle of the wheel before the coming of Columbus. However, since the publication of the Book of Mormon, considerable archaeological evidence has come forth to reinforce its claims that there were horses on the American continents before the time of Columbus and that these early peoples did know the principle of the wheel."[9]

Alma 18:12–17 • The king and his servants fear Ammon, but he perceives their thoughts and sets them at ease. After making the king's horses ready, Ammon went in unto him, but noticing that the king's countenance had changed "he was about to return out of his presence" (v. 12). Before he could do so, "one of the king's servants said unto him, Rabbanah, which is, being interpreted, powerful or great king . . . the king desireth thee to stay" (v. 13).

This title of respect for Ammon has a Semitic connection. The Lamanite word *Rabbanah* meant "powerful or great king," and many Semitic words have essentially the same meaning. In the New Testament, respected leaders were called rabboni (John 20:16), and the Jewish word *rabbi* meant "one who teaches or leads."

Daniel H. Ludlow said about Hebrew in the New World, "That the spoken language of both the Nephites and the Lamanites is derived from the Hebrew is made quite clear in several places in the Book of Mormon. In fact, even as late as the fourth century AD one Book of Mormon prophet said, '. . . if our plates had been sufficiently large we should have written in Hebrew' (Mormon 9:33)."[10]

Ammon respectfully responded, "What wilt thou that I should do for thee, O king? And the king answered him not for the space of an hour, according to their time, for he knew not what he should say unto him" (v. 14). He asked again, "What desirest thou of me? But the king answered him not" (v. 15). At first, we might find this prolonged silence strange, but we should also asked ourselves, "What would I do if I found myself unexpectedly standing before my God (or thought I was doing so)? Would we be silent, overwhelmed at the experience, or even fearful? This is the circumstance that King Lamoni found himself in at this moment.

By the power of the Spirit, Ammon "perceived the thoughts of the king. And he said unto him: Is it because thou hast heard that I defended thy servants and thy flocks, and slew seven of their brethren with the sling and with the sword, and smote off the arms of others, in order to defend thy flocks and thy servants; behold, is it this that causeth thy marvelings?" (v. 16). This was precisely why the king feared him, but Ammon put him at ease, saying, "Behold, I am a man, and am thy servant; therefore, whatsoever thou desirest which is right, that will I do" (v. 17). This astonished the king even more, that Ammon could discern his thoughts, but he finally summoned the courage to ask, "Who art thou? Art thou that Great Spirit, who knows all things? Ammon answered and said unto him: I am not" (vv. 18–19).

Alma 18:18–23 • Sufficiently impressed and humbled, the king promises to listen to the message of Ammon. The king not only wondered how Ammon could read his thoughts, but also by what power he had defeated those who had sought to scatter his flocks (v. 20). He promised Ammon, if he would disclose his source of power, that he would give him anything he desired (v. 21). This was the teaching opportunity Ammon had been seeking, and he did not waste it. "Now Ammon being wise, yet harmless, he said unto Lamoni: Wilt thou hearken unto my words, if I tell thee by what power I do these things? And this is the thing that I desire of thee" (v. 22). Lamoni said, "Yea, I will believe all thy words. And thus he was caught with guile" (v. 23).

The word *guile*, as used here, is an interesting one. Daniel H. Ludlow observes, "Although the word guile is frequently used to mean 'deceitful cunning' or 'treachery,' it can also denote the use of strategy. It is evidently used in the latter sense in Alma 18:23; in other words, Ammon planned or used strategy in arranging the questions he asked King Lamoni."[11] Ammon had a plan from the beginning to win the hearts of the Lamanites so that he could save their souls. He was not just "lucky" or even unexpectedly "blessed." He had a plan, and the Lord helped him accomplish it. It was a gentle and, at the same time, wise approach, consistent with the Lord's advice to his missionary disciples in Judea: "Behold, I send you forth as sheep in the midst of wolves: be ye therefore wise as serpents, and harmless as doves" (Matthew 10:16).

Teaching the First Principles with Simplicity

Ammon had also carefully considered the order of his teachings to the king. It was not haphazard or random. In fact, it was so effective that the missionary discussions used for decades by our missionaries throughout the world were originally developed using Ammon's methods as a model. He used a careful sequence that led the king from point to point until he had a full understanding of the basic saving principles of the gospel. These were, in order:

▷ Our relationship to God
▷ The creation and fall of Adam and Eve
▷ God's dealings with his children through prophets
▷ The history of the Lamanites and Nephites
▷ The plan of redemption
▷ The coming of Jesus Christ

It is also important to note that Ammon taught from the scriptures (Alma 18:36, 38). As a people, the Lamanites had been largely ignorant of the scriptures, which presented a quite different view of things than the traditions of their fathers under which they had lived for centuries.

Alma 18:24–35 • Our relationship to God. Ammon began with the fundamental fact that there is a God in heaven who created all things—including ourselves, his children (vv. 24–29). Ammon knew that the king believed in a Great Spirit, and he started from that point in leading him along to a knowledge of the truth. As Bruce R. McConkie noted, "According to Lamanite traditions, God is the Great Spirit. It is obvious that by this designation the Lamanites had in mind a personal being, for King Lamoni mistakenly supposed that Ammon was the Great Spirit (Alma 18:2–28; 19:25–27). Both Ammon and Aaron, using the same principle [used] by Paul on Mars Hill (Acts 17:22–31), [used this belief to teach] that the Great Spirit was the God who created the heavens and the earth. (Alma 18:8–29; 22:8–11)."[12] Ammon further taught the king that God dwells in heaven with his angels (vv. 30–33).

Ammon next explained his own (and the king's) relationship to God. He said, "I am a man; and man in the beginning was created after the image of God, and I am called by his Holy Spirit to teach these things unto this people, that they may be brought to a knowledge of that which is just and true" (v. 34). The marvelous abilities the king had observed in him were because "of that Spirit [which] dwelleth in me, which giveth me knowledge, and also power according to my faith and desires which are in God" (v. 35).

Alma 18:34–36 • The creation, the fall, and the history of God's dealings with man. Ammon then proceeded to rehearse the history of God's dealings with his children. "He began at the creation of the world, and also the creation of Adam, and told him all the things concerning the fall of man, and rehearsed and laid before him the records and the holy scriptures of the people, which had been spoken by the prophets, even down to the time that their father, Lehi, left Jerusalem" (vv. 34–36).

Alma 18:37–38 • The history of the Lamanites from Laman and Lemuel until then. Ammon explained how the Nephites and Lamanites fit into the overall picture of the earth's history and purpose. He "rehearsed unto them . . . all the journeyings of their fathers in the wilderness, and all their sufferings with hunger and thirst, and their travail. . . . And he also rehearsed unto them concerning the rebellions of Laman and Lemuel, and the sons of Ishmael . . . and he expounded unto them all the records and scriptures from the time that Lehi left Jerusalem down to the present time" (vv. 37–38). This may have been the first time that Lamoni and his people had heard "the other side of the story" of Nephi's dealings with Laman and Lemuel. Up to this point, they knew only what the traditions of their fathers had told them. Now they knew the truth.

Alma 18:39 • The plan of redemption and the coming of Jesus Christ. And finally, Ammon "expounded unto them the plan of redemption, which was prepared from the foundation of the world; and he also made known unto them concerning the coming of Christ, and all the works of the Lord did he make known unto them" (v. 39). This was the crowning principle—the one that gives meaning and purpose to everything else and the one that offers hope to all of God's children, including the Lamanites.

Bruce R. McConkie said that the Creation, the Fall, and the Atonement are "the three pillars of eternity" and the "greatest events that have ever occurred in all eternity." He went on to say, "If we can gain an understanding of them, then the whole eternal scheme of things will fall into place, and we will be in a position to work out our own salvation. . . . These three are the foundations upon which all things rest. Without any one of them all things would lose their purpose and meaning and the plans and designs of Deity would come to naught."[13]

The logic of Ammon's teaching method is impressive. But the real power of conversion came through the Spirit. Ammon was sensitive to the promptings of the Spirit and followed them with exactness. And when he bore witness of these things, it penetrated beyond the king's intellectual understanding to the center of his soul. Missionaries teach, but only the Spirit converts.

Brigham Young said,

> Let one go forth who is careful to prove logically all he says by numerous quotations from the revelations, and let another travel with him who can say, by the power of the Holy Ghost, Thus saith the Lord, and tell what the people should believe— what they should do—how they should live, and teach them to yield to the principles of salvation—though he may not be capable of producing a single logical argument, though he may tremble under a sense of his weakness, cleaving to the Lord for strength, as such men generally do, you will invariably find that the man who testifies by the power of the Holy Ghost will convince and gather many more of the honest and upright than will the merely logical reasoner.[14]

The Results of King Lamoni's Conversion
(Alma 19–20)

A Lot of Falling Down

Alma 18:40–42 • King Lamoni is deeply touched, seeks forgiveness, and faints. Believing what Ammon had taught him, the king "began to cry unto the Lord, saying: O Lord, have mercy; according to thy abundant mercy which thou hast had upon the people of Nephi, have upon me, and my people" (vv. 40–41). And then "he fell unto the earth, as if he were dead" (v. 42).

This kind of spiritual exhaustion or trance was not entirely new. There are several examples in the Book of Mormon of people so overcome by the spirit that it overcame their natural bodies. At the time the angel appeared unto Alma and the sons of Mosiah to call them to repentance, Alma became weak and could not speak nor move for three days (Mosiah 27, Alma 36). And upon realizing his responsibility for the burning alive of many righteous women and children in Ammonihah, Zeezrom became weak and was confined to bed with a burning fever (Alma 11–12, 15).

Alma 19:6 • Ammon understands from personal experience what is happening. "He knew that King Lamoni was under the power of God; he knew that the dark veil of unbelief was being cast away from his mind, and the light which did light up his mind . . . was the light of the glory of God." He knew this because he and his brothers, along with Alma, had been there himself, on the verge of destruction and physically overcome while their souls were being purged of wickedness. He knew from experience that the Spirit of the Lord may have a very dramatic effect on those who have been especially wicked. "This light had infused such joy into his soul, the cloud of darkness having been dispelled, and that the light of everlasting life was lit up in his soul, yea, he knew that this had overcome his natural frame, and he was carried away in God."

Alma 19:1–5, 7–11 • The queen shows her great faith. After the king had lain motionless for two days and two nights, his wife and servants assumed he was dead and were about to take him to a sepulcher for burial (v. 1). Before doing so, "the queen having heard of the fame of Ammon . . . sent and desired that he should come in unto her. . . . Ammon did as he was commanded, and went in unto the queen, and desired to know what she would that he should do" (vv. 2–3). She expressed her faith in his priesthood power and requested that he go in and see her husband (vv. 4–5). A debate had ensued among those around the king, some saying, "He is not dead" and others saying, "He is dead and . . . he stinketh, and . . . he ought to be placed in the sepulchre" (v. 5). Apparently, in that day, one of the few ways one could be sure that a man was dead was if his body started to decompose. The queen said, "as for myself, to me he doth not stink" (v. 5).

Ammon wanted only to be helpful to her and went in to investigate the king's condition. He found that he was not dead and told the queen, "He sleepeth in God, and on the morrow he shall rise again; therefore bury him not" (vv. 6–8). When he asked if she believed him, she expressed her faith that "it shall be according as thou hast said" (v. 9). He blessed her for her faith, observing that "there has not been such great faith among all the people of the Nephites" (v. 10)—a sad commentary on the faithless state of Ammon's own people. The queen watched continually over her husband's body throughout the night and into the next day, when she knew that he would awake from his coma and arise (v. 11).

Alma 19:12–13 • The king revives and bears witness of Christ. At the promised hour the next day, the king "arose, . . . stretched forth his hand unto the woman, and said, Blessed be the name of God, and blessed art thou. For as sure as thou livest, behold, I have seen my Redeemer" (vv. 12–13). This man, once the sovereign over a wicked and degenerate people, was now a personal witness of the Lord Jesus Christ. He went on to testify that "he shall come forth, and be born of a woman, and he shall redeem all mankind who believe on his name" (v. 13). Overcome with joy, both the king and his queen sunk down with joy (presumably to their knees), "being overpowered by the Spirit" (v. 13).

Alma 19:14 • All three are so overcome that they fall again to the earth. Ammon, observing this wonderful scene, was also overcome with joy. His prayers were being answered right before his eyes; "the Lamanites, his brethren, who had been the cause of so much mourning among the Nephites, or among all the people of God because of their iniquities and their traditions" were now changed. "He fell upon his knees, and began to pour out his soul in prayer and thanksgiving to God for what he had done for his brethren; and he was also overpowered with joy; and thus they all three had sunk to the earth."

Alma 19:15–16 • The servants are also overcome by the Spirit and fall to the earth. The king's servants who stood around this scene "also began to cry unto God, for the fear of the Lord had come upon them also" (v. 15). We can well imagine why. People are falling down all around them, overcome with the Spirit, which must have been a powerful presence in the room where they stood. "And it came to pass that they did call on the name of the Lord, in their might, even until they had all fallen to the earth" (v. 16).

Alma 19:17 • Abish, the Lamanite Woman. The only one who did not faint was "one of the Lamanitish women, whose name was Abish, she having been converted unto the Lord for many years, on account of a remarkable vision of her father" (v. 16). Daniel H. Ludlow said,

> If for no other reason, Abish, the Lamanitish woman, is distinguished because her actual name appears in the Book of Mormon. She is one of only three women in the entire Nephite-Lamanite-Mulekite-Jaredite records to have her name in the Book of Mormon. The other two are Sariah, the wife of Lehi (1 Nephi 2:5), and Isabel, the harlot (Alma 39:3).
>
> The brief account of the conversion of Abish is not clear. The statement that Abish had been converted 'unto the Lord for many years, on account of a remarkable vision of her father' (Alma 19:16) may have two possible interpretations. One interpretation is that Abish herself had this vision and in her vision she saw her father. Another possible interpretation is that the vision was actually had by the father of Abish. Regardless of which interpretation is correct, this conversion of Abish plays an important role in converting large numbers of Lamanites.[15]

Alma 19:18–21 • Others who were not present have a variety of reactions. Some murmured and accused Ammon (a Nephite) of murder (vv. 18–19). Some said the king was evil and brought this upon himself (v. 20). And some of the one-armed thieves from the incident at the water place of Sebus sought revenge against Ammon (v. 21). We can be somewhat sympathetic with their confusion because, after all, they were not present when all this happened, and all they knew was that the king and queen and their servants were lying comatose on the floor, next to the body of Ammon. How to explain it? They could only conjecture, and of course their conjecturing were largely self-serving—fitting in nicely with their own prejudices and suspicions.

Alma 19:22–23 • Ammon, though helplessly comatose, is divinely protected from his

enemies. One of the thieves from the incident at the waters of Sebus, presumably the brother of their gang's leader (who was the only one who had been slain by Ammon with the sword), stepped forward to take his revenge on Ammon. But "as he lifted the sword to smite him, behold, he fell dead" (v. 22). Here we see the exactness with which the Lord keeps his promises. Mormon (who is summarizing this event for us) observes, "Now we see that Ammon could not be slain, for the Lord had said unto Mosiah, his father: I will spare him, and it shall be unto him according to thy faith—therefore, Mosiah trusted him unto the Lord" (v. 23).

Alma 19:24–27 • Seeing the miraculous sparing of Ammon, the people remain divided. Having seen Ammon's would-be attacker struck dead, nobody dared to touch him. Some thought he might be the Great Spirit, and others thought he had been sent to them by God (v. 25). Some believed that he was an awful monster sent by the Nephites to torment them (v. 26). And some thought he was sent by the Great Spirit to afflict and torment them for their wickedness (the first thing that the king had assumed before his conversion) (v. 27). As evidence, they cited the consistent way in which the Nephites had been blessed while the Lamanites had been cursed and ineffective in their battles.

Alma 19:28–29 • Abish tries to resolve the contention by reviving the queen and king. The argument among these parties became quite heated. We can imagine the panic they must have felt as they tried to make sense of what was literally lying in front of them. "And while they were thus contending, the woman servant [Abish] who had caused the multitude to be gathered together came, and when she saw the contention which was among the multitude she was exceedingly sorrowful, even unto tears" (v. 28). She took the queen by the hand as if she were about to raise her up from the ground, "and as soon as she touched her hand she arose and stood upon her feet, and cried with a loud voice, saying: O blessed Jesus, who has saved me from an awful hell! O blessed God, have mercy on this people!" (v. 29), showing that the queen had now also been converted and redeemed.

Alma 19:30–33 • The king revives again and teaches and testifies to his people. The queen was filled with joy and spoke "many words which were not understood" (perhaps speaking in tongues, and perhaps speaking of things she had seen which the people could not comprehend—or both). Then "she took the king, Lamoni, by the hand, and behold he arose and stood upon his feet" (v. 30). Seeing the contention among his people over what had happened, he rebuked them and rehearsed unto the them the teachings he had received from Ammon, causing many of them to believe and be converted (v. 31). Nevertheless, "there were many among them who would not hear his words; therefore they went their way" (v. 32). Last of all, "when Ammon arose he also administered unto them, and also did all the servants of Lamoni; and they did all declare unto the people the selfsame thing—that their hearts had been changed; that they had no more desire to do evil" (v. 33).

This lost desire to do evil reminds us of the people who heard King Benjamin's address, experienced a "mighty change" by "the Spirit of the Lord," and had "no more disposition to do evil, but to do good continually" (Mosiah 5:2; also see Alma 13:12 and 1 John 3:9).

President Joseph F. Smith said of his own conversion, "The feeling that came upon me was that of pure peace, of love and of light. I felt in my soul that if I had sinned—and surely I was not without sin—that it had been forgiven me; that I was indeed cleansed from sin; my heart was touched, and I felt that I would not injure the smallest insect beneath my feet. I felt as if I wanted to do good everywhere to everybody and to everything. I felt a newness of life, a newness of desire to do that which was right. There was not one particle of desire for evil left in my soul."[16]

Alma 19:34–36 • Mormon's summary of God's love for all of his children. All of those who had experienced these changing visions declared to the people "that they had seen angels and had conversed with them; and . . . they had told them things of God, and of his righteousness" (v. 34). As a result of these witnesses, many Lamanites believed and were baptized, chose righteousness, and established the Church among them (v. 35).

At this point in the narrative, Mormon inserts an editorial comment on what happened as a result of this "falling down" conversion incident at King Lamoni's palace: "And thus the work of the Lord did commence among the Lamanites; thus the Lord did begin to pour out his Spirit upon them; and we see that his arm is extended to all people who will repent and believe on his name" (v. 36).

LAMONI'S FATHER IS CONVERTED

Alma 20:1–5 • Lamoni wants to share the gospel with his father, the king over all the Lamanites. What is the first desire of any person who has tasted the sweet fruits of the gospel and of redemption? For Lehi, standing at the tree of life, it was that his family might also partake, which I presume we can all understand. We want those most dear to us to have the same happiness that we have found. And in the case of the newly-converted King Lamoni, it was no different. He "desired that Ammon should go with him to the land of Nephi, that he might show him unto his father" (v. 1).

However, when Ammon inquired of the Lord concerning the matter, the answer was, "Thou shalt not go up to the land of Nephi, for behold, the king will seek thy life; but thou shalt go to the land of Middoni; for behold, thy brother Aaron, and also Muloki and Ammah are in prison" (v. 2). Ammon's first responsibility was to his own family—his brother and his missionary companions.

The Book of Mormon does not specifically state how many companions accompanied the four sons of Mosiah on their mission, but it clearly indicates there were additional missionaries (Mosiah 28:1; Alma 22:35), and at least two of them, Muloki and Ammah, are mentioned here by name—Muloki and Ammah, companions to Ammon's brother Aaron. All of the others remain nameless in the abridged Book of Mormon record, though they may have been in the original records from which Mormon was working.

When Ammon told Lamoni that his brother and his companions were in prison at Middoni and that he had been commanded to go and deliver them, Lamoni offered to help. "I will go with thee to the land of Middoni," he said, "for the king of the land of Middoni, whose name is Antiomno, is a friend unto me" (vv. 3–4). When Lamoni asked how Ammon knew his brother was in prison, he answered, "No one hath told me, save it be God" (v. 5).

Alma 20:8–16 • Lamoni's father is hostile toward his son and Ammon. Apparently, the Lord had in mind the answering of both Lamoni's and Ammon's needs, because on the way to Middoni, they "met the father of Lamoni, who was king over all the land" (v. 8). By this time, Lamoni had already missed the feast his father had expected him to attend, and he demanded to know why (v. 9). What's more, he wanted to know why his son was traveling with "this Nephite, who is one of the children of a liar" (v. 10). Lamoni respectfully rehearsed unto his father all that had occurred since the coming of Ammon among them, and was greatly astonished to find that it made his father furious (vv. 11–13). Said he, "Lamoni, thou art going to deliver these Nephites, who are sons of a liar. Behold, he robbed our fathers; and now his children are also come amongst us that they may, by their cunning and their lyings, deceive us, that they again may rob us of our property" (v. 13).

Lamoni's father then commanded his son to slay Ammon with the sword, and forbid him to go to the land of Middoni. Instead he was to return immediately to the land of Ishmael over which he presided as king (vv. 13–14). Lamoni responded, "I will not slay Ammon, neither will I return to the land of Ishmael, but I go to the land of Middoni that I may release the brethren of Ammon, for I know that they are just men and holy prophets of the true God" (v. 15). Hearing this, Lamoni's father drew his sword, intending to kill his own son for his disobedience (v. 16).

Alma 20:20–25 • Ammon protects and defends Lamoni. As Lamoni's father raised his sword to slay his son, Ammon intervened and wounded the king's arm so that he could not use it—arms being a favorite target for Ammon in battle (v. 20). Thus disabled, the king began to plead with Ammon to spare his life (v. 21). Ammon responded that he would not spare him unless he would free his brother and his companions from prison, and the king readily agreed (vv. 22–23). Seeing the king's willingness to grant him whatever he wanted, Ammon added a second condition—"that Lamoni may retain his kingdom, and that ye be not displeased with him, but grant that he may do according to his own desires in whatsoever thing he thinketh" (v. 24). With this, the king rejoiced that his life had been spared (v. 25).

Alma 20:26–27 • Ammon's selfless example again convinces a king. Lamoni's father was astonished by Ammon's love for his son Lamoni and also that he had not requested anything more than that he would free his missionary brethren and spare Lamoni's life. These were selfless requests, not the kind of self-serving grabbing for power or wealth that most men might have done. He said, "Because this is all that thou hast desired, that I would release thy brethren, and suffer that my son Lamoni should retain his kingdom, behold, I will grant unto you that my son may retain his kingdom from this time and forever; and I will govern him no more" (v. 26).

The blinding effect of Lamanite traditions, which had caused the king to see all of them as self-serving liars, was thus dispelled, and he wanted to know more concerning the teachings of these Nephites. He asked that Ammon and his brothers come to see him in his own kingdom "for I shall greatly desire to see thee" (v. 27).

Alma 20:28–30 • Ammon and the two kings proceed on to Middoni and free Ammon's brethren. Ammon's brother Aaron and his companions had not been as blessed in their attempts to teach the Lamanites. They had fallen into the hands of "a more hardened and a more stiffnecked people; therefore they would not hearken unto their words, and they had cast them out, and had smitten them, and had driven them from house to house, and from place to place, even until they had arrived in the land of Middoni; and there they were taken and cast into prison, and bound with strong cords, and kept in prison for many days" (v. 30). When Ammon found them there, he was "exceedingly sorrowful, for behold they were naked, and their skins were worn exceedingly because of being bound with strong cords. And they also had suffered hunger, thirst, and all kinds of afflictions" (v. 29). But Lamoni was able to convince his fellow-king to release them, and they were set free (vv. 28–29).

The Missions of Aaron and His Brethren
(Alma 21–22)

At this point in the record, Mormon inserts the experiences of Aaron and his missionary companions during the time that Ammon was having so much success on his mission to Lamoni and his people. When the missionaries separated at the beginning of their missions, Aaron and his companions headed toward the land and city the Lamanites called Jerusalem, which bordered on the land called Mormon (Alma 21:1). The land called Mormon is presumably the area where the waters of Mormon were located, in which Alma the Elder had once baptized so many (Mosiah 18:5).

REJECTED AT JERUSALEM AND MIDDONI

Alma 21:1–3 • The city of Jerusalem contains apostate Nephites. The city had been built by Lamanites, Amalekites, and the people of Amulon—the latter two groups being apostate Nephites. Mormon said, "The Lamanites of themselves were sufficiently hardened, but the Amalekites and the Amulonites were still harder; therefore they did cause the Lamanites that they should harden their hearts, that they should wax strong in wickedness and their abominations" (v. 3). This is the first mention of the Amalekites in the Book of Mormon, and the exact source of their name is never made clear. The Amulonites were descendants and the followers of Amulon, the wicked priest of King Noah (Mosiah 23:31–35; 24:3–4).

Alma 21:4–8 • The Order of Nehors. Both of these groups of apostate Nephites believed in the teachings of the anti-Christ named Nehor (Alma 1:1–16). They were so hardened in their wickedness that only one Amalekite and no Amulonites were converted by the four sons of Mosiah and their companions (Alma 23:14). These groups believed that simply meeting together constituted worship (v. 6). They believed that God would save all men (v. 6). And they denied Christ, saying that no man could know of things to come (vv. 7–8).

Alma 21:12–14 Aaron and his brethren are imprisoned at Middoni. Having experienced limited success in Jerusalem because of the hardness of the hearts of the people there, Aaron and his brethren traveled on to the city of Middoni (v. 12). There Aaron and some of his companions were cast into prison, while others escaped into the surrounding area (v. 13). Those who were imprisoned "suffered many things" until they were finally delivered by the arrival of Lamoni and Ammon (v. 14).

THE REQUIREMENTS FOR REDEMPTION

Alma 21:15–17 • After their release from prison, Aaron and his brethren immediately begin to preach the gospel, with considerable success. Following the promptings of the Spirit, they preached in whatever synagogues of the Amalekites and assemblies of the Lamanites "where they could be admitted" (v. 16). They "brought many to the knowledge of the truth" and "they did convince many of their sins, and of the traditions of their fathers, which were not correct" (v. 17).

Alma 22:1–4 • Aaron is led by the Spirit to the palace of King Lamoni's father. Ammon's earlier example in sparing the life of Lamoni's father now bore additional fruit. Aaron and his missionary companions, after finishing their proselyting in Middoni, were led next to the land of Nephi, "even to the house of the king which was over all the land," which was the father of Lamoni (v. 1). They identified themselves as "the brethren of Ammon," whom this same king had recently helped to be delivered out of prison (v. 2). Following the same tactic as their brother Ammon had used with Lamoni, Aaron and his brothers offered to become the king's servants (v. 3). The king refused this offer and said instead "I will insist that ye shall administer unto me; for I have been somewhat troubled in mind because of the generosity and the greatness of the words of thy brother Ammon; and I desire to know the cause why he has not come up out of Middoni with thee" (v. 3). Aaron explained, "the Spirit of the Lord has called him another way" and "he has gone to the land of Ishmael, to teach the people of Lamoni" (v. 4).

Alma 22:5–6 • The king remembers and is troubled by Ammon's call to repentance. The teachings of Ammon had remained with this great king of all the Lamanites, and he needed answers. He asked, "What is this that ye have said concerning the Spirit of the Lord? Behold, this is the thing which doth trouble me" (v. 5) and "What is this that Ammon said—If ye will repent ye shall be saved, and if ye will not repent, ye shall be cast off at the last day?" (v. 6).

Alma 22:7–14 • Aaron's method of teaching Lamoni's father is similar to Ammon's teaching of Lamoni (Alma 18:24–39). Aaron started with the "Great Spirit." "Believest thou that there is a God?" he asked. "And the king said, I know that the Amalekites say that there is a God, and I have granted unto them that they should build sanctuaries, that they may assemble themselves together to worship him. And if now thou sayest there is a God, behold I will believe" (v. 7). The king was obviously willing to be taught, and Aaron rejoiced at the opportunity. "Behold, assuredly as thou livest, O king, there is a God" (v. 8). Aaron then proceeded to identify God as the Great Spirit in whom the king already believed (v. 9). Aaron taught the king that this Great Spirit "created all things both in heaven and in earth" (v. 10). He then "began from the creation of Adam, reading the scriptures unto the king—how God created man after his own image, and that God gave him commandments, and that because of transgression, man had fallen" (v. 12). He expounded upon the Fall of man and the plan of redemption, which had been "prepared from the foundation of the world, through Christ, for all whosoever would believe on his name" (v. 13). He explained that man could not save himself from his fallen state but that "the sufferings and death of Christ atone for their sins, through faith and repentance," and he also taught the king concerning the resurrection (v. 14).

Alma 22:15–16 • Still troubled by the prospect of being "cast off" forever, the king asks what he must do to obtain redemption. Aaron's answer was that he must (1) "bow down before God," (2) "repent of all thy sins," and (3) "call on [God's] name in faith."

Alma 22:17–18 • The king's humble prayer: "I will give away all my sins to know thee." Hearing Aaron's instruction to humble himself and pray, the king immediately did so. The king "did bow down before the Lord, upon his knees; yea, even he did prostrate himself upon the earth, and cried mightily" unto the Lord (v. 17). The words of his prayer show the depth of his concern for his salvation and his willingness to repent: "O God, Aaron hath told me that there is a God; and if there is a God, and if thou art God, wilt thou make thyself known unto me, and I will give away all my sins to know thee, and that I may be raised from the dead and be saved at the last day. And now when the king had said these words, he was struck as if he were dead" (v. 18).

Likening the king's situation to our own, we might appropriately ask, "Are there any sins I am not willing to give up in order to know God and obtain redemption?" The first time I seriously contemplated this question for myself, I was as deeply concerned as the king. After all, there were certain "little sins" that I rather liked to indulge in and hoped that God would simply wink at, knowing that "I'm only human" and they were "not serious."

For example, I enjoyed watching football games on a Sunday afternoon, and I knew that many others did as well—including many of my ward and stake priesthood leaders. Surely this was "no big deal." A wise high priest group leader on one particular Super Bowl Sunday taught a lesson about this humble Lamanite king's willingness to give up all his sins to know the Lord, and I found myself distressed a bit at his counsel. My reasoning was that if, once a year, on Super Bowl Sunday, I chose to join in this nationwide event, surely it would not deny me my exaltation. There are much worse sins that I never commit, and I have given great portions of my life in service to the kingdom. And besides, I was doing it with my four sons, so it was an important family activity and bonding opportunity. It wasn't completely evil.

As the high priest leader continued his lesson, he mentioned the rich young man who had "done all . . . things" since his youth and yet lacked one thing (Luke 18:21–22). And he reminded us that this great Lamanite king seemed willing to give away *all* his sins in order to know the Lord (Alma 22:18). He asked, "Are there some little inappropriate things we really don't want to give up?" And if so, then what are we forfeiting in exchange for them?" This was not a matter that was going to be decided for me in that moment during a priesthood lesson. But in response to my later prayers, the Spirit made it clear that, for me, deliberately committed "little sins" were not appropriate. I came to understand this important principle: One sin, however minor, deliberately committed and un-repented, is sufficient to keep me out of the celestial kingdom of God.

Ezra Taft Benson said, "Each of us must surrender our sins if we are to really know Christ. For we do not know Him until we become like Him. There are some, like this king, who must pray until they, too, have 'a wicked spirit rooted' from them so they can find the same joy."[17]

Mosiah 5:13 • Three additional reasons a person may not know the Lord. Earlier in the Book of Mormon, King Benjamin said that a man cannot know a Master (1) whom "he has not served," (2) who "is a stranger unto him," or (3) who "is far from the thoughts and intents of his heart." I believe this is about the motivation behind our choices. If we truly love the Lord, and wish to know him, then we will abandon willful sins, and we will do so for appropriate reasons. We will do so, not out of fear but out of our pure love for Him, our desire to serve Him, and our willingness to keep him at the center of our thoughts and hearts.

The same high priest group leader who had pricked my conscience about my favorite "little sins" also provided, as part of another lesson, an interesting chart about our motivations for keeping the commandments. I offer a simplified version of it below. All of these motivations are fine, and keeping the commandments is important no matter what our motivations. But ultimately, we should seek to be motivated by pure charity.

	Sabbath Holiness	**Tithing**	**Temple Attendance**
Charity	Because I love God and wish to serve others	Because I wish to help build the kingdom	Because I wish to help exalt the living and dead

Obedience	Because the Lord commands it	Because the Lord commands it	Because the Lord commands it
Reward	Rest, increased spirituality, and other blessings	Financial blessings (10 − 1 = 11)	Enjoying the peace and spirit of the temple
Appearances	So others will see me at Church on Sunday	So others will see that I pay my tithing	So others will see me there on temple night
Fear	Avoid the curses upon the land	Avoid being burned at the last day	Avoid being denied eternal exaltation

Alma 22:18–21 • Like his son Lamoni, the king is physically overcome by the Spirit. As had happened with Lamoni after he was taught by Ammon, when the king had expressed his desire to know the Lord and give away all his sins, "he was struck as if he were dead" (v. 18). His servants ran and told the queen, who "when she saw him lay as if he were dead and also Aaron and his brethren standing as though they had been the cause of his fall, she was angry with them, and commanded that her servants, or the servants of the king, should take them and slay them" (v. 19). The servants, who knew what had happened, did not dare lay hands on the missionaries, and "when the queen saw the fear of the servants she also began to fear exceedingly, lest there should some evil come upon her," and she suggested that they go and get "the people, that they might slay Aaron and his brethren" (vv. 20–21).

Alma 22:22–27 • At this point, Aaron "put forth his hand and raised the king from the earth, and said unto him: Stand. And he stood upon his feet, receiving his strength" (v. 22). The king then proceeded to "minister unto them, insomuch that his whole household were converted unto the Lord" (v. 23). He ministered also to the multitude who had assembled, who were "pacified towards Aaron and those who were with him" (v. 25). All of these were thereafter taught by Aaron and his companions (v. 26). The king also sent a proclamation among all his people, the Lamanites, that the missionaries should not be harmed and that the people should listen carefully to what they taught them (v. 27; Alma 23:1–3).

Notes
1. Carlos E. Asay, in Conference Report, Oct. 1976. 58.
2. J. Golden Kimball, in Thomas E. Cheney, *The Golden Legacy* (Salt Lake City: Peregrine Smith, 1973), 75.
3. J. Golden Kimball, *The Golden Legacy: A Folk History of J. Golden Kimball* (Salt lake City: Peregrine Smith, 1974), 49.
4. *Teachings of the Prophet Joseph Smith,* Joseph Fielding Smith, sel. (Salt Lake City: Deseret Book, 1976), 174.
5. David O. McKay, *The Improvement Era*, Oct. 1960, 703.
6. Annique Juqant, *The New Era*, Mar. 1987, 22.
7. Ezra Taft Benson, *Come unto Christ* (Salt Lake City: Deseret Book, 1983), 95.
8. *The Neal A. Maxwell Quote Book*, Cory H. Maxwell, ed. (Salt Lake City: Bookcraft, 1997), 1.
9. Daniel Ludlow, *A Companion to Your Study of the Book of Mormon* (Salt Lake City: Deseret Book, 1976), 206–9.
10. Ibid., 207.

11. Ibid.
12. Bruce R. McConkie, *Mormon Doctrine*, 2nd ed. (Salt Lake City: Bookcraft, 1966), 340.
13. Bruce R. McConkie, "The Three Pillars of Eternity" (devotional, Brigham Young University, Provo, Utah, Feb. 17, 1981).
14. Brigham Young, *Discourses of Brigham Young*, John A. Widtsoe, comp. (Salt Lake City: Deseret Book, 1941), 330.
15. Daniel Ludlow, *A Companion to Your Study of the Book of Mormon* (Salt Lake City: Deseret Book, 1976), 207.
16. Joseph F. Smith, *Gospel Doctrine*, 5th ed. (Salt Lake City: Deseret Book, 1939), 96.
17. Ezra Taft Benson, in Conference Report, Oct. 1983, 63.

LESSON 26
"Converted unto the Lord"
ALMA 22–29

Book of Mormon Geography
and the Anti-Nephi-Lehies

Book of Mormon Geography

The Book of Mormon can be frustrating for those who seek definitive answers concerning its geography. Neither Nephi nor Mormon intended their writings to be primarily historical, archaeological, or scientific. They are religious texts, and every incident selected to be included on the plates had a teaching purpose. If, in doing so, they spoke of geography, it was only to give a sense of direction and general location, not to provide a road map.

At this point in the Book of Mormon we receive considerably more detail about geography than in any other single place, so we will pause and consider the general layout of Book of Mormon sites. The accompanying map was created by Daniel H. Ludlow to achieve this purpose without any attempt to correlate it to any particular geography in North, Central, or South America.

Alma 22:27–34 • Nephite and Lamanite lands

▷ The Lamanites occupied an area south of the land of Zarahemla, from the sea east to the west. These

Possible Book of Mormon Sites

This map shows relative locations of important events and is not to be compared to any actual geographical locations. This map was originally developed by Daniel H. Ludlow and is used with permission.

21

Lamanite areas were divided from Nephite lands by borders of mountainous wilderness. Nephite lands (Zarahemla and Bountiful) were at a lower elevation than the south wilderness and the land of Nephi, which are described as being "up" from there (v. 27).

▷ Lamanites also occupied the area west of the land of Zarahemla, by the seashore. Their areas of habitation in their own lands extended all the way to the west seashore, which was the place where Lehi landed originally (v. 28).

▷ Lamanites also lived to the east of the land of Zarahemla, near the seashore in what was called the land of Bountiful. Thus, the Nephites were nearly surrounded by Lamanites living to their west, south, and east (v. 29).

▷ To the north of the land of Zarahemla was the land of Desolation, so called because it was the area where the Jaredites first landed and where they were eventually utterly destroyed (v. 30).

▷ These two lands were not literally north and south of each other, only generally so. The Jaredites migrated southward into the land of Bountiful, so called because of the many animals that migrated there for its plentiful food (v. 31).

▷ The land northward (Desolation) was divided from the land southward (Bountiful) by "a small neck of land," and "it was only the distance of a day and half's journey" from "the line Bountiful and the land Desolation" (v. 32).

Daniel H. Ludlow said,

> Some students of the Book of Mormon interpret this verse to mean that the entire narrow neck of land separating the land northward from the land southward could be traversed by a Nephite in a day and a half. However, a careful reading of this verse does not necessarily justify this conclusion. The historian's statement concerning a line "from the east to the west sea" does not necessarily mean the same as though he had said that the line existed from the east sea to the west sea. The statement may mean that it was a day and a half's journey for a Nephite from the east of the line to the west sea.
>
> In Helaman 4:7 the author mentions this same area again: "And there they did fortify against the Lamanites, from the west sea, even unto the east; it being a day's journey for a Nephite, on the line which they had fortified." Again, note that the word sea does not follow the word east. Also, a Nephite can now travel this distance in only one day's journey, and it is quite clear the distance being covered is "the line which they had fortified" and not necessarily the distance between two seas.[1]

Eventually, the Nephites occupied the land Bountiful in order to protect themselves from invasion by the Lamanites from the southeast (v. 33). The Lamanites were thus confined to the land of Nephi and to the borders formed by wilderness on the north, west, and east of the land of Zarahemla, and were eventually driven from the east wilderness (v. 34).

SOME CAUTIONS ABOUT BOOK OF MORMON GEOGRAPHY

These are a few of the clues to Book of Mormon geography that we have to work with, and we must be careful not to over-estimate what we think they tell us. Dr. Ludlow's map is useful because it establishes the relative locations of Book of Mormon cities and lands without insisting that they could have existed in any one specific part of the hemisphere.

As discussed in the chapter of this series corresponding to lesson 5, we assume that when Lehi's family left the land Bountiful in Arabia, they sailed eastward across the Indian and Pacific

Oceans and landed on the west coast of the Americas. We assume this because Mormon describes the area inhabited by most of the Lamanites in 77 BC as "the wilderness on the west, in the land of Nephi . . . west of the land of Zarahemla, in the borders by the seashore . . . in the place of their fathers' first inheritance" (Alma 22:28). This would seem to suggest a west coast landing.

As for what part of America—North America, Central America (Mesoamerica), or South America—the only *official* statements that have been made by Church authorities say that we do not know. Among scholars and members there are proponents for all three of these theories, and every one of them has a quote or two from an apostle or prophet in support of their claims. What are we to make of such contradictory statements by General Authorities and scholars on this topic? The only logical conclusion is that what they are telling us when they make these statements is their *opinion* (to which they are entitled), but their statements on this topic are *not doctrine*. If the answer to this question is revealed in the future, we will hear it from the heads of the Church in an official manner. But this has not yet happened, and until it does we should not teach our opinions as if they are doctrine.

President George Q. Cannon said,

> We are greatly pleased to notice the increasing interest taken by the Saints in this holy book [the Book of Mormon]. It contains the fullness of the gospel of Christ, and those who prayerfully study its sacred pages can be made wise unto salvation. It also unravels many mysteries connected with the history of the ancient world, more particularly of this western continent, mysteries which no other book explains. But valuable as is the Book of Mormon both in doctrine and history, yet it is possible to put this sacred volume to uses for which it was never intended, uses which are detrimental rather than advantageous to the cause of truth, and consequently to the work of the Lord.
>
> We have been led to these thoughts from the fact that the brethren who lecture on the lands of the Nephites or the geography of the Book of Mormon are not united in their conclusions. No two of them, so far as we have learned, are agreed on all points, and in many cases the variations amount to tens of thousands of miles. These differences of views lead to discussion, contention and perplexity; and we believe more contention is caused by these divergences than good is done by the truths elicited.
>
> How is it that there is such a variety of ideas on this subject? Simply because the Book of, Mormon is not a geographical primer. It was not written to teach geographical truths. What is told us of the situation of the various lands or cities of the ancient Jaredites, Nephites and Lamanites is usually simply an incidental remark connected with the doctrinal or historical portions of the work; and almost invariably only extends to a statement of the relative position of some land or city to contiguous or surrounding places, and nowhere gives us the exact situation or boundaries so that it can be definitely located without fear of error. . . .
>
> Of course, there can be no harm result from the study of the geography of this continent at the time it was settled by the Nephites, drawing all the information possible from the record which has been translated for our benefit. But beyond this we do not think it necessary, at the present time, to go [any further], because it is plain to be seen, we think, that evils may result therefrom.[2]

The Anti-Nephi-Lehies Are Converted
(ALMA 23–26)

A PROCLAMATION BY THE KING OF THE LAMANITES

Alma 23:1–3 • The king of the Lamanites issues a proclamation to his people after his conversion. He prohibited anyone from interfering with or persecuting the sons of Mosiah as they went forth preaching the gospel.

Alma 23:4–7 • Thousands of Lamanites are converted to the gospel, not a single one of which ever falls away. At the time these missionaries came among them, the Lamanites were "an idle people, full of mischief and subtlety" (2 Nephi 5:24). Enos said they were "wild . . . ferocious . . . bloodthirsty . . . full of idolatry and filthiness" (Enos 1:20). And Jarom said they "loved murder and would drink the blood of beasts" (Jarom 6). Thus, it was no exaggeration when Mormon said concerning their missions that the work "was great, for they had undertaken to preach the word of God to a wild and a hardened and a ferocious people" (Alma 17:14). And now, literally thousands of them had been converted and were thereafter continuously faithful. The equivalent in our own day would be for missionaries to have penetrated the mountainous hideouts of terrorists sworn to our utter destruction, converting thousands of them to the gospel of Jesus Christ.

Marion G. Romney said,

> In the twenty-third and twenty-fourth chapters of Alma we have a dramatic account of the power of the gospel changing almost a whole nation from a bloodthirsty, indolent, warlike people into industrious, peace-loving people. Of these people the record says that thousands were brought to a knowledge of the Lord, and that as many as were brought to a knowledge of the truth never did fall away. . . . That is the great message I want to leave here. It is the softening of the hearts that this gospel does to the people who receive it. . . . Now this remarkable transformation wrought in the hearts of these thousands of people was done in a very short period of time under the influence and power of the gospel of Jesus Christ. It would do the same thing today for all the peoples of the earth if they would but receive it.[3]

Alma 23:8–18 • Converted Lamanites are blessed "to be a very industrious people; . . . and the curse of God did no more follow them." We see this same willingness to be industrious today among Lamanite peoples who are flocking into the Church more quickly than any other people on the earth.

Spencer W. Kimball said concerning the rising of the Lamanites in our own day,

> The Lamanite people are increasing in numbers and influence. When the Navajos returned from Fort Sumner after a shameful and devastating captivity, there were only 9,000 of them left; now there are more than 100,000. There are nearly 130 million Lamanites worldwide. Their superstitions are giving way. They are becoming active politically and responsible in their communities wherever they dwell. Their employment and standard of living are increasing. . . .
>
> The Church has been established among them to a degree, and it will continue to be established on an ever-increasing scale. . . . They attend their meetings faithfully. They have the priesthood among them. There are branch presidents, quorum leaders, bishops, stake presidents, high councilors, mission presidents, and leaders in all phases of the work among them. They are attending the temple and receiving the ordinances necessary for exaltation. They are intelligent and faithful; they are a great people and a blessed people. . . .
>
> And can we not exercise our faith to expand this work even further? Enos prayed a prayer of mighty faith and secured a promise from the Lord that the Lamanite would be preserved. How glorious it would be if a million Latter-day Saint families were on their knees daily asking in faith that the work among these their brethren would be hastened, that the doors might be opened.
>
> The Lamanites must rise again in dignity and strength to fully join their brethren and sisters of the household of God in carrying forth his work in preparation for that day when the Lord Jesus Christ will return to lead his people, when the millennium will be ushered in, when the earth will

be renewed and receive its paradisiacal glory and its lands be united and become one land. For the prophets have said, "The remnant of the house of Joseph shall be built upon this land; and it shall be a land of their inheritance; and they shall build up a holy city unto the Lord, like unto the Jerusalem of old; and they shall no more be confounded, until the end come when the earth shall pass away" (Ether 13:8).[4]

EVIDENCE OF THEIR TRUE CONVERSION

Alma 23:6 • The Lamanite converts who were taught by the sons of Mosiah are "converted unto the Lord." They were not just attracted by the personalities of missionaries, the influence of friends, or the appeal of social programs. Sadly, this is sometimes how it is with people who are baptized too quickly without understanding fully their baptismal covenants. For example, in Europe in the early 1960s missionaries were eagerly baptizing young people whom they had invited to play baseball. They invited them to be baptized after they had won their confidence. These "baseball baptisms" brought some strong people into the Church who remain today as faithful members and priesthood leaders. Unfortunately, they also brought into the Church many young people who had an inadequate understanding of what membership entailed, and they quickly fell away. While I was serving as a missionary in one city in England in 1969, we identified more than 250 members of record who did not understand what they were doing when they were baptized and did not wish to be members of the Church.

This was not the case with the Lamanite converts who were taught by the sons of Mosiah. They were truly "converted unto the Lord," and they remained faithful throughout their lives.

President Gordon B. Hinckley said in the priesthood session of general conference in 1997,

> Each year a substantial number of people become members of the Church, largely through missionary efforts. Last year there were 321,385 converts comprised of men, women, and children. This is a large enough number, and then some, in one single year to constitute 100 new stakes of Zion. One hundred new stakes per year. Think of it! This places upon each of us an urgent and pressing need to fellowship those who join our ranks.

> It is not an easy thing to become a member of this Church. In most cases it involves setting aside old habits, leaving old friends and associations, and stepping into a new society which is different and somewhat demanding. With the ever-increasing number of converts, we must make an increasingly substantial effort to assist them as they find their way. Every one of them needs three things: (1) A friend, (2) a responsibility, and (3) nurturing with 'the good word of God' (Moroni 6:4). It is our duty and opportunity to provide these things. . . .

> The challenge now is greater than it has ever been because the number of converts is greater than we have ever before known. A program for retaining and strengthening the convert will soon go out to all the Church. I plead with you, brethren; I ask of you, each of you, to become a part of this great effort. Every convert is precious. Every convert is a son or daughter of God. Every convert is a great and serious responsibility.[5]

Alma 23:16–18 • They "were desirous . . . that they might be distinguished from their brethren" by adopting the name Anti-Nephi-Lehies (vv. 16–17; Alma 27:27–30). The precise meaning of the name Anti-Nephi-Lehies is not known. Daniel H. Ludlow said, "The "Nephi-Lehi" part of the title probably had reference to the lands of Nephi and Lehi (or the people then living in those lands) rather than to the descendants of Nephi or Lehi. However, Dr. Hugh Nibley has found "a Semitic and common Indo-European root corresponding to anti that means 'in the face of' or 'facing,' as of one facing a mirror, and by extension either 'one who opposes' or 'one who imitates.'"⁶ Thus the term *Anti-Nephi-Lehies* might refer to those who imitate the teachings of the descendants of Nephi and Lehi, rather than those who are against such teachings, which is how we would usually interpret the prefix *anti* today.

Later this group of converted Lamanites began to be called Ammonites, after the leader of the Nephite missionaries—Ammon—who had converted them (Alma 27:26). Still later, their children referred to themselves as Nephites (Alma 53:16).

Alma 24:6–10, 23 • They refused to ever again take up arms against anyone. They had previously been guilty of murder but now, because of sacred covenants, refused to kill again—even in self-defense (Alma 24:16–27; 27:2–3, 23–24, 27–30). They considered their swords "weapons of rebellion" (Alma 23:7) and vowed never to use them again.

Alma 24:12–17 • "They took their swords . . . and they did bury them up deep in the earth." They resolved to "stain our swords no more with the blood of our brethren" (v. 12), fearing that if they did "they [could] no more be washed bright through the blood of the Son of our great God, which [should] be shed for the atonement of our sins" (v. 13.). They were profoundly thankful and rejoiced, "God has had mercy on us, and made these things known unto us that we might not perish . . . because he loveth our souls [and] he loveth our children" (v. 14). They resolved to hide their swords "deep in the earth" (v. 16) to keep them bright "as a testimony to our God at the last day . . . that we have not stained our swords in the blood of our brethren since he imparted his word unto us and has made us clean thereby" (v. 15). And "if our brethren destroy us, behold, we shall go to our God and shall be saved" (v. 16).

It is significant that they buried their weapons rather than simply promising not to use them. It is entirely possible that this served as the source of the "bury-the-hatchet" tradition of peace, which was a common practice among some of the tribes of Native Americans when Columbus and other white men came to their lands. It is also possible that the tradition of never engaging in war among certain native tribes in Mexico is connected to the Ammonites who migrated northward to escape the Nephite-Lamanite wars (Helaman 3:4).

Jerry L. Ainsworth observes that "when the Spaniards arrived on this continent and began exploiting the Indians and destroying their culture, they encountered a group of Indians on the west coast of Mexico that would not fight. These Indians claimed a history of never having fought and stated they would not commence at that point. . . . Mexican history records that before AD 1600 the Pacific Ocean was called El Mar del Sur—the 'sea South'; [but] around AD 1600 it was renamed El Oceano de los Pacificos—the 'Ocean of the Peaceful People' (México a Traves de los Siglos, 2:459)."⁷

D&C 58:42–43 • When we truly repent of our sins, we "confess them and forsake them." The Ammonites' burying of their weapons was a symbolic gesture of forsaking the sins they committed with them, which is an essential part of repentance. The Lord promises in this latter-day revelation that he will forgive us of our sins and "remember them no more" if we will confess and *forsake* them.

Isaiah 2:4–5 • The Millennium will be ushered in with similar covenants of peace. Isaiah records that the Lord's people will "beat their swords into plowshares, and their spears into pruninghooks: nation shall not lift up sword against nation, neither shall they learn war any more." The peace of the Millennium will result from the firm commitment of those within that society to never wage war of any kind.

Alma 24:18–19 • Mormon praises the commitment of these Lamanites. "And this they did, it being in their view a testimony to God, and also to men, that they never would use weapons again for the shedding of man's blood; and this they did, vouching and covenanting with God, that rather than shed the blood of their brethren they would give up their own lives; and rather than take away from a brother they would give unto him; and rather than spend their days in idleness they would labor abundantly with their hands. And thus we see that, when these Lamanites were brought to believe and to know the truth, they were firm, and would suffer even unto death rather than commit sin."

Alma 24:19 An example of how Book of Mormon writers corrected writing errors. Mormon writes, "They buried their weapons of peace, or they buried the weapons of war, for peace." Mormon was writing on "plates of ore" that he made with his own hands. Making corrections would have been difficult if not impossible. This verse shows how he corrected himself when necessary.

Alma 24:1–2 • As a result of their conversion, the Anti-Nephi-Lehies faced very difficult circumstances, including their own certain death when they would not take up arms to defend themselves. The Amalekites, Amulonites, and Lamanites in the lands of Amulon, Helam, Jerusalem, and in all of the surrounding area "who had not been converted and had not taken upon them the name of Anti-Nephi-Lehi, were stirred up by the Amalekites and by the Amulonites to anger" against the Anti-Nephi-Lehies who had converted (v. 1). Their hatred is described as "exceedingly sore against them, even insomuch that they began to rebel against their king," and they "took up arms against the people of Anti-Nephi-Lehi" (v. 2).

Alma 24:20–27 • When the unconverted Lamanites see that their brethren would die rather than defend themselves their hearts are "swollen with mercy." They had come into the land "for the purpose of destroying the king, and to place another in his stead and also of destroying the people of Anti-Nephi-Lehi out of the land" (v. 20). When they arrived they found the people of Anti-Lehi-Nephi had "prostrated themselves before them to the earth, and began to call on the name of the Lord; and thus they were in this attitude when the Lamanites began to fall upon them, and began to slay them with the sword" (v. 21). Because of this lack of resistance, they killed 1,005 of them as they lay upon the ground before them (v. 22).

At first it must have seemed too easy, and we can imagine their bloodthirstiness as they slaughtered vast numbers of people whom they considered traitors to their Lamanite nation. But when they "saw that their brethren would not flee from the sword, neither would they turn aside to the right hand or to the left, but that they would lie down and perish, and praised God even in the very act of perishing under the sword . . . they did forbear from slaying them; and there were many whose hearts had swollen in them for those of their brethren who had fallen under the sword, for they repented of the things which they had done" (vv. 23–24). They threw down their weapons and refused to take them up again, being "stung for the murders which they had committed" and began to lay down themselves and be similarly killed rather than continue to slay their brethren (v. 25).

As it turned out, more attackers were converted that day than the number of Anti-Nephi-Lehies who had died, and Mormon comments that "those who had been slain were righteous people, therefore we have no reason to doubt but what they were saved" (v. 26). Mormon observes further that "there was not a wicked man slain among them; but there were more than a thousand brought to the knowledge of the truth" (v. 27), demonstrating that the Lord works in a number of ways (some not so obvious) to bring the gospel to his children, whether in this world or the next.

It is often the case that the Lord uses terrible tragedies to further his saving work among his children. Ezra Taft Benson said, "I have seen, at close range, the manner in which the Lord has turned disasters—war, occupation, and revolution—into blessings."[8] The recent massive tsunami in Indonesia opened doors to the Church in those nations through the humanitarian aid that we sent to their suffering people. And similar good will has been established through the providing of wells to drought-stricken areas of Africa, relief supplies to Hurricane Katrina victims in Louisiana and Alabama, and medical and dental care to impoverished people in Central and South America. If we look beyond the suffering, we see the hand of God moving over his children to provide for their eternal salvation.

Alma 24:28–30 • The killers are mostly apostate Nephites, not Lamanites. We should not be surprised to learn that the greatest number of those who slaughtered these defenseless Lamanites were apostate Nephites—"Amalekites and Amulonites, the greatest number of whom were after the order of the Nehors" (v. 28). And not a single one of these Amalekites or Amulonites, or those who were of the order of Nehor, were converted to the Lord through this experience (v. 29).

Mormon observes, "And thus we can plainly discern, that after a people have been once enlightened by the Spirit of God, and have had great knowledge of things pertaining to righteousness, and then have fallen away into sin and transgression, they become more hardened, and thus their state becomes worse than though they had never known these things" (v. 30).

On one occasion,

> when the Prophet [Joseph Smith] had ended telling how he had been treated [by apostates], Brother Behunnin remarked: "If I should leave this Church I would not do as those men have done: I would go to some remote place where Mormonism had never been heard of[,] settle down, and no one would ever learn that I knew anything about it."
>
> The great Seer immediately replied: "Brother Behunnin, you don't know what you would do. No doubt these men once thought as you do. Before you joined this Church you stood on neutral ground. When the gospel was preached good and evil were set before you. You could choose either or neither. There were two opposite masters inviting you to serve them. When you joined this Church you enlisted to serve God. When you did that you left the neutral ground, and you never can get back on to it. Should you forsake the Master you enlisted to serve it will be by the instigation of the evil one, and you will follow his dictation and be his servant."
>
> He emphasized the fact that a man or woman who had not taken sides either with Christ or belial could maintain a neutral position, but when they enlisted under either the one or the other they left the neutral ground forever.[9]

Seeking Safety Among the Nephites
(ALMA 27–28)

A PROPOSED REFUGE IN ZARAHEMLA

Alma 27:1–5 • Ammon and his brethren urge the Anti-Nephi-Lehies to go to the land of Zarahemla, where the Nephites live. The true Lamanites (those who were actual descendants of Laman and Lemuel), concluded that "it was in vain to seek their destruction [the destruction of the

Anti-Nephi-Lehies], [and] they returned again to the land of Nephi" (v. 1). But the Amalekites were not satisfied and "because of their loss, were exceedingly angry. And when they saw that they could not seek revenge from the Nephites, they began to stir up the people in anger against their brethren, the people of Anti-Nephi-Lehi" and "they began again to destroy them" again (v. 2). And once again, the Anti-Nephi-Lehies "refused to take their arms, and they suffered themselves to be slain according to the desires of their enemies" (v. 3).

Ammon and his brethren were greatly concerned about the danger and loss of life being suffered by these people "whom they so dearly beloved, and among those who had so dearly beloved them—for they were treated as though they were angels sent from God to save them from everlasting destruction" (v. 4). They therefore said to the king of the Lamanites who was among them, "Let us gather together this people of the Lord, and let us go down to the land of Zarahemla to our brethren the Nephites, and flee out of the hands of our enemies, that we be not destroyed" (v. 5).

Alma 27:6–10 • The king is reluctant to take his people to Zarahemla because he fears the Nephites will see them as enemies and destroy them. He said, "Behold, the Nephites will destroy us, because of the many murders and sins we have committed against them" (v. 6). Ammon offered to inquire of the Lord concerning the matter and asked, "If he say unto us, go down unto our brethren, will ye go?" And this good and faithful Lamanite king, who had been willing to do whatever the Lord required in order to be saved, again showed his great faith: "Yea, if the Lord saith unto us go, we will go down unto our brethren, and we will be their slaves until we repair unto them the many murders and sins which we have committed against them" (vv. 7–8). Ammon reassured him, "It is against the law of our brethren, which was established by my father, that there should be any slaves among them; therefore let us go down and rely upon the mercies of our brethren" (v. 9). And the king responded, "Inquire of the Lord, and if he saith unto us go, we will go; otherwise we will perish in the land" (v. 10).

Alma 27:11–14 • The king is persuaded to go to Zarahemla by a revelation from God. Ammon proceeded to inquire of the Lord, and he received a commandment: "Get this people out of this land, that they perish not; for Satan has great hold on the hearts of the Amalekites, who do stir up the Lamanites to anger against their brethren to slay them; therefore get thee out of this land; and blessed are this people in this generation, for I will preserve them" (vv. 11–12). Ammon related this instruction from the Lord to the king, and "they gathered together all their people, yea, all the people of the Lord, and did gather together all their flocks and herds, and departed out of the land, and came into the wilderness which divided the land of Nephi from the land of Zarahemla, and came over near the borders of the land" (vv. 13–14). At that point they stopped while Ammon and his brothers went into the city to see if the Nephites would allow these converted Lamanites to live among them (v. 15).

Alma 27:16–19 • It was during this journey to Zarahemla with the converted Anti-Nephi-Lehies that the reunion of Alma and the sons of Mosiah occurs (Alma 17:1–2). As Ammon and his brothers were "going forth into the land . . . he and his brethren met Alma . . . and behold, this was a joyful meeting" (v. 16). Ammon was so full of joy at this reunion that "he was swallowed up in the joy of his God, even to the exhausting of his strength; and he fell again to the earth" (v. 17). The same joy was felt by Alma, Aaron, Omner, and Himni, "but behold their joy was not that to exceed their strength" (vv. 18–19). We will discuss this reunion in greater detail below.

Alma 27:20–26 • When Ammon asks them to admit the Anti-Nephi-Lehies into their land, the Nephites give them the land of Jershon in the east, near the land of Bountiful. Alma led the sons of Mosiah back to the land of Zarahemla, where they reported to the chief judge all that had happened to them on their missions among the Lamanites (v. 20). The chief judge then sent a proclamation among the people to determine whether they would permit the Anti-Nephi-Lehies to live among them (v. 21). The people agreed to accept them, "saying: Behold, we will give up the land of Jershon, which is on the east by the sea . . . south of the land Bountiful" (v. 22). The word *Jershon* is an interesting one, which is taken from the Hebrew language and means "the land of the expelled, or of the strangers." It is yet another piece of evidence of the authenticity and truthfulness of the Book of Mormon.

The Nephites also agreed to place their armies between the land of Jershon and the land of Nephi (where the Lamanites lived) in order to protect the Anti-Nephi-Lehies (v. 23). The only condition was that they "give [the Nephites] a portion of their substance to assist [them] that [they] may maintain [their] armies" (v. 24). This was acceptable because although the Anti-Nephi-Lehies were under covenant not to bear arms, they could contribute to support the Nephite armies that protected them.

At this point, Alma accompanied the sons of Mosiah back to the camp where the Anti-Nephi-Lehies were waiting, where he told them of the marvelous conversion that he and the sons of Mosiah had experienced so many years before (v. 25). They received the news of being accepted by the Nephites with great joy and went down into the land of Jershon and took possession of it. They were "called by the Nephites the people of Ammon," by which name they were thereafter known throughout the remainder of the Book of Mormon (v. 26).

A Great Tragedy in Jershon

Alma 28:1–3 • After the people of Ammon settle in the land of Jershon, the Lamanites again attack them, no doubt encouraged to do so by the hateful apostate Nephites among them (v. 1). Although the Lamanites were eventually defeated, many Ammonites as well as Nephites died in this war (v. 3). One of the battles is described by Mormon as "such an one as never had been known among all the people in the land from the time Lehi left Jerusalem" with "tens of thousands of the Lamanites . . . slain and scattered abroad" (v. 2).

Alma 28:4–6 • The Nephites mourn greatly over their dead. There was "great mourning and lamentation . . . among all the people of Nephi" (v. 4), including "widows mourning for their husbands, . . . fathers mourning for their sons, . . . the daughter for the brother, . . . [and] the brother for the father," all of them "mourning for their kindred who had been slain" (v. 5). Mormon describes it as "a sorrowful day; yea, a time of solemnity, and a time of much fasting and prayer" (v. 6). The Nephites had made and were continuing to make a great sacrifice on behalf of the Ammonites—people who had once been their bitter enemies but who were now their fellow members of the Church.

Alma 28:11–12 • Some mourners fear for the salvation of their dead. The bodies of many were buried, while the bodies of thousands more were "moldering in heaps upon the face of the earth" (v. 11). Thousands mourned out of fear for the salvation of their loved ones, while others mourned the loss of loved ones but rejoiced in the knowledge that they would eventually be "raised to dwell at the right hand of God, in a state of never-ending happiness" (v. 12).

D&C 42:45 • The Lord expects us to weep for the loss of those that die, but more especially for those that have no hope of a glorious resurrection.

The Prophet Joseph Smith said, "The only difference between the old and young dying is, one lives longer in heaven and eternal light and glory than the other, and is freed a little sooner from this miserable, wicked world. . . . More painful to me are the thoughts of annihilation than death. If I have no expectation of seeing my father, mother, brothers, sisters and friends again, my heart would burst in a moment, and I should go down to my grave. The expectation of seeing my friends in the morning of the resurrection cheers my soul and makes me bear up against the evils of life. It is like their taking a long journey, and on their return we meet them with increased joy."[10]

Alma 28:13–14 • Mormon emphasizes two points as he summarizes the missionary labors of the sons of Mosiah and the subsequent battles between the Lamanites and the Nephites.

1. There is a great inequality of man due to sin, transgression, and the power of the devil. Satan devises cunning plans to ensnare the hearts of men and lead them to destruction (v. 13), and all too often he succeeds. This leads to great sorrow because of the death and destruction this produces among men (v. 14).

2. There is a great need for righteous men to labor diligently in the vineyards of the Lord and lead men back to God. This leads to great joy as men receive and follow the light of Christ (v. 14).

Ammon And Alma Rejoice
(ALMA 26, 29)

At this point, we pause to reflect upon the great rejoicing felt by Alma and the sons of Mosiah when they met again after more than fourteen years of separation (Alma 17:4). You will recall that they ran into each other while the sons of Mosiah were bringing the Anti-Nephi-Lehies (Ammonites) into the Land of Zarahemla for their safety (Alma 27:16–19 above).

AMMON'S FEELINGS ABOUT THEIR SUCCESS

Alma 26:1–4 • The "marvelous light of God." Ammon wondered out loud, "How great reason have we to rejoice; for could we have supposed when we started from the land of Zarahemla that God would have granted unto us such great blessings?" (v. 1). He then listed the blessings they had received as "our brethren, the Lamanites, were in darkness, yea, even in the darkest abyss, but . . . many of them are brought to behold the marvelous light of God!" and "we have been made instruments in the hands of God to bring about this great work" as "thousands of them do rejoice, and have been brought into the fold of God" (vv. 2–4). Truly, nobody could have anticipated such results when they set out for their missions fourteen years earlier.

Bruce R. McConkie said, "Whenever the gospel is on earth, it is the true light (1 John 2:8). Those who accept the gospel of Christ are thus called 'out of darkness into his marvellous light' (1 Peter 2:9; Alma 26:3, 15). Paul was sent to the Gentiles, 'To open their eyes, and to turn them from darkness to light' (Acts 26:18), 'the light of the glorious gospel of Christ, . . . the light of the knowledge of the glory of God' (2 Corinthians 4:4–6). Those who accept the gospel have their souls 'illuminated by the light of the everlasting word' (Alma 5:7). Our Lord 'brought life and immortality to light through the gospel' (2 Timothy 1:10)."[11]

31

Alma 26:5–7 • The "sheaves" of missionary work. Sheaves are stalks and heads of grain bound together in bundles. Ammon compared the gathering of their Lamanite converts into the Church as being like gathering sheaves of wheat for the Lord. "Behold, the field was ripe, and . . . ye did thrust in the sickle, and did reap with your might, . . . and behold the number of your sheaves!" (v. 5). He continues the analogy: "And they shall be gathered into the garners, that they are not wasted. Yea, they shall not be beaten down by the storm at the last day; yea, neither shall they be harrowed up by the whirlwinds; but when the storm cometh they shall be gathered together in their place, that the storm cannot penetrate to them; yea, neither shall they be driven with fierce winds whithersoever the enemy listeth to carry them" (v. 6). He was speaking of their spiritual protection at the last day, saying, "Behold, they are in the hands of the Lord of the harvest, and they are his; and he will raise them up at the last day" (v. 7).

Alma 26:10–12 • Aaron rebukes Ammon for boasting. He was concerned that Ammon's expressions of joy "doth carry thee away unto boasting" (v. 10). But Ammon explained his intent: "I do not boast in my own strength, nor in my own wisdom; but behold, my joy is full, yea, my heart is brim with joy, and I will rejoice in my God" (v. 11). He knew his place in the process. "Yea, I know that I am nothing; as to my strength I am weak; therefore I will not boast of myself, but I will boast of my God, for in his strength I can do all things; yea, behold, many mighty miracles we have wrought in this land, for which we will praise his name forever" (v. 12).

Ammon was making a careful distinction between what he and his brothers did and what the Lord did in saving so many Lamanite souls. In like manner, missionaries today need to make the extremely important distinction between what they themselves do personally and what the Lord has blessed them to be able to do. When we enjoy success, we must be careful to give all the glory to God. It is he, through the Spirit, who converts. Missionaries plant, but the Lord of the harvest reaps the results in their hearts.

Wilford Woodruff said,

> We have no chance to be lifted up in the pride of our hearts with regard to the position we occupy. If the President of the Church or either of his counselors or of the apostles or any other man feels in his heart that God cannot do without him, and that he is especially important in order to carry on the work of the Lord, he stands upon slippery ground. I heard Joseph Smith say that Oliver Cowdery, who was the second apostle in his Church, said to him, "If I leave this Church it will fall."
>
> Said Joseph, "Oliver, you try it." Oliver tried it. He fell; but the kingdom of God did not. I have been acquainted with other apostles in my day and time who felt that the Lord could not do without them; but the Lord got along with his work without them. I say to all men Jew and Gentile, great and small, rich and poor—that the Lord Almighty has power within himself, and is not dependent upon any man, to carry on his work; but when he does call men to do his work they have to trust in him.[12]

Alma 26:13–15 • Ammon explains that he is rejoicing over God's miraculous deliverance of so many people from their otherwise certain destruction. Said he, "Behold, how many thousands of our brethren has he loosed from the pains of hell; and they are brought to sing redeeming love, and this because of the power of his word which is in us, therefore have we not great reason to rejoice?" (v. 13). He answers that "we have reason to praise him forever, for he is the Most High God, and has loosed our brethren from the chains of hell. Yea, they were encircled about with everlasting darkness and destruction; but behold, he has brought them into his everlasting light

. . . and they are encircled about with the matchless bounty of his love" (vv. 14–15). And they—the sons of Mosiah—had been privileged to be "instruments in his hands of doing this great and marvelous work" (v. 15).

Brigham Young said,

> I had only traveled a short time to testify to the people, before I learned this one fact, that you might prove doctrine from the Bible till doomsday, and it would merely convince a people, but would not convert them. You might read the Bible from Genesis to Revelation, and prove every iota that you advance, and that alone would have no converting influence upon the people. Nothing short of a testimony by the power of the Holy Ghost would bring light and knowledge to them—bring them in their hearts to repentance. Nothing short of that would ever do. You have frequently heard me say that I would rather hear an Elder, either here or in the world, speak only five words accompanied by the power of God, and they would do more good than to hear long sermons without the Spirit. That is true, and we know it.[13]

Alma 26:23–26 • Ammon reflects upon the prejudice of the Nephites when they first said they wanted to go on a mission to the Lamanites. Several times in earlier chapters I have compared their mission to a theoretical one today where young missionaries might volunteer to go into the training camps of terrorists in an effort to convert them to the gospel of Jesus Christ—people who not only do not believe in Christ but who are devoted to killing all of us in the name of their misguided religious and cultural beliefs.

Ammon asked, "Now do ye remember, my brethren, that we said unto our brethren in the land of Zarahemla, we go up to the land of Nephi, to preach unto our brethren, the Lamanites, and they laughed us to scorn?" (v. 23). Did they seriously believe they could teach the gospel to "as stiffnecked a people as they are; whose hearts delight in the shedding of blood; whose days have been spent in the grossest iniquity; whose ways have been the ways of a transgressor from the beginning?" (v. 24). It certainly must have sounded preposterous to any rational Nephite of the time.

The nay-sayers said that the Nephites' best strategy was to "take up arms against them, that [they] destroy them and their iniquity out of the land, lest they overrun [them] and destroy [them]" (v. 25). But the gospel proved to be more effective than all the weapons the Nephites possessed. These faithful young men went into the wilderness "not with the intent to destroy our brethren, but with the intent that perhaps we might save some few of their souls" (v. 26).

Surely, this applies to our time as well. Spencer W. Kimball said, "What are we to fear when the Lord is with us? Can we not take the Lord at his word and exercise a particle of faith in him? Our assignment is affirmative: . . . to carry the gospel to our enemies, that they might no longer be our enemies."[14]

Alma 26:27–30 • Ammon reflects on how patience and trust in the Lord helped them experience a good outcome from a difficult situation. Their missions were not easy; they were very difficult. But Ammon recalls, "When our hearts were depressed, and we were about to turn back, behold, the Lord comforted us, and said, Go amongst thy brethren, the Lamanites, and bear with patience thine afflictions, and I will give unto you success" (v. 27). This has a familiar ring to the words of the Lord to Joseph Smith in Liberty Jail: "My son, peace be unto thy soul; thine adversity and thine afflictions shall be but a small moment; And then, if thou endure it well, God shall exalt thee on high" (D&C 121:7–8). He had earlier commanded his latter-day Church to follow the Prophet Joseph Smith "in all patience and faith. For by doing these things the gates of hell shall not prevail against you; yea, and the Lord God will disperse the powers of darkness from before you, and cause the heavens to shake for your good, and his name's glory" (D&C 21:5–6).

Neal A. Maxwell said,

> Patience is not indifference. Actually, it is caring very much, but being willing, nevertheless, to submit both to the Lord and to what the scriptures call the "process of time." Patience is tied very closely to faith in our Heavenly Father. Actually, when we are unduly impatient, we are suggesting that we know what is best—better than does God. Or, at least, we are asserting that our timetable is better than his. Either way we are questioning the reality of God's omniscience. . . .

> We read in Mosiah about how the Lord simultaneously tries the patience of his people even as he tries their faith (Mosiah 23:21). One is not only to endure—but to endure well and gracefully—those things which the Lord "seeth fit to inflict upon [us]" (Mosiah 3:19), just as did a group of ancient American Saints who were bearing unusual burdens but who submitted "cheerfully and with patience to all the will of the Lord" (Mosiah 24:15).

> Paul, speaking to the Hebrews, brings us up short by writing that even after faithful disciples have "done the will of God, . . . ye have need of patience" (Hebrews 10:36). How many times have good individuals done the right thing only to break, or wear away, under the subsequent stress, canceling out much of the value of what they have already so painstakingly done? Sometimes that which we are doing is correct enough but simply needs to be persisted in patiently—not for a minute or a moment but sometimes for years. Paul speaks of the marathon of life and how we must "run with patience the race that is set before us" (Hebrews 12:1). Paul did not select the hundred-yard dash for his analogy!

> The Lord has twice said, "And seek the face of the Lord always, that in patience ye may possess your souls, and ye shall have eternal life" (D&C 101:38 and Luke 21:19). Could it be that only when our self-control has become total do we come into true possession of our own souls? . . . Clearly, without patience, we will learn less in life. We will see less. We will feel less. We will hear less. Ironically, rush and more usually mean less. The pressures of now, time and time again, go against the grain of the gospel with its eternalism. There is also in patience a greater opportunity for that discernment which sorts out the things that matter most from the things that matter least . . .

> Patience permits us to cling to our faith in the Lord when we are tossed about by suffering as if by surf. When the undertow grasps us, we will realize that even as we tumble we are somehow being carried forward; we are actually being helped even as we cry for help! One of the functions of the tribulation of the righteous is that "tribulation worketh patience" (Romans 5:3). What a vital attribute patience is, if tribulation is worth enduring to bring about its development!

> Patience is, therefore, clearly not fatalistic, shoulder-shrugging resignation; it is accepting a divine rhythm to life; it is obedience prolonged.[15]

The sons of Mosiah were very patient in all of their sufferings. They "suffered every privation [as they] traveled from house to house, relying upon the mercies of the world—not upon the mercies of the world alone but upon the mercies of God." They wrote, "And we have entered into their houses and taught them, and we have taught them in their streets; yea, and we have taught them upon their hills; and we have also entered into their temples and their synagogues and taught them; and we have been cast out, and mocked, and spit upon, and smote upon our cheeks; and we have been stoned, and taken and bound with strong cords, and cast into prison; and through the power and wisdom of God we have been delivered again. And we have suffered all manner of afflictions, and all this, that perhaps we might be the means of saving some soul; and we supposed that our joy would be full if perhaps we could be the means of saving some" (vv. 28–30).

Alma 26:35–37 • Ammon speaks of the great power, knowledge, and mercy of God. He asked, "Now have we not reason to rejoice? Yea, I say unto you, there never were men that had so great reason to rejoice as we, since the world began" (v. 35). He said that his personal joy "is carried away, even unto boasting in my God; for he has all power, all wisdom, and all understanding; he comprehendeth all things, and he is a merciful Being, even unto salvation, to those who will repent and believe on his name" (v. 35). God is not a thundering destroyer of the wicked but a patient father who gives his children—even those as wicked as were the Lamanites—every opportunity to repent and be saved. This is the kind of being that Ammon is praising here.

"Now if this is boasting," he said, "even so will I boast; for this is my life and my light, my joy and my salvation, and my redemption from everlasting wo. Yea, blessed is the name of my God, who has been mindful of this people, who are a branch of the tree of Israel . . . lost . . . in a strange land" (v. 36). Indeed, Ammon reminds us that "God is mindful of every people, whatsoever land they may be in; yea, he numbereth his people, and his bowels of mercy are over all the earth" and for this Ammon "will give thanks unto my God forever" (v. 37).

The Prophet Joseph Smith said,

> There are but a very few beings in the world who understand rightly the character of God. The great majority of mankind do not comprehend anything, either that which is past, or that which is to come, as it respects their relationship to God. They do not know, neither do they understand the nature of that relationship; and consequently they know but little above the brute beast, or more than to eat, drink and sleep. This is all man knows about God or his existence, unless it is given by the inspiration of the Almighty.
>
> If a man learns nothing more than to eat, think and sleep, and does not comprehend any of the designs of God; the beast comprehends the same things. It eats, drinks, sleeps, and knows nothing more about God; yet it knows as much as we, unless we are able to comprehend by the inspiration of Almighty God. If men do not comprehend the character of God, they do not comprehend themselves.[16]

ALMA'S FEELINGS ABOUT THEIR SUCCESS

Alma 27:16–19 • This scripture returns to the account of the reunion of Alma and the sons of Mosiah (see also Alma 17:1–2). Notice the number of times Mormon used the word *joy* to describe the feelings of those involved. Alma felt joy on meeting the sons of Mosiah after fourteen years of separation, and his joy was like that felt by Ammon, for he did not rejoice in his own successes alone, but also in those of his friends (v. 16). Ammon felt this joy to such an extent that it exhausted his strength, causing him to fall to the earth (v. 17). "Now was not this exceeding joy?" asks Mormon. "Behold, this is joy which none receiveth save it be the truly penitent and humble seeker of happiness" (v. 18). Aaron, Omner, and Himni also felt this joy, but it "was not that to exceed their strength" as it had been for Ammon and Alma (v. 19).

D&C 18:15–16 • The joy that comes from bringing a soul unto Christ. The Lord tells us in this latter-day revelation that if you were to labor your entire life and managed to bring only one soul to him "how great shall be your joy with him in the kingdom of my Father!" (v. 15). And if your joy would be great by bringing just one soul, "how great will be your joy if you should bring many souls unto me!" (v. 16).

I came to understand this doctrine in a very personal way on my mission. I was, at the time, a district leader serving in a small town in the Midlands of England. In addition to our leadership responsibilities, my companion and I labored diligently to teach the gospel in our assigned area.

Over a period of many months we literally knocked on every door in that town and had not had an opportunity to baptize a single soul. I remember well our feelings as we returned home on that final day, knowing we had now covered the entire area without success. We walked into our landlady's residence and flopped down in her living room chairs, completely discouraged.

"What's the matter, boys?" she asked. "You look very sad." Her name was Ivy Fields, and she was a wonderful old woman who had nurtured several sets of missionaries in her home over time. This was a woman who took the time to iron our thick woolen ski socks after washing them. "You don't have to do that," I protested one morning. "Those are ski socks. You couldn't put a wrinkle in them if you tried." "Well," she retorted with some disgust, "I would think that if my own sons were away in America that their landlady would iron their socks." She was just that kind of loving, motherly woman. And now she was wondering why we were so sad.

"Ivy," I said, "we've been all over this town for months, and we haven't had an opportunity to give our message to one believing soul. Nobody will listen to us." She walked forward and put her hand on my shoulder. "Well, what is it that you boys teach?" My companion and I looked at each other with deer-in-the-headlights eyes. Here, under our own rented roof was the one soul in this entire town who was interested, and we had never thought to ask her. We proceeded to teach her the gospel, and she was baptized shortly thereafter.

In response to her conversion, her family more-or-less disowned her, a seventy-two-year-old mother and grandmother who was now very much on her own. After I returned home, we continued to write letters and eventually she came to America and joined with my family here. She eventually passed away here and is buried in the Holladay Cemetery in Salt Lake City. On her stone we placed the simple epitaph: "Ivy Alice Branch Field. Our English Mum." I have no doubt that this one soul will bring me great joy in the eternities to come.

Alma 29:1–2 • "O that I were an angel." The joy that comes from converting just one soul makes us wish that we could convert the world. This was certainly the feeling of Alma as he wished he had the converting power of an angel. "O that I were an angel, and could have the wish of mine heart," he said, "that I might go forth and speak with the trump of God, with a voice to shake the earth, and cry repentance unto every people! Yea, I would declare unto every soul, as with the voice of thunder, repentance and the plan of redemption, that they should repent and come unto our God, that there might not be more sorrow upon all the face of the earth." What missionary in any age cannot relate to this?

Alma 29:3–8 • God gives men what they want, whether it is good or evil. Alma continued, "But behold, I am a man, and do sin in my wish; for I ought to be content with the things which the Lord hath allotted unto me" (v. 3). He confessed that God is just and that "he granteth unto men according to their desire, whether it be unto death or unto life . . . according to their wills" (v. 4). God will not force any man to heaven, and Alma realized that he will respect the agency of all his children. Those who "knoweth not good from evil" will be held blameless for their choices, "but he that knoweth good and evil, to him it is given according to his desires, whether he desireth good or evil, life or death, joy or remorse of conscience" (v. 5). This demonstrates the justice of God. Every child gets the wish of his heart and, in the end, will be accountable for what he has chosen.

Under these circumstances, Alma asked, "Why should I desire more than to perform the work to which I have been called? Why should I desire that I were an angel, that I could speak unto all the ends of the earth? For behold, the Lord doth grant unto all nations, of their own nation and tongue, to teach his word" (vv. 6–8).

As part of this observation, Alma said that God allots to all men as much as "he seeth fit that they should have" (v. 8). Henry D. Moyle said, "I believe that we, as fellow workers in the priesthood, might well take to heart the admonition of Alma and be content with that which God hath allotted us. We might well be assured that we had something to do with our 'allotment' in our pre-existent state. This would be an additional reason for us to accept our present condition and make the best of it. It is what we agreed to do. . . . We had our own free agency in our pre-mortal existence, and whatever we are today is likely the result of that which we willed to be heretofore."[17]

Alma 29:8 • All of God's children are taught in their own tongue, often by missionaries of their own nation. Spencer W. Kimball said,

> Since about 92% of all missionaries in the field are Americans, we must call to the attention of all members in other lands that we need far more local missionaries. This scripture [Alma 29:8] indicates, brethren, that every nation is to furnish its own missionaries and we expect that to follow. . . . It is all nations of their nation and tongue. We need far more, thousands more Brazilians to preach in Brazil in Portuguese; thousands more Mexicans to preach in Spanish—Chileans, Peruvians, Bolivians, Colombians, Argentines, Venezuelans to proselyte in Spanish—hundreds more of local men to preach in Scandinavian, German, French, Filipino, Indian and all nationalities in all tongues and nations. . . . Since the local men can better represent their own people without problems of language, visas, and other rights and services, we need soon hundreds of more young men of every race and nation.[18]

Alma 29:9–16 • Alma rejoices in being an instrument in the hands of God. He said, "I know that which the Lord hath commanded me, and I glory in it. I do not glory of myself, but I glory in that which the Lord hath commanded me; yea, and this is my glory, that perhaps I may be an instrument in the hands of God to bring some soul to repentance; and this is my joy" (v. 9). As he contemplates the conversion of so many people, including Lamanites, he said, "Then is my soul filled with joy; then do I remember what the Lord has done for me, yea, even that he hath heard my prayer" (v. 10). Clearly, Alma had prayed for the power to teach and baptize. He also remembers God's "merciful arm which he extended towards me" (v. 10), not forgetting how close he and his friends the sons of Mosiah came to being utterly destroyed through their foolish rebellions against the Church.

Alma reflected upon God's mercy to his ancestors, "For I surely do know that the Lord did deliver them out of bondage, and by this did establish his church; yea, the Lord God, the God of Abraham, the God of Isaac, and the God of Jacob, did deliver them out of bondage" (v. 11). He is speaking of the children of Israel in Egypt (v. 12). "Yea . . . and that same God hath called me by a holy calling [to be a prophet], to preach the word unto this people, and hath given me much success, in the which my joy is full" (v. 13). He also rejoices in the success of the sons of Mosiah who "have labored exceedingly, and have brought forth much fruit; and how great shall be their reward!" (v. 15).

Alma 29:17 • "That they may go no more out." Alma's final wish was that their converts would remain faithful: "And now may God grant unto these, my brethren, that they may sit down in the kingdom of God; yea, and also all those who are the fruit of their labors that they may go no more out, but that they may praise him forever." It does little good in the long run if a person is baptized and then falls away. The Lord said to his disciples about their own missionary labors, "Ye have not chosen me, but I have chosen you, and ordained you, that ye should go and bring forth fruit, and that your fruit should remain" (John 15:16).

This reminds us of what President Hinckley has said about retaining converts. "The greatest tragedy in the Church . . . is the loss of those who join the Church and then fall away. With very few exceptions it need not happen."[19]

President Hinckley also said, "We are becoming a great global society. But our interest and concern must always be with the individual. Every member of this church is an individual . . . Our great responsibility is to see that each is `remembered and nourished by the good word of God' (Moroni 6:4), that each has opportunity for growth and expression and training in the work and ways of the Lord, that none lacks the necessities of life, that the needs of the poor are met, that each member shall have encouragement, training, and opportunity to move forward on the road of immortality and eternal life."[20]

He later observed, "Unfortunately, with this acceleration in conversions, we are neglecting some of these new members. . . . There is no point in doing missionary work unless we hold on to the fruits of that effort. The two must be inseparable. You cannot disregard the converts. . . . They need nurturing with the good word of God. They come into the Church with enthusiasm for what they have found. We must immediately build on that enthusiasm. . . . I am satisfied the Lord is not pleased with us. . . . I invite every member to reach out in friendship and love for those who come into the Church as converts."[21]

Prophecies and Promises Fulfilled
(ALMA 25)

Alma 25:1–2 • The Lord's prophecies of the destruction of Ammonihah are fulfilled. He had commanded Alma to "return to the city of Ammonihah, and preach again unto the people of the city . . . [and] say unto them, except they repent the Lord God will destroy them" (Alma 8:16). And in an earlier lesson we saw how this prophecy was fulfilled by their utter destruction at the hands of the Lamanites (Alma 16:2). Now we get the rest of the story, as we read here that it was the armies of Lamanites who had failed to destroy the people of Anti-Nephi-Lehi that then turned on the people of Ammonihah "and destroyed them" (vv. 1–2).

Alma 25:3–12 • Abinadi's prophecies regarding the posterity of the wicked priests of Noah are fulfilled. In many subsequent battles between the Nephites and Lamanites, the Lamanites were "driven and slain" (v. 3). "And among the Lamanites who were slain were almost all the seed of Amulon and his brethren, who were the priests of Noah" (v. 4). The few who survived "fled into the east wilderness, and . . . usurped the power and authority over the Lamanites" (v. 5). Many of the Lamanites over whom they now ruled, "after having suffered much loss and so many afflictions [in their wars with the Nephites], began to be stirred up in remembrance of the words which Aaron and his brethren had preached to them in their land . . . and thus there were many of them converted in the wilderness" (v. 6). This greatly angered their Amulonite overlords, who then caused that all those Lamanites that believed in these things should perish by fire because of their belief (vv. 5, 7), thus fulfilling a prophecy of Abinadi that the seed of the priests of Noah [the Amulonites] would "cause many to be put to death, in the like manner as he was [by fire]" (v. 12; Mosiah 17:15).

The Lamanites, having had enough of the vicious behavior of the Amulonites, rose up against them and "began to hunt the seed of Amulon and his brethren and began to slay them [as they] fled into the east wilderness" (vv. 8–9). This fulfilled yet another prophecy of Abinadi, who predicted that the children of the priests of Noah would be "scattered abroad and slain, even as a sheep having no shepherd is driven and slain by wild beasts" (v. 12; Mosiah 17:17).

Alma 25:13–16 • The converted Lamanites believe the prophecies of the coming of Christ.
The Lamanites who thus overthrew their Amulonite oppressors, "returned again to their own land; and many of them came over to dwell in the land of Ishmael and the land of Nephi, and did join themselves to the people of God, who were the people of Anti-Nephi-Lehi. And they did also bury their weapons of war, according as their brethren had and they began to be a righteous people; and they did walk in the ways of the Lord, and did observe to keep his commandments and his statutes" (vv. 13–14).

Mormon here observed that the converted Lamanites "did keep the law of Moses; for it was expedient that they should keep the law of Moses as yet, for it was not all fulfilled. But notwithstanding the law of Moses, they did look forward to the coming of Christ, considering that the law of Moses was a type of his coming, and believing that they must keep those outward performances until the time that he should be revealed unto them" (v. 15). He adds further that "the law of Moses did serve to strengthen their faith in Christ; and thus they did retain a hope through faith, unto eternal salvation, relying upon the spirit of prophecy, which spake of those things to come" (v. 16).

These converted Lamanites understood, as had the righteous Nephites before them, that actual salvation did not come through obedience to the law of Moses alone (Mosiah 13:27–33). Rather, they correctly understood that the law of Moses served an important purpose until the Savior completed his mission in mortality. Through observance of this law, they could look forward to the coming of Christ, with the law serving as a type (or representation) of Christ and his mission.

Alma 25:17 • God fulfilled all his promises to the sons of Mosiah. Ammon, Aaron, Omner, and Himni saw their success among the Lamanites as a fulfillment of their prayers and the Lord's promises to them. From the very beginning of their missions, the sons of Mosiah had received comfort and counsel from the Lord. He visited and comforted them with his Spirit, and he counseled them to press forward despite their challenges and to "be patient in long-suffering and afflictions, that [they] may show forth good examples" (Alma 17:10–11). He had promised, if they would do this, "I will make an instrument of thee in my hands unto the salvation of many souls" (Alma 17:11; see also Alma 17:35–39; 19:22–23; 26:1–4). Mormon observes now, at the end of their missions, that these promises were fulfilled "in every particular."

This is perhaps the greatest lesson that emerges from this section of the Book of Mormon— that God always keeps his promises. A second and equally important conclusion is that he will redeem any willing soul who turns to him, whatever their former state of wickedness. His primary interest is in saving his children, not destroying them. And we should join him in this saving work with the same charitable attitude.

Spencer W. Kimball said, "If we are to fulfill the responsibility given to us by the Lord on the Mount of Olives to go into all the world and preach the gospel to every creature, then we will need to open the doors to these nations. . . . We've hardly scratched the surface. We need far more missionaries, and we need more countries that will think of us as being their friends and will give us an opportunity to come into their nations and give to their people the finest thing in the world—the gospel of Christ—which can be their salvation and their great happiness. . . . We will make them good citizens, we will make them good souls, and we will make them happy and joyous."[22]

Notes

1. Daniel H. Ludlow, *A Companion to Your Study of the Book of Mormon* (Salt lake City: Deseret Book, 1976), 209.
2. George Q. Cannon, "The Book of Mormon Geography," *Juvenile Instructor*, Jan. 1890, 18–19.
3. Marion G. Romney, in Conference Report, Oct. 1948, 75.
4. Spencer W. Kimball, "Our Paths Have Met Again," *Ensign*, Dec. 1975, 5, 7.
5. Gordon B. Hinckley, "Converts and Young Men," *Ensign*, May 1997, 47–48.
6. Daniel H. Ludlow, *A Companion to Your Study of the Book of Mormon* (Salt Lake City: Deseret Book, 1976), 209.
7. Jerry L. Ainsworth, *The Lives and Travels of Mormon and Moroni* (Peacemakers Publishing, 2000), 133.
8. Ezra Taft Benson, *The Teachings of Ezra Taft Benson* (Salt Lake City: Bookcraft, 1988), 168.
9. Daniel Tyler, "Recollections of the Prophet Joseph Smith," *Juvenile Instructor*, Aug. 1892, 492.
10. Joseph Smith Jr., *History of The Church of Jesus Christ of Latter-day Saints*, B. H. Roberts, ed., 2nd ed. (Salt Lake City: The Church of Jesus Christ of Latter-day Saints), 4:554, 5:362.
11. Bruce R. McConkie, *Mormon Doctrine*, 2nd ed., (Salt Lake City: Bookcraft, 1966), 144–45.
12. Wilford Woodruff, *The Discourses of Wilford Woodruff*, G. Homer Durham, comp. (Salt Lake City: Bookcraft, 1946), 123–24.
13. Brigham Young, *Discourses of Brigham Young*, John A. Widtsoe, comp. (Salt Lake City: Deseret Book, 1954), 330.
14. Spencer W. Kimball, "The False Gods We Worship," *Ensign*, Jun. 1976, 6.
15. Neal A. Maxwell (address to BYU students, Provo, UT, Nov. 27, 1979); *Ensign*, October 1980, 28–31.
16. Joseph Smith, *Teachings of the Prophet Joseph Smith*, Joseph Fielding Smith, sel. (Salt Lake City: Deseret Book, 1976), 343.
17. Henry D. Moyle, in Conference Report, Oct. 1952, 71.
18. Spencer W. Kimball, regional representatives' seminar, Salt Lake City, Utah, Sept. 30, 1977.
19. Gordon B. Hinckley, regional representatives' seminar, Salt lake City, Utah, April 3, 1987.
20. Gordon B. Hinckley, "This Work Is Concerned with People," *Ensign*, May 1995, 52.
21. Gordon B. Hinckley, *Ensign*, "Some Thoughts on Temples, Retention of Converts, and Missionary Service," November 1997, 50–51.
22. Spencer W. Kimball, in Conference Report, Oct. 1978, 66; *Ensign*, Nov. 1978, 45–46.

"All Things Denote There Is a God"

Korihor and the Zoramites

The Purpose and Effects of Adversity

After the needless slaughter of thousands of fathers, husbands, and brothers, along with innocent women and children during the most recent Lamanite wars, the Nephites were humbled and began to pull their society back to order. Adversity can have that effect upon people, but it can also turn some people away.

Spencer W. Kimball said, "One time or another we all face adversity's chilling wind. One man flees from it, and like an unresisting kite falls to the ground. Another yields no retreating inch, and the wind that would destroy him lifts him as readily to the heights. We are not measured by the trials we meet, only by those we overcome."[1]

One important factor in this difference is the degree of a person's faith in God. The focus of this lesson is on two groups of people who experienced the same misery and misfortune as other Nephites, but whose reactions were markedly different. For some, humility led to faith, self-mastery, and salvation. For others, faithlessness led to apostasy.

Korihor the Anti-Christ

(ALMA 30)

WHAT IS AN ANTI-CHRIST?

1 John 2:22; 1 John 4:2–3 • An anti-Christ is one who denies the existence of Christ or of the Father or refuses to confess his knowledge of them.

The Bible Dictionary defines an anti-Christ as "anyone or anything that counterfeits the true gospel or plan of salvation and that openly or secretly is set up in opposition to Christ" ("Anti-Christ," 609).

Bruce R. McConkie said, "An antichrist is an opponent of Christ; he is one who is in opposition to the true gospel, the true Church, and the true plan of salvation. (1 John 2:19; 4:4–6.) He is one who offers salvation to men on some other terms than those laid down by Christ. Sherem (Jacob 7:1–23), Nehor (Alma 1:2–16), and Korihor (Alma 30:6–60) were antichrists who spread their delusions among the Nephites."[2]

Alma 30:1–5 • The Nephites live in peace for nearly two years after establishing the people of Ammon in the land of Jershon and driving the warring Lamanites out of the land (74–73 BC). They buried their numberless dead and then engaged in fasting, mourning, and prayer (vv. 1–2). They were strict in their obedience to the commandments and in the ordinances of the law of Moses (v. 3), and as a result the Lord blessed them with continual peace (vv. 4–5).

Alma 30:6–12 • Korihor (an anti-Christ) comes among the people, preaching against Christ and his prophets. It was toward the latter end of the year 73 BC that Korihor "came . . . into the land of Zarahemla, and he was Anti-Christ, for he began to preach unto the people against the prophecies which had been spoken by the prophets, concerning the coming of Christ" (v. 6). According to Nephite law "the law could have no hold upon him" because of his beliefs (vv. 7, 12). People were free to choose whom they would serve spiritually (v. 8). If they committed crimes such as murder, robbery, theft, or adultery, they were punished according to the laws of the land (vv. 9–10). But "there was no law against a man's belief; therefore, a man was punished only for the crimes which he had done; therefore all men were on equal grounds" (v. 11). Korihor was free, therefore, to go around and "preach unto the people that there should be no Christ" (v. 12).

The False Teachings of Korihor
(ALMA 30)

The teachings of Korihor have a familiar ring to them. They are the same arguments made by the secular philosophers and religionists of our own time. There is perhaps no greater example of the Book of Mormon's applicability to our time than Korihor's philosophies.

DISRESPECT FOR ANYONE WHO DARES TO DISAGREE WITH HIM

Secularists object to the pious life-styles of believers, claiming that nobody is more righteous than another—they are simply "different." And yet, there is no class of people more self-righteous than secularists, who truly do believe that they are the only class of people worthy of respect. Those who disagree with them are silly, foolish, or even crazy.

Alma 30:13–14 • Anyone who disagrees with him is "foolish."
Alma 30:16 • Believing otherwise "is the effect of a frenzied mind."
Alma 30:31 • Anyone who disagrees with him is "silly."

A STRICTLY RATIONAL AND SCIENTIFIC APPROACH TO TRUTH.

Alma 30:13 • "No man can know of anything which is to come." (Note: It is contradictory for him to say that no one can know of things to come and then predict that there will be no Christ—a future event. Secularists often violate their own rules.)

Alma 30:15 • "Ye cannot know of things which ye do not see; therefore ye cannot know that there shall be a Christ." To the strictly scientific mind, if something cannot be directly observed (and the observation replicated by others), then it does not exist. The universe (the laws of physics) are self-existent and operate according to fixed principles (for example, the law of gravity). Fair enough, though we could make a long list of things scientists once denied were true and now embrace (such as the existence of other planets in the universe).

However, when scientists go beyond their observations and try to explain what is *behind* what they see, they go too far. Observing how planets behave is one thing; claiming that there is no intelligent mind behind those motions is another, and is completely unscientific.

C. S. Lewis wrote,

> Wherever there have been thinking men both views turn up. And note this too. You cannot find out which view is the right one by science in the ordinary sense. Science works by experiments. It watches how things behave. Every scientific statement in the long run, however complicated it looks, really means something like, "I pointed the telescope to such and such a part of the sky at 2:20 on January 15th and saw so-and-so," or, "I put some of this stuff in a pot and heated it to such-and-such a temperature and it did so-and-so." Do not think I am saying anything against science: I am only saying what its job is. And the more scientific a man is, the more (I believe) he would agree with me that this is the job of science—and a very useful and necessary job it is too. But why anything comes to be there at all, and whether there is anything behind the things science observes—something of a different kind—this is not a scientific question. If there is "Something Behind," then either it will have to remain altogether unknown to men or else make itself known in some different way. The statement that there is any such thing, and the statement that there is no such thing, are neither of them statements that science can make. And real scientists do not usually make them.[3]

A New Morality and the Shedding of Old Inhibitions:

Alma 30:17 • "Whatsoever a man [does is] no crime." This is the part of secularist thinking that is most popular, because it claims to "set us free" from consequences. If there be no God then there is no sin, and it's perfectly okay to think or to do whatever we want without fear of any kind of accountability or punishment.

"Eat, drink, and be merry!" "You only live once!" "It's your life, so live it to the full—on the edge, without restraint, and with gusto!" "Make your own rules!" "Go for it!" "Live, and let live!" But it's all a lie. Simple observation shows us that there *are* consequences of our choices, and we *do* eventually pay a price in our health and happiness. History tells us that the consequences do come, both to individuals and to the societies in which they live. We can fool ourselves, but we can't escape the law of the harvest. It is as sure and as irrevocable as the law of gravity.

Strict Materialism as the Measure of a Man's Success

Alma 30:17 • "Every man prosper[s] according to his genius, and . . . every man conquer[s] according to his strength." This tenet enthrones pride. If I'm doing better than you it is because I am smarter than you, stronger than you, more valuable than you. The name of the game is competition. The idea is to win, and because there are no rules (see above), anything is permissible so long as I come out on top. If you are not as able and powerful as I am, then I may use you to enhance my wealth and position. "Lead, follow, or get out of the way!" The prideful press their way through the crowd, grasping what they believe is rightfully theirs, without concern for how much pain and suffering they may cause along the way.

Alma 30:18 • "When a man [is] dead that [is] the end thereof." Secular naturalists deny that there is any purpose to life. Bertrand Russell is one of the most revered proponents of the naturalistic viewpoint, and his philosophies are built around this "purposeless" notion. E. A. Burtt summarizes Russell's ideas as follows:

> To Russell, man is but the chance and temporary product of a blind and purposeless nature, an irrelevant spectator of her doings, almost an alien intruder on her domain. No high place in a cosmic teleology is his; his ideals, his hopes, his mystic raptures, are but the creations of his own errant and enthusiastic imagination, without standing or application to a real world interpreted mechanically in terms of space, time, and unconscious, though eternal atoms. His mother earth is but a speck in the boundlessness of space, his place even on the earth but insignificant and precarious, in a word, he is at the mercy of brute forces that unknowingly happened to throw him into being, and promise ere long just as unknowingly to snuff out the candle of his little day. Himself and all that is dear to him will in course of time become "buried in a universe of ruins."[4]

ACCUSING ALMA AND THE CHURCH OF EXPLOITING PEOPLE FOR THEIR MONEY

Alma 30:27 • "Ye keep them down . . . in bondage, that ye may glut yourselves with [their] labors." The hypocrisy of this claim is breathtaking. Korihor knew full-well that Alma and his associates supported themselves temporally and did not rely upon any form of tax or welfare from the people. They were lay ministers whose only desire was to serve and to save the people. On the other hand, Korihor was profiting from his preaching, which teachings he himself later explained "were pleasing unto the carnal mind; and I taught them, even until I had much success, insomuch that I verily believed that they were true; and for this cause I withstood the truth, even until I have brought this great curse upon me" (Alma 30:53).

Alma 30:18 • His teachings cause people to be proud of their wickedness. False prophets appeal to so many people because the faithless can use their teachings to feel justified in doing as they wish. This is precisely what happened to those who followed Korihor. He "set them free" from consequences and empowered them to do whatever they wanted in the pursuit of wealth, power, and prestige.

How to Respond to Anti-Christs
(ALMA 30)

How should we deal with anti-Christs like Korihor? The response of the people, of the high priests, and of Alma provides an example of how we should deal with the anti-Christs of our own day.

1. Do not engage in arguments (vv. 19–21).
After spreading his false teachings in Zarahemla, Korihor attempted to preach the same things among the people in Jershon and Gideon. While the people of Zarahemla listened to Korihor's false teachings, the people of Ammon and the people in Gideon would not.

2. If the anti-Christ is a Church member, hold him or her accountable (vv. 21–22).

The people of Ammon delivered him to their high priest, Ammon, and the people of Gideon delivered him to their high priest, Giddonah. The fact that he was delivered to the high priests would seem to indicate that Korihor was a member of the Church. He was probably being tried for his membership because he was teaching many false doctrines (vv. 23–24, 27–28). He denounced the Church leaders who were trying him and went on to denounce the Fall, the Atonement, and revelation.

The Prophet Joseph Smith said, "I will give you one of the Keys of the mysteries of the Kingdom. It is an eternal principle, that has existed with God from all eternity: That man who rises up to condemn others, finding fault with the Church, saying that they are out of the way, while he himself is righteous, then know assuredly, that that man is in the high road to apostasy; and if he does not repent, will apostatize, as God lives."[5]

Korihor challenges their testimonies, saying, "Ye do not know that they are true" (Alma 30:24).

McConkie and Millet said, "The doubter errs grossly through generalizing beyond his own experiences. What he has not experienced, no one else can. Because he does not know, no one knows; because he cannot feel, surely no one has felt; because he is lacking in evidence concerning the coming of a Christ, unquestionably the evidence amassed by every believing soul is either insufficient or naively misinterpreted. Those who dare not believe dare not allow others to believe."[6]

I have experienced this kind of thinking-for-other-people behavior. Once, while working on my graduate degrees, I was challenged by a professor who said with some disdain, "You Mormons are not Christians, and you do not believe in Christ." I responded, "Who are you to tell me what I believe? You have no idea what I believe. I believe in Christ. He is my king and my beloved Savior, and I know that he lives. I do most certainly believe in him, and you are not the arbiter of who is and who is not a Christian. I suggest that you speak for yourself." He apologized.

The Savior said, "By this shall all men know that ye are my disciples, if ye have love one to another" (John 13:35). If that is the measure by which a disciple of Christ is discerned, then the hateful behavior of those would loudly and publicly call into question our discipleship and faith in Christ are not his disciples. The pharisees rejected Christ himself with the same spirit of accusation. We should not engage in any portion of their behavior, nor respond with the same spirit. The Lord said, "Ye shall know them by their fruits" (Matthew 7:16).

Korihor was delivered to Alma, the chief judge over all the land, and "went on to blaspheme" (vv. 29–30). The word *blaspheme*, as used here, means "to speak evil of or to revile against God." Bruce R. McConkie said, "Blasphemy consists in either or both of the following: 1. Speaking irreverently, evilly, abusively, or scurrilously against God or sacred things; or 2. Speaking profanely or falsely about Deity. Among a great host of impious and sacrilegious speaking that constitute blasphemy are such things as: taking the name of God in vain; evil-speaking about the Lord's anointed; belittling sacred temple ordinances, or patriarchal blessings, or sacramental administrations; claiming unwarranted divine authority; and promulgating with profane piety a false system of salvation."[7]

3. Know the truth (vv. 31–35). Anti-Christs often distort or fabricate facts to suit their purposes, hoping that their fallacies will never be questioned. If we know the facts, then we can withstand such behavior. Alma responded to Korihor's accusations against Church leaders by providing the facts of the situation. He testifies of the fruits of the gospel (vv. 34–35). One of the most important evidences of the truthfulness of the gospel is the joy it produces in the hearts of people.

4. Bear personal testimony (vv. 39–40). Our personal witnesses cannot be assailed by any other person. This is why a personal testimony is so vital to our ability to overcome difficulties and challenges and to endure to the end.

5. Seek the guidance of the Holy Ghost (vv. 41–42). Alma was able to discern through he Spirit that Korihor was lying and knew what he was saying was not true.

Alma 30:43 • Korihor demands a sign that will prove God's existence. This is the standard response of a secularist to the testimony of the faithful: "Show me a sign, that I may be convinced that there is a God, yea, show unto me that he hath power, and then will I be convinced of the truth of thy words."

D&C 63:7–12 • Faith is not generated by signs. Signs come only to those who already believe, to help and sustain them and reward their faith. They do not come to the faithless in order to convince them.

Boyd K. Packer said, "In a world filled with skepticism and doubt, the expression 'seeing is believing' promotes the attitude, 'You show me, and I will believe.' We want all of the proof and all of the evidence first. It seems hard to take things on faith. When will we learn that in spiritual things it works the other way about—that believing is seeing? Spiritual belief precedes spiritual knowledge. When we believe in things that are not seen but are nevertheless true, then we have faith."[8]

Joseph F. Smith said, "It is not by marvelous manifestations unto us that we shall be established in the truth, but it is by humility and faithful obedience to the commandments and laws of God. When I as a boy first started out in the ministry, I would frequently go out and ask the Lord to show me some marvelous thing, in order that I might receive a testimony. But the Lord withheld marvels from me, and showed me the truth, line upon line, precept upon precept, here a little and there a little, until he made me to know the truth from the crown of my head to the soles of my feet, and until doubt and fear had been absolutely purged from me."[9]

The Prophet Joseph Smith said, "Jesus put forth [a] saying that he who seeketh a sign is an adulterous person; and that principal is eternal, undeviating, and firm as the pillars of heaven; for whenever you see a man seeking after a sign, you may set it down that he is an adulterous man."[10]

Alma 30:44 • "All things denote there is a God." Alma cited "all these thy brethren," the prophets, the scriptures, and the entire material universe as sufficient proof that there is an all-knowing and all-powerful God.

Gordon B. Hinckley said, "Can any man who has walked beneath the stars at night, can anyone who has seen the touch of spring upon the land doubt the hand of divinity in creation? So observing the beauties of the earth, one is wont to speak as did the Psalmist: 'The heavens declare the glory of God; and the firmament sheweth his handywork. Day unto day uttereth speech, and night unto night sheweth knowledge.' (Ps. 19:1–2.) All of beauty in the earth bears the fingerprint of the Master Creator."[11]

Alma 30:45–50 • Alma provides a sign—Korihor is struck permanently dumb. Korihor rejected all of the witnesses Alma has cited, saying, "Except ye shall show me a sign" (v. 45). Knowing that the only signs given to the wicked are those that will condemn them, Alma grieved for the wickedness of Korihor but said, "It is better that thy soul should be lost than that thou shouldst be the means of bringing many souls down to destruction, by thy lying and by thy flattering words; therefore if thou shalt deny again, behold God shall smite thee, that thou shalt become dumb, that thou shalt never open thy mouth any more, that thou shalt not deceive this people any more" (vv. 46–47). Korihor said again that he would not believe in God, and Alma therefore gave him his sign. "This will I give unto thee for a sign, that thou shalt be struck dumb, according to my words; and I say, that in the name of God, ye shall be struck dumb, that ye shall no more have utterance" (vv. 48–49). And immediately Korihor was struck dumb (v. 50).

Alma 30:51–53 • Korihor admits that he has always known there is a God. He acknowledged that he was now dumb and could not speak, saying, "Nothing save it were the power of God could bring this upon me" and then admitted "I always knew there was a God (vv. 51–52). He also acknowledged that he had chosen to follow Satan because it was "pleasing unto the carnal mind" and brought him "much success" (v. 53). And he said that his great success eventually convinced him of his own false doctrines, saying "I verily believed that they were true; and for this cause I withstood the truth, even until I have brought this great curse upon me" (v. 53).

Alma 30:54–59 • The curse remains with him and eventually he is trampled to death while begging in the streets. Korihor begged Alma to "pray unto God, that the curse might be taken from him" (v. 54), but Alma refused, saying, "If this curse should be taken from thee thou wouldst again lead away the hearts of this people; therefore, it shall be unto thee even as the Lord will" (v. 55). Where there are no consequences, there is little motivation to do what is right. If Korihor had been quickly healed, it would have been too easy to forget the severity of his punishment and to even deny that it was of God. This could not be a temporary condition. It was a permanent punishment for a man who was given many opportunities to admit his fault and repent of his blasphemy. He chose not to do so.

Now unable to secure a following for his swelling oratory, Korihor "was cast out, and went about from house to house begging for his food" (v. 56). His situation was widely known and those who had followed him were warned to repent "lest the same judgments would come unto them" (v. 57). Not surprisingly, "they were all convinced of the wickedness of Korihor; therefore they were all converted again unto the Lord; and this put an end to the iniquity after the manner of Korihor" (v. 58). Korihor eventually made his way to a city of apostate Nephites called Zoramites led by a man named Zoram (perhaps thinking he would be welcomed there). But "as he went forth amongst them, behold, he was run upon and trodden down, even until he was dead" (v. 59).

Alma 30:60 • Mormon editorializes about the story of Korihor. In the end, Satan will not support those who follow him but will abandon them. Mormon observes, "And thus we see the end of him who perverteth the ways of the Lord; and thus we see that the devil will not support his children at the last day, but doth speedily drag them down to hell" (v. 60).

Janette C. Hales said, "Satan does not support those who follow him. He can't! It's the Lord who sustains; the Spirit sustains; righteousness sustains. That sustenance is not Satan's to give."[12]

Alma's Mission to the Zoramites
(Alma 31)

The Apostate Zoramite Religion

Alma 31:1–4 • The Zoramites pose a threat to Nephite peace. The Zoramites, a group of Nephites who had separated themselves from the faithful, were "perverting the ways of the Lord," and their leader Zoram was encouraging them to "bow down to dumb idols" (v. 1). This caused Alma great sorrow (v. 2) because he knew from experience that this could only lead to destruction. Had it not been so at Ammonihah? The Book of Mormon records that he was sick at heart and "exceedingly sorrowful" (vv. 1–2).

The area where the Zoramites had settled was called "Antionum, which was east of the land of Zarahemla . . . nearly bordering upon the seashore . . . south of the land of Jershon, [and bordering] upon the wilderness south, which wilderness was full of the Lamanites" (v. 3; refer to the map at the beginning of lesson 26). Their proximity to the Lamanites caused the Nephites great concern, fearing that they would ally themselves with the Lamanites "and that it would be the means of great loss on the part of the Nephites" (v. 4).

Alma 31:5–7 • Alma organizes a mission to the Zoramites. How could Alma best deal with this threat? Was military force the answer? It certainly had not been the answer when the sons of Mosiah went forth to pacify and convert the Lamanites. Alma believed that "the preaching of the word had a great tendency to lead the people to do that which was just—yea, it had had more powerful effect upon the minds of the people than the sword, or anything else" (v. 5). He concluded that "it was expedient that they should try the virtue of the word of God" among the Zoramites (v. 5).

Marion G. Romney said, "There are no armaments, no governmental schemes, no international organizations, and no mechanisms for the control of weapons which can preserve an unrighteous people. . . . Alma has given us compelling evidence of his conviction that repentance is more effectual than arms in maintaining peace. You will recall that he was the elected chief judge of the Nephite nation. As such he was the governor of the people of Nephi and commander-in-chief of their armies. Seeing many of them dissenting and conniving with the enemy, he, notwithstanding his power to strengthen and command his armies, placed the affairs of state in other hands that he himself might cry repentance unto the dissenters."[13]

Ezra Taft Benson said, "The gospel is the only answer to the problems of the world. We may cry peace. We may hold peace conferences. And I have nothing but commendation for those who work for peace. But it is my conviction that peace must come from within. It cannot be imposed by state mandate. It can come only by following the teachings and the example of the Prince of Peace."[14]

President Benson also said, "The Lord works from the inside out. The world works from the outside in. The world would take people out of the slums. Christ takes the slums out of the people, and then they take themselves out of the slums. The world would mold men by changing their environment. Christ changes men, who then change their environment. The world would shape human behavior, but Christ can change human nature."[15]

With regard to the best way to change men's lives, Boyd K. Packer said, "True doctrine, understood, changes attitudes and behavior. The study of the doctrines of the gospel will improve behavior quicker than a study of behavior will improve behavior."[16]

Alma took as his missionary companions three of the sons of Mosiah—Ammon, Aaron, and Omner—leaving the fourth, Himni, to watch over the church in Zarahemla. He also took Amulek and Zeezrom and two of his sons—Shiblon and Corianton (vv. 6–7).

Alma 31:8–11 • The Zoramites became apostate for two primary reasons: (1) They were dissenters (politically and religiously); and (2) they were disobedient to the commandments and became apostates from the Church.

Alma 31:12–21 • The beliefs of the Zoramite religion were similar in many ways to the anti-Christ and the secular views espoused by Korihor, but without denying the existence of a God. These were truly the philosophies of men, mingled with some scripture.

▷ They did not keep the law of Moses (v. 9).
▷ They had forsaken daily prayer (v. 10).
▷ They had perverted the ways of the Lord (v. 11).
▷ They practiced their religion only one day per week (v. 12).
▷ They believed God was, is, and always will be a spirit (v. 15).
▷ They did not believe in the traditions of their fellow Nephites (v. 16).
▷ They taught that "there shall be no Christ" (v. 16).
▷ They believed they would be saved but everyone else would not (v. 17).
▷ They believed others were bound by "foolish traditions" (v. 17).
▷ They saw themselves as "a chosen and a holy people" (v. 18).

Alma 31:21 • The Rameumptom. Zoramites offered their public prayers from a "holy stand" in their synagogue, which they called Rameumptom. This is yet another evidence of the authenticity of the Book of Mormon.

Ram is Hebrew for a high place where one can be seen (e.g., the town Ramallah in the Judean hills and the hill Ramah in the Book of Mormon). *Mptom* is Hebrew for "a threshhold."

The need to be seen doing righteous things such as praying is not unique to the Zoramites. It is quite common in the world today. K. Douglas Bassett observed,

> Our society may well be as guilty as the wealthy Zoramites of using fashion as "the science of appearances, inspiring us with the desire to seem rather than to be" (Edwin Hubbell Chapin). In our day the costly apparel syndrome may be identified as one aspect of the modern-day term "conspicuous consumption." The word conspicuous alludes to the visual side of vanity—the need to be seen, to be recognized. Consumption refers to that which we take in or that which we consume. Conspicuous consumption may be defined as that which we take to ourselves in order to be recognized and approved by others. By its very definition, the person trapped in conspicuous consumption, especially as it applies to "costly apparel," must be focused on the opinions of others, because what is "in" today may be "out" tomorrow. Vanity then becomes its own punishment, because there is never time to be satisfied—the eyes and opinions of others can turn so quickly to embrace someone else. For us, the disease that afflicted the Zoramites encompasses more than clothing. It can include cars, houses, boats, diplomas, and anything else that has a foundation where the need for the approval of man carries more weight than the need to be accepted by God.[17]

Alma 31:22–25 • The character of the Zoramite people was what we would expect of a largely secular and materialistic people.

> ▷ Elitist—They believed they were the only people God loved (v. 22).
> ▷ Shallow—They practiced their religion only on the Sabbath (v. 23).
> ▷ Worldly—They loved gold and silver (v. 24).
> ▷ Proud—They engaged in great boasting (v. 25).

Alma 31:19, 24, 34 • Alma and his brethren are astonished by the Zoramites' false worship. The Book of Mormon says that when they had "heard these prayers, they were astonished beyond all measure" (v. 19), and Alma's "heart was grieved; for he saw that they were a wicked and a perverse people; yea, he saw that their hearts were set upon gold, and upon silver, and upon all manner of fine goods" (v. 24). He prayed, "O Lord, wilt thou grant unto us that we may have success in bringing them again unto thee in Christ" (v. 34).

Alma 31:30–35 • Alma's prayer is a model for missionaries everywhere. He prays for his own capacity to do the work and to teach with power, but also prays for the redemption of the Zoramites, whom he calls "precious."

v. 30 • "Give me strength, that I may bear with mine infirmities."
v. 31 • "Wilt thou comfort my soul in Christ."
v. 32 • "Give unto me success, and also my fellow laborers."
v. 32 • "Wilt thou comfort [my fellow laborers'] souls in Christ."
vv. 34–35 • "[Help us bring the Zoramites] unto thee."
v. 35 • "[The Zoramites'] souls are precious."
v. 35 • "Give unto us . . . power and wisdom."

D&C 18:10–14 • The worth of souls is great in the sight of God, and his joy is great in the "soul that repenteth."

The Prophet Joseph Smith said, "Souls are as precious in the sight of God as they ever were, and the Elders were never called to drive any down to hell, but to persuade and invite all men everywhere to repent, that they may become the heirs of salvation."[18]

Alma 31:36–39 • Alma gives blessings to his missionaries and they proceed to teach correct principles to the people. Alma "clapped his hands upon" (blessed) all of the missionaries who were with him, and "they were filled with the Holy Spirit" (v. 36). They then separated from each other and began to travel and teach without purse or scrip (v. 37). The scripture records that "the Lord provided for them that they should hunger not, neither should they thirst; yea, and he also gave them strength, that they should suffer no manner of afflictions, save it were swallowed up in the joy of Christ," which was what Alma had promised them in his blessings to them before they departed (v. 38).

This is not to suggest that they had no difficulties or challenges. The promise was that their afflictions would be "swallowed up in the joy of Christ."

Neal A. Maxwell said,

> Why is non-endurance a denial of the Lord? Because giving up is a denial of the Lord's loving capacity to see us through "all these things"! Giving up suggests that God is less than He really is . . . . So much of life's curriculum consists of efforts by the Lord to get and keep our attention. Ironically, the stimuli He uses are often that which is seen by us as something to endure. Sometimes

50

what we are being asked to endure is His "help"—help to draw us away from the cares of the world; help to draw us away from self-centeredness; attention-getting help when the still, small voice has been ignored by us; help in the shaping of our souls; and help to keep the promises we made so long ago to Him and to ourselves. . . .

Whether the afflictions are self-induced, as most of them are, or whether they are of the divine-tutorial type, it matters not. Either way, the Lord can help us so that our afflictions, said Alma, can be "swallowed up in the joy of Christ" (Alma 31:38). Thus, afflictions are endured and are overcome by joy. The sour notes are lost amid a symphony of salvational sounds. Our afflictions, brothers and sisters, may not be extinguished. Instead they can be dwarfed and swallowed up in the joy of Christ. This is how we overcome most of the time—not the elimination of affliction, but the placing of these in that larger context.[19]

Notes

1. Spencer W. Kimball, in Conference Report, Oct. 1974.

2. Bruce R. McConkie, *Mormon Doctrine*, 2nd ed. (Salt Lake City: Bookcraft, 1966), 39–40.

3. C. S. Lewis, *Mere Christianity* (New York: Macmillan, 1960), 32.

4. E.A. Burtt, *The Metaphysical Foundations of Modern Physical Science* (London: Routledge & Kegan Paul, 1950), 10.

5. Joseph Smith, *Teachings of the Prophet Joseph Smith*, Joseph Fielding Smith, sel. (Salt Lake City: Deseret Book, 1976), Joseph Fielding Smith, sel. (Salt Lake City: Deseret Book, 1976), 156–157.

6. Joseph Fielding McConkie and Robert L. Millet, *Doctrinal Commentary on the Book of Mormon* (Salt Lake City: Deseret Book, 1987), 2:86.

7. Bruce R. McConkie, *Mormon Doctrine*, 2nd ed. (Salt Lake City: Bookcraft, 1966), 90.

8. Boyd K. Packer, *Faith* (Salt Lake City: Deseret Book, 1983), 43.

9. Joseph F. Smith, *Joseph F. Smith, Gospel Doctrine, 5th ed. (Salt Lake City: Deseret Book, 1939),*, 5th ed. (Salt Lake City: Deseret Book, 1939), 7.

10. Joseph Smith, *Teachings of the Prophet Joseph Smith*, Joseph Fielding Smith, sel. (Salt Lake City: Deseret Book, 1976), 156–57.

11. Gordon B. Hinckley, in Conference Report, Apr. 1978, 90.

12. Janette C. Hales, devotional, Brigham Young University, Provo, UT, March 16, 1993.

13. Marion G. Romney, in Conference Report, Apr. 1950, 87–88.

14. Eazra Taft Benson, *Title of Liberty* (Salt Lake City: Deseret Book, 1964), 213–14.

15. Ezra Taft Benson, *Ensign*, Nov. 1985, 6.

16. Boyd K. Packer, in Conference Report, Oct. 1986, 20.

17. Neal A. Maxwell, "Doctrines of the Book of Mormon," in *1991 Sperry Symposium*, 18–19.

18. Joseph Smith, *Teachings of the Prophet Joseph Smith*, Joseph Fielding Smith, sel. (Salt Lake City: Deseret Book, 1976), 77.

19. Neal A. Maxwell, fireside address, Brigham Young University, Provo, Utah, December 2, 1984.

LESSON 28
"The Word Is in Christ unto Salvation"
ALMA 32–35

Nourishing the Word with Faith

When Alma and his brethren first encountered the Zoramites, they discovered that the poor had been humbled through their afflictions (Alma 32:1–7). Though it may not have felt like it to them, this was a great blessing. Humility prepared their hearts to hear and believe the truth (Alma 32:8–16, 24–25). Those who were not thus humbled rejected the words of Alma and his companions and reaped destruction and damnation.

Spencer W. Kimball said, "Being human, we would expel from our lives physical pain and mental anguish and assure ourselves of continual ease and comfort, but if we were to close the doors upon sorrow and distress, we might be excluding our greatest friends and benefactors. Suffering can make saints of people as they learn patience, longsuffering, and self-mastery."[1]

How to Exercise Faith
(ALMA 32)

THE NEED FOR PROPER PREPARATION AND PATIENCE

Alma 32:8–16, 24–25 • Humility prepares our hearts to hear and believe the truth. We must first be teachable. When we figure that we already know, then we are not receptive to anything new. This is precisely why the Lord calls faithful youngsters, like the Prophet Joseph Smith at age fifteen, to do great things. And it is also why the missionaries usually have more success among the poor and humble than among the wealthy and mighty.

Alma 32:17–18, 21 • Faith is not to have a perfect knowledge, but to believe and to hope. If, when we begin, we are expecting to know "of a surety," then we may be disappointed. The power of faith is phenomenal; just the amount of faith represented by a tiny mustard seed can move mountains. But it cannot be feigned. As the fictional Huckleberry Finn found out, "You can't pray a lie." Either you truly do believe or you don't.

Also, you cannot exercise faith about something for which you have a perfect knowledge. The Prophet Joseph Smith defined faith as "the assurance which men have of the existence of things which they have not seen, and the principle of action in all intelligent beings."[2] Faith involves a degree of trust—primarily in God but also in others. Faith requires us to be believing when we don't know for sure (John 20:27). Faith is one of the characteristics possessed by our Heavenly Father, and if we wish to be like him we must possess faith also.

The Prophet Joseph Smith said that God literally controls the universe through his faith:

> The principle of power which existed in the bosom of God, by which the worlds were framed, was faith; and that it is by reason of this principle of power existing in the Deity, that all created things exist; so that all things in heaven, on earth, or under the earth, exist by reason of faith as it existed in him.
>
> Had it not been for the principle of faith the worlds would never have been framed, neither would man have been formed of the dust. It is the principle by which Jehovah works, and through which he exercises power over all temporal as well as eternal things. Take this principle or attribute—for it is an attribute—from the Deity, and he would cease to exist.
>
> Who cannot see, that if God framed the worlds by faith, that it is by faith that he exercises power over them, and that faith is the principle of power? And if the principle of power, it must be so in man as well as in the Deity?[3] (Joseph Smith, comp., *Lectures on Faith* [1985], 1:15–17.)

Alma 32:22–23 • Remember that God is merciful and kind and will reward our faith. To have faith in God, we must trust him and believe him. Alma reminded us that God wants us to succeed and will, without fail, reward our exercise of faith (v. 22). We need not worry that he will let us down. If we approach him with fear or with doubt, he cannot help us because faith is the very power by which he will reveal his will to us and move events and circumstances for our good. If we have not faith, we cut off the power line by which the answers can come. Alma also assured us that all of God's children—men, women, and children—will receive the revelation they seek if they will exercise their faith (v. 23).

Alma 32:26 • Be patient. Alma reminded us that nobody can know perfectly at first. It takes time. We live in a world where "instant gratification" is expected, but faith does not develop in a moment. Indeed, patience is an element of faith, and we show our faith by patiently waiting upon God for an answer or a blessing. My wife and I once prayed for a righteous blessing for thirty-two years before God saw fit to grant it. We always knew he would; we just didn't know when, and we had to learn to be patient and to exercise our faith.

Neal A. Maxwell said,

> Patience is tied very closely to faith in our Heavenly Father. Actually, when we are unduly impatient, we are suggesting that we know what is best—better than does God. Or, at least, we are asserting that our timetable is better than his. Either way we are questioning the reality of God's omniscience. . . .
>
> There is also a dimension of patience which links it to a special reverence for life. Patience is a willingness, in a sense, to watch the unfolding purposes of God with a sense of wonder and awe rather than pacing up and down within the cell of our circumstance. Too much anxious opening of the oven door and the cake falls instead of rising! So it is with us. If we are always selfishly taking our temperature to see if we are happy, we won't be. When we are impatient, we are neither reverential nor reflective because we are too self-centered. Whereas faith and patience are companions, so are selfishness and impatience. . . .
>
> I remember as a child going eagerly to the corner store for what we then called the "all-day sucker." It would not have lasted all day under the best of usage, but it could last quite awhile. The trick was to resist the temptation to bite into it, to learn to savor rather than to crunch and chew. The same savoring was needed with a precious square of a milk chocolate bar. Make the

treat last, especially in depression times! In life, however, even patiently stretching out sweetness is sometimes not enough; in certain situations, enjoyment must actually be deferred. A patient willingness to defer dividends is a hallmark of individual maturity. . . .

Clearly, without patience, we will learn less in life. We will see less. We will feel less. We will hear less. Ironically, rush and more usually mean less. The pressures of now, time and time again, go against the grain of the gospel with its eternalism. . . . Patience is, therefore, clearly not fatalistic, shoulder-shrugging resignation; it is accepting a divine rhythm to life; it is obedience prolonged.[4]

Dallin H. Oaks said, "The Lord will speak to us through the Spirit in his own time and in his own way. Many people do not understand this principle. They believe that when they are ready and when it suits their convenience, they can call upon the Lord and he will immediately respond, even in the precise way they have prescribed. Revelation does not come that way. . . . The principle stated in [D&C 88:68] applies to every communication from our Heavenly Father: 'It shall be in his own time, and in his own way, and according to his own will.' We cannot force spiritual things."[5]

Boyd K. Packer said,

Sometimes you may struggle with a problem and not get an answer. What could be wrong? It may be that you are not doing anything wrong. It may be that you have not done the right things long enough. Remember, you cannot force spiritual things. . . . Put difficult questions in the back of your minds and go about your lives. Ponder and pray quietly and persistently about them. The answer may not come as a lightning bolt. It may come as a little inspiration here and a little there, "line upon line, precept upon precept" (D&C 98:12). Some answers will come from reading the scriptures, some from hearing speakers. And, occasionally, when it is important, some will come by very direct and powerful inspiration. The promptings will be clear and unmistakable.[6]

AN EXPERIMENT WITH A SEED

Alma gave the Zoramites a procedure by which they could first develop and then exercise their faith. He used the analogy of planting a small seed, nourishing it, and then watching it grow. The process he outlined follows.

Alma 32:27 • Be willing to try. Simply desire to believe, even if you can do nothing more. Give place in your heart for the word of God to be planted.

Alma 32:28 • You will begin to feel swelling motions in your breast. If you do not cast the seed out through disbelief, and if you do not resist the Spirit (through unworthiness, etc.), you will begin to feel the familiar "burning in your bosom" that confirms the correctness of your choice to pursue increased faith. Remember, however, that this is only a beginning. We must be cautious about seeking for signs—expecting manifestations rather than staying focused on exercising faith and letting the Spirit communicate to both our hearts and our minds in the Lord's own way and time.

S. Dilworth Young said, "If I am to receive revelation from the Lord, I must be in harmony with him by keeping his commandments. Then as needed, according to his wisdom, his word will come into my mind through my thoughts, accompanied by a feeling in the region of my bosom. It is a feeling which cannot be described, but the nearest word we have is 'burn' or 'burning.' Accompanying this always is a feeling of peace, a further witness that what one heard is right. Once one recognizes this burning, this feeling, this peace, one need never be drawn astray in his daily life or in the guidance he may receive."[7]

Alma 32:29–33 • A growing confirmation will come that the seed (the word) is good. The fact that our efforts bring us peace will increase our faith in the process but will not give us a perfect knowledge (v. 29). What we can know at the beginning of this process is that the seed of faith "swelleth, and sprouteth, and beginneth to grow," which demonstrates that the seed of our faith is good (vv. 30–32). All of this has been accomplished by the simple act of our giving our faith a chance—by experimenting with faith as Alma suggested (v. 33).

Alma 32:34–36 • Continue to be patient. Alma warned that we should not expect our understanding or faith to be perfect at this point. We do have a perfect knowledge of one thing—that the seed of faith is rewarding and good. We no longer have to have faith in that principle because we now know it. It has "swelled [our] souls, and . . . sprouted up" and "[our] understanding doth begin to be enlightened, and [our] mind doth begin to expand" (v. 34). Nevertheless, having experienced this beginning amount of spiritual light does not make our knowledge perfect (v. 35). We have exercised only that amount of faith that is required to "try the experiment to know if the seed was good" (v. 36), and that is all we know so far.

Alma 32:37–40 • Nourish your "seedling" and it will grow and strengthen. A growing testimony must continue to be nourished. Alma encouraged us to "nourish it with great care, that it may get root, that it may grow up, and bring forth fruit unto us" (v. 37). If we do not nourish it, it will die. Alma warned, "If ye neglect the tree, and take no thought for its nourishment, behold it will not get any root; and when the heat of the sun cometh and scorcheth it, because it hath no root it withers away, and ye pluck it up and cast it out" (v. 38). When this happens, it is not because the seed of faith was not good nor that the fruit of it would not have been desirable, "but it is because your ground is barren, and ye will not nourish the tree" and we can therefore never experience its fully ripened fruit (vv. 39–40).

Alma 32:41–43 • The seed becomes a tree if we are diligent and patient in nourishing it, and we will eventually "pluck the fruit thereof" (v. 42). The fruit of the tree of faith is eternal life, "which is most precious, which is sweet above all that is sweet, and which is white above all that is white, yea, and pure above all that is pure; and ye shall feast upon this fruit even until ye are filled, that ye hunger not, neither shall ye thirst" (v. 42). These fruits are the "rewards of your faith, and your diligence, and patience, and long-suffering, waiting for the tree to bring forth fruit unto you" (v. 43).

1 Nephi 15:36 • Nephi also said the fruit of the tree of life (eternal life) is more precious than any other thing. He calls this fruit the "most precious and most desirable above all other fruits . . . and . . . the greatest of all the gifts of God."

Alma's Teachings Concerning Christ
(ALMA 33–35)

PRINCIPLES OF PROPER WORSHIP
(ALMA 33)

Alma 33:1 • The people ask how they should exercise their faith. Alma responded to their question, but not until verse 23. First, he dispelled two false beliefs: (1) that they could worship only in a synagogue, and (2) that there was no Christ.

Alma 33:2–11 • When and where we may worship. The people believed that they could not worship God because they had been cast out of their synagogues (v. 2). Alma quoted the prophet Zenos to show that God can be worshiped anywhere and anytime (vv. 3–11).

Alma 33:14–16 • Whom we should worship. Alma established the reality of the Lord through the testimony of Zenos and Zenock. He asked how the Zoramites could read the scriptures and yet disbelieve in the Son of God (v. 14), because Zenos and Zenock had both spoken plainly concerning his coming (vv. 15–16).

Alma 33:19–22 • Alma instructs them to believe in the Redeemer, his Atonement, and the ultimate judgment all of us will face. The Savior "was spoken of by Moses; yea, and behold a type was raised up in the wilderness, that whosoever would look upon it might live. And many did look and live" (v. 19).

This makes reference to the brass serpent that Moses made and raised in the wilderness (Numbers 21:9), which was a type, or symbol, of Jesus Christ (see also John 3:14–15; Helaman 8:13–15). Alma explained that few of the Israelites in Moses' time "understood the meaning" of the serpent "because of the hardness of their hearts." Indeed, "there were many who were so hardened that they would not look, [and] therefore they perished. Now the reason they would not look is because they did not believe that it would heal them" (v. 20). He then asked, "O my brethren, if ye could be healed by merely casting about your eyes that ye might be healed, would ye not behold quickly, or would ye rather harden your hearts in unbelief, and be slothful . . . that ye might perish?" (v. 21).

Alma closed the analogy by encouraging the Zoramites, "Cast about your eyes and begin to believe in the Son of God, that he will come to redeem his people, and that he shall suffer and die to atone for their sins; and that he shall rise again from the dead which shall bring to pass the resurrection, that all men shall stand before him, to be judged at the last and judgment day, according to their works" (v. 22). This is the heart of the gospel.

The Prophet Joseph Smith explained that "the fundamental principles of our religion are the testimony of the apostles and Prophets, concerning Jesus Christ, that He died, was buried, and rose again the third day, and ascended into heaven; and all other things which pertain to our religion are only appendages to it."[8]

Alma 33:23 • Along the way, our burdens will be made light through faith in Christ. There is no promise of ease in the pursuit of eternal life. Alma's prayer was, "God grant unto you that your burdens may be light, through the joy of his Son." Eternal life is within the grasp of every child of God. Alma concludes his list of the principles of proper worship with the observation, "And even all this can ye do if ye will." In other words, it's not an impossible task to obtain eternal life.

D&C 14:7 • Christ reassures us that we will obtain eternal life if we endure to the end. He writes, "And, if you keep my commandments and endure to the end you shall have eternal life, which gift is the greatest of all the gifts of God." Sometimes we despair of ever achieving the level of perfection necessary to obtain the celestial kingdom. Satan would have us believe that it is not possible . . . so why even try? When we think like this, we are forgetting the one indispensable ingredient that makes it all possible—the Atonement of Jesus Christ. If we love him and serve him and do our very best to obey him, then he will do the rest by redeeming us from our sins. Because of Jesus Christ, we can and will achieve exaltation. And this truly is "the greatest of all the gifts of God" to his children.

Alma 34:1–5 • The great question: Does salvation come through Christ or through something else? Our eternal salvation rests on the answer. As Alma concluded his teaching and sat down, his missionary companion, Amulek, arose and addressed this vital question (v. 1). After offering support to all the teachings of Alma concerning faith, Amulek began his sermon by saying, "We have beheld that the great question which is in your minds is whether the word be in the Son of God, or whether there shall be no Christ" (v. 5). He said to the Zoramites (who had ceased believing in the atonement), "It is impossible that ye should be ignorant of the things which have been spoken concerning the coming of Christ, who is taught by us to be the Son of God; yea, I know that these things were taught unto you bountifully before your dissension from among us" (v. 2). Salvation was and is and always will be through Jesus Christ, and in no other way.

Bruce R. McConkie said, "The issue is not whether men shall worship, but who or what is to be the object of their devotions. . . . There is no salvation in worshiping a false god. It does not matter one particle how sincerely someone may believe that God is a golden calf, or that he is an immaterial, uncreated power that is in all things; the worship of such a being or concept has no saving power. Men may believe with all their souls that images or powers or laws are God, but no amount of devotion to these concepts will ever give the power that leads to immortality and eternal life."[9]

Alma 34:8–10 • Amulek testifies concerning Christ and our need to develop faith in him. Amulek gave his personal witness of the Savior and his Atonement—"that Christ shall come among the children of men, to take upon him the transgressions of his people, and that he shall atone for the sins of the world; for the Lord God hath spoken it" (v. 8). Under the great plan of salvation, we are permitted to act for ourselves and to learn by experience to distinguish good from evil. This inevitably leads to errors as we stumble along through life. Therefore, Amulek taught that "it is expedient that an atonement should be made . . . or else all mankind must unavoidably perish." This is because all mankind becomes "hardened . . . fallen and . . . lost, and must perish except it be through the atonement" (v. 9).

Alma 34:10, 13–16 • Amulek calls Christ's Atonement an "infinite and eternal sacrifice." The Atonement of Jesus Christ would be a "great and last sacrifice," and then there would be "a stop to the shedding of blood" (v. 13). All blood sacrifices since the days of Adam, including those required by the law of Moses, had been offered in symbolism of the great and eternal sacrifice of Jesus Christ that was to come in the meridian of time. Once the Lord accomplished his infinite Atonement, the law of Moses was "all fulfilled, every jot and tittle" (v. 13). Indeed, the Atonement "is the whole meaning of the law, every whit pointing to that great and last sacrifice; and that great and last sacrifice will be the Son of God" (v. 14). This "great and last sacrifice" was "not a sacrifice of man, neither of beast, neither of any manner of fowl" nor a "human sacrifice," but an "infinite and eternal sacrifice" (vv. 10, 14) wrought by the only being in the universe capable of doing it—the Lord Jesus Christ.

Bruce R. McConkie said, "Man cannot resurrect himself; man cannot save himself; human power cannot save another; human power cannot atone for the sins of another. The work of redemption must be infinite and eternal; it must be done by an infinite being; God himself must atone for the sins of the world."[10]

Tad R. Callister, in his excellent book *The Infinite Atonement* explores in depth what an *infinite* atonement means. Here are just a few of the reasons he provides for why the Atonement is infinite:

> ▷ The Being who performed the Atonement (Christ) is infinite (58–60).
> ▷ The power of the Atonement is unlimited and eternal (61–66).
> ▷ The Atonement applies to all time—from the infinite past to infinite future (72–81).
> ▷ The Atonement covers all living things on all of God's planets everywhere (83–94).
> ▷ It's depth is complete—covering all of our sin, sorrow, adversity, sickness, and pain (95–116).
> ▷ The suffering of Christ was infinite in scope—beyond our understanding (117–156).
> ▷ The Savior's motivation for doing it—his love for us—was also infinite (157–160).[11]

The Savior's Atonement brings "salvation to all those who shall believe on his name," which was the intent and purpose of it from the beginning (v. 15). Through this Atonement, "mercy . . . overpowereth justice," providing a means by which we may have faith (in Christ) and repent (v. 15). As we do so, "mercy can satisfy the demands of justice, and encircles [us] in the arms of safety, while he that exercises no faith unto repentance is exposed to the whole . . . demands of justice" (v. 16). Therefore, although Christ suffered for all men, "only unto him that has faith unto repentance" is redemption made (v. 16).

ACQUIRING THE ATTRIBUTES OF GODLINESS
(ALMA 34)

To be with God we must be like him. And in order to become like him we need two things: (1) a correct understanding of his character and attributes, and (2) the acquisition of those same character traits in our own lives.

The Prophet Joseph Smith said, "Correct ideas of the character of God are necessary in order to . . . exercise . . . faith in him unto life and salvation. . . . The real design which the God of heaven had in view in making the human family acquainted with his attributes, was, that they, through the ideas of the existence of his attributes, might be enabled to exercise faith in him, and, through the exercise of faith in him, might obtain eternal life. . . . Having said so much, we shall proceed to examine the attributes of God. . . . We have, in the revelations which he has given to the human family, the following account of his attributes."[12]

The Prophet then proceeded to list the following six attributes and read the scriptures shown associated with them here.

> ▷ Knowledge (Acts 15:18; Isaiah 46:9–10)
> ▷ Faith or Power (Hebrews 11:3; Genesis 1:1; Isaiah 14:24, 27)
> ▷ Justice (Psalm 89:14; Isaiah 45:21; Zephaniah 3:5; Zechariah 9:9)
> ▷ Judgment (Psalm 89:14; Deuteronomy 32:4; Psalm 9:7; Psalm 9:16)
> ▷ Mercy (Psalm 89:14; Exodus 34:6; Nehemiah 9:17)
> ▷ Truth (Psalm 89:14; Exodus 34:6; Deuteronomy 32:4; Psalm 31:5)

Alma 34:17–41 Acquiring the attributes of godliness. Amulek listed some of the same attributes of godliness and added others. His point was that we must acquire these attributes if we wish to be exalted.

> ▷ **Faith** (v. 17). Amulek challenged the Zoramites, "Exercise your faith unto repentance"

which would happen when they "beg[a]n to call upon his holy name, that he would have mercy upon" them.

▷ **Prayer** (vv. 18–28). We can and should pray everywhere and all the time. Amulek suggested praying at work ("in your fields . . . over all your flocks") as well as at home, where we should pray "morning, mid-day, and evening" (vv. 20–21). "But this is not all," he said, "ye must pour out your souls in your closets, and your secret places, and in your wilderness" (v. 26). And when we are not engaged in formal prayer, we are instructed, "Let your hearts be full, drawn out in prayer unto him continually" (v. 27). This is what the apostle Paul meant when he advised the Thessalonian Saints to "pray without ceasing" (1 Thessalonians 5:17).

Amulek also taught that we can and should pray about everything. He suggested prayer "against the power of your enemies" (v. 22), "against the devil, who is an enemy to all righteousness" (v. 23), "over the crops of your fields, that ye may prosper in them" (v. 24), and "over the flocks of your fields, that they may increase" (v. 25), "for your welfare" (v. 27), and "for the welfare of those who are around you" (v. 27).

▷ **Charity** (vv. 28–29). Amulek then offered a word of caution about prayer. We must be charitable if we expect our prayers to be answered. He said, "For after ye have done all these things, if ye turn away the needy, and the naked, and visit not the sick and afflicted, and impart of your substance, if ye have, to those who stand in need, . . . behold, your prayer is vain, and availeth you nothing, and ye are as hypocrites who do deny the faith" (v. 28), and "if ye do not remember to be charitable, ye are as dross, which the refiners do cast out, (it being of no worth) and is trodden under foot of men" (v. 29).

Marion G. Romney said, "Defining [what he calls the Royal law], the apostle James said, 'If ye fulfil the royal law according to the scripture, Thou shalt love thy neighbour as thyself . . . (James 2:8). We must have this law in mind in all that we do. . . . Amulek . . . tells the people to pray . . . and tells them where to pray and how to pray and what to pray for . . . and then he says that after ye have done all these things, if ye turn away the needy, and the naked, and visit not the sick and afflicted, and impart not your substance . . . behold, your prayer is vain, and availeth you nothing, and ye are as hypocrites who do deny the faith."[13]

▷ **Humility** (v. 37). Amulek taught that God expects us to "work out . . . our salvation with fear before God" (v. 37). Fear of God does not mean being afraid; it means honoring and obeying and worshiping him appropriately. He commands, "No more deny the coming of Christ" (v. 37), "Contend no more against the Holy Ghost, but . . . receive it" (v. 38), "Take upon you the name of Christ" (v. 38), and "Humble yourselves even to the dust, and worship God, in whatsoever place ye may be in, in spirit and in truth" (v.38).

▷ **Gratitude** (v. 38). We are also required to be thankful, and to recognize the source of our blessings. Amulek counseled, "Live in thanksgiving daily, for the many mercies and blessings which he doth bestow upon you" (v. 38). In latter-day revelation, the Lord said, "And in nothing doth man offend God, or against none is his wrath kindled, save those who confess not his hand in all things, and obey not his commandments" (D&C 59:21). When we think we are "self-made," we offend the God who made us.

▷ **Prayerfulness** (v. 39). Amulek advised to be "watchful unto prayer continually." Apparently, this is the only way to avoid being "led away by the temptations of the devil, that he may . . . overpower you." Nephi gave the same counsel, noting that "the Spirit . . . teacheth a man to pray" but "the evil spirit teacheth not a man to pray, but teacheth him that he must not pray" (2 Nephi 32:8). We increase our power to be righteous when we pray, and that dis-empowers Satan, who, Amulek observed, "rewardeth you no good thing."

Brigham Young said about overcoming the influence of Satan, "Do you want to know how to pray in your families? I have told you, a great many times, how to do when you feel as though you have not a particle of the Spirit of prayer with you. Get your wives and your children together, lock the door so that none of them will get out, and get down on your knees; and if you feel as though you want to swear and fight, keep on your knees until they [your knees] are pretty well wearied."[14]

▷ **Forgiveness** (v. 40). Amulek exhorted the Zoramites, "Have patience, and . . . bear with all manner of afflictions. . . . Do not revile against those who do cast you out because of your exceeding poverty, lest ye become sinners like unto them" (v. 40). This is a challenging doctrine that suggests that the sin of refusing to forgive is as serious (or more so) than any sins that may be committed against us.

The Prophet Joseph Smith said, "I advise all of you to be careful what you do, or you may by-and-by find out that you have been deceived. . . . If a spirit of bitterness is in you, don't be in haste. You may say, 'That man is a sinner!' Well, if he repents, he shall be forgiven."[15] The Lord said, "I, the Lord, will forgive whom I will forgive, but of you it is required to forgive all men" (D&C 64:10).

Spencer W. Kimball said, "We may get angry with parents, or a teacher, or the bishop, and dwarf ourselves into nameless anonymity as we shrivel and shrink under the venom and poison of bitterness, little realizing the suffering of the hater, the latter cheats himself. . . . To terminate activity in the Church just to spite leaders or to give vent to wounded feelings is to cheat ourselves."[16] I once heard a brother compare this to "drinking poison and hoping the other person will die." It makes no sense at all.

▷ **Patience and Hope** (v. 41). The Lord expects us to "have patience, and bear with [our] afflictions, with a firm hope that [we] shall one day rest from all [our] afflictions" (v. 41). The Lord does not promise the righteous that they will be free from affliction and adversity, only that he will give them power to overcome their obstacles and learn and grow through the experience. To the Prophet Joseph Smith suffering in Liberty Jail the Lord said, "All these things shall give thee experience, and shall be for thy good" (D&C 122:7).

M. Russell Ballard said, "If we do our best to keep the commandments of God, come what may, we will be all right. Of course, that does not necessarily mean that we will be spared personal suffering and heartache. Righteousness has never precluded adversity. But faith in the Lord Jesus Christ—real faith, whole-souled and unshakable—is a power to be reckoned with in the universe. . . . It can be a source of inner strength, through which we find peace, comfort, and the courage to cope."[17]

Orson F. Whitney said, "No pain that we suffer, no trial that we experience is wasted. It ministers to our education, to the development of such qualities as patience, faith, fortitude and humility. All that we suffer and all that we endure, especially when we endure it patiently, builds up our characters, purifies our hearts, expands our souls, and makes us more tender and charitable, more worthy to be called the children of God, . . . and it is through sorrow and suffering, toil and tribulation, that we gain the education that we come here to acquire."[18]

George Q. Cannon said,

> Every Latter-day Saint who gains a celestial glory will be tried to the very uttermost. If there is a point in our character that is weak and tender, you can and may depend upon it that the Lord will test us to the utmost before we can get through and receive that glory and exaltation which He has in store for us as a people . . .
>
> No matter how serious the trial, how deep the distress, how great the affliction, [God] will never desert us. He never has, and He never will. He cannot do it. It is not His character. He is an unchangeable being; the same yesterday, the same today, and He will be the same throughout the eternal ages to come. We have found that God. We have made Him our friend, by obeying His Gospel; and He will stand by us. We may pass through the fiery furnace; we may pass through deep waters; but we shall not be consumed nor overwhelmed. We shall emerge from all these trials and difficulties the better and the purer for them, if we only trust in our God and keep His commandments.[19]

Alma 34:30–31 • We must bring forth the "fruit" of repentance. Amulek called upon the Zoramites to "come forth and bring fruit unto repentance" (v. 30) and "harden not [their] hearts any longer" (v. 31). He promised that if they would do this, "immediately shall the great plan of redemption be brought about" (v.31). Joseph Fielding McConkie and Robert L. Millet explain that "neither the profession of faith nor the confession of sin supplants the need for works of righteousness. As the tree is known by its fruits, so the repentant soul is known by its deeds."[20]

Alma 34:31–33 • The "day of this life" is the time to repent, and we must not procrastinate. Amulek proclaimed, "Now is the time and the day of your salvation. . . . For behold, this life is the time for men to prepare to meet God; yea, behold the day of this life is the day for men to perform their labors" (v. 31–32). He continued, "Do not procrastinate the day of your repentance until the end" because "this day of life . . . is given us to prepare for eternity, [and] if we do not improve our time while in this life, then cometh the night of darkness wherein there can be no labor performed" (v. 33).

What, then, is "the day of this life?" Alvin R. Dyer said, "The day of this life is from the day of mortal birth until the end of the period of the spirit world. It is not at the end of this mortal life. This is why we preach the gospel in the spirit world so that the work can be done for people vicariously here upon the earth, within the recognized day of this life."[21]

However, Bruce R. McConkie made it clear that this does not mean people will have a "second chance" at salvation if they reject the gospel or their covenants during their mortal lives. "Whenever the gospel is offered to any person or group, they then have the obligation to believe and obey its doctrines; otherwise, they do not become inheritors of its blessings. The doctrine of salvation for the dead great and glorious as it is, does not mean that those who reject the truth, or who disobey their gospel covenants in this life, shall have a second chance to gain salvation by accepting and living the law in the spirit world. Salvation for the dead is for those who die without a knowledge of the gospel and who would have received it, with all their hearts, had it been presented to them in this mortal life."[22]

Elder McConkie explained on another occasion,

There are those who believe that the doctrine of salvation for the dead offers men a second chance for salvation. I knew a man, now deceased, not a member of the Church, who was a degenerate old reprobate who found pleasure, as he supposed, in living after the manner of the world. A cigarette dangled from his lips, alcohol stenched his breath, and profane and bawdy stories detailed his lips. His moral status left much to be desired.

His wife was a member of the Church, as faithful as she could be under the circumstances. One day she said to him, "You know the Church is true; why won't you be baptized?" He replied, "Of course I know the Church is true, but I've no intention of changing my habits in order to join it. I prefer to live the way I do. But that doesn't worry me in the slightest. I know that as soon as I die, you will have someone go to the temple and do the work for me and everything will come out alright in the end anyway."

He died and she had the work done in the temple. We do not sit in judgment and deny vicarious ordinances to people. But what will it profit him? There is no such thing as a second chance to gain salvation. This is the time and the day of our probation. After this day of life, which is given us to prepare for eternity, then cometh the night of darkness wherein there can be no labor performed.

For those who do not have an opportunity to believe and obey the holy word in this life, the first chance to gain salvation will come in the spirit world. If those who hear the word for the first time in the realms ahead are the kind of people who would have accepted the gospel here, had the opportunity been afforded them, they will accept it there. Salvation for the dead is for those whose first chance to gain salvation is in the spirit world.[23]

Alma 34:34 • The same spirit that inhabits your body now will inhabit it in eternity. We will not suddenly change when we face the "awful crisis" of our time having expired. We cannot say, "I will repent, . . . I will return to my God. . . . For that same spirit which doth possess your bodies at the time that ye go out of this life, that same spirit will have power to possess your body in that eternal world" (v. 34).

Elder Melvin J. Ballard explained,

[Until a person] learns to overcome the flesh, his temper, his tongue, his disposition to, indulge in the things God has forbidden, he cannot come into the celestial kingdom of God-he must overcome either in this life or in the life to come. But this life is the time in which men are to repent. Do not let any of us imagine that we can go down to the grave not having overcome the corruptions of the flesh and then lose in the grave all our sins and evil tendencies. They will be with us. They will be with the spirit when separated from the body. The spirit only can repent and change, and then the battle has to go forward with the flesh afterwards. It is much easier to overcome and serve the Lord when both flesh and spirit are combined as one. . . . Every man and woman who is putting off until the next life the task of correcting and overcoming the weakness of the flesh are sentencing themselves to years of bondage, for no man or woman will come forth in the resurrection until they have completed their work, until they have overcome, until they have done as much as they can do.[24]

The Results of Their Preaching to the Zoramites
(Alma 35)

Alma 35:1–7 • The "more popular part of the Zoramites" cast out the people who believe in the words of Alma and his brethren. When Amulek had finished his sermon, the missionaries "withdrew themselves from the multitude [in the land of Zoram] and came over into the land of

Jershon" (vv. 1–2). After their departure "the more popular part of the Zoramites . . . consulted together concerning the words which had been preached unto them, [and] they were angry because of the word, for it did destroy their craft [and[they would not hearken unto the words" (v. 3). They gathered the people together and asked each of them how they felt about the missionaries' words without disclosing their intentions (vv. 4–5). And then they "cast out of the land" all of those who "weree in favor of the words which had been spoken by Alma and his brethren" (v. 6). There were many such persons, and after being cast out they "came over also into the land of Jershon" where Alma and his companions ministered unto them (vv. 6–7).

Alma 35:8–9 • The people of Ammon (the Anti-Nephi-Lehies) receive the Zoramites who have been cast out. Unsatisfied with his own intolerance, the "chief ruler of the Zoramites" requested that the people of Ammon also cast out those Zoramites who had joined with them (v. 8) and "breathed out many threatenings against them" (v. 9). However, "the people of Ammon did not fear their words [and] did not cast them out." Instead "they did receive all the poor of the Zoramites that came over unto them; and they did nourish them, and did clothe them, and did give unto them lands for their inheritance; and they did administer unto them according to their wants" (v. 9). This is just one of several instances in the Book of Mormon where Lamanites (in this case the Ammonites) are more Christlike than Nephites (in this case the Zoramites). Righteousness is not racial, and the Nephites were not always the most blessed of these peoples.

Alma 35:10–13 • The Zoramites ally themselves with the Lamanites, and war breaks out against the Nephites. As had happened several times before in Book of Mormon history, the proud and angry Nephites living in the land of Zoram turned against their own people and joined with the Lamanites, stirring them up to anger against both the Zoramites they had cast out of their city and the Ammonites who had given them refuge. In 74 BC, the Lamanites "began to make preparations for war" (vv. 10–11). To protect themselves, "the people of Ammon departed out of the land of Jershon, and came over into the land of Melek" while the armies of the Nephites established themselves in the land of Jershon (v. 13), and war between the Lamanites and Nephites broke out the very next year (73 BC).

Alma 35:10–15 • Alma and his missionary companions return to Zarahemla. Their missions had been fruitful, "having been instruments in the hands of God of bringing many of the Zoramites to repentance," but all of those who had done so "were driven out of their land" and took up residence in the land of Jershon, where they had to take up arms to defend themselves (v. 14). This was the cause of much sorrow for Alma, "being grieved for the iniquity of his people, yea for the wars, and the bloodsheds, and the contentions which were among them." He recognized that the reason for these difficulties was that "the hearts of the people began to wax hard, and . . . they began to be offended because of the strictness of the word," for which "his heart was exceedingly sorrowful" (v. 15).

Notes
1. Spencer W. Kimball, *Faith Precedes the Miracle* (Salt Lake City: Deseret Book, 1972), 98.
2. Joseph Smith, *Lectures on Faith* (Salt Lake City: Deseret Book, 1985), 1:9.
3. Ibid.
4. Neal A. Maxwell, address to BYU students, Provo, Utah, November 27, 1979; *Ensign*, October 1980, 28–31.

5. Dallin H. Oaks, *Ensign*, March 1997, 10–11.
6. Boyd K. Packer, in Conference Report, Oct. 1979, 29–30; *Ensign*, Nov. 1979, 21.
7. S. Dilworth Young, "The Still Small Voice," *Ensign*, May 1976, 23.
8. Joseph Smith, *Teachings of the Prophet Joseph Smith*, Joseph Fielding Smith, sel. (Salt Lake City: Deseret Book, 1976), 121.
9. Bruce R. McConkie, in Conference Report, October 1971, 167.
10. Bruce R. McConkie, *A New Witness for the Articles of Faith* (Salt Lake City: Deseret Book, 1985), 111–12.
11. Tad R. Callister, *The Infinite Atonement* (Salt Lake City, UT: Deseret Book, 2000).
12. Joseph Smith, *Lectures on Faith* (Salt Lake City: Deseret Book, 1985), 4:1–10.
13. Marion G. Romney, in Conference Report, April 1978, 142.
14. Brigham Young, in *Journal of Discourses* (London: Latter-day Saints' Book Depot, 1854–86), 4:200.
15. in James R. Clark, comp., *Messages of the First Presidency of The Church of Jesus Christ of Latter-day Saints* (Salt Lake City: Bookcraft, 1965–75), 1:222.
16. Spencer W. Kimball, *The Teachings of Spencer W. Kimball*, Edward L. Kimball, ed. (Salt Lake City: Bookcraft, 1982), 242–43.
17. M. Russell Ballard, *Ensign*, November 1992, 32.
18. Orson F. Whitney, *Improvement Era*, March 1966, 211.
19. Brian H. Stuy, ed., *Collected Discourses*, 5 vols. (Burbank, CA, and Woodland Hills, UT: BHS Publishing, 1987–1992), 2:185.
20. Joseph Fielding McConkie and Robert L. Millet, *Doctrinal Commentary on the Book of Mormon*, 4 vols. (Salt Lake City: Bookcraft, 1987–1992), 3:100.
21. Alvin R. Dyer, *The Meaning of Truth*, rev. ed. (Salt Lake City: Deseret Book, 1973), 69.
22. Bruce R. McConkie, *Doctrinal New Testament Commentary* (Salt Lake City: Bookcraft, 1966–73), 2:423.
23. Bruce R. McConkie, "The Seven Deadly Heresies" (fireside address, Brigham Young University, Provo, Utah, June 1, 1980).
24. Melvin J. Ballard, "The Three Degrees of Glory" (sermon, Ogden, Utah, September 22, 1922).

LESSON 29
"Give Ear to My Words"
ALMA 36–39

Alma's Letters to His Sons

This lesson consists of the doctrine and advice that Alma gave to his three sons. Alma 36–37 contains his charge to Helaman. Alma 38 contains his blessing and counsel to Shiblon. Alma 39–42 contains Alma's counsel to Corianton.

Alma himself had rejected the counsel of his father for a while (Mosiah 26:1). He had also been guilty of very serious sins and of prideful rhetoric that turned people away from the Church (Mosiah 27:8). He wanted his sons to avoid the mistakes he had made in his youth (Alma 37:35), and to accomplish this he chose to counsel his sons individually (Alma 35:16). He communicated with each son "separately" through letters, telling each one specifically what he individually needed to hear.

Righteous parents often face the challenge of dealing with unrighteous children. Parents are obligated to teach their children and encourage them to live the gospel, but they must also respect their children's agency and do not force them to live righteously. We can observe Alma's efforts to do this as we read these chapters.

Alma's Message to Helaman
(ALMA 36–37)

ALMA BEARS HIS TESTIMONY

Alma 36:1–3, 30 • "[If ye] keep the commandments of God ye shall prosper in the land." Alma gave this promise to his son Helaman both as he began and ended his letter (vv. 1, 30). He counseled his son, "Do as I have done. . . . Hear my words and learn of me" (v. 2–3), which is what all righteous parents want their children to do. Alma knew from personal experience that "whosoever shall put their trust in God shall be supported in their trials, and their troubles, and their afflictions" (v. 3). He reminded Helaman of the captivity of their fathers, "for they were in bondage, and none could deliver them except it was . . . God . . . and he surely did deliver them in their afflictions" (v. 2). He promised that the same God will help us in our individual trials and make it possible for us to be "lifted up at the last day" (v. 3).

Alma 36:4–5 • Alma's knowledge and testimony came not in a temporal way, but "of God."
His witness was not just his heartfelt opinion; it came from God at the time of his conversion
(v. 4). Alma testified, "God has, by the mouth of his holy angel, made these things known unto
me, not of any worthiness of myself" (v. 5). He later bore the same witness to his son Shiblon
(Alma 38:6).

ALMA'S PERSONAL EXAMPLE

Alma used his personal experience to illustrate the principles he sought to teach his sons.
As part of this process, he revealed many important facts concerning his own repentance and
conversion. The original historical account of these events is contained in Mosiah 27:7–37, and
we discussed them at some length in lesson 20. In Alma 36:5–26, we read Alma's retelling of the
story to his son Helaman, and in Alma 38:7–8 we find Alma's retelling of a few facts of the story
to his son Shiblon. As part of this recitation of his own life, Alma encouraged Helaman to follow
his example:

Alma 36:2–3 • "Do as I have done. . . . Hear my words and learn of me"
Alma 36:29–30 • "Remember what I have done. . . . Know as I do know"

Alma 36:6–13 • Alma tells Helaman of his own sins. He did this to help Helaman to avoid
similar problems, to emphasize the validity of his counsel, and to reinforce the seriousness of his
parental concern.

Alma and his friends, the sons of Mosiah, "went about . . . seeking to destroy the Church of
God" (Alma 36:6). Mormon called Alma the Younger "a very wicked and an idolatrous man"
(Mosiah 27:8) and called all of these young men "the very vilest of sinners" (Mosiah 28:4).
Alma the Younger himself said, "I had rebelled against my God, and . . . had not kept his holy
commandments . . . and I had murdered many of his children, or rather led them away unto
destruction" (Alma 36:13–14).

Mormon also described Alma the Younger as a flatterer—a man "of many words" (Mosiah
27:8) who caused great dissension in the Church and weakened it (Mosiah 27:9). We can only
imagine the damage that was done by the prophet's own son denying the truth of what his father
was teaching. And worse, they were trying to "destroy the Church of God" and "lead astray the
people of the Lord." They were "rebelling against God" and "even the king" (Mosiah 27:10).
Little wonder that Alma's father, Alma the Elder, spent much time praying for the redemption of
his son (Mosiah 27:14).

Alma told his son Helaman, "God sent his holy angel to stop us by the way. And behold,
he spake unto us, as it were the voice of thunder, and the whole earth did tremble beneath our
feet; and we all fell to the earth, for the fear of the Lord came upon us" (vv. 6–7). The angel
commanded Alma and his companions to "seek no more to destroy the Church of God" (v. 9), and
Alma said, "[For three days and nights thereafter] I could not open my mouth, neither had I the
use of my limbs" (v. 10). The experience left Alma "racked with eternal torment, for [his] soul was
harrowed up to the greatest degree and racked with all [his] sins" (v. 12). Realizing that he had
"rebelled against [his] God, and . . . had not kept his holy commandments," he was "tormented
with the pains of hell" (v. 13).

Alma 36:14–16 • Alma describes the "pains of hell" that he experienced. Alma was
experiencing the "pains of hell" because, as he puts it, "So great had been my iniquities, that the

very thought of coming into the presence of my God did rack my soul with inexpressible horror" (v. 14). He wished, "[That I] could be banished and become extinct both soul and body, that I might not be brought to stand in the presence of my God, to be judged of my deeds" (v. 15). These, he explains are "the pains of a damned soul" (v. 16).

Alma 36:17–20 • Alma tells how he became redeemed. While he was "racked with torment" and "harrowed up by the memory of [his] many sins," he remembered the teachings of his father concerning "Jesus Christ, a Son of God, [who would come] to atone for the sins of the world" (v. 17). He cried within his heart, "O Jesus, thou Son of God, have mercy on me, who am in the gall of bitterness, and am encircled about by the everlasting chains of death" (v. 18). Immediately, the pain and guilt and memory of his sins left him. Of this experience he recalled, "Oh, what joy, and what marvelous light I did behold; yea, my soul was filled with joy as exceeding as was my pain!" (vv. 19–20).

Alma 36:21–24 • Alma compares the "exquisite and . . . bitter" pain caused by his sins to the "exquisite and sweet . . . joy" felt through the redemption of Christ. He wrote of the moment he realized he had been forgiven: "There could be nothing so exquisite and so bitter as were my pains . . . there can be nothing so exquisite and sweet as was my joy" (v. 21). He saw a vision of God sitting upon his throne, and he wrote, "My soul did long to be there" (v. 22). His "limbs did receive their strength again, and [he] stood upon [his] feet" and he bore witness "unto the people that [he] had been born of God" (v. 23). While this all might seem rather instantaneous, Alma's conversion was genuine and permanent, as evidenced by the fact that "from that time even until now, [he has] labored without ceasing, that [he] might bring souls unto repentance" (v. 24).

Alma 36:24–26 • Alma's motivation for serving God is purely charitable—as had been the motivations of the sons of Mosiah in serving missions among the Lamanites—"that I might bring them [those he taught] to taste of the exceeding joy of which I did taste; that they might also be born of God, and be filled with the Holy Ghost" (v. 24). He received "great joy in the fruit of [his] labors." He wrote, "Many have been born of God, and have tasted as I have tasted, and have seen eye to eye as I have seen; therefore they do know of these things of which I have spoken" (vv. 25–26).

Alma 36:27–29 • The Lord gives his servants inner peace in spite of trials. Alma testified that he had been "supported under trials and troubles of every kind, yea, and in all manner of afflictions" (v. 27). He testified, "Yea, God has delivered me from prison, and from bonds, and from death; yea, and I do put my trust in him, and he will still deliver me" (v. 27). Notice that Alma did not expect to avoid difficulties but rejoiced in the support he received from God while experiencing them.

Alma's hope for the future was strong, knowing that God "will raise [him] up at the last day, to dwell with him in glory; yea, and [he] will praise him forever" (v. 28). He reflected upon the many times that God had delivered His people out of bondage—from Egypt and later from Jerusalem when Lehi's family was warned to escape (vv. 28–29). "I have always retained in remembrance their captivity," Alma said to his son, "and ye also ought to retain in remembrance, as I have done" (v. 29).

Each of us must also become "converted" as Alma was, even if we have already been baptized members of the Church. Both new converts and members must know for themselves, and to obtain such a witness must achieve the elements of conversion that Alma listed in his letter to Helaman.

> ▷ A clear realization of sins and iniquities (v. 13).
> ▷ A deep godly sorrow for sins (vv. 12–16).
> ▷ Suffering and torment for sins (vv. 12–13).
> ▷ An appeal to the Savior (vv. 17–18).
> ▷ Forgiveness, spiritual enlightenment, and great joy (vv. 19–23).
> ▷ A life of righteousness and service (vv. 24–26).

Bruce R. McConkie said,

> Any accountable person can gain a testimony of the gospel by obedience to that law upon which the receipt of such knowledge is predicated. This is the formula:
> 1. He must desire to know the truth of the gospel, of the Book of Mormon, of the Church, or of whatever is involved.
> 2. He must study and learn the basic facts relative to the matter involved. "Search the scriptures" (John 5:39). "Search these commandments" (D&C 1:37).
> 3. He must practice the principles and truths learned, conforming his life to them. "My doctrine is not mine, but his that sent me. If any man will do his will, he shall know of the doctrine, whether it be of God, or whether I speak of myself" (John 7:16–17).
> 4. He must pray to the Father in the name of Christ, in faith, and the truth will then be made manifest by revelation "by the power of the Holy Ghost. And by the power of the Holy Ghost ye may know the truth of all things" (Moroni 10:3–5; 1 Corinthians 2).[1]

Elder McConkie also said, "Every devoted, obedient, and righteous person on earth has and does receive revelation from God. Revelation is the natural inheritance of all the faithful. . . . To the faithful the Lord promises: 'Assuredly as the Lord liveth, who is your God and your Redeemer, even so surely shall you receive a knowledge of whatsoever things you shall ask in faith, with an honest heart, believing that you shall receive . . .' (D&C 8:1–3; 46:7; Matt. 7:7–8; James 1:5). . . . With reference to their own personal affairs, the Saints are expected (because they have the gift of the Holy Ghost) to gain personal revelation and guidance rather than to run to . . . church leaders to be told what to do."[2]

Revelation does not always consist of visitations from angels or hearing their voices. There are a number of ways and circumstances through which we receive personal revelation, each of which may be accompanied by a witness from the Spirit that they are from God. Here are just a few examples:

> ▷ While studying the scriptures, alone or with others
> ▷ While listening to prophets or others speak
> ▷ During personal interviews
> ▷ During or following prayer
> ▷ While meditating upon the things of God
> ▷ In dreams
> ▷ In patriarchal blessings
> ▷ In fathers' blessings
> ▷ In special priesthood blessings

Revelation comes by a "still, small voice" that communicates to both our minds and

our hearts (D&C 8:2). The Spirit enlightens our minds with new ideas or insights, flashes of inspiration, and strong feelings or impressions (D&C 128:1). The spirit touches our hearts with a feeling of peace or "burning" within our bosom. This is usually manifested as a *confirmation* that what we are thinking is correct and is of God, not as a independent *sign* (D&C 85:6; 6:15; 11:13–14).

The Prophet Joseph Smith said revelation may come as "sudden strokes of ideas" that flow into our minds as "pure intelligence."[3] Hence, the need to "study it out" in our minds and then take it to the Lord for confirmation (D&C 9:7–8). This is the process by which most revelation comes to us, and we must learn to understand it properly if we wish to avoid frustration or deception.

May I be so bold as to suggest that when we read the Book of Mormon and then take Moroni's challenge to "ask of God" whether it be true, we have more to do than to simply ask and then wait for some kind of feeling in our breast? I have encountered many people who have been frustrated when they have read the Book of Mormon, asked the Lord if it was true, and then felt . . . nothing. Could this seeking for a feeling be a form of sign-seeking? I personally think so.

If I understand the Prophet Joseph Smith's description of the process (and who would know better than he), we have to seriously consider what we are reading *while we're reading it*, and ponder its passages in our minds and hearts. "Is this of God?" It is. "Did Joseph Smith write this himself?" He was not capable of it, and especially not the hundreds of genuine linguistic, cultural, and geographic details that have since that day been shown to be absolutely accurate. Nobody knew those things in Joseph Smith's day, especially not an uneducated farm boy on the western frontier of New York in 1830. And finally, and most important, "Have I felt the Spirit as I have read it?" Yes, I have.

I can testify that the Spirit has whispered to me many times that what I was reading in the Book of Mormon is from God. I have both *thought* it and *felt* it as I read it. And is that not a witness? It is. The Lord said, "Did I not speak peace to your mind concerning the matter? What greater witness can you have than from God?" (D&C 6:23). I think we need to recognize the witnesses we have already received (while reading) and not seek for something more spectacular and immediate at the end. In my experience, that is not how it works.

Dallin H. Oaks said,

> Some [people] have looked exclusively for the great manifestations that are recorded in the scriptures and have failed to recognize the still, small voice that is given to them. . . . We need to know that the Lord rarely speaks loudly. His messages almost always come in a whisper. . . .
>
> Not understanding these principles of revelation, some people postpone acknowledging their testimony until they have experienced a miraculous event. They fail to realize that with most people . . . gaining a testimony is not an event but a process. . . .
>
> Visions do happen. Voices are heard from beyond the veil. I know this. But these experiences are exceptional. . . . Most of the revelation that comes to leaders and members of the Church comes by the still, small voice or by a feeling rather than by a vision or a voice that speaks specific words we can hear. I testify to the reality of that kind of revelation, which I have come to know as a familiar, even daily, experience to guide me in the work of the Lord.[4]

Boyd K. Packer said, "These delicate, refined spiritual communications are not seen with our eyes nor heard with our ears. And even though it is described as a voice, it is a voice that one feels more than one hears."[5] Hence, we need to pay attention to what we're thinking and feeling while we're reading the Book of Mormon.

I have felt many such witnesses while studying and teaching the Book of Mormon for over thirty-two years. Time and again I have recognized in my mind the authenticity of the record, and the impossibility of Joseph Smith's having written it himself in six weeks' time. At other times, the beauty of some of its passages has been almost overwhelming; a flood of light has filled my mind and a rushing, swelling peace has filled my bosom. And other times it has been much more subdued, but nevertheless present, quietly speaking peace to both my mind and my heart. I testify to you, my readers and friends, that this Book of Mormon is of God. By revelation I both *know* it in my mind and *feel* it in my heart and soul. It anchors my testimony. It is tangible, physical proof of the restoration. And it contains the words of God as given through some of his most choice servants, such as Alma.

THE IMPORTANCE OF SCRIPTURE

Alma 37:1–3 • Alma delivers the sacred records to his son Helaman. He gave him the records he had been entrusted with and commanded him, "Keep a record of this people, according as I have done, upon the plates of Nephi, and keep all these things sacred which I have kept," noting that "it is for a wise purpose that they are kept" (vv. 1–2). He describes their contents as "engravings" of the "holy scriptures" plus the "genealogy of [thier] forefathers, even from the beginning" (v. 3).

Alma 37:4–5 • The brass plates will retain their brightness and eventually go forth to all nations. Alma prophesied that they would be "handed down from one generation to another, and be kept and preserved by the hand of the Lord until they should go forth unto every nation, kindred, tongue, and people" (v. 4). He also promised that the plates of brass (and all the other plates of the Nephites) would "retain their brightness" (be timeless) because they contain holy writ (v. 5; 1 Nephi 5:19).

Bruce R. McConkie said,

> The value of the Brass plates to the Nephites cannot be overestimated. By means of them they were able to preserve the language (1 Nephi 3:19), most of the civilization, and the religious knowledge of the people from whence they came. (1 Nephi 22:30.) By way of contrast, the Mulekites, who were led out of Jerusalem some 11 years after Lehi's departure, and who had no record equivalent to the Brass plates, soon dwindled in apostasy and unbelief and lost their language, civilization, and religion (Omni 14–18).
>
> From prophet to prophet and generation to generation the Brass plates were handed down and preserved by the Nephites (Mosiah 1:16; 28:20; 3 Nephi 1:2). At some future date the Lord has promised to bring them forth, undimmed by time and retaining their original brightness, and the scriptural accounts recorded on them are to "go forth unto every nation, kindred, tongue, and people" (Alma 37:3–5; 1 Nephi 5:18–19).[6]

Daniel H. Ludlow said,

> The brass plates were similar to our Old Testament down to the time of Jeremiah except that they were more complete and comprehensive (1 Nephi 13:23). Joseph Smith did not translate directly from the brass plates of Laban, but he did translate two records that contained some of the writings on the brass plates. These were (1) the small plates of Nephi, which frequently quoted directly from the brass plates, and (2) the plates of Mormon, which contained a few writings from the brass plates that Mormon included in his abridgment of the large plates of Nephi. Therefore, through our present Book of Mormon a portion of the brass plates has already gone forth "unto all nations, kindreds, tongues, and people," just as Lehi prophesied (1 Nephi 5:17–19).[7]

Alma 37:6–7 • By "small and simple things" the Lord accomplishes his eternal purposes.
Alma calls keeping the sacred records a "small and simple thing" (v. 6). It might have seemed mundane—as does the keeping of our personal journals today—but it is through "small and simple things [that] great things [are] brought to pass; and small means in many instances doth confound the wise" (v. 6) and "bringeth about the salvation of many souls" (v. 7).

Wilford Woodruff said, "I have never spent any of my time more profitably for the benefit of mankind than in my journal writing, for a great portion of the Church history has been compiled from my journals and some of the most glorious gospel sermons, truths, and revelations that were given from God to this people through the mouth of the Prophets Joseph and Brigham, Heber and the Twelve could not be found upon the earth on record only in my journals and they are compiled in the Church history and transmitted to the Saints of God in all future generations. Does not this pay me for my troubles? It does."[8]

Spencer W. Kimball said,

> Your own private journal should record the way you face up to challenges that beset you. Do not suppose life changes so much that your experiences will not be interesting to your posterity. . . . Your journal should contain your true self rather than a picture of you when you are "made up" for a public performance. There is a temptation to paint one's virtues in rich color and whitewash the vices, but there is also the opposite pitfall of accentuating the negative. Personally I have little respect for anyone who delves into the ugly phases of the life he is portraying, whether it be his own or another's. The truth should be told, but we should not emphasize the negative. Even a long life full of inspiring experiences can be brought to the dust by one ugly story. . . . What could you do better for your children and your children's children than to record the story of your life, your triumphs over adversity, your recovery after a fall, your progress when all seemed black, your rejoicing when you had finally achieved? . . . Get a notebook, my young folks, a journal that will last through all time, and maybe the angels may quote from it for eternity. Begin today and write in it your goings and comings, your deepest thoughts, your achievements and your failures, your associations and your triumphs, your impressions and your testimonies. Remember, the Savior chastised those who failed to record important events.[9]

Alma 37:11–19 • Alma did not fully understand the reason for keeping and preserving their records. Alma admitted, "[The reasons for keeping the records] are not yet fully made known unto me" (v. 11). "I [can] only say they are preserved for a wise purpose," he tells his son, "which purpose is known unto God" (v. 12). He emphasized the sacredness of the trust given to Helaman and promised that heaven would protect the records (vv. 13–14). He warned his son that if he was disobedient to God, the records would be taken away from him (v. 15), but that if he was obedient God would bless him and would fulfill all his promises regarding the sacred record (vv. 16–17). But he did know that God will "preserve these things for a wise purpose in him, that he might show forth his power unto future generations" (v. 18) as well as to the Nephites and Lamanites their own day (v. 19).

Reasons the scriptures are important (Alma 37:1–19). In the course of giving the sacred records to his son Helaman, Alma identified a number of reasons their records (and all scriptures) are important:

 ▷ They contain the scriptures and a genealogy of their forefathers (v. 3).
 ▷ They fulfill prophecy (vv. 4–5).
 ▷ They confound the wise (v. 6).

- ▷ They bring about the salvation of many souls (v. 7).
- ▷ They "enlarge the memory of this people" (v. 8).
- ▷ They convince many (e.g., the Lamanites) of errors in their traditions (vv. 8–9, 19).
- ▷ They bring men to a knowledge of God (vv. 8–9).
- ▷ They bring men to repentance (vv. 9–10).
- ▷ They show the power of God to future generations (vv. 14, 18–19).

Alma 37:21–31 • Helaman is to withhold information on the twenty-four gold plates from his people concerning the Jaredites' wicked oaths and plans, which, if known, might corrupt the people. Alma described them as "mysteries and . . . works of darkness, . . . the secret works of those people who have been destroyed . . . yea, all their murders, and robbings, and their plunderings, and all their wickedness and abominations" (v. 21). Helaman was charged not to make these things known "unto this people" and to also carefully guard and preserve "these interpreters" (the Urim and Thummim) (v. 21). The Nephites had already begun to "work in darkness . . . secret murders and abominations" and were under threat of destruction if the did not repent (v. 22), and the Lord did not want any further wickedness to be revealed to them.

The Lord's prophecy concerning the destruction of the Jaredites had already been fulfilled. Alma notes here that they "did not repent; therefore they have been destroyed, and thus far the word of God has been fulfilled; yea, their secret abominations have been brought out of darkness and made known unto us" (vv. 24–26). But the Lord did not want these things made known to the current (and perhaps equally wicked) generation, so Alma commanded his son to "retain all their oaths, and their covenants, and their agreements in their secret abominations . . . and all their signs and their wonders . . . lest peradventure they should fall into darkness also and be destroyed" (v. 27).

Alma notes that "there is a curse upon all this land, that destruction shall come upon all . . . workers of darkness, according to the power of God, when they are fully ripe" (v. 28). For this reason, he wants his son to "keep these secret plans of their oaths and their covenants from this people, and only their wickedness and their murders and their abominations shall ye make known unto them" (v. 29). Instead he is to "teach them to abhor such wickedness and abominations and murders" and remind them that the Jaredites were destroyed precisely because of these things (v. 29).

Alma 37:23 • An interpretive stone and also "interpreters" will be given to the Lord's servant Gazelem. The unveiling of secret works of darkness (both in Alma's day and also in our own) will be accomplished through the Lord's "servant Gazelem" by means of "a stone, which shall shine forth in darkness unto light" (v. 23). The name Gazelem in an authentic one, providing yet another evidence of the accuracy of the Book of Mormon.

- ▷ Gaz   A stone
- ▷ Aleim   A name of God as a revelator
- ▷ Gaz-Aleim   "A seer who uses a stone"

Urim and Thummim: Alma also explained the role of the interpreters (the Urim and Thummim, which were also stones) in revealing to prophets the secret plans and oaths of the wicked (v. 23). In other words, the Urim and Thummim were not only used for the purpose of translation of ancient records but were also a means whereby prophets could obtain information that was crucial to their missions and their safety.

Orson Pratt said, "The same instrument was in use, many hundred years after the days of Aaron, by the Prophets of Israel. David inquired by means of an instrument of that kind, concerning his enemies, who pursued him from city to city, asking the Lord certain questions—whether his enemies would come to the city where he happened to be, and whether he would be delivered up to them by the people of that city; and the Lord gave him all necessary instruction, and by this means he was delivered out of the hands of his enemies from time to time."[10]

Priddy Meeks (1795–1886), a possessor of the gift of healing and one of the early pioneers, was living in Illinois when he and his family joined the Church. He moved his family to Nauvoo and became acquainted with the Prophet Joseph Smith. On one occasion he asked the prophet concerning the "stone" (which he says was the same as the stones of the Urim and Thummim) that the Prophet possessed and that he showed to Brother Meeks. He says that the Prophet told him that "in time of war the Nephites had the advantage of their enemies by looking in the seerstone which would reveal whatever they wished to know."[11]

I have heard Eldred G. Smith, Patriarch emeritus to the Church and direct descendant of Hyrum Smith, relate on three occasions (in firesides) that the Prophet Joseph Smith used it for the same purpose. He says that the prophet kept the Urim and Thummim with him all the time during the early days of his ministry so that he could know when his enemies were coming and could take appropriate action in hiding the plates. The Prophet Joseph Smith received many of his early revelations contained in the Doctrine and Covenants through the Urim and Thummim. So it was used for multiple purposes in the early days of the restoration.

Alma 37:32–34 • Helaman is to teach the gospel, not mysteries. As opposed to the secret works of darkness of the wicked, Helaman was to teach the people "an everlasting hatred against sin and iniquity" (v. 32). He was to preach repentance and faith, humility, meekness, and "to withstand every temptation of the devil, with their faith on the Lord Jesus Christ" (v. 33). He was to teach them to "never be weary of good works, but to be meek and lowly in heart; for such shall find rest to their souls" (v. 34).

This instruction reminds me of the warning I received, along with a room full of other new missionaries, in 1968 from Bruce R. McConkie. I was seated at the front of one of the classroom rows of desks when Elder McConkie came to our training session in the old missionary home in Salt Lake City (where the Conference Center now stands) to address us. He stood directly in front of me and began his remarks with a powerful command that literally rattled the pencil that was sitting on top of my desk. "Thou shalt not discuss tenets!" he thundered. We were all now focused on him with wide-eyed amazement. And then he quoted from Alma and other scriptures (without benefit of notes) to explain what he meant. Missionaries are called to teach, not to argue. We should never delve into the mysteries—things we don't know or don't understand—with investigators. Our responsibility is to teach faith, repentance, baptism, and the receipt of the Holy Ghost. And every thing we say and do should have reference to and be focused upon the one thing that matters most: the birth, teachings, Atonement, death, and resurrection of Jesus Christ. If it does not have to do with these core principles, it has no place in our teaching and testifying.

Alma 37:35–37 • "Counsel with the Lord in all thy doings, and he will direct thee for good." Alma encouraged his son, "Learn wisdom in thy youth." He was to do so by praying for the Lord's guidance in all things and keeping the commandments of God (v. 35). Everything he did and everywhere he went was to be done in the name of the Lord, and all his thoughts and desires ("affections of thy heart") were to be "placed upon the Lord forever" (v. 36). He was to "counsel with the Lord" about everything—"when thou liest down at night lie down unto the Lord, that he may watch over you in your sleep; and when thou risest in the morning let thy heart be full of thanks unto God." If he does all of these things, Alma promises he will be "lifted up at the last day" (v. 37).

We may conclude from these verses that nothing is too inconsequential to take to our God. If it's important to us, it's important to our loving Father in Heaven. Though his thoughts are higher than our thoughts, and his ways are higher than our ways (Isaiah 55:9), he still understands our mortal experiences and wishes to help us. Alma's advice—"counsel with the Lord in all thy doings"—makes it clear that we can take everything that concerns us to the Lord, in humility and faith. And the great God of our universe will hear and answer us, always in a way that will be for our good.

Alma 37:38–42 • Alma describes the "small means" by which the Liahona provided directions to Lehi's family. Alma had access to information concerning Lehi's journey in the wilderness that we do not now possess. His discussion of the Liahona here is interesting because of the additional information it provides to us. He calls it "a ball, or director—or our fathers called it Liahona, which is, being interpreted, a compass; and the Lord prepared it" (v. 38). It was made by very curious workmanship and functioned as a guide to the Lehites on their journey to the new world (v. 39). It was more than just a compass that indicated what direction was north, south, east, and west (as we would understand the term *compass* today), although it may well have included such information since Nephi was able to give very specific descriptions of the direction they were traveling (e.g., "nearly a south-southeast direction" [1 Nephi 16:13]).

But it was more than a direction-giving device. It "did work for them according to their faith in God; therefore, if they had faith to believe that God could cause that those spindles should point the way they should go, behold, it was done; therefore they had this miracle, and also many other miracles wrought by the power of God, day by day" (v. 40). This would make it as much of a spiritual barometer as a compass. If it stopped working they knew that they were in need of repentance and increased faith. This process was referred to by Alma as "miracles . . . worked by small means," which, because of their smallness ("no big deal" as we would say it), "they were slothful, and forgot to exercise their faith and diligence" (v. 41). When they did this, "those marvelous works ceased, and they did not progress in their journey" (v. 41). During those times when they were slothful or disobedient or had insufficient faith, they were stuck (they "tarried") in the wilderness and "did not travel a direct course, and were afflicted with hunger and thirst, because of their transgressions" (v. 42).

Why the Lehites considered the Liahona a "small thing." Dr. Hugh Nibley explained,

> The meaning is perfectly clear: though Lehi's people enjoyed daily demonstrations of God's power, the device by which that power operated seemed so ordinary (Alma included it among "small and simple things . . . very small means" [Alma 37:6–7]) that in spite of the "marvellous works" it showed them they tended to neglect it. . . .
>
> [To understand why, we] turn to Mr. Fahd's study of belomancy in the ancient Near East. "Belomancy is the practice of divination by shooting, tossing, shaking, or otherwise manipulating rods, darts, pointers, or other sticks, all originally derived from arrows. . . . These old practices might have some connection with the Liahona. For the most common use of divination arrows, and probably their original purpose, was, according to . . . Fahd, [giving] direction [to] travelers in

the desert. [These] 'arrows' used in divination . . . were devoid of heads and feathers, being mere shafts or pointers. . . ."

But why arrows? Because, as we have shown elsewhere, the shooting of arrows is a universal form of divination. Other substitutes for shooting were shaking or drawing from a bag or quiver, "balancing on the finger, or spinning on a pivot. . . ." In the New World . . . the "arrows or darts are tossed . . . or shot . . . at an arrow tossed or shot to the ground so that they fall one across the other." More often than not, the arrows in question were mere sticks or pointers . . . All this shaking, tossing, and shooting emphasizes the divinatory [function] of arrows as pointers, but along with that they also conveyed their message . . . by the writing that was upon them. . . .

The original and natural number of arrows used in divination seems to have been two. . . . The . . . arrangement was that two arrows designated the advisability or inadvisability of a journey; they were designated as "the safr [Go ahead!] and the khadr [Stay where you are!]" [The most] regular consultants of the arrows were those faced with travel-problems. . . .

It would be an obtuse reader indeed who needed [me] to spell out for him the resemblance between ancient arrow-divination and the Liahona: two "spindles or pointers" bearing written instructions provide superhuman guidance for travelers in the desert. What more could you want? But what is the relationship between them? On this the Book of Mormon is remarkably specific. Both Nephi and Alma go out of their way to insist that the Liahona did not work itself (i.e., it was not a magic thing, but worked only by the power of God and only for appointed persons who had faith in that power).

Moreover, while both men marvel at the wonderful workmanship of the brass ball in which the pointers were mounted, they refer to the operation of those pointers as "a very small thing," so familiar to Lehi's people that they hardly gave it a second glance. So contemptuous were they of the "small means" by which "those miracles were worked" for their guidance and preservation that they constantly "forgot to exercise their faith," so that the compass would work. This suggests that aside from the workmanship of the mounting, there was nothing particularly strange or mystifying about the apparatus, which Alma specifies as a "temporal" thing. . . .

Was the Liahona, then, just old magic? No, it is precisely here that Nephi and Alma are most emphatic—unlike magic things, these pointers worked solely by the power of God, and then, too, for only those designated to use them. Anybody about to make a journey could consult the mantic arrows at the shrines, and to this day throughout the world mantic arrows are still being consulted. But it is clear from Alma's words that in his day the Liahona had been out of operation for centuries, having functioned only for a true man of God and only for one special journey.[12]

Are we sometimes guilty of taking important but "small" things for granted? Do we neglect our daily prayers, our daily scripture study, our family home evenings, or other things we have been continuously counseled to do, because we see them as "small" things that do not produce spectacular and immediate results? M. Russell Ballard said, "We observe vast sweeping world events; however, we must remember that the purposes of the Lord in our personal lives generally are fulfilled through the small and simple things, and not the momentous and spectacular."[13]

Alma 37:43–47 • Alma compares the scriptures to the Liahona, and the "simple" symbol of Moses' brass serpent. Just as the Lehites were sometimes slow to give heed to the Liahona—a simple temporal device—and did not prosper, "so it is with things which are spiritual" (v. 43). The scriptures (the "word of Christ") may also seem to be a small thing, but they "will point to you a straight course to eternal bliss, as it was for our fathers to give heed to this compass" (v. 44). The symbolism ("type") of the Liahona's leading the Lehites to the land of promise applies equally well to the scriptures as they "carry us beyond this vale of sorrow into a far better land of promise" (v. 45).

Alma also references the brass serpent that Moses raised up in the wilderness as a healing device for the Israelites. Just as the Lehites had sometimes failed to exercise faith in the Liahona's ability to guide them safely to the promised land, so also the children of Israel neglected to look upon this symbol of Christ to avoid death, because it was too simple (see also Numbers 21:5–9; 1 Nephi 17:41). With regard to studying the scriptures, Alma said, "Do not let us be slothful because of the easiness of the way" because "the way is prepared, and if we will look we may live forever" (v. 46).

Alma then finishes up with a quick summary. Helaman is to "take care of these sacred things," "look to God and live," "go unto this people and declare the word," and be sober." With that, Alma closes his letter: "My son, farewell" (v. 47).

Alma's Message to Shiblon
(ALMA 38)

ALMA'S TESTIMONY AND PRAISE FOR SHIBLON

Alma 38:1–5 • Alma's praise and promises for his son Shiblon. It is important for parents to recognize and praise their children, which Alma did here for his son Shiblon. He began with the same promise he made to Helaman—"Inasmuch as ye shall keep the commandments of God ye shall prosper in the land" (v. 1). He then expressed his "great joy" in Shiblon "because of your steadiness and your faithfulness unto God," that he had "commenced in your youth to look to the Lord your God" (v. 2). He also praised him by saying, "Because of thy faithfulness and thy diligence, and thy patience and thy long-suffering among the people of the Zoramites" (v. 3). Shiblon had accompanied his father on the mission among the Zoramites and had experienced both "bonds" and stoning with patience until the Lord delivered him (v. 4). Alma promised him, "Put your trust in God even so much ye shall be delivered out of your trials, and your troubles, and your afflictions, and ye shall be lifted up at the last day" (v. 5).

Alma 38:6–9 • Alma bears his testimony to Shiblon. Alma related very briefly his conversion experience as he bore his powerful testimony to Shiblon. He wanted his son to know that he was not just speaking his opinion of the truthfulness of the gospel: "but it is the Spirit of God which is in me which maketh these things known unto me; for if I had not been born of God I should not have known these things" (v. 6). He declared, "[I had] seen an angel face to face, and he spake with me, and his voice was as thunder, and it shook the whole earth." The angel commanded Alma to stop his destructive work against the Church (v. 7). He also related that he "was three days and three nights in the most bitter pain and anguish of soul" because of his sins, which were not remitted "until [he] did cry out unto the Lord Jesus Christ for mercy . . . and [he] did find peace to [his] soul" (v. 8). He testified, "There is no other way or means whereby man can be saved, only in and through Christ," whom Alma calls "the life and the light of the world . . . the word of truth and righteousness" (v. 9).

ALMA'S COUNSEL FOR MISSIONARIES AND TEACHERS

Alma 38:10–15 • Alma counsels Shiblon about missionary work and teaching. He knew that

Shiblon would continue to be a faithful missionary, so he offered advice that applies to all who would seek to teach the gospel to others.

▷ Be "diligent and temperate" (devoted but not extreme) (v. 10).
▷ Avoid pride and "boasting in your own wisdom" (v. 11).
▷ Use "boldness, but not over-bearance" (v. 12).
▷ "Bridle all your passions" (anger, lust, etc.) (v. 12).
▷ Be motivated by ("filled with") love (v. 12).
▷ "Refrain from idleness" (don't be lazy) (v. 12).
▷ Don't be like the Zoramites—making a show of your religion (v. 13).
▷ Don't be arrogant or think you are better than others (v. 14).
▷ Be sober (serious) in your work (v. 15).

He closes his short epistle with words of blessing—"May the Lord bless your soul, and receive you at the last day into his kingdom, to sit down in peace"—and words of encouragement—"Now go, my son, and teach the word unto this people. . . . My son, farewell" (v. 15).

Alma's Message to Corianton

Alma's counsel to his son Corianton comprises chapters 39 through 42 of the book of Alma. The first chapter contains his admonition to his son to repent and is covered here at the end of lesson 29. Alma 40–42 contains his explanation to Corianton of the great plan of redemption and will be covered in the following lesson, which is lesson 30.

Alma Admonishes Corianton to Repent
(Alma 39)

Alma 39:1–4 • Corianton had been proud and immoral on his mission. Alma's counsel for him was somewhat different from the counsel he gave to his brothers because Corianton had committed serious sins. Unlike his steady and faithful brother, Helaman, Corianton had not given heed to his father's counsel (v. 1). Specifically, he had boasted in his own strength and wisdom (v. 2) and had been immoral with the harlot Isabel while serving a mission (v. 3). While he was not her only conquest—she "did steal away the hearts of many"—Alma maintains, "This was no excuse for thee, my son. Thou shouldst have tended to the ministry wherewith thou wast entrusted" (v. 4).

Alma 39:5–8 • Alma teaches concerning the hierarchy of sins. He wished his son had not been immoral, and wrote, "I would not dwell upon your crimes, to harrow up your soul, if it were not for your good" (v. 7). But he reminds his son, "Ye cannot hide your crimes from God; and except ye repent they will stand as a testimony against you at the last day" (v. 8).

As part of this discussion, Alma called unchastity the "most abominable above all sins save it be the shedding of innocent blood or denying the Holy Ghost" (v. 5). This would place unchastity third among the hierarchy of sins. He said, "If ye deny the Holy Ghost when it once has had place in you, and ye know that ye deny it, behold, this is a sin which is unpardonable" (v. 6), which would make it the most serious of all sins. And he called murder a sin for which "it is not easy . . . to obtain forgiveness" (v. 6). To understand this teaching, we must understand the nature of these three sins and the meaning of the words *pardonable* and *forgivable*.

The ranking of these sins, and the reasoning behind the ranking, are as follows. The penalties for these sins and reasons why they rank as they do, are explained below.

	Sin Against the Holy Ghost	Murder	Adultery and Fornication
Nature of the Sin	Unpardonable	Unforgivable	Most grievous
Penalty	Suffering endures forever	Suffering to the end of Millennium	Only one opportunity to repent
Reasoning	Denying an open vision of Christ	Once taken, life cannot be restored	Once taken, virtue is lost

The sin against the Holy Ghost—the unpardonable sin. Alma ranked this as the most serious of all sins, and one for which there is neither forgiveness nor pardon. To understand what this means we must understand the concept of "pardoning."

Prisoners receive pardon when they have served their allotted time and paid their allotted price for their crimes. At the time of pardon, the suffering ceases and the prisoner is set free. For a crime that is unpardonable, the prisoner is never set free—his suffering continues without ever ceasing. So it is with the unpardonable sin. One who is guilty of this sin will suffer forever, without ceasing. There will never be a time when he or she has paid the price and suffering will cease. It will never cease. Only the most serious of all sins could be worthy of such endless punishment, and such is the case if you "deny the Holy Ghost when it once has had place in you, and ye know that ye deny it" (Alma 39:6).

The unpardonable sin is more than just having a testimony and then later denying it. It is more than receiving the priesthood and then turning against the Church. It is a sin that is committed only by those who have had an open vision of the Savior and then turned against him as though it had never happened. It is defined in D&C 76:31 as follows:

(1) They "know my power, and
(2) have been made partakers thereof, and
(3) suffered themselves through the power of the devil to be overcome, and
(4) to deny the truth, and
(5) defy my power."

The Prophet Joseph Smith said, "What must a man do to commit the unpardonable sin? He must receive the Holy Ghost, have the heavens opened unto him, and know God, and then sin against Him. After a man has sinned against the Holy Ghost, there is no repentance for him. He has got to say that the sun does not shine while he sees it; he has got to deny Jesus Christ when the heavens have been opened unto him, and to deny the plan of salvation with his eyes open to the truth of it; and from that time he begins to be an enemy. This is the case with many apostates of the Church of Jesus Christ of Latter-day Saints."[14]

When one commits this sin, he becomes a "son of perdition"—perdition being another name for Cain, who walked and talked with Jehovah and yet willfully turned against him. The number of people who have or will become sons of perdition is very limited.

Murder—the unforgivable sin. To understand the concept of unforgivable sin, we must understand what it means to be forgiven. We are forgiven for a crime when we are not required to pay any price for it. We are not considered guilty when we are forgiven, and we go on living as if the crime had never taken place. This is what happens when the Lord forgives us of our sins. He pays the price for us and he "remembers them no more" (D&C 48:42). Though our sins be "as red as scarlet," they shall be "as white as snow" in the Lord's eyes (Isaiah 1:18). All sins are forgivable except murder and the sin against the Holy Ghost.

For crimes that are forgivable, the prisoner must personally pay the price. There is no avoiding it. But after he has paid the price, he will eventually receive pardon, so his suffering will not be endless. In our society, for example, a murderer is usually not forgiven. He must serve his allotted time, but after having done so he is pardoned and released from prison. Such is the case with the sin of murder. It is not forgivable. The Atonement of Jesus Christ cannot atone for it, and the murderer will have to suffer in "hell" for a while for this very serious sin. But at some point—known only to God—the murderer will have paid his price and will be set free from spiritual prison.

The General Handbook of Instruction for the Church defines murder as "the deliberate and unjustified taking of human life."[15] The Prophet Joseph Smith said concerning this sin: "A murderer . . . one that sheds innocent blood, cannot have forgiveness."[16]

Bruce R. McConkie said, "Murder, the unlawful killing of another human being with malice aforethought, is the second most serious sin. It is an abomination in the sight of God because it, like unchastity, involves the unlawful tampering with human life. It is a 'sin unto death' (see 1 John 5:16–17), an offense which is called the unforgivable sin."[17]

Harold B. Lee said, "One of the most serious of all sins and crimes against the Lord's plan of salvation is the sin of murder or the destruction of human life. It seems clear that to be guilty of destroying life is the act of 'rebellion' against the plan of the Almighty by denying an individual thus destroyed in mortality, the privilege of a full experience in this earth-school of opportunity. It is in the same category as the rebellion of Satan and his hosts and therefore it would not be surprising if the penalties to be imposed upon a murderer were to be of similar character as the penalties meted out to those spirits which were cast out of heaven with Satan."[18]

Spencer W. Kimball said,

> Another scriptural character responsible for murder—and this in conjunction with adultery—was the great King David. For his dreadful crime, all his life afterward he sought forgiveness. Some of the Psalms portray the anguish of his soul, yet David is still paying for his sin. He did not receive the resurrection at the time of the resurrection of Jesus Christ. Peter declared that his body was still in the tomb (see Acts 2:29-34). . . .
>
> Perhaps one reason murder is so heinous is that man cannot restore life. Man's mortal life is given him in which to repent and prepare himself for eternity, and should one of his fellowmen terminate his life and thus limit his progress by making his repentance impossible, it would be a ghastly deed, a tremendous responsibility for which the murderer might not be able to atone in his lifetime.[19]

Murder is not forgivable but is eventually pardonable. Joseph F. Smith said, "But even David, though guilty of adultery and murder of Uriah, obtained the promise that his soul should not be left in hell, which means, as I understand it, that even he shall escape the second death."[20]

The Prophet Joseph Smith underlined the seriousness of the sin of murder by using David as an example of what happens to a murderer:

"A murderer, for instance, one that sheds innocent blood, cannot have forgiveness. David sought repentance at the hand of God carefully with tears, for the murder of Uriah; but he could only get it through hell: he got a promise that his soul should not be left in hell. Although David was a king, he never did obtain the spirit and power of Elijah and the fullness of the Priesthood; and the Priesthood that he received, and the throne and kingdom of David is to be taken from him and given to another by the name of David in the last days, raised up out of his lineage."[21]

Unchastity—the most serious of all forgivable sins. Unchastity is forgivable, though it is the most serious of all sins except the sin against the Holy Ghost and murder.

The Lord said, "Thou shalt not commit adultery; and he that committeth adultery, and repenteth not, shall be cast out [excommunicated]. But he that has committed adultery and repents with all his heart, and forsaketh it, and doeth it no more, thou shalt forgive; But if he doeth it again, he shall not be forgiven, but shall be cast out" (D&C 42:24–26). Thus adultery is both pardonable and forgivable, but if committed again after a person understands the law, it is unforgivable.

Boyd K. Packer reminds us that the power of procreation is central to the plan of salvation:

> There was provided in our bodies—and this is sacred—a power of creation, a light, so to speak, that has the power to kindle other lights. This gift was to be used only within the sacred bonds of marriage. Through the exercise of this power of creation, a mortal body may be conceived, a spirit enter into it, and a new soul born into this life.
>
> This power is good. It can create and sustain family life, and it is in family life that we find the fountains of happiness. . . . [It] "is a gift from God our Father. In the righteous exercise of it as in nothing else, we may come close to him. . . ."
>
> The power of creation—or may we say procreation—is not just an incidental part of the plan: it is essential to it. Without it the plan could not proceed. The misuse of it may disrupt the plan.
>
> Much of the happiness that may come to you in this life will depend on how you use this sacred power of creation. . . . If [Satan] can entice you to use this power prematurely, to use it too soon, or to misuse it in any way, you may well lose your opportunities for eternal progression. . . .
>
> God has declared in unmistakable language that misery and sorrow will follow the violation of the laws of chastity. . . . Crowning glory awaits you if you live worthily. The loss of the crown may well be punishment enough. Often, very often, we are punished as much by our sins as we are for them.
>
> Protect and guard your gift. Your actual happiness is at stake. Eternal family life . . . can be achieved because our Heavenly Father has bestowed this choicest gift of all upon you—this power of creation. It is the very key to happiness.[22]

Alma 39:9–14 • Alma's counsel concerning sexual sin. His advice to his son is good advice for any person seeking to repent of unchastity or to avoid the problem in the first place.

> ▷ To "go no more after the lusts of your eyes" (v. 9) means to choose not to respond to immoral images or suggestions. And Daniel H. Ludlow explains that to "cross yourself" (v. 9) is akin to the Lord's command to "take up your cross"—to deny ourselves of all unrighteousness (3 Nephi 12:30; Matthew 16:24; JS—Matthew 16:26).[23]
>
> ▷ "Counsel with your elder brothers" (v. 10) means to counsel with righteous family members, friends, or priesthood leaders to help strengthen our resistance to temptation.
>
> ▷ "Suffer not yourself to be led away by any vain or foolish thing" (v. 11). Moral sins often occur while engaged in silly, loud, or boastful behavior (such as wild parties, drinking, and so forth).
>
> ▷ Consider your influence on others (vv. 11–12). Moral sin is not a strictly personal matter, because our immorality can also encourage others to sin. Corianton was encouraging the Zoramites to sin through his bad example.

- ▷ Forsake your sins (v. 13). "Turn to the Lord with all your mind, might, and strength" means to reject all former wickedness and be devoted to the Lord and his purposes.
- ▷ Confess your sins (v. 13). "Acknowledge your faults and that wrong which ye have done," both to those you have harmed and to the Church. Moral sins require confession to the bishop.
- ▷ Forsake all forms of worldliness (v. 14). "Seek not after riches nor the vain things of this world." Worldliness drives away the spirit and weakens our resolve and self-confidence. The Lord draws a clear connection between virtue and self-esteem in modern-day revelation: "Let virtue garnish thy thoughts unceasingly; then shall thy confidence wax strong in the presence of God" (D&C 121:45).

Alma 39:15–19 • Alma teaches Corianton of the hope he can have for forgiveness through Christ's atonement. Alma assured his son that Christ would come and atone for the sins of the world, including Corianton's adultery (v. 15). With a touch of irony, he reminded Corianton that this message—the coming and redemption of Christ—is what he was supposed to have been teaching to others (v. 16). If people's minds are sufficiently prepared for the Savior's coming, then they will be saved when he appears (v. 16). The good news for Corianton, however, is that he does not have to wait for that day. "Behold, I say unto you, is not a soul at this time as precious unto God as a soul will be at the time of his coming? Is it not as necessary that the plan of redemption should be made known unto this people as well as unto their children?" (vv. 17–18). Corianton can be forgiven of his sins if he will sincerely repent and turn with faith unto the Savior.

Finally, making reference to his own earlier redemption from equally serious sins, Alma concludes this part of his letter by asking, "Is it not as easy at this time for the Lord to send his angel to declare these glad tidings unto us as unto our children, or as after the time of his coming?" (v. 19). The answer, of course, is yes. The Lord had seen fit to send an angel to redeem Alma, and the Lord has provided the means by which *all* of his children can be redeemed from sins if they will repent and turn to him.

Notes

1. Bruce R. McConkie, *Mormon Doctrine*, 2nd ed. (Salt Lake City: Bookcraft, 1966), 786–87.
2. Ibid., 644–45.
3. Joseph Smith, *Teachings of the Prophet Joseph Smith*, Joseph Fielding Smith, sel. (Salt Lake City: Deseret Book, 1976), 151.
4. Dallin H. Oaks,, "Teaching and Learning by the Spirit," *Ensign*, March 1997, 11–12, 14.
5. Boyd K. Packer, *That All May Be Edified* (Salt Lake City: Bookcraft, 1982), 335.
6. Bruce R. McConkie, *Mormon Doctrine*, 2nd ed., (Salt Lake City: Bookcraft, 1966), 103.
7. Daniel H. Ludlow, *A Companion to Your Study of the Book of Mormon* (Salt Lake City: Deseret Book, 1976), 57.
8. Wilford Woodruff, "Diary," March 17, 1857, quoted in Dean C. Jessee, "The Kirtland Diary of Wilford Woodruff," in *BYU Studies* 12, no. 4 (1971–1972).
9. Spencer W. Kimball, *The Teachings of Spencer W. Kimball*, Edward L. Kimball, ed. (Salt Lake City: Bookcraft, 1982), 350–51.
10. Orson Pratt, in *Journal of Discourses* (London: Latter-day Saints' Book Depot, 1854), 18:156.
11. Richard H. Cracroft and Neal E. Lambert, comps., *A Believing People: Literature of the Latter-day Saints* (Salt Lake City: Bookcraft, 1979), 116.
12. Hugh Nibley, *Since Cumorah* (Salt Lake City, Utah: Deseret Book, 1967), 283-95.

13. M. Russell Ballard, *Ensign*, May 1990, 6.
14. Joseph Smith, *Teachings of the Prophet Joseph Smith*, Joseph Fielding Smith, sel. (Salt Lake City: Deseret Book, 1976), 358.
15. *The General Handbook of Instruction* (Salt lake City: The Church of Jesus Christ of Latter-day Saints), 10.
16. Joseph Smith, *Teachings of the Prophet Joseph Smith*, Joseph Fielding Smith, sel. (Salt Lake City: Deseret Book, 1976), 339.
17. Bruce R. McConkie, *A New Witness for the Articles of Faith* (Salt Lake City: Deseret Book, 1985), 339.
18. Harold B. Lee, *The Teachings of Harold B. Lee*, Clyde J. Williams, ed. (Salt Lake City: Bookcraft, 1996), 198.
19. Spencer W. Kimball, *The Miracle of Forgiveness* (Salt Lake City: Bookcraft, 1969), 127–29.
20. Joseph F. Smith, *Gospel Doctrine, Selections from the Sermons and Writings of Joseph F. Smith*, John A. Widtsoe, comp. (Salt Lake City: Deseret Book, 1939), 433.
21. Joseph Smith, *History of The Church of Jesus Christ of Latter-day Saints*, 2nd ed., B. H. Roberts, ed. (Salt Lake City: The Church of Jesus Christ of Latter-day Saints, 1844), 6:253.
22. Boyd K. Packer, in Conference Report, Apr. 1972, 136–39.
23. Daniel H. Ludlow, *A Companion to Your Study of the Book of Mormon* (Salt Lake City: Deseret Book, 1976), 223.

"The Great Plan of Happiness"

The Great Plan of Happiness

These three chapters of Alma are perhaps the most plain in all of scripture concerning the plan of salvation. The context of these teachings is Alma's teachings to his son Corianton. Alma had spoken plainly concerning Corianton's sins, but also concerning the opportunity for forgiveness if he would turn to the Lord with all his heart, might, mind, and strength and rely upon the Savior's Atonement to save him. Hearing this doctrine, Corianton is now worried about a number of things that directly affect his standing before the Lord.

▷ Death and the resurrection (Alma 40:1).

▷ The principles of repentance and restoration (Alma 41:1).

▷ The principles of justice and mercy (Alma 42:1).

In response, Alma teaches Corianton about our Heavenly Father's plan, which he variously refers to as:

▷ "The plan of restoration" (Alma 41:2).

▷ "The great plan of salvation" (Alma 42:5).

▷ "The great plan of happiness" (Alma 42:8).

▷ "The plan of redemption" (Alma 42:11).

▷ "The great plan of mercy" (Alma 42:31).

Neal A. Maxwell said, "The Lord has described his plan of redemption as the Plan of Happiness. . . . Conversationally, we reference this great design almost too casually at times; we even sketch its rude outlines on chalkboards and paper as if it were the floor plan for an addition to one's house. However, when we really take time to ponder the Plan, it is breathtaking and overpowering!"[1]

Alma does not discuss the plan of salvation in either chronological or topical order, but discusses individual concepts in multiple places in these three chapters. For purposes of clarity in teaching and understanding, I have organized his teachings into discrete topics. We begin with what happens at death.

Death and the Spirit World
(ALMA 40)

Alma 40:11–14, 21 • Between death and resurrection, our spirits go to either "paradise" or spirit prison. Alma told his son that he had learned about death and the spirit world from an angel (v. 11), but he does not say who the angel was nor when he appeared. He learned from the angel that "the spirits of all men, as soon as they are departed from this mortal body . . . whether they be good or evil, are taken home to that God who gave them life" (v. 11). This is similar to what we read in Ecclesiastes 12:7: "Then shall the dust return to the earth as it was, and the spirit shall return unto God who gave it."

Are the spirits of those who die "taken home to God" literally? No, these scriptures should not be interpreted to mean that the spirit, at the time of death, goes into the immediate presence of the Lord.

Brigham Young said,

> When you lay down this tabernacle, where are you going? Into the spiritual world. . . . Where is the spirit world? It is right here. Do the good and evil spirits go together? Yes, they do. Do they both inhabit one kingdom? Yes, they do. Do they go to the sun? No. Do they go beyond the boundaries of the organized earth? No, they do not. They are brought forth upon this earth, for the express purpose of inhabiting it to all eternity. Where else are you going? No where else, only as you may be permitted. . . .
>
> It reads that the spirit goes to God who gave it. Let me render this scripture a little plainer; when the spirits leave their bodies they are in the presence of our Father and God; they are prepared then to see, hear and understand spiritual things. But where is the spirit world? It is incorporated within this celestial system. Can you see it with your natural eyes? No. Can you see spirits in this room? No. Suppose the Lord should touch your eyes that you might see, could you then see the spirits? Yes, as plainly as you now see bodies with your natural eyes.[2]

George Q. Cannon said, "Alma, when he says that 'the spirits of all men, as soon as they are departed from this mortal body, . . . are taken home to that God who gave them life,' has the idea, doubtless, in his mind that our God is omnipresent—not in His own personality but through His minister, the Holy Spirit. He does not intend to convey the idea that they are immediately ushered into the personal presence of God. He evidently uses that phrase in a qualified sense."[3]

Joseph Fielding Smith said,

> These words of Alma as I understand them, do not intend to convey the thought that all spirits go back into the presence of God for an assignment to a place of peace or a place of punishment and before him receive their individual sentence. "Taken home to God," simply means that their mortal existence has come to an end, and they have returned to the world of spirits, where they are assigned to a place according to their works with the just or with the unjust, there to await the resurrection. "Back to God" is a phrase which finds an equivalent in many other well-known conditions. For instance: a man spends a stated time in some foreign mission field. When he is released and returns to the United States, he may say, "It is wonderful to be back home"; yet his home may be somewhere in Utah or Idaho or some other part of the West.[4]

Heber C. Kimball said, "As for my going into the immediate presence of God when I die, I do not expect it, but I expect to go into the world of spirits and associate with my brethren, and preach the Gospel in the spiritual world, and prepare myself in every necessary way to receive my body again, and then enter through the wall into the celestial world."[5]

THE SPIRIT WORLD

Alma calls the spirit world "a space between death and the resurrection of the body, and a state of the soul in happiness or in misery until the time which is appointed of God that the dead shall come forth, and be reunited, both soul and body" (v. 21). And there they "remain . . . [the wicked in spirit prison, and] the righteous in paradise, until the time of their resurrection" (v. 14).

The Prophet Joseph Smith said, "There has been much said . . . about the words of Jesus (when on the cross) to the thief, saying, 'This day shalt thou be with me in paradise.' 'King James' translators make it out to say paradise. But what is paradise? It is a modern word: it does not answer at all to the original word that Jesus made use of. . . . There is nothing in the original word in Greek from which this was taken that signifies paradise; but it was 'This day thou shalt be with me in the world of spirits.'"[6]

Robert L. Millet said, "The transition from time into eternity is immediate. As the physical self breathes its last breath, the spirit self passes through a veil separating this world from the next. At this point the spirit experiences what might be called a 'partial judgment.' Those who have been true and faithful to their trust in mortality, Alma explained, are received into paradise, 'a state of rest, a state of peace, where they shall rest from all their troubles and from all care, and sorrow (Alma 40:12).'"[7]

Bruce R. McConkie said, "Death itself is an initial day of judgment for all persons, both the righteous and the wicked. When the spirit leaves the body at death, it is taken home to that God who gave it life, meaning that it returns to live in the realm of spiritual existence (Eccles. 12:7). At that time the spirit undergoes a partial judgment and is assigned an inheritance in paradise or in hell to await the day of the first or second resurrection."[8]

Joseph Fielding Smith said, "All spirits of men after death return to the spirit world. There, as I understand it, the righteous—meaning those who have been baptized and who have been faithful—are gathered in one part and all the others in another part of the spirit world."[9]

The location of the spirit world. Do the spirits of the dead go to a far distant place, or are they nearby? According to modern apostles and prophets, the spirit world is right here on earth.

Brigham Young said, "Where is the spirit world? . . . It is right here. . . . Do [spirits] go beyond the boundaries of this organized earth? No, they do not. They are brought forth upon this earth, for the express purpose of inhabiting it to all eternity. . . . When the spirits leave their bodies they are in the presence of our Father and God; they are prepared then to see, hear and understand spiritual things. . . . If the Lord would permit it, and it was His will that it should be done, you could see the spirits that have departed from this world, as plainly as you now see bodies with your natural eyes."[10]

The Prophet Joseph Smith said, "The spirits of the just are exalted to a greater and more glorious work; hence they are blessed in their departure to the world of spirits. Enveloped in flaming fire, they are not far from us, and know and understand our thoughts, feelings, and motions, and are often pained therewith."[11]

Ezra Taft Benson said, "The spirit world is not far away. Sometimes the veil between this life and the life beyond becomes very thin. Our loved ones who have passed on are not far from us."[12]

Parley Pratt said, "[The spirit world] is here on the very planet where we were born; or in other words, the earth and other planets of like sphere, have their inward or spiritual spheres, as well as their outward, or temporal. The one is peopled by temporal tabernacles, and the other by spirits. A veil is drawn between the one sphere and the other, whereby all the objects in the spiritual sphere are rendered invisible to those in the temporal."[13]

Paradise

Paradise is a state of happiness, rest, and peace. Alma taught that "the spirits of those who are righteous are received into a state of happiness, which is called paradise, a state of rest, a state of peace, where they shall rest from all their troubles and from all care, and sorrow" (v. 12).

Joseph F. Smith said, "Paradise is the abode of the righteous in the world of spirits (2 Nephi 9:13; Alma 60:13; Moroni 10:34), a 'state of happiness,' a place hereafter where the spirits of the faithful expand in wisdom, where they have respite from all their troubles, and where care and sorrow do not annoy."[14]

Brigham Young said, "Here, we are continually troubled with ills and ailments of various kinds. In the spirit world we are free from all this and enjoy life, glory, and intelligence; and we have the Father to speak to us, Jesus to speak to us, and angels to speak to us, and we shall enjoy the society of the just and the pure who are in the spirit world until the resurrection."[15]

President Young also said,

> What will be the nature of our pursuits in a state of being in which we shall possess more vigor and a higher degree of intelligence than we possess here? Shall we have labor? Shall we have enjoyment in our labor? Shall we have any object of pursuit, or shall we sit and sing ourselves away to everlasting bliss? . . .
>
> I would like to say to you, my friends and brethren, if we could see things as they are, and as we shall see and understand them, this dark shadow and valley [of mortal life] is so trifling that we shall turn round and look upon it and think, when we have crossed it, why this is the greatest advantage of my whole existence, for I have passed from a state of sorrow, grief, mourning, woe, misery, pain, anguish and disappointment into a state of existence where I can enjoy life to the fullest extent as far as that can be done without a body. My spirit is set free, I thirst no more, I want to sleep no more, I hunger no more, I tire no more, I run, I walk, I labor, I go, I come, I do this, I do that, whatever is required of me, nothing like pain or weariness. I am full of life, full of vigor, and I enjoy the presence of my Heavenly Father, by the power of his Spirit.[16]

There is only progress in the spirit world, never regression. Another important thing to understand about spirit paradise is that the spirits who dwell there never become less faithful or fall from grace in any way.

Bruce R. McConkie said,

> What we are saying is that when the Saints of God chart a course of righteousness, when they gain sure testimonies of the truth and divinity of the Lord's work, when they keep the commandments, when they overcome the world, when they put first in their lives the things of God's kingdom: when they do all these things, and then depart this life—though they have not yet become perfect—they shall nonetheless gain eternal life in our Father's kingdom; and eventually they shall be perfect as God their Father and Christ His Son are perfect. There is no equivocation, no doubt, no uncertainty in our minds. Those who have been true and faithful in this life will not

fall by the wayside in the life to come. If they keep their covenants here and now and depart this life firm and true in the testimony of our blessed Lord, they shall come forth with an inheritance of eternal life.[17]

SPIRIT PRISON

Spirit prison is a place of spiritual darkness and fearful anticipation. Alma taught that "the spirits of the wicked, yea, who are evil . . . shall be cast out into outer darkness [where] there shall be weeping, and wailing, and gnashing of teeth, and this because of their own iniquity, being led captive by the will of the devil." The wicked are those who "have no part nor portion of the Spirit of the Lord; for behold, they chose evil works rather than good; therefore the spirit of the devil did enter into them, and take possession of their house" (v. 13).

This outer darkness of which Alma spoke should not be confused with the punishment that awaits the sons of perdition. In this case, *outer darkness* means what we call the spirit prison. This is a place of spiritual "darkness, and a state of awful, fearful looking for the fiery indignation of the wrath of God upon them" (v. 14).

Brigham Young said, "What is the condition of the righteous? They are in possession of the spirit of Jesus—the power of God. . . . Jesus will administer to them; angels will administer to them; and they have a privilege of seeing and understanding more than you or I have, in the flesh; but they have not got their bodies [back] yet. . . . What is the condition of the wicked? They are in prison. Are they happy? No."[18]

Bruce R. McConkie said, "So complete is the darkness prevailing in the minds of these spirits, so wholly has gospel light been shut out of their consciences, that they know little or nothing of the plan of salvation, and have little hope within themselves of advancement and progression through the saving grace of Christ."[19]

LIFE AND WORK IN THE SPIRIT WORLD

D&C 138:29–34 • In 1918, President Joseph F. Smith received a vision of the spirit world, which shed further light on this important subject.

Christ did not visit the spirit prison when he went there (v. 29).

▷ He organized missionary work from among the righteous in paradise to take the gospel to those in spirit prison (vv. 30–31).

▷ The message is one of liberty—the opportunity to be freed from captivity (v. 31).

▷ These missionaries are sent to those who died without a knowledge of truth (v. 32).

▷ These missionaries are also sent to those who died in sin (v. 32).

▷ Their message is faith, repentance, vicarious baptism, and the gift of the Holy Ghost by the laying on of hands (v. 33).

▷ Spirits receiving this message are required to exercise faith and repentance just like persons living on this earth (v. 34).

This revelation confirms that in spirit prison there is a lack of knowledge about God, Christ, and the plan of salvation, just as there is in mortality. In other words, when people who are unfamiliar with the saving truths of the gospel die, they do not suddenly know the truth of all things. They are received into a place populated by people just like them, believing the same things they believed on earth and possessed of the same virtues and weaknesses they had as mortals. The only thing they know more than they knew here is that there is life after death. Other than that, they remain in the same spiritual darkness they experienced here. Only their acceptance of the missionaries and their message can change their condition and permit them to enter into the paradise enjoyed by the righteous. In this way, they can be judged like men in the flesh even though they are now living in the spirit (v. 34).

D&C 138:57–59 • When righteous persons pass away, they do missionary work among the billions of souls who need to hear the gospel in the spirit world. While the righteous do indeed rest from all sorrow, pain, sickness, and disability, they do not sit idly on clouds playing harps, as some suppose. So what do they do with their time there?

President Smith said in this revelation (D&C 138): "I beheld that the faithful elders of this dispensation, when they depart from mortal life, continue their labors in the preaching of the gospel of repentance and redemption, through the sacrifice of the Only Begotten Son of God, among those who are in darkness and under the bondage of sin in the great world of the spirits of the dead" (v. 57). They can be redeemed through repentance and obedience to the ordinances of gospel, including those of the temple (v. 58). As part of this process of repentance, they will pay "the penalty of their transgressions," be "washed clean" (through vicarious baptism), and "shall receive a reward according to their works, for they are heirs of salvation" (v. 59).

The Resurrection
(ALMA 40)

THE RESURRECTION IS LITERAL

Alma 40:21 • Alma speaks of "the time which is appointed of God that the dead shall come forth, and be reunited, both soul and body, and be brought to stand before God, and be judged according to their works" (v. 21). This is no "spiritual resurrection" as many churches and pastors teach, but a real and literal reuniting of the body and the spirit. "The soul shall be restored to the body, and the body to the soul" said Alma to his son (v. 23).

Bruce R. McConkie said, "The resurrection is the creation of an immortal soul; it consists in the uniting or reuniting of body and spirit in immortality. . . . Resurrected beings have bodies of flesh and bones, tangible, corporeal bodies, bodies that occupy space, digest food, and have power, outwardly, to appear as mortal bodies do (Luke 24)."[20]

Job testified of the literal nature of the resurrection when he said, "And though after my skin [meaning "after my death"] worms destroy this body, yet in my flesh shall I see God: Whom I shall see for myself, and mine eyes shall behold . . . though my reins [internal organs] be consumed within me" (Job 19:26–27).

Ezekiel also testified concerning a vision he received of the resurrection: "As I prophesied, there was a noise, and behold a shaking, and the bones came together, bone to his bone . . . [and] the sinews and the flesh came up upon them, and the skin covered them above: but there was no breath in them. Then said [the Lord] unto me, Prophesy . . . and breathe upon these slain, that they may live. So I prophesied as he commanded me, and the breath came into them, and they lived, and stood up upon their feet, an exceeding great army" (Ezekiel 37:7–10).

The Prophet Joseph Smith received a vision similar to Ezekiel's:

Would you think it strange that I relate what I have seen in vision in relation [to] this interesting theme. Those who have died in Jesus Christ, may expect to enter into all that fruition of Joy when they come forth, which they have pursued here. So plain was the vision I actually saw men before they had ascended from the tomb as though they were getting up slowly. They take each other by the hand [and they say] my father and my son, my Mother and my daughter, my brother and my sister. . . . By the vision of the Almighty I have seen it. . . . The expectation of seeing my friends in the morning of the resurrection cheers my soul and makes me bear up against the evils of life. It is like their taking a long journey, and on their return we meet them with increased joy.

God has revealed His Son from the heavens and the doctrine of the resurrection also; and we have a knowledge that those we bury here God will bring up again, clothed upon and quickened by the Spirit of the great God; and what mattereth it whether we lay them down, or we lay down with them, when we can keep them no longer? Let these truths sink down in our hearts, that we may even here begin to enjoy that which shall be in full hereafter.[21]

THE RESURRECTION IS UNIVERSAL

Alma 40:1–2, 5 • There is "a time appointed that all shall come forth from the dead" (v. 4). Corianton was worried about the resurrection (v. 1), I suppose because of his own precarious status before the Lord and because nothing of the kind had ever happened in the history of the world. Alma reassured him that there will be a resurrection and that it will be universal—"a time appointed that all shall rise from the dead" (v. 5). This means that every person who has ever lived on this earth will be resurrected (see also Alma 11:42–44).

Bruce R. McConkie said, "Nothing is more absolutely universal than the resurrection. Every living being will be resurrected. 'As in Adam all die, even so in Christ shall all be made alive' (1 Cor. 15:22). Those who live and die before the millennial era, all in their proper order, will have their bodies and spirits reunited in resurrected immortality. The righteous who live after the Second Coming shall be changed from mortality to immortality in the twinkling of an eye, their bodies and spirits being united inseparably."[22]

THE RESURRECTION IS PERFECT

Alma 40:23 • All things shall be "restored to their proper and perfect frame." When the soul and body are reunited, "every limb and joint shall be restored to its body; yea, even a hair of the head shall not be lost; but all things shall be restored to their proper and perfect frame" (v. 23). This means that the precise "frame" for each of us (our genetic code) will be duplicated in our resurrected bodies. We will look like ourselves—like we do in mortality—though in a perfected state, without deformity or loss of any kind.

The Prophet Joseph Smith said, "All men will come from the grave as they lie down, whether old or young; there will not be added unto their stature one cubit, neither taken from it; all will be raised by the power of God, having spirit in the bodies, and not blood."[23]

Joseph F. Smith said,

Deformity will be removed; defects will be eliminated, and men and women shall attain to the perfection of their spirits, to the perfection that God designed in the beginning. . . . The physical defects, some of which may have resulted before birth, are defects which are due to some physical and mortal condition and not an inheritance from the spirit world. . . . The body will come forth as it is laid to rest. . . . As it is laid down, so will it arise, and changes to perfection will come by the law of restitution. But the spirit will continue to expand and develop (*Joseph F. Smith, Gospel Doctrine, 5th ed. (Salt Lake City: Deseret Book, 1939),*, 23–24, 447–448, 623–624).

You will come forth from your graves, these same mortal bodies as they are now, bearing the marks just as much as Christ's body bore the marks that were upon him. They will come forth from their graves, but they will be immediately immortalized, restored to their perfect frame, limb and joint. And the poor, unfortunate creature who has lost a leg or an arm or a finger will have it restored to its proper frame, every joint to its place, and every part to its part, and it will be made perfect (Alma 40:23).[24]

Joseph Fielding Smith said, "Death is a purifying process as far as the body is concerned. We have reason to believe that the appearance of old age will disappear and the body will be restored with the full vigor of manhood and womanhood."[25]

He also said,

A little sound thinking will reveal to us that it would be inconsistent for our bodies to be raised with all kinds of imperfections. Some men have been burned at the stake for the sake of truth. Some have been beheaded, and others have had their bodies torn asunder; for example, John the Baptist was beheaded and received his resurrection at the time of the resurrection of our Redeemer. It is impossible for us to think of him coming forth from the dead holding his head in his hands; our reason says he was physically complete in the resurrection. He appeared to the Prophet Joseph Smith and Oliver Cowdery with a perfect resurrected body.

When we come forth from the dead our spirits and bodies will be reunited inseparably, never again to be divided, and they will then be assigned to the kingdom to which they belong. All deformities and imperfections will be removed, and the body will conform to the likeness of the spirit, for the Lord revealed, "that which is spiritual being in the likeness of that which is temporal; and that which is temporal in the likeness of that which is spiritual; the spirit of man in the likeness of his person, as also the spirit of the beast, and every other creature which God has created" (D&C 77:2). . . . A man who has lost a leg in childhood will have his leg restored. . . . Deformities and the like will be corrected, if not immediately at the time of the uniting of the spirit and body, so soon thereafter [almost instantly] that it will make no difference.[26]

Melvin J. Ballard said, "He will return this house [our body] to us, not as it was, old and decrepit, but strong, and vigorous and beautiful, for I believe with the prophets, that in the resurrection from the dead whether it shall take place immediately at the resurrection or thereafter when the restitution of all things comes, there will be no maimed or crippled bodies (Alma 40:23). When you see men and women in the resurrection, we shall see them in the very bloom of their glorious manhood and womanhood, and he has promised all who would keep his commandments and obey the gospel of the Lord Jesus Christ, the restoration of their houses, glorified, immortalized, celestialized, fitted to dwell in the presence of God."[27]

Children will be resurrected as children, not as adults. Joseph F. Smith said, "The body will come forth as it is laid to rest, for there is no growth or development in the grave. . . . [But] the body, after the resurrection, will develop to the full stature of man."[28]

"Joseph Smith taught the doctrine that the infant child that was laid away in death would come up in the resurrection as a child; and, pointing to the mother of a lifeless child, he said to her: 'You will have the joy, the pleasure, and satisfaction of nurturing this child, after its resurrection, until it reaches the full stature of its spirit.' There is restitution, there is growth, there is development, after the resurrection from death. I love this truth. It speaks volumes of happiness, of joy and gratitude to my soul. Thank the Lord he has revealed these principles to us."[29]

Joseph Fielding Smith said, "Children will arise as children, for there is no growth in the grave. Children will continue to grow until they reach the full stature of their spirits."[30]

Alvin R. Dyer said, "Children who die as to natural death in their infancy, or before the age of accountability . . . will have the exceptional joy of having their tabernacles of flesh and bone mature and grow to the full stature of their spirit bodies under more favorable conditions of existence during the Millennium."[31]

THE SEQUENCE OF THE RESURRECTION

Alma 40:3–4, 19–21 • Alma is uncertain of the sequence of the resurrection. Alma had "inquired diligently of God . . . concerning the resurrection" (v. 3) and had been reassured that "all shall come forth from the dead" (v. 4). But Alma said that the precise time when this would happen "no one knows; but God" (v. 4). He taught that the spirits of all men stay in the spirit world until the resurrection, when they will be "reunited, both soul and body, and be brought to stand before God, and be judged according to their works" (v. 21).

Alma was uncertain about whether "all [would] be reunited at once, the wicked as well as the righteous" (v. 19). He taught that the resurrection of those who lived and died before the resurrection of Christ would occur "before the resurrection of those who die after the resurrection of Christ" (v. 19), but he was uncertain about whether it would occur at the same time as the resurrection of Christ or at some later time. Note the contrast between Alma's uncertainty about the sequence of the resurrection—how many resurrections there will be, and in what order—and the clarity with which he taught concerning the spirit world, which information had been made known to him by an angel (Alma 40:11–14, 21). He was careful to differentiate between revealed doctrine and his personal opinions.

Alma gave his opinion that the righteous who lived before Christ's day would be resurrected "at the resurrection of Christ, and his ascension into heaven" (v. 20), but whether this was correct or not, Alma said, "I do not say" (v. 21). As we know today, he was correct: "The graves were opened; and many bodies of the Saints which slept arose, and came out of the graves after his resurrection, and went into the holy city, and appeared unto many" (Matthew 27:52–53).

Bruce R. McConkie said, "To those who lived before the resurrection of Christ, the day of his coming forth from the dead was known as the first resurrection. Abinadi and Alma, for instance, so considered it (Mosiah 15:21–25; Alma 40). To those who have lived since that day, the first resurrection is yet future and will take place at the time of the Second Coming (D&C 88:96–102). We have no knowledge that the resurrection is going on now or that any persons have been resurrected since the day in which Christ came forth excepting Peter, James, and Moroni, all of whom had special labors to perform in this day which necessitated tangible resurrected bodies."[32]

D&C 76:51–86 • The sequence and circumstances of the resurrection.

Those who inherit the celestial kingdom are resurrected first (vv. 51–70).
   ▷ They accepted Jesus Christ and also the gospel in this life (v. 52).
   ▷ They are faithful saints "made perfect" through the Atonement of Christ (v. 69).
   ▷ They are those who overcome all things through faith (vv. 53, 60).
   ▷ They are those who are "sealed" (verified as worthy) by the Holy Spirit (v. 53).
   ▷ They are anointed priests and kings (receive temple ordinances) (vv. 56–57).

- ▷ Their names are written in heaven (in the Lamb's book of life) (v. 68).
- ▷ They will rise in the first resurrection at the beginning of the Millennium (vv. 64–65).
- ▷ They will descend with Christ when he comes again to reign on the earth (v. 63).
- ▷ They will be resurrected with celestial bodies, whose glory is compared to the brightness of the sun (v. 70).
- ▷ They will receive a fulness of God's glory (v. 56).
- ▷ They will inherit all things from the Father (vv. 55, 59).
- ▷ As sons of God, they will themselves become gods (v. 58).
- ▷ They will dwell in the presence of God and Christ forever in "the heavenly place, the holiest of all" (vv. 62, 66–67).

Those who inherit the terrestrial kingdom are resurrected second (vv. 71–79).
- ▷ They accepted Christ but rejected the Church (v. 75).
- ▷ They rejected the gospel in mortality but accepted it in the spirit world (v. 74).
- ▷ They are "honorable men" who were deceived by philosophies of the world (v. 75).
- ▷ They are members of the Church who "are not valiant" in their testimonies (v. 79).
- ▷ They are those who "died without law" (heathen and pagan people who do not hear the gospel in this life, and who would not accept it if they did because they love their unclean practices) (v. 72).
- ▷ They dwell in spirit prison until and unless they accept the gospel (D&C 138:31, 34).
- ▷ They will be resurrected after all celestial beings have risen, during the Millennium.
- ▷ They will be resurrected with terrestrial bodies, whose glory differs from celestial bodies "as the moon differs from the sun" (vv. 71, 78).
- ▷ For the rest of eternity, they will be visited from time to time by the Son but will never again see the Father (v. 77).

Those who inherit the telestial kingdom are resurrected last (vv. 81–86).
- ▷ They rejected both Christ and the gospel of Christ (the Church) (v. 82).
- ▷ They did not deny Holy Spirit (they are not sons of Perdition) (v. 83).
- ▷ They are thrust down to hell (spirit prison) until the end of the Millennium (v. 84).
- ▷ The are resurrected at the end of the Millennium (v. 85; D&C 88:100–101).
- ▷ They will be resurrected with telestial bodies, whose glory differs from terrestrial bodies "as the glory of the stars differs from that of the glory of the moon" (v. 81).
- ▷ For the rest of eternity, they will be visited by angels from the terrestrial world and the Holy Spirit, but will never again see the Father or the Son (v. 86).

The Doctrine of Restoration
(ALMA 40–41)

Alma 41:1–2 • Alma refers to resurrection as a "restoration." One reason for calling it a *restoration* is because "the soul shall be restored to the body, and the body to the soul; yea, and every limb and joint shall be restored to its body" (Alma 40:23). Alma went on to speak of the perfection of this restoration: "yea, even a hair of the head shall not be lost; but all things shall be restored to their proper and perfect frame" (Alma 40:23).

A second reason for calling the resurrection a "restoration" is because "all things [will] be restored to their proper order" (Alma 41:2). Each individual spirit will "be restored to its body, and . . . every part of the body [will] be restored to itself" (Alma 41:2). I will not receive your body nor will you receive mine. Each of us will inherit an eternal and perfected version of the body we have possessed in mortality. There is no suggestion anywhere in scripture that this new body must be made from the same elements that the original was, but our resurrected bodies will be carbon copies of the original, according to the "perfect frame" of our personal and unique genetic codes. We will not all look alike in the eternities.

Bruce R. McConkie said, "As seen from these scriptures, the resurrection is a restoration, both a restoration of body and spirit and a restoration to the individual of the same mental and spiritual acquirements and attitudes he had in this life."[33]

Alma 41:3–6 • Alma explains the doctrine of restoration. Alma called it "requisite with the justice of God" that all men "should be judged according to their works" (v. 3). If some were judged and punished and others ignored or let off lightly, then it would be unfair and inequitable and God could not be said to be "just." This is why God "cannot look upon sin with the least degree of allowance" (Alma 45:16; D&C 1:31) and why all sins must and will be punished.

The good news in this process is that everyone will be judged not only on whether their "works were good in this life" but also on whether or not "the desires of their hearts were good" (v. 3). I find great comfort in this doctrine, since I know that in my heart I truly desire to do and to be good, even though my performance doesn't always show it, and I am in constant need of repentance. God knows our hearts, and we will be judged with the desires of our hearts in mind. If our works and our desires are found to be good, we will "be restored unto that which is good" in the resurrection (v. 3). On the other hand, "if their works are evil they shall be restored unto them for evil" (v. 4). For those who sin and repent of those sins, "If he hath repented of his sins, and desired righteousness until the end of his days, even so he shall be rewarded unto righteousness" (v. 6). All of this is according to the doctrine or principle of restoration that Alma taught.

Alma 41:4–7 • Men "are their own judges." Alma went on to explain how the judgment will occur. Contrary to popular belief, we will not need to stand before God to be judged by Him. The judgment will have already occurred at the moment of resurrection by virtue of the kind of being we are at that time. "Therefore, all things shall be restored to their proper order, every thing to its natural frame . . . raised to endless happiness to inherit the kingdom of God, or to endless misery to inherit the kingdom of the devil. . . . The one raised to happiness according to his desires of happiness, or good according to his desires of good; and the other to evil according to his desires of evil" (vv. 4–5). In other words, at the time of resurrection we will *be* whatever we truly *desired to be*, and God will not need to decree our fate through some formal process—we will rise in the resurrection *as we are*. And that will be determined by *ourselves*, not by God or any other person or being. As we've been taught, "They are their own judges, whether to do good or do evil" (v. 7). Could anything be more just and fair? I think not. In the end, we will inherit whatever we have made of ourselves—period.

True enough, we will stand before God eventually, but that will only be to confirm that what we have inherited as our eternal reward is a "just" result of what we have made of ourselves. This is the moment when "every knee shall bow and every tongue confess" that Jesus is the Christ and that our judgment has been just (Romans 14:11; Philippians 2:11; Mosiah 16:1; Mosiah 27:31; D&C 76:110–11; 88:104).

Alma 41:10–13 • Wickedness can never produce happiness. With the doctrine of restoration in mind, Alma warned his son, "Do not suppose, because it has been spoken concerning restoration, that ye shall be restored from sin to happiness. Behold, I say unto you, wickedness never was happiness" (v. 10). This shows us that the doctrine of restoration is closely associated with the law of the harvest. We don't plant corn and get beans. And we don't sow wickedness and then expect happiness.

We are all prone to weakness, being "in a state of nature, . . . in a carnal state, . . . in the gall of bitterness and in the bonds of iniquity" (v. 11). Because of our fallen natures, we are "without God in the world, and . . . have gone contrary to the nature of God," and therefore we are "in a state contrary to the nature of happiness" (v. 11). Alma posed the question of whether a person can be "restored" to a condition that is "in a state opposite to [his] nature" (v. 12). And his answer was clear: "O, my son, this is not the case; but the meaning of the word restoration is to bring back again evil for evil, or carnal for carnal, or devilish for devilish—good for that which is good; righteous for that which is righteous; just for that which is just; merciful for that which is merciful" (v. 13). We cannot escape the natural harvest of what we have made of ourselves in the end.

The Prophet Joseph Smith said, "Happiness is the object and design of our existence; and will be the end thereof, if we pursue the path that leads to it; and this path is virtue, uprightness, faithfulness, holiness, and keeping all the commandments of God. But we cannot keep all the commandments without first knowing them, and we cannot expect to know all, or more than we now know unless we comply with or keep those we have already received."[34]

The Prophet further taught, "In obedience there is joy and peace unspotted, unalloyed; and as God has designed our happiness. . . . He never will institute an ordinance or give a commandment to His people that is not calculated in its nature to promote that happiness which He has designed, and which will not end in the greatest amount of good and glory to those who become the recipients of his law and ordinances."[35]

Alma 41:14–15 • Whatever we "send out" to others will return to us again at the day of resurrection. Alma advised his son, "See that you are merciful unto your brethren; deal justly, judge righteously, and do good continually" because if you do, "ye shall have mercy restored unto you again; ye shall have justice restored unto you again; ye shall have a righteous judgment restored unto you again; and ye shall have good rewarded unto you again" (v. 14). Teaching this same doctrine, the Lord said, "With what measure ye mete, it shall be measured to you again" (Matthew 7:2; 3 Nephi 14:2). In other words, if I judge others with a "narrow yardstick" that allows for little tolerance and forgiveness, then that same yardstick will be used to measure my own performance. On the other hand, if I am tolerant and willing to forgive weakness in others then I will likewise be judged that way myself. "For that which ye do send out shall return unto you again, and be restored; therefore, the word restoration more fully condemneth the sinner, and justifieth him not at all" (Alma 41:15).

The Law of Justice
(ALMA 42)

Alma 42:1 • Corianton feels that punishment is "unfair." He was troubled by his father's teachings that "the sinner should be consigned to a state of misery." He thought it unfair (v. 1).

This is a common attitude in our own day, that negative consequences or punishments are "mean" or "cruel" and that the natural consequences of our behavior are not necessary. "I'm sorry" should be enough.

This reminds me of an event early on in my own family's history. My oldest son, when he was very young, did his best imitation of Picasso on our living room wall with his crayons. We wanted to teach him that this was not appropriate, but rather than yelling at him or spanking him, we introduced him to the law of the harvest—that there are consequences for our choices. I provided him (a little six-year-old) with a bucket of soapy water and a soft cloth and told him, "Clean it off the wall, and don't stop until it's all gone." A brief protest to his mother did not spring him from his fate, and he began scrubbing.

A half-hour later he was still at it, and one of our neighbors stopped by our house. When she saw our little boy scrubbing the wall and learned the reason for it, she said with some distress, "Oh, how mean! He's just a little boy! He didn't know any better." I smiled and escorted her out of earshot of my son for a moment. "How do you suppose he'll learn to 'know any better'?" I asked. "I'm teaching him one of the most important lessons of life—that there are consequences for our choices, and that if we make mistakes we have to fix them. I guarantee you that after that wall's clean, he will never draw on it again." And he didn't, because he knew the consequences and had learned his lesson.

Consequences are not "unfair"; they are essential. It was Satan who wanted to spare us of any consequences, and one-third of our Father's children thought that was an excellent idea. But our loving Father knew that there would be no growth without consequences. He allowed us to *learn by our own experience* to distinguish good from evil. Such an approach will inevitably lead to mistakes on our part, but there is simply no other way to learn and to grow. So he provided us with the opportunity to make mistakes, learn, repent, and then be forgiven for those mistakes—all the while not forfeiting the eternal lessons we learn from the consequences we have suffered.

Alma 42:6–7, 10 • Our agency makes us "subjects" who can control their destiny through the choices we make. Alma explained that we will all die, and therefore if there were no way to repent we would be "cut off from the face of the earth . . . and [become] lost forever . . . [a] fallen man" (v. 6). Satan knew this, and that is why he worked so hard to facilitate the Fall of Adam and Eve. If he could do that (which he did) and then get Jesus to fail (which he did not), then we would have been in Satan's power forever, without any hope of redemption from our fallen state.

By virtue of our fallen state, Alma taught that we are "cut off both temporally and spiritually from the presence of the Lord; and thus . . . [become] subjects to follow after [our] own will" (v. 7). There is great import in this statement. Alma was saying that it was necessary for us to be separated from our Father's presence in order to be able to freely exercise our agency and learn from our choices. Alma was also teaching that we are "subjects" and not "objects" as we exercise our will and make choices. We are not objects being "acted upon" by fate or by inescapable forces, but rather we are subjects fully in charge of our choices and our behavior (see also 2 Nephi 2:13, 26).

This is not a popular notion in our world today, where it seems that everything we do and say is blamed on an outside force of some kind. "Don't blame me; I'm not my fault" actually became the title of a book, and it captures the blame game that is so often played by those who refuse to acknowledge their own responsibility for their choices. Those who debate nature vs. nurture in explaining human behavior are both looking for an outside explanation on which to blame (or credit) the outcome. The truth, Alma said, is that we are not objects, but subjects, and we choose to be whatever we ultimately become.

True enough, our temporary separation from God renders us "carnal, sensual, and devilish, by nature," said Alma, but we have been given the power to overcome that nature by virtue of our choices, and "this probationary state became a state for [us] to prepare . . . a preparatory state" in which we can choose to rise above carnality (v. 10). If it were not so, then being punished for the mistakes we make would indeed be unfair and unjust. But the very existence of the law of justice tells us that we are in charge of our choices.

Alma 42:16–21 • Justice requires a penalty for sin; otherwise, there would be no incentive to keep the commandments. Or, as Alma put it, "repentance could not come unto men except there were a punishment" (v. 16). This principle is as "eternal as the life of the soul," as is the principle that happiness results from obedience (v. 16).

Alma explained this by asking a series of interrelated questions, which establish the following relationships between principles (v. 17):

> ▷ Without sin, there would be no need for repentance.
> ▷ Without law, there would be no sin.
> ▷ Without punishment, there would no purpose for law.

However, as Alma reminded his son, there is punishment for violations of eternal law, and those violations—called sin—produce a "remorse of conscience unto man," which then leads him to repent (v. 18). The key to the entire process is what Alma calls punishment but which we could simply call consequences. For example, if there were no law against murder and no severe punishment attached to it, nobody "would . . . be afraid he would die if he should murder" (v. 19). And "if there was no law given against sin men would not be afraid to sin" (v. 20). And in general, if there were no laws or commandments, neither justice nor mercy would be possible or even necessary because "they would have no claim" upon any of us (v. 21).

Phrased more simply, Alma's dissertation on justice tells us that in order to learn and grow and eventually obtain happiness, we must learn by experience to make righteous choices. Without laws (commandments), there would be no choices and therefore no agency. And without consequences for our choices, there would be no motivation to choose righteously. Commandments provide choices, choices enable agency, and consequences provide incentive to keep commandments and to repent. They are all interrelated.

Bruce R. McConkie said, "Since mortal man is on probation to prepare himself for eternity, and since he is endowed with the great gift of free agency, it follows that he must be held accountable for his disobedience. Otherwise this sphere of existence would not provide the test nor give the experience which would qualify him to return to the presence of God hereafter. . . . Justice and judgment are the penalty affixed for disobedience (D&C 82:4); none are exempt from the justice of God (D&C 107:84); and perfect justice will be administered to all men in the day of judgment. (2 Nephi 9:46)."[36]

Of course, consequences are not always in the form of punishment. There are also consequences for righteous choices. Hence obedience brings joy while disobedience brings sorrow and pain. Either way, consequences provide incentive to make good choices. This is explained in D&C 130:20–21, where the Prophet Joseph Smith explained that "there is a law, irrevocably decreed in heaven before the foundations of this world, upon which all blessings are predicated—and when we obtain any blessing from God, it is by obedience to that law upon which it is predicated." (see also Alma 42:22).

Alma 42:11–14, 22–23 • Without mercy, we would be banned from God's presence forever. Alma explained that the entire plan of redemption was designed to provide a way to satisfy the demands of justice and still make it possible for us to be forgiven of our mistakes. Since we all sin (Romans 3:23), without the Savior's Atonement, "there was no means to reclaim men from this fallen state, which man had brought upon himself because of his own disobedience" (v. 12) and we would have all been eternally damned—shut off from the presence of God with no hope of returning to him.

Without some means of "repentance of men in this probationary state . . . mercy could not take effect except it should destroy the work of justice" (v. 13). And mercy cannot rob justice. Every sin must be punished and justice must prevail. Otherwise, God would not be a just God, and he would "cease to be God" (v. 13). And since "all mankind were fallen, and they were in the grasp of justice . . . the justice of God [would consign] them forever to be cut off from his presence" (v. 14). There would be no hope for any of us. But God will not cease to be God, and he has provided a way for justice to be served, and mercy also.

Alma explained, "There is a law given, and a punishment affixed, and a repentance granted" (which provides mercy to us). Without the opportunity for repentance, "justice claimeth the creature and executeth the law, and the law inflicteth the punishment" (which provides justice). "If not so, the works of justice would be destroyed, and God would cease to be God" (v. 22). We simply could not worship such an unjust God.

"But God ceaseth not to be God," said Alma, "and mercy claimeth the penitent . . . because of the atonement" (v. 23). So God provided a way for both justice and mercy to be served.

Alma 42:13, 22, 25 • God cannot and will not cease to be God. Robert L. Millet said,

> In seeking to dramatize the absolute necessity for God's justice to be meted out where appropriate, Alma spoke to Corianton of a most unusual hypothetical situation. . . . "Now the work of justice could not be destroyed; if so, God would cease to be God." Alma explained further that "there is a law given, and a punishment affixed, and a repentance granted; which repentance, mercy claimeth; otherwise, justice claimeth the creature and executeth the law, and the law inflicteth the punishment; if not so, the works of justice would be destroyed, and God would cease to be God" (Alma 42:13, 22, 25).
>
> Some have taken these verses to mean that it is indeed possible for God to cease to be God; that if he should, by some bizarre means, fail to function in perfectness, he would be unseated and removed from his place of preeminence; that the forces in the universe would demand his abdication from the heavenly throne. Such ideas are to some quite stimulating. They are, nonetheless, erroneous and misleading. . . .
>
> God cannot and will not cease to be God. His title, his status, and his exalted position are forever fixed and immutable. Nor need the Saints of God spend a particle of a second worrying and fretting about the Almighty falling from grace. Joseph Smith explained in the Lectures on Faith (lecture 4) that for the Saints to do so is to err in doctrine as to the true nature of God and thus fall short of that dynamic faith which leads to life and salvation. Alma's hypothetical case is just that—purely hypothetical. He is arguing toward the impossible, the absurd, to emphasize the logical certainty of the principle that mercy cannot rob justice. It is as if Alma had said, "It is as ridiculous to suppose that mercy can rob justice and that men and women can break the laws of God with impunity, as it is to suppose that God can cease to be God." In fact, Alma concludes, "God ceaseth not to be God, and mercy claimeth the penitent, and mercy cometh because of the atonement" (Alma 42:23).[37]

The Law of Mercy
(ALMA 42)

Alma 42:15 • God has provided a way for both mercy and justice to be served. God himself has provided a way out of this situation through the law of mercy. Justice must be served, and that means that a penalty must be paid of all sins. Therefore, "the plan of mercy could not be brought about except an atonement should be made." In order for us to obtain mercy and be forgiven, somebody else must satisfy the demands of justice, "therefore God himself atoneth for the sins of the world, to bring about the plan of mercy, to appease the demands of justice, that God might be a perfect, just God, and a merciful God also."

Mosiah 15:7–9 • The Atonement of Jesus Christ "appeased the demands of justice." When Christ was "led, crucified, and slain, the flesh becoming subject even unto death" (v. 7), he "breaketh the bands of death, having gained the victory over death; giving the Son power to make intercession for the children of men" (v. 8), and "satisfied the demands of justice" (v. 9).

D&C 19:16–19 • The severity of Christ's suffering teaches us much about the price that must be paid for sins in order for justice to be satisfied. Sin is not a "small thing" when considered in this light, though it may sometimes seem that way to us because of our ability to avoid such suffering through the Atonement of Christ: "For behold, I, God, have suffered these things for all, that they might not suffer if they would repent; but if they would not repent they must suffer even as I; which suffering caused myself, even God, the greatest of all, to tremble because of pain, and to bleed at every pore, and to suffer both body and spirit—and would that I might not drink the bitter cup, and shrink" (vv. 16–19).

D&C 45:3–5 • Christ has intervened on our behalf to make our exaltation possible. I am always touched by this powerful scripture in the Doctrine and Covenants where the Savior tells us what he will say on our behalf at the day of judgment. I imagine myself standing next to my blessed Brother as he invokes his own suffering to appease the law of justice and make it possible for me to inherit the celestial blessings I desire. The compassion in his words touches me every time I read it: "Listen to him who is the advocate with the Father, who is pleading your cause before him— Saying: Father, behold the sufferings and death of him who did no sin, in whom thou wast well pleased; behold the blood of thy Son which was shed, the blood of him whom thou gavest that thyself might be glorified; Wherefore, Father, spare these my brethren that believe on my name, that they may come unto me and have everlasting life" (vv. 3–5).

John Taylor said,

> The Savior thus becomes master of the situation—the debt is paid, the redemption made, the covenant fulfilled, justice satisfied, the will of God done, and all power is now given into the hands of the Son of God—the power of the resurrection, the power of the redemption, the power of salvation, the power to enact laws for the carrying out and accomplishment of this design. Hence life and immortality are brought to light, the Gospel is introduced, and He becomes the author of eternal life and exaltation, He is the Redeemer, the Resurrector, the Savior of man and the world . . . Is justice dishonored? No; it is satisfied, the debt is paid. Is righteousness departed from? No; this is a righteous act. All requirements are met. Is judgment violated? No; its demands are fulfilled.[38]

Alma 42:2–10 • God has provided redemption from both spiritual and physical death.

Spiritual death—separation from the presence of God—occurred when Adam and Eve were expelled from the garden of Eden. For their own protection, they were prevented by "cherubim, and a flaming sword which turned every way" from partaking of the fruit of the tree of life, which would have made them immortal and thus ended immediately their mortal condition. This would have left them "no space for repentance," refuting the promises of God, and frustrating the entire plan of salvation (vv. 2–3, 5). "And thus we see, that there was a time granted unto man to repent, yea, a probationary time, a time to repent and serve God" (v. 4). That is the purpose of our time on earth.

Physical death was a natural consequence of Adam and Eve's partaking of the forbidden fruit, and they would eventually "be cut off from the face of the earth" (v. 6), as will all of us. Should this occur before there was sufficient time and opportunity to repent, they (and we) would have become "lost forever . . . [a] fallen man" (v. 6). But God determined to grant unto them (and us) the power to make choices and sufficient time to repent from whatever bad choices we might make (v. 7). Physical death cannot be avoided without destroying the "great plan of happiness" (v. 8). It is part of God's plan, and when coupled with a resurrection, provides an eternal and glorified body for us to inhabit throughout eternity.

Our spirits never die like our physical bodies do (v. 8), but they experience a form of death when they are separated from the presence of the Lord (v. 9). Therefore, God has provided a means of redemption for both our bodies (resurrection) and our spirits (the Atonement of Jesus Christ) (v. 9). And "this probationary state became a [time] for them to prepare; it became a preparatory state" (v. 10).

Alma 42:23–26 • Alma teaches that "mercy cometh because of the atonement" and the resurrection of the dead. The Father's plan "bringeth to pass the resurrection of the dead" to redeem us from physical death, and "the resurrection of the dead bringeth back men into the presence of God" redeeming us from spiritual death (v. 23). In this way, "justice exerciseth all his demands, and also mercy claimeth all which is her own" (v. 24). I find it interesting that justice is represented as a male ("he") and mercy as a female ("she") in this passage, don't you?

In summary, Alma asked, "What, do ye suppose that mercy can rob justice? I say unto you, Nay; not one whit. If so, God would cease to be God" (v. 25). Justice would be robbed if a person were forgiven for sins he had not repented, so only "the truly penitent are saved" (v.24). And thus "God bringeth about his great and eternal purposes, which were prepared from the foundation of the world. And thus cometh about the salvation and the redemption of men, and also their destruction and misery" (v. 26).

Alma 42:27–31 • We need godly sorrow for our sins. Alma reminded his son that "whosoever will come may come and partake of the waters of life freely; and whosoever will not come the same is not compelled to come," but either way there will be consequences—"in the last day it shall be restored unto him according to his deeds" (vv. 27–28). Alma admonished his son not to be troubled by the law of justice and whether it was "fair" or not, but to "only let your sins trouble you, with that trouble which shall bring you down unto repentance" (v. 29).

Alma said to his son, "Do not endeavor to excuse yourself in the least point because of your sins, by denying the justice of God; but do you let the justice of God, and his mercy, and his long-suffering have full sway in your heart; and let it bring you down to the dust in humility" (v. 30; see also 2 Corinthians 7:8–10). In other words, stop making excuses and questioning the wisdom and fairness of God; instead humble yourself and repent.

Spencer W. Kimball explained,

> When we become fully aware of the seriousness of the wrong we have done, we decide with all our heart to do whatever is necessary to rid ourselves of the effects of the sin. We are totally sorry. We are willing to pay penalties, to suffer even to excommunication if necessary. Paul wrote, "For Godly sorrow worketh repentance to salvation not to be repented of: but the sorrow of the world worketh death (2 Corinthians 7:10)." If one is sorry only because someone found out about his sin, his repentance is not complete. Godly sorrow causes one to want to repent even though he has not been caught by others and makes him determined to do right no matter what happens. This kind of sorrow brings righteousness and will work toward forgiveness.[39]

Spencer W. Kimball also said,

> Often people indicate that they have repented when all they have done is to express regret for a wrong act. But true repentance is marked by that godly sorrow that changes, transforms, and saves. To be sorry is not enough. Perhaps the felon in the penitentiary, coming to realize the high price he must pay for his folly, may wish he had not committed the crime. That is not repentance. The vicious man who is serving a stiff sentence for rape may be very sorry he did the deed, but he is not repentant if his heavy sentence is the only reason for his sorrow. That is the sorrow of the world.
>
> The truly repentant man is sorry before he is apprehended. He is sorry even if his secret is never known. . . . Repentance of the godly type means that one comes to recognize the sin and voluntarily and without pressure from outside sources begins his transformation.[40]

Alma closed his epistle to Corianton with a call for his son to return to his ministry: "O my son, ye are called of God to preach the word unto this people. And now, my son, go thy way, declare the word with truth and soberness, that thou mayest bring souls unto repentance, that the great plan of mercy may have claim upon them. And may God grant unto you even according to my words. Amen" (v. 31).

It is gratifying to find that Corianton evidently responded to his father's teachings and call for him to repent, because we do indeed find him serving faithfully as a missionary later on (Alma 49:30).

Notes
1. Neal A. Maxwell, "Thanks Be to God," *Ensign*, July 1982, 51.
2. Brigham Young, in *Journal of Discourses* (London: Latter-day Saints' Book Depot, 1854), 3:367–69.
3. George Q. Cannon, *Gospel Truth: Discourses and Writings of President George Q. Cannon*, Jerreld L. Newquist, ed. (Salt Lake City: Deseret Book, 1987]), 57–58.
4. Joseph Fielding Smith, *Answers to Gospel Questions*, Joseph Fielding Smith Jr., comp. (Salt Lake City: Deseret Book, 1957–1966), 2:84–86.
5. Heber C. Kimball, in *Journal of Discourses* (London: Latter-day Saints' Book Depot, 1854), 3:112–113.
6. Joseph Smith, *Teachings of the Prophet Joseph Smith*, Joseph Fielding Smith, sel. (Salt Lake City: Deseret Book, 1976), Joseph Fielding Smith, sel. (Salt Lake City: Deseret Book, 1976), 309.
7. Robert L. Millet, in Kent Jackson, ed., Kent P. Jackson, ed., *Studies in Scripture, Vol. 8: Alma 30 to Moroni* (Salt Lake City: Deseret Book, 1988), 69.
8. Bruce R. McConkie, *Mormon Doctrine*, 2nd ed. (Salt Lake City: Bookcraft, 1966), 402.
9. Joseph Fielding Smith, *Doctrines of Salvation*, Bruce R. McConkie, comp. (Salt Lake City: Deseret Book, 1954–56), 2:230.

10. Brigham Young, in *Journal of Discourses* (London: Latter-day Saints' Book Depot, 1854), 3:369–68.

11. Joesph Smith, *Teachings of the Prophet Joseph Smith*, Joseph Fielding Smith, sel. (Salt Lake City: Deseret Book, 1976), 326.

12. Ezra Taft Benson, *God, Family, Country: Our Three Great Loyalties* (Salt Lake City: Deseret Book, 1974), 22.

13. Parley P. Pratt, *Key to the Science of Theology/A Voice of Warning* (Salt Lake City: Deseret Book, 1965), 126–27.

14. Joseph F. Smith, *Gospel Doctrine*, 5th ed. (Salt Lake City: Deseret Book, 1939), 448.

15. Brigham Young, *Discourses of Brigham Young*, John A. Widtsoe, comp. (Salt Lake City: Deseret Book, 1954), 380–81.

16. Brigham Young, in *Journal of Discourses* (London: Latter-day Saints' Book Depot, 1854), 17:142.

17. Bruce R. McConkie, *Ensign*, Nov. 1976, 107.

18. Brigham Young, in *Journal of Discourses* (London: Latter-day Saints' Book Depot, 1854), 3:95.

19. Bruce R. McConkie, *Mormon Doctrine*, 2nd ed. (Salt Lake City: Bookcraft, 1966), 551–52.

20. Ibid., 637.

21. Joseph Smith, *History of The Church of Jesus Christ of Latter-day Saints*, B. H. Roberts, ed. (Salt Lake City: The Church of Jesus Christ of Latter-day Saints, 1932–1951), 5:361–62.

22. Bruce R. McConkie, *Mormon Doctrine*, 2nd ed. (Salt Lake City: Bookcraft, 1966), 638.

23. Joseph Smith, *Teachings of the Prophet Joseph Smith*, Joseph Fielding Smith, sel. (Salt Lake City: Deseret Book, 1976), 199–200.

24. Joseph F. Smith, quoted in Roy W. Doxey, comp., *Latter-day Prophets and the Doctrine and Covenants* (Salt Lake City: Deseret Book, 1978), 3:168.

25. Joseph Fielding Smith, *Answers to Gospel Questions*, Joseph Fielding Smith Jr., comp. (Salt Lake City: Deseret Book, 1957–1966), 4:187.

26. Joseph Fielding Smith, *Doctrines of Salvation*, Bruce R. McConkie, comp. (Salt Lake City: Deseret Book, 1954–56), 2:289, 293.

27. Bryant S. Hinckley, *Sermons and Missionary Services of Melvin J. Ballard* (Salt Lake City: Deseret Book, 1949), 186.

28. Joseph F. Smith, *Gospel Doctrine*, 5th ed. (Salt Lake City: Deseret Book, 1939), 23, 447–48.

29. *Ensign*, April 1977, 7.

30. Joseph Fielding Smith, *Answers to Gospel Questions*, Joseph Fielding Smith Jr., comp. (Salt Lake City: Deseret Book, 1957–1966), 4:189.

31. Alvin R. Dyer, *Who Am I?* (Salt Lake City: Deseret Book, 1966), 482–83.

32. Bruce R. McConkie, *Mormon Doctrine*, 2nd ed. (Salt Lake City: Bookcraft, 1966), 637–43.

33. Ibid., 641.

34. Joseph Smith, *Teachings of the Prophet Joseph Smith*, Joseph Fielding Smith, sel. (Salt Lake City: Deseret Book, 1976), 255–56.

35. Joseph Smith, *History of The Church of Jesus Christ of Latter-day Saints*, B. H. Roberts, ed. (Salt Lake City: The Church of Jesus Christ of Latter-day Saints, 1932–1951), 5:135.

36. Bruce R. McConkie, *Mormon Doctrine*, 2nd ed. (Salt Lake City: Bookcraft, 1966), 406–7.

37. Robert L. Millet, in Kent Jackson, ed., *Studies in Scripture, Vol. 8: Alma 30 to Moroni* (Salt Lake City: Deseret Book, 1988), 64–65.

38. John Taylor, *The Mediation and Atonement* (Salt Lake City: Deseret News, 1882), 171.

39. Spencer W. Kimball, *Repentance Brings Forgiveness* (Latter-day Tracts [Pamphlets], 1984), 8.

40. Spencer W. Kimball, *The Miracle of Forgiveness* (Salt Lake City: Bookcraft, 1969), 153.

"Firm in the Faith of Christ"
ALMA 43–52

Captain Moroni and the Causes of War

War in the Book of Mormon

Mormon and Moroni saw much war, and they saw thousands killed in battle. Of the 522 pages in the Book of Mormon, nearly one third (170 pages, 68 chapters) is devoted to recording the wars between the Lamanites and the Nephites. Beginning with Alma 35, with the exception of the next seven chapters (Alma 36–42), the Book of Mormon contains 44 consecutive chapters dealing with wars and their consequences. Thus began one of the longest periods of war in Nephite history.

I remember well my earliest experiences of reading these chapters in the Book of Mormon. *How negative and depressing!* I thought. *Why is there so much concerning war in a sacred book of scripture?* As I came to understand that this portion of the Book of Mormon was taken from the large plates of Nephi, which were primarily historical in nature, I could understand why they did not seem as uplifting as 1 and 2 Nephi, which were taken from the more spiritual small plates. Still, I wondered why Mormon included so much about military strategy, details about battles, and horrific bloodshed." I knew that Mormon had selected specific events for his book and ignored others. Why were these included?

As the years have passed and our world has become more and more saturated with war and terrorism, it has become more clear to me why these chapters are relevant to our day. These Nephites lived during times of horrific religious wars, and so do we. Their responses are instructive to us today. This portion of the Book of Mormon teaches us how to live righteously in times of war.

D&C 87:3–6 • The relevance to us of the Book of Mormon war chapters. In our day "war shall be poured out upon all nations . . . until the consumption decreed hath made a full end of all nations." Mormon knew we would live in a day of "wars and rumors of wars" (D&C 45:26) and desired to give us important information about how to live as Saints in an age of war.

In D&C 87—the "prophecy on war"—the Prophet Joseph Smith predicted the Civil War nearly thirty years before it came to pass, including when, where, and why it would occur (vv. 3–4). He also predicted difficulties later on, when the "remnants who are left of the land [the Lamanites] will marshal themselves, and shall become exceedingly angry, and shall vex the Gentiles with a sore vexation" (v. 5). We have not yet seen that day, though we have certainly seen a rise in tension and even anger with Lamanite peoples in recent years.

The prophecy on war concludes with these sobering words: "And thus, with the sword and by bloodshed the inhabitants of the earth shall mourn; and with famine, and plague, and earthquake, and the thunder of heaven, and the fierce and vivid lightning also, shall the inhabitants of the earth be made to feel the wrath, and indignation, and chastening hand of an Almighty God, until the consumption decreed hath made a full end of all nations" (v. 6).

Ezra Taft Benson said, "In the Book of Mormon we find a pattern for preparing for the Second Coming. A major portion of the book centers on the few decades just prior to Christ's coming to America. By careful study of that time period, we can determine why some were destroyed in the terrible judgments that preceded His coming and what brought others to stand at the temple in the land of Bountiful and thrust their hands into the wounds of His hands and feet. From the Book of Mormon we learn how disciples of Christ live in times of war."[1]

The Lord's Commandments Concerning War
(ALMA 43)

Alma 35:3–15 • Background to the Nephite wars. We may recall from lesson 28 that the Nephites feared that the Zoramite dissenters would join with the Lamanites, and Alma preached the word of God to them to keep this from happening (vv. 4–5). The Zoramites who believed in Alma's preaching were cast out by the unbelieving Zoramites, who feared the loss of their wealth and power if conversion were widespread (vv. 3–6). The people of Ammon, also known as the Anti-Nephi-Lehies, provided for the welfare of these cast-out Zoramites, which stirred up the apostate Zoramites to anger against them (vv. 9–10). The Zoramites, as had been feared, allied themselves with the Lamanites and made preparations for war (v. 11).

The people of Ammon "departed out of the land of Jershon," allowing the armies of the Nephites to occupy the area and contend with the armies of the Lamanites and Zoramites" (v. 13). As war broke out, the converted Zoramites took up arms "to defend themselves, and their wives, and children, and their lands" (v. 14). The people of Ammon, who could not engage in war because of their covenant never to do so again, gave to the Nephites "a large portion of their substance to support their armies," but other than that, "the Nephites were compelled, alone, to withstand against the Lamanites" (Alma 43:13).

Alma was "grieved for the iniquity of his people," without which they could have avoided "the wars, and the bloodsheds, and the contentions which were among them" (v. 15). He observed that in the midst of so much wickedness and violence "the hearts of the people began to wax hard," and "his heart was exceedingly sorrowful"(v. 15). Knowing that the only possibility for peace would come from sincere repentance, Alma sent his sons, including a repentant Corianton (Alma 49:30), among the Nephites to call them to repentance (Alma 43:1–2).

NEPHITE AND LAMANITE MOTIVATIONS

Alma 43:3–5, 8 • Zerahemnah leads the Lamanites into war against the Nephites. The apostate Zoramites and the Lamanites moved into the land of the Zoramites in preparation for an attack upon the Nephites (vv. 4–5), with Zerahemnah (an apostate Zoramite) as their commander. He had prepared the Lamanites for war by stirring up their anger toward the Nephites. His goals were not only to conquer the Nephites, but to gain greater power over the Lamanites as well (v. 8).

Alma 43:13, 6–7 • The Zoramites and Amalekites were formerly Nephites. By this time (74 BC) the distinction between a Lamanite and a Nephite was one of righteousness rather than race or bloodline. The Lamanites had become "a compound of Laman and Lemuel, and the sons of Ishmael, and all those who had dissented from the Nephites, who were Amalekites and Zoramites, and the descendants of the priests of Noah" (v. 13). Among these people, the apostate Nephites were much worse than those who had never known the truth (Alma 24:30). They had become enemies to righteousness and to God (Mosiah 2:36–37) and they were more hardened and ferocious than the Lamanites (Alma 47:36). Because they were "of a more wicked and murderous disposition than the Lamanites," Zerahemnah appointed chief captains over the Lamanites from among these bitter and apostate Amalekites and Zoramites (vv. 6–7).

The Prophet Joseph Smith said to a convert who boasted that if he ever left the Church he would leave it alone and not oppose it, "Before you joined this Church you stood on neutral ground. . . . There were two opposite masters inviting you to serve them. When you joined this Church you enlisted to serve God. When you did that you left the neutral ground, and you never can get back on to it. Should you forsake the Master you enlisted to serve it will be by the instigation of the evil one, and you will follow his dictation and be his servant."[2]

Alma 43:9–10, 23, 28, 30 • Nephite motivations for war were righteous. They engaged only in defensive warfare, never going on the offensive. In fact, in the entire Book of Mormon, the first record of the Nephites initiating a battle is in Mormon 4:1–4, after they themselves had become wicked. They went to war only to (1) defend their homes and families, (2) preserve their liberties, and (3) maintain their right to worship God, which they knew they would lose if they were defeated by the Lamanites (vv. 9–10).

Bruce R. McConkie said, "Self-defense is as justifiable where war is concerned as where one man seeks to take the life of another. . . . Righteous men are entitled, expected, and obligated to defend themselves; they must engage in battle when there is no other way to preserve their rights and freedoms and to protect their families, homes, land, and the truths of salvation which they have espoused."[3]

Moroni, the captain of the Nephite armies, sent spies to watch the movements of the Lamanite army but also asked the prophet Alma to enquire of the Lord "whither the armies of the Nephites should go to defend themselves against the Lamanites" (v. 23). He wanted Nephite strategies and tactics to be righteous, as well as their motivations (v. 30).

Alma 43:29, 43–44 • Lamanite motivations for war were unrighteous. "It was their intention to destroy their brethren, or to subject them and bring them into bondage that they might establish a kingdom unto themselves over all the land" (v. 29). They wanted to do this at least partly because of their intense hatred for righteous Nephites, inspired primarily by their apostate Nephite commanders, the Zoramites and Amalekites (v. 44). In their fierce anger and rage, they attacked and fought with unprecedented strength and courage. Mormon says that "never had the Lamanites been known to fight with such exceedingly great strength and courage, no, not even from the beginning" (v. 43). They "fought like dragons" and used such force that "they did smite in two many of their head-plates, and they did pierce many of their breastplates, and they did smite off many of their arms" (v. 44). Nevertheless, they were not fighting for a righteous cause, and as a result, more often than not, they ended up defeated.

Alma 43:45–47 • The Lord's commandments concerning war. The Lord reveals here his commandments concerning war and bloodshed. He commanded the Nephites to defend themselves, "Inasmuch as ye are not guilty of the first offense, neither the second" (v. 46). They were also commanded to defend their families "even unto bloodshed" (v. 47). Note that this suggests a defensive cause and not an offensive one. And for this purpose only, the Nephites fought in defense of themselves, their families, their lands, country, rights, and religion (v. 47).

THE CHURCH'S TEACHINGS CONCERNING WAR

We live in a time of war. War has been "poured out upon all nations," and bloodshed takes place somewhere on earth every single day, just as the Prophet Joseph Smith predicted (D&C 87:3). There have been two worldwide wars in the past century, and multiple regional conflicts and a war on terror that have all involved members of the Church. In all of these conflicts, brave men and women have given their lives to defend our freedoms, but they have also taken the lives of enemies. And whenever this occurs, the question arises, is this murder? Both the Book of Mormon, in Alma 43, and modern-day prophets, make it clear that such killing is justified in the eyes of the Lord and is not a violation of his commandments.

During World War II the First Presidency said,

> The members of the Church have always felt under obligation to come to the defense of their country when a call to arms was made. . . . We have felt honored that our brethren have died nobly for their country; the Church has been benefitted by their service and their sacrifice.
>
> Nevertheless, we have not forgotten that on Sinai, God commanded, "Thou shalt not kill"; nor that in this dispensation the Lord has repeatedly reiterated that command. . . . But all these commands, from Sinai down, run in very terms against individuals as members of society, as well as members of the Church, for one man must not kill another as Cain killed Abel; they also run against the Church as in the case of securing land in Zion, because Christ's Church should not make war, for the Lord is a Lord of peace. He has said to us in this dispensation: "Therefore, renounce war and proclaim peace. . . ." (D&C 98:16.)
>
> Thus the Church is and must be against war. The Church itself cannot wage war, unless and until the Lord shall issue new commands. It cannot regard war as a righteous means of settling international disputes; these should and could be settled—the nations agreeing—by peaceful negotiation and adjustment.[4]

David O. McKay said, "We love peace, but not peace at any price. There is a peace more destructive of the manhood of living man than war is destructive of the body. Chains are worse than bayonets."[5]

Charles W. Penrose, who was a member of the First Presidency, said, "It is not right for us to engage in the shedding of human blood, for vengeance or retaliation. But when the Lord commands or inspires his servants to counsel the sons and daughters of Israel to lend their aid in the work of righteous warfare, that is different. . . . We are to arise in our might and in our strength and go forth to victory; not with a desire to shed blood, not with the desire to destroy our fellow creatures, but in self defense and because we do want to maintain and hand down to our posterity those sacred principles of liberty that have been revealed from on high."[6]

David O. McKay said,

> There are . . . two conditions which may justify a truly Christian man to enter—mind you, I say enter, not begin—a war:
>
> (1) An attempt to dominate and to deprive another of his free agency, and,
>
> (2) Loyalty to his country. Possibly there is a third, [namely], Defense of a weak nation that is being unjustly crushed by a strong, ruthless one.
>
> Paramount among these reasons, of course, is the defense of man's freedom. . . .
>
> To deprive an intelligent human being of his free agency is to commit the crime of the ages. . . . So fundamental in man's eternal progress is his inherent right to choose, that the Lord would defend it even at the price of war. Without freedom of thought, freedom of choice, freedom of action within lawful bounds, man cannot progress. . . .
>
> The greatest responsibility of the state is to guard the lives, and to protect the property and rights of its citizens; and if the state is obligated to protect its citizens from lawlessness within its boundaries, it is equally obligated to protect them from lawless encroachments from without—whether the attacking criminals be individuals or nations.[7]

Captain Moroni's Uncommon Charity in War

Alma 43:17–22 • The military strategy and techniques used by Captain Moroni were wise, especially for such a young (just twenty-five years old) man (v. 17). He prepared his people with breastplates, arm-shields, thick clothing, and helmets (v. 19), and they went into battle "armed with swords, and with cimeters, and all manner of weapons of war" (v. 18). By contrast, the Lamanite armies "had only their swords and their cimeters, their bows and their arrows, their stones and their slings; and they were naked, save it were a skin which was girded about their loins" (v. 20). All, that is, except the Zoramites and the Amalekites, who were not so scantily dressed (v. 20). The Lamanite armies "were not armed with breastplates, nor shields—therefore, they were exceedingly afraid of the armies of the Nephites because of their armor, notwithstanding their number being so much greater than the Nephites" (v. 21). They did not engage the Nephites in battle at Jershon but went instead through the wilderness to the land of Manti, where the River Sidon originated, hoping to take possession of that area (v. 22).

Alma 43:27–35 • In actual battle, Moroni used decoy and encircling tactics to confuse and defeat the enemy. Dr. Hugh Nibley has commented extensively on the evidence of experienced war leadership in the strategies used by the Nephites—a subject that Joseph Smith knew absolutely nothing about.

Captain Moroni "caused that his army should be secreted in the valley which was near the bank of the river Sidon, which was on the west of the river Sidon in the wilderness" (v. 27). He also "placed spies round about, that he might know when the camp of the Lamanites should come" (v. 28). He "divided his army and brought a part over into the valley, and concealed them on the east, and on the south of the hill Riplah" (v. 31). The rest of the army "he concealed in the west valley, on the west of the river Sidon, and so down into the borders of the land Manti. And thus having placed his army according to his desire, he was prepared to meet them" (vv. 32–33).

When the Lamanite armies "came up on the north of the hill, where a part of the army of Moroni was concealed . . . [they] passed the hill Riplah, and came into the valley, and began to cross the river Sidon" (vv. 34–35). At that point, the Nephite army "which was concealed on the

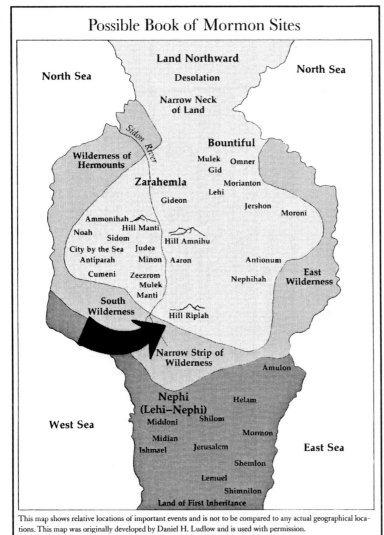

Possible Book of Mormon Sites

North Sea

Land Northward

Desolation

North Sea

Narrow Neck of Land

Sidon River

Wilderness of Hermounts

Bountiful

Mulek Omner
Gid

Zarahemla

Morianton

Lehi

Gideon

Jershon

Moroni

Ammonihah

Hill Manti

Noah

Sidom

Hill Amnihu

City by the Sea

Judea

Antiparah

Minon

Aaron

Antionum

Cumeni

Zeezrom

Nephihah

East Wilderness

Mulek

Manti

South Wilderness

Hill Riplah

Narrow Strip of Wilderness

Amulon

Nephi (Lehi–Nephi)

Helam

West Sea

Middoni

Shilom

Midian

Mormon

Ishmael

Jerusalem

East Sea

Shemlon

Lemuel

Shimnilon

Land of First Inheritance

This map shows relative locations of important events and is not to be compared to any actual geographical locations. This map was originally developed by Daniel H. Ludlow and is used with permission.

south of the hill, which was led by a man whose name was Lehi, . . . [came] forth and encircled the Lamanites about on the east in their rear" (v. 35).

Alma 43:53–54 • The Nephites surround the Lamanites and have a chance to destroy them, but Captain Moroni stops the bloodshed. When the Lamanites saw "the men of Lehi on the east of the river Sidon, and the armies of Moroni on the west of the river Sidon, that they were encircled about by the Nephites, they were struck with terror" (v. 53). There was no way of escape, and they would certainly have been destroyed had the Nephites chosen to fall upon them. But Captain Moroni, "when he saw their terror, commanded his men that they should stop shedding their blood" (v. 54). His wanted to subdue and disarm the Lamanites, not to destroy them, and he hoped to achieve his objective of ending the Lamanite threat without further loss of life.

Alma 44:1–4 • Like Captain Moroni, we should not hate our enemies but should seek their best interests as well as our own. The Nephites withdrew a bit, and Moroni called out to Zerahemnah, the apostate Nephite who led the Lamanite armies, "Zerahemnah, . . . we do not desire to be men of blood. Ye know that ye are in our hands, yet we do not desire to slay you" (v. 1). He contrasted Nephite and Lamanite motives for war: "We have not come out to battle against you that we might shed your blood for power; neither do we desire to bring any one to the yoke of bondage. But this is the very cause for which ye have come against us; yea, and ye are angry with us because of our religion" (v. 2).

Captain Moroni was more interested in converting the Lamanites than destroying them. He called out to them, "Ye behold that the Lord is with us; and ye behold that he has delivered you into our hands. And now I would that ye should understand that this is done unto us because of our religion and our faith in Christ" (v. 3). The Lamanites had sought to destroy their faith, but had failed. Captain Moroni said to them, "Now ye see that ye cannot destroy this our faith . . . the true faith of God" (vv. 3–4). Furthermore, "God will support, and keep, and preserve us, so long as we are faithful unto him, and unto our faith, and our religion; and never will the Lord suffer that we shall be destroyed except we should fall into transgression and deny our faith" (v. 4).

Rather than fall upon them and wipe them out, Captain Moroni was seeking here to convert and save them. What military leader in ancient or modern history would have done the same? Can we imagine General Eisenhower calling out to the German forces on D-Day, offering to stop the assault if they would repent? Captain Moroni was indeed a rare and special military leader. There has never been another one like him. But if there were such military leaders today, the ugliness of war could, in fact, be diminished.

Joseph F. Smith said, "Would the nations of the earth that are at war with each other be at war as they are, if the Spirit of God Almighty had pervaded their souls and moved and actuated them in their designs? No; not at all. Worldly ambition, pride, and the love of power, determination on the part of rulers to prevail over their competitors in the national games of life, wickedness at heart, desire for power, for worldly greatness, have led the nations of the earth to quarrel with one another and have brought them to war and self-destruction. I presume there is not a nation in the world today that is not tainted with this evil more or less."[8]

Spencer W. Kimball said, "Victory and defeat alike leave countries devastated and the conqueror and the conquered reduced. Wickedness brings war, and war vomits destruction and suffering, hate and bloodshed upon the guilty and the innocent. This impressive book [the Book of Mormon] should convince all living souls of the futility of war and the hazards of unrighteousness."[9]

The First Presidency said, "If men of good will can bring themselves to do so, they may save the world from a holocaust, the depth and breadth of which can scarcely be imagined. We are confident that when there is enough of a desire for peace and a will to bring it about, it is not beyond the possibility of attainment."[10]

All these things notwithstanding, we know from the words of the prophets that the world will not repent of its hatred and lust for power until and unless its inhabitants turn to the gospel of Jesus Christ and worship him as their Prince of Peace.

David O. McKay said, "No peace, even though temporarily obtained, will be permanent unless it is built upon the solid foundation of eternal principles. The first of these [is] . . . when we sincerely accept God as our Father and make Him the center of our being. . . . Of equal importance is the acceptance of the Son of God as the Savior of mankind. . . . Men may yearn for peace, cry for peace, and work for peace, but there will be no peace until they follow the path pointed out by the living Christ."[11]

Alma 44:6–7 • Captain Moroni demands that the Lamanites take an oath never to attack the Nephites again. He commanded them "by all the desires . . . for life" to lay down their weapons, promising, "We will seek not your blood, but we will spare your lives, if ye will go your way and come not again to war against us" (v. 6). But if they will not do so, Moroni says, "Behold, ye are in our hands, and I will command my men that they shall fall upon you, and inflict the wounds of death" (v. 7). Again, I would ask, can we even imagine a military leader promising to let an opposing army go home in peace if they will promise never to attack again? This is precisely what Captain Moroni did in these circumstances, and it demonstrates the charity Captain Moroni had for all men, including his enemies.

This does not mean he was weak or unwilling to fight. He said that if they did not promise to go home in peace, they would "become extinct," and their arrogance in assuming that they could subject the Nephites to bondage would be turned on their own heads. "Then we will see who shall have power over this people," he said. "We will see who shall be brought into bondage" (v. 7).

Alma 44:8–9 • Zerahemnah refuses to make an oath never to attack the Nephites again, because he knows he would break it. He came forward and "delivered up his sword and his cimeter, and his bow into the hands of Moroni." As he did so he said, "Behold, here are our weapons of war; we will deliver them up unto you, but we will not suffer ourselves to take an oath unto you, which we know that we shall break, and also our children" (v. 8). This demonstrates the binding power of a man's word within their culture—that if a man promised something (even to his enemy) he simply would not break that covenant. He offered to give the Nephites all of their weapons and to depart into the wilderness but without making any such promise of peace. He said, "Otherwise we will retain our swords, and we will perish or conquer" (v. 8). Zerahemnah did not believe that God had protected the Nephites, only that their armor and their tactics had prevailed (v. 9).

Alma 44:10–24 • Lamanites who refuse to take the oath are killed. The survivors finally submit to Captain Moroni's terms and are driven from the land. Moroni promptly returned the Lamanites' weapons to them and said, "Behold, we will end the conflict" (v. 10). Just as Zerahemnah could not break his own word about making war upon the Nephites, neither could Captain Moroni break his own word. "I cannot recall the words which I have spoken," he said, "therefore as the Lord liveth, ye shall not depart except ye depart with an oath that ye will not return again against us to war . . . [and] as ye are in our hands we will spill your blood upon the ground" (v. 11).

In anger, Zerahemnah picked up his sword and "rushed forward that he might slay Moroni" (v. 12). But before he could do so, one of Moroni's soldiers "smote [his sword] even to the earth, and it broke by the hilt" (v. 12). He then proceeded to scalp Zerahemnah with a blow from his sword, and "his scalp . . . fell to the earth," sending Zerahemnah scampering into the midst of his soldiers (v. 12). Picking up the scalp from the ground with the point of his sword, Moroni's soldier warned Zerahemnah's soldiers that unless they gave up their weapons and made an oath of piece that "so shall [they] fall to the earth" (v. 14). Many of them were struck with fear, came forward with the weapons, and departed into the wilderness with a covenant of peace (v. 15).

All of this only made Zerahemnah more angry, and he stirred up the remainder of his army to fight with the Nephites (v. 16). Captain Moroni then gave the command to his own army to fall upon them and kill them, which they did with considerable ease since the Lamanites had no armor to protect them (vv. 17–18). Seeing that they would be utterly destroyed unless they submitted to Moroni's terms, Zerahemnah then cried out that they would make a covenant of peace if Moroni would let them depart in peace (v. 19). Hearing this, Moroni called upon his army to cease slaying them, and they collected their weapons and let the Lamanites depart into the wilderness (v. 20). It had been a bloody war on both sides of the conflict, and their dead were too great to number to bury (v. 21). They simply cast the dead bodies into the River Sidon, which eventually carried them out to sea (v. 22). The Nephites then returned to their homes and enjoyed peace and security for a while (v. 23).

Alma 43:23, 49–50 • In times of war, we should not become bloodthirsty or angry, but maintain our righteousness and exercise faith in Christ. In Alma 43–44, Captain Moroni set the example by seeking to know the Lord's will concerning their military actions (v. 23), rather than relying solely upon the Nephites' own military strength. He also made sure that the Nephites fought only *defensive* wars (Alma 48:14) and solely for the purpose of defending "liberty and their freedom from bondage" (v. 49). Because of their righteous approach, the Nephites were able to "stand against the Lamanites with power" and defeat them (v. 50).

Bruce R. McConkie said, "Self-defense is as justifiable where war is concerned as where one man seeks the life of another, with the obvious conclusion that (from the standpoint of those called upon to engage in armed conflict) some wars are righteous and others are unrighteous. Righteous men are entitled, expected, and obligated to defend themselves; they must engage in battle when there is no other way to preserve their rights and freedoms and to protect their families, homes, land, and the truths of salvation which they have espoused. In many wars, perhaps most, both sides are equally at fault and neither is justified. But there have been and yet will be wars in which the balances of eternal justice will show that one side had the favor of Deity and the other did not."[12]

The Prophet Alma Departs
(ALMA 45)

Alma 44:24 • Chapter 44 ends the record kept by Alma. The end of this chapter marks the end of the eighteenth year of the reign of the judges (73 BC) and the end of Alma's record concerning his people, which was written upon the plates of Nephi. Of course, the version of these stories that we have received was summarized and rewritten with commentary by Mormon nearly five hundred years later, but this marks the end of the events which he read and took from the writings of Alma himself.

Alma 45:2–8 • Alma turned the record over to his eldest son, Helaman. Alma interviewed his son concerning his faith in the records of their fathers (the plates), his faith in Jesus Christ, and his willingness to keep the commandments of God. Then, having confidence that Helaman had sufficient faith and would be obedient, he commended the records into his hands and blessed him.

Alma 45:10–17 • Before leaving his people for the last time, Alma prophesies their future. He predicted that wickedness would bring about the Nephites' complete destruction. He predicted the precise time when they would begin to apostatize—"four hundred years from the time that Jesus Christ shall manifest himself unto them" (v. 10). He predicted that they would "see wars and pestilences, . . . famines and bloodshed, even until the people of Nephi shall become extinct" (v. 11). These things would come upon them "because they shall dwindle in unbelief and fall into the works of darkness, and lasciviousness, and all manner of iniquities" (v. 12). He said that "the fourth generation [after Christ's coming] shall not all pass away before this great iniquity shall come" (v. 12). He said it will result in the utter destruction of the descendants of the Nephites, and "whosoever remaineth, and is not destroyed in that great and dreadful day, shall be numbered among the Lamanites, and shall become like unto them" (vv. 13–14).

Alma then restated the long-standing prophetic "cursing and the blessing" on this land (v. 16; compare Ether 2:8–12) and also blessed his sons, blessed the earth "for the righteous' sake" (v. 15), and blessed the Church and its faithful members (v. 17). These words of blessing are the final words we hear from Alma the Younger, and it is interesting to note that when Mormon recorded these words in his abridgment nearly five hundred years later, he had already witnessed the complete fulfillment of Alma's prophecies.

Alma 45:18–19 • Alma departs for the city of Melek and is never heard of again. He left Zarahemla and traveled in the direction of the land of Melek but "was never heard of more" and "as to his death or burial we know not of" (v. 18). Mormon observed that "he was a righteous man; and the saying went abroad in the Church that he was taken up by the Spirit, or buried by the hand of the Lord, even as Moses" (v. 19). Not knowing precisely what this means, he notes that "the scriptures saith the Lord took Moses unto himself; and we suppose that he has also received Alma in the spirit, unto himself" (v. 19). The only certain thing he can say is, "We know nothing concerning his death and burial" (v. 19).

ALMA WAS TRANSLATED

Joseph Fielding Smith said, "There are several important prophets who were granted the privilege of remaining on the earth. John the Revelator was one of these, and in the Doctrine and Covenants, section seven, is an account of this. Elijah evidently was another, for no living soul could have received the resurrection until after our Redeemer had opened the graves. The scriptural inference is that Moses also was translated as was Alma. . . . It is a very reasonable thought to believe that both Moses and Alma, like Elijah and John, were translated to accomplish some work which the Lord had in store for them at some future day."[13]

Bruce R. McConkie said, "Moses, Elijah, and Alma the younger, were translated. The Old Testament account that Moses died and was buried by the hand of the Lord in an unknown grave is an error (Deut. 34:5–7). It is true that he may have been 'buried by the hand of the Lord,' if that expression is a figure of speech which means that he was translated. But the Book of Mormon account, in recording that Alma 'was taken up by the Spirit,' says, 'the scriptures saith the Lord took Moses unto himself; and we suppose that he has also received Alma in the spirit, unto himself' (Alma 45:18–19)."[14]

Elder McConkie also said,

Enoch and his city were all translated and taken up into heaven without tasting death. So also were Moses and Elijah and Alma and many others of whom we have no record. Indeed the whole focus of life among the worthy saints from the day of Enoch to the day of Abraham was so to live that they would be caught up and receive an inheritance in that city whose builder and maker was God. All these were with Christ in his resurrection; that is, they received their resurrected and immortal bodies at that time. John the Revelator and the Three Nephites and others whose identity is unknown have been translated since the day of Christ. They are all carrying on their ministries of preaching and prophesying and will do so until the Second Coming, when they will receive their resurrected and immortal bodies.[15]

Captain Moroni's Righteous Leadership
(ALMA 45–48)

THE NEPHITES FOLLOW WISE AND RIGHTEOUS LEADERS

Alma 48:11–13 • Mormon's glowing appraisal of Captain Moroni. It should be no surprise that Mormon chose the name Moroni for his own son nearly five hundred years later. They turned out to have a lot in common. Both Moronis lead their armies at a very young age—Captain Moroni was only twenty-five years old (Alma 43:17; Moroni 2:1–2). Additionally, they were both men of great faith and courage. Mormon describes Captain Moroni as:

- ▷ a strong and a mighty man (v. 11)
- ▷ a man of a perfect understanding (v. 11)
- ▷ a man who did not delight in bloodshed (v. 11)
- ▷ a man whose soul did joy in the liberty and the freedom of his country and his brethren (v. 11)
- ▷ a man whose heart did swell with thanksgiving to his God, for the many privileges and blessings that he bestowed upon his people (v. 12)
- ▷ a man who did labor exceedingly for the welfare and safety of his people (v. 12)
- ▷ a man who was firm in the faith of Christ (v. 13)
- ▷ a man who had sworn with an oath to defend his people, his rights, his country, and his religion, even to the loss of his blood (v. 13)

Alma 48:14–16 • Moroni and the Nephites look to the Lord for strength in war, knowing he will guide them if they keep his commandments. "They were taught to defend themselves against their enemies, even to the shedding of blood if it were necessary; yea, and they were also taught never to give an offense, yea, and never to raise the sword except it were against an enemy, except it were to preserve their lives" (v. 14). They believed that if they followed these instructions God would prosper them and watch over them (v. 15). And if, in the end, war became necessary, God would guide them in their tactics, warn them concerning their enemies, and deliver them from danger (v. 16).

PRIDE AND DISSENSION LEAD TO WAR

Alma 45:20–22 • Helaman and his brethren go throughout the land, preaching and reorganizing the Church. At the beginning of the nineteenth year of the reign of the judges (73 BC), Helaman went out among the people to preach to them (v. 20). This was necessary, he felt, because of the dissensions and disturbances that had arisen among his people because of their wars with the Lamanites (v. 21). We have experienced similar dissensions in our own day over the war in Iraq and other conflicts that have divided us. Helaman knew that the gospel was the only answer to this problem. Helaman and his companions went throughout the land and appointed priests and teachers among the people (v. 22).

Alma 45:23–24 • Many do not listen to them. Because of the prevailing atmosphere of dissension, many "would not give heed to the words of Helaman and his brethren" (v. 23). They had grown arrogant and proud "because of their exceedingly great riches." Believing more in themselves than their God and his prophets, they "would not give heed to their words, to walk uprightly before God" (v. 24).

Alma 46:1–7 • The leader of the dissenters is Amalickiah, a large and strong man who wanted to be king (vv. 3–4). He divided the people by appealing to local leaders who were also seeking for power (v. 4), and together they sought to overthrow their form of government, promising power to those who would support them in their quest (v. 5). And through this process, he undermined their faith in God and in the preaching of Helaman (v. 6). The end result of these dissensions was an "exceedingly precarious and dangerous" situation, despite the fact that they had so recently rejoiced in God's deliverance of them from their enemies (v. 7). They had quickly forgotten God.

Alma 46:8–10 • Mormon comments on what we learn from these events. He used the phrase "thus we see" to conclude two things about the Nephites: how quickly the people had forgotten God (v. 8) and what a negative impact just one wicked man can have (vv. 9–10).

D&C 98:9–10 • A similar caution from the Lord in our own day. We are not immune from these same problems that infected the Nephites. The Lord warns that "when the wicked rule the people mourn" (v. 9), and says, concerning our leaders, "Honest men and wise men should be sought for diligently, and good men and wise men ye should observe to uphold; otherwise whatsoever is less than these cometh of evil" (v. 10).

This entire episode among the Nephites is very reminiscent of our own day. In the midst of a terrible war against bloodthirsty enemies, our nation has quickly disintegrated from a united and humble people seeking wisdom and protection from God in the year 2001 to a people who are viciously divided over nearly every public policy. The contending parties have little good to say about their opposition, and the end goal seems only to be maintaining or obtaining power at any cost. The people have grown weary of such endless fighting among our leaders and are wishing for strong and wise leaders who can help us find our way out of the morass of hatred and spite. The Lord's advice is to seek men to lead us who are honest, good, and wise, warning us that anything less will only lead to more evil.

CAPTAIN MORONI RAISES THE TITLE OF LIBERTY

Alma 46:11–15 • Moroni creates the title of liberty to produce unity and mobilize the people to defend themselves. Consider what was written on the title of liberty—a flag made from a torn piece of Captain Moroni's coat (vv. 11–12). Note the order of the things Moroni wanted them to remember, because it illustrates well the causes for which they were going to war: (1) their God, (2) their religion, (3) their freedom and peace, and (4) their families (v. 12). Moroni fastened his flag upon a pole, strapped on his armor, and then offered a heartfelt prayer to God, asking that he would protect their liberties so long as there were any believing souls left in the land (v. 13).

He referred to all such believers as "Christians," a name derived from the fact that they believed in a coming Messiah who would be called Christ (vv. 14–15). In the Old World, New Testament scholars suggest that the early Saints were called Christians by their detractors but that this name eventually became one of respect (Acts 11:26).

Alma 46:18–26 • The title of liberty symbolizes Joseph's coat of many colors. Those who subscribed to the cause written upon the title of liberty made a covenant to "maintain their rights, and their religion, that the Lord God may bless them" (v. 20). As Moroni went forth among the people, many were gathered to him, tearing their garments as a token of the covenant they were making (v. 21). They cast their torn garments at the feet of Moroni with an oath that if they were to break their covenants then God could rend them as they had their garments and trod them under foot as they were now doing to their garments (vv. 21–22).

Seizing this teaching moment, "Moroni said unto them: Behold, we are a remnant of the seed of Jacob; yea, we are a remnant of the seed of Joseph, whose coat was rent by his brethren into many pieces; yea, and now behold, let us remember to keep the commandments of God, or our garments shall be rent by our brethren, and we be cast into prison, or be sold, or be slain" (v. 23). This draws a clear connection between Moroni's torn coat and the coat of their ancestor Joseph, whose coat was also torn.

The story about the preserved remnant of Joseph's coat is not included in our present Bible. The Nephites may have had these words on the brass plates or learned of them by revelation. In either case, this illustrates how the Book of Mormon not only confirms but often expands on the Bible, which speaks only of Joseph's brothers taking his blood-soaked garment back to show their father Jacob (Genesis 37:23, 31–33).

Moroni goes on to say that a portion of Joseph's coat "was preserved and had not decayed" (v. 24). Moroni quotes Jacob as prophesying, "Even as this remnant of garment of my son hath been preserved, so shall a remnant of the seed of my son be preserved by the hand of God, and be taken unto himself, while the remainder of the seed of Joseph shall perish, even as the remnant of his garment" (vv. 24–26).

Dr. Hugh Nibley said,

> In the tenth century of our era the greatest antiquarian of the Moslem world, Muhammad ibn-Ibrahim ath-Tha'labi, collected in Persia a great many old tales and legends about the prophets of Israel. . . . Among other things, Tha'labi tells a number of stories, which we have not found anywhere else, about Jacob and the garment of Joseph. In one, Joseph's brethren bring his torn garment to their father as proof that he is dead, but Jacob after examining the garment, ("and there were in the garment of Joseph three marks of tokens when they brought it to his father") declares that the way the cloth is torn shows him that their story is not true. . . .
>
> Aside from the great symbolic force of the tale, there can be no doubt that the story told by Moroni as one familiar to all the people actually was one that circulated among the Jews in ancient times. . . . It was totally unknown to the world in which Joseph Smith lived.
>
> These interesting little details are typical apocryphal variations on a single theme, and the theme is the one Moroni mentions; the rent garment of Joseph is the symbol both of his suffering and his deliverance, misfortune and preservation. Such things in the Book of Mormon illustrate the widespread ramifications of the Book of Mormon culture, and the recent declaration of Albright and other scholars that the ancient Hebrews had cultural roots in every civilization of the Near East. This is an acid test that no forgery could pass; it not only opens a window on a world we dreamed not of, but it brings to our unsuspecting and uninitiated minds a first glimmering suspicion of the true scope and vastness of a book nobody knows.[16]

Nephite-Lamanite Wars Continue
(ALMA 46–50)

MORONI'S UNCOMMON CHARITY TOWARD PRISONERS

Alma 46:28–33 • Moroni prevents Amalickiah and his armies from fleeing to the land of Nephi. Amalickiah knew that the Nephite army was more numerous than his own, and he also knew that his own men were doubtful concerning the justice of the cause to which he had recruited them. Therefore, he sought to retreat to the land of Nephi (vv. 28–29). Moroni knew that if he allowed this to happen Amalickiah would only seek again to stir up the hearts and minds of the Lamanites in that land against the Nephites (v. 30). So he took his armies and headed off their retreat. Amalickiah escaped with a small number of his men, but the rest were brought back to the land of Zarahemla (vv. 31–33).

Alma 46:34–39 • Moroni's response to the captured Alamickiahites is humane, just, and remarkable for two reasons:

1. His prisoners of war were given a chance to swear their allegiance to the government and then be freed, even though the war still continued. Those who would not make such a covenant were put to death (v. 35).
2. It illustrates once again the great importance these people placed on making and keeping oaths. A simple oath was sufficient to trust his captives.

Moroni then "caused the title of liberty to be hoisted upon every tower which was in all the land, which was possessed by the Nephites" (v. 36). They enjoyed peace in the land until "nearly the end of the nineteenth year of the reign of the judges" in 72 BC (v. 37), and especially in the Church, which for "four years. . . [had] much peace and rejoicing" (v. 38).

Alma 46:40–41 • Comments on the climate. Mormon observed that "there were some who died with fevers, which at some seasons of the year were very frequent in the land—but not so much so with fevers, because of the excellent qualities of the many plants and roots which God had prepared to remove the cause of diseases, to which men were subject by the nature of the climate" (v. 40), which suggests a tropical or subtropical climate in and around Zarahemla. Other than this passage, very little information is provided in the Book of Mormon about the climate where the Nephites and Lamanites lived.

AMALICKIAH'S UNBRIDLED DESIRE FOR POWER

Alma 47:1, 4, 8 • Amalickiah becomes king of the Lamanites by treachery. He laid a very subtle plan to "dethrone the king of the Lamanites" (v. 4) "and take possession of the kingdom" (v. 8.) He stirred up the Lamanites to anger against the people of Nephi, and "the king of the Lamanites sent a proclamation throughout all his land, among all his people, that they should gather themselves together again to go to battle against the Nephites" (v. 1). It was his plan "to gain favor with the armies of the Lamanites, that he might place himself at their head and dethrone the king and take possession of the kingdom" (v. 8).

Alma 48:1–6 • Amalickiah wants to rule over the Nephites as well. He had managed to obtain the throne of kingship among the Lamanites, and now he wanted to rule over all the lands—both Lamanite and Nephite (vv. 1–2). He prepared to attack by amassing a large army of Lamanites and stirring them up to hatred for the Nephites (v. 3). For his leaders of the army he appointed Zoramites—apostate Nephites—who hated the Nephites and knew well the Nephites' strengths and weaknesses (v. 5).

MORONI'S WISE PREPARATIONS FOR WAR

Alma 48:7–9; Alma 49:2–4, 13, 18 • Moroni's careful preparation for war. Moroni prepared the Nephites for Amalickiah's attack by strengthening their defenses. They built "walls of stone to

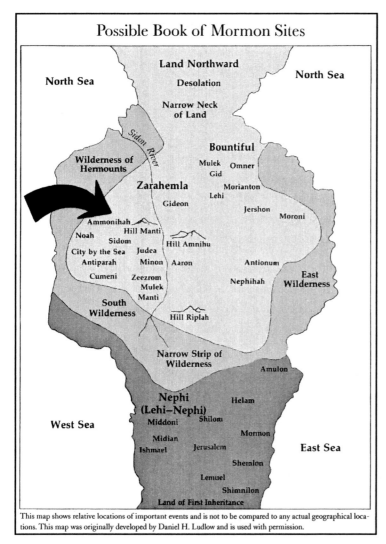

Possible Book of Mormon Sites

North Sea

Land Northward
Desolation

North Sea

Narrow Neck
of Land

Sidon River

Wilderness of
Hermounts

Bountiful

Mulek   Omner
Gid

Zarahemla

Morianton
Lehi

Gideon

Jershon

Moroni

Ammonihah
Noah   Hill Manti
        Sidom
City by the Sea   Judea
Antiparah   Minon
Cumeni   Zeezrom
          Mulek
          Manti
South
Wilderness

Hill Amnihu

Aaron

Antionum

Nephihah

East
Wilderness

Hill Riplah

Narrow Strip of
Wilderness

Amulon

Nephi
(Lehi–Nephi)
Middoni
Midian
Ishmael

Helam

Shilom

Mormon

Jerusalem

Shemlon

Lemuel

Shimnilon

Land of First Inheritance

West Sea

East Sea

This map shows relative locations of important events and is not to be compared to any actual geographical locations. This map was originally developed by Daniel H. Ludlow and is used with permission.

encircle them about, round about their cities and the borders of their lands" (Alma 48:8). "And in their weakest fortifications he did place the greater number of men; and thus he did fortify and strengthen the land which was possessed by the Nephites" (Alma 48:9). He "stationed an army by the borders of the city [Ammonihah]" and "cast up dirt round about to shield them from the arrows and the stones of the Lamanites" (Alma 49:2). Because they had destroyed it once before, the Lamanites thought Ammonihah would be easy to conquer, but "how great was their disappointment; for behold, the Nephites had dug up a ridge of earth round about them, which was so high that the Lamanites could not cast their stones and their arrows at them that they might take effect, neither could they come upon them save it was by their place of entrance" (Alma 49:4).

Moroni had "built forts of security, for every city in all the land round about" (Alma 49:13). So when the Lamanites left Ammonihah and "marched forward to the land of Noah with a firm determination . . . [to] destroy the people of that city . . . because of the highness of the bank which had been thrown up, and the depth of the ditch which had been dug round about" (Alma 49:13, 18).

The contrast between Moroni's and Amalickiah's leadership is apparent in these events. One was seeking his own power and the other sought the welfare of the people.

Amalickiah	Moroni
Desired power over people (Alma 46:2–5)	Desired welfare of the people (Alma 48:11–12)
Gained power by fraud, deceit, and murder (Alma 46:9–10)	Prepared the people to defend themselves (Alma 48: 7–10, 14–15)
Lead his followers to wickedness (Alma 46:9–10)	Exercised faith in Christ (Alma 48:13–15)
	Was spiritually powerful (Alma 48:17)

Alma 50:1–6 • Moroni continues to strengthen Nephite defenses. These successes did not lull the Nephites into complacency. They "did not stop making preparations for war," but instead continued "in digging up heaps of earth round about all the cities, throughout all the land which

was possessed by the Nephites" (v. 1). They created a pit or mote with the earth mounded up on the inside to a considerable height. Then, on top of the mound they placed "timbers, yea, works of timbers built up to the height of a man, round about the cities" (v. 2). On top of these wooden breastworks they placed "a frame of pickets . . . [that] were strong and high" (v. 3). At the corners of these fortifications Moroni "caused towers to be erected that overlooked those works of pickets, and he caused places of security to be built upon those towers, that the stones and the arrows of the Lamanites could not hurt them" (v. 4). From the top of these towers, "they could cast stones . . . according to their pleasure and their strength, and slay him who should attempt to approach near the walls of the city" (v. 5). This was done in "every city in all the land" (v. 6).

In recent years, archaeologists have been surprised to find earthen fortifications that are precisely like those described in the Book of Mormon. Prior to that, no knowledge of such things had ever existed in our own time, let alone in 1829 when Joseph Smith translated the Book of Mormon. Fortified earthworks patterned after the style of Moroni's fortification have been discovered at several places in Peten, Guatemala, Belize, and the southern Yucatan peninsula.

Jerry L. Ainsworth said,

> Several ancient sites qualify as candidates for the city of Bountiful. Of these, Palenque, in the state of Chiapas, in southern Mexico, seems the most likely. One reason is that the city of Bountiful was surrounded by a large earthen wall of "an exceeding height." The Nephite army commander, Moroni, utilized Lamanite prisoners in digging that city's fortification (Alma 53:4). . . . I have observed remnants of such timber work on an inner bank of a ditch near the city of Emiliano Zapata in the area of Palenque. The Spanish dictionary defines *palenque* as "a wooden barrier or stockade." A wooden barrier apparently at one time encircled the area of Palenque. A town in the same area, Palizada, has a similar name. *Palizada* means "a place fenced with sticks" or "a wall of timber."[17]

Alma 49:25–28 • The differing reaction among the Lamanites and Nephites. When the Lamanites attempted to attack these fortified cities, many were slain, including their chief captains. They returned defeated to the land of Nephi "to inform their king, Amalickiah, who was a Nephite by birth, concerning their great loss" (v. 25). This news made him "exceedingly angry with his people, because he had not obtained his desire over the Nephites" (v. 26). He proceeded to "curse God, and also Moroni, swearing with an oath that he would drink his blood" (v. 27). At the same time, "the people of Nephi did thank the Lord their God, because of his matchless power in delivering them from the hands of their enemies" by instructing Moroni to fortify their cities (v. 28). The Nephites had been protected by their temporal preparation, but also because they kept the commandments of God and followed the wise counsel of their leaders.

Alma 49:29–30 • Obedience to their prophets brings peace to the Nephites. At this point, the Nephites began to enjoy "continual peace among them, and exceedingly great prosperity in the Church because of their heed and diligence which they gave unto the word of God" (v. 30). Their prophets included Helaman and his sons Shiblon, Ammon, and Corianton (who had evidently repented after being chastised by their father—see Alma 39–42). They were assisted by "all those who had been ordained by the holy order of God, being baptized unto repentance, and sent forth to preach among the people" (v. 30).

Alma 50:19–22 • Mormon summarizes what we learn from these events. With another "thus we see" editorial, Mormon noted, "How merciful and just are all the dealings of the Lord, to the fulfilling of all his words unto the children of men" (v. 19). He quoted the Lord's promise to Lehi that "inasmuch as [his descendants] shall keep my commandments they shall prosper in the land . . . [but if not] they shall be cut off from the presence of the Lord" (v. 20). Mormon saw the fulfillment of this prophecy among the people of Nephi, "for it has been their quarrelings and their contentions, yea, their murderings, and their plunderings, their idolatry, their whoredoms, and their abominations . . . which brought upon them their wars and their destructions" (v. 21). Meanwhile, "those who were faithful in keeping the commandments of the Lord were delivered at all times, whilst thousands of their wicked brethren have been consigned to bondage, or to perish by the sword, or to dwindle in unbelief, and mingle with the Lamanites" (v. 22).

THE NEED FOR A STRONG DEFENSE AND SPIRITUAL STRENGTH

The Book of Mormon teaches that a people must prepare to defend themselves if they are to remain free, for war may sometimes be required to defend that freedom. It also teaches that mere physical defenses and armaments are not sufficient preparation.

John A. Widtsoe said,

> Preparedness is today on every tongue. There is danger ahead, and defenses must be set up. Preparedness is not a new word to Latter-day Saints. For one hundred and ten years our voice has been one of warning to prepare against the commotion and calamities of the last days. We have taught and continue to teach that full preparedness and complete defense against the devastation by evil is the acceptance of the Gospel of Jesus Christ. When every knee shall bow and every tongue confess that Jesus is the Christ we may look for the peace of Eden, but not before.
>
> Our land is setting up defenses of powder and steel. That is well enough. But there are intangible defenses more powerful which direct the use of material defenses. These must be fostered, if our preparedness shall be adequate.[18]

Alma 49:30; Alma 50:23 • While righteous, the Nephites were prosperous and happy, even in times of war. They enjoyed "continual peace among them, and exceedingly great prosperity in the Church because of their heed and diligence which they gave unto the word of God" (Alma 49:30). Mormon says, "Behold there never was a happier time among the people of Nephi, since the days of Nephi, than in the days of Moroni [71–68 BC]" (Alma 50:23). Surely this is how we should live today in the midst of worldwide conflict. The Book of Mormon, once again, shows itself to be the best resource we have for knowing how to live righteously in times of trouble and war.

King-men and Freemen
(ALMA 50–52)
THE ROLE OF THE GOVERNMENT IN MAINTAINING PEACE

Nephihah, the second chief judge, died in the twenty-fourth year of the reign of the judges (68 BC). Pahoran, his son, was appointed to replace him. The sacred oath and ordinance that was administered to Pahoran shows the Nephite concept of the role of government.

Alma 50:39 • As chief judge, Pahoran took upon himself the responsibilities to:
 ▷ Judge righteously

- ▷ Keep peace and freedom
- ▷ Grant the people the privilege to worship the Lord
- ▷ Support and maintain the cause of God
- ▷ Bring the wicked to justice

RENEWED CONTENTION AMONG THE NEPHITES

Alma 50:26–35 • Morianton and his people rebel against the government. Eventually, divisions among the Nephites began to arise again. The people who possessed the land of Morianton "did claim a part of the land of Lehi; therefore there began to be a warm contention between them ... [and] the people of Morianton took up arms against their brethren, and they were determined by the sword to slay them" (v. 26). The people in the land of Lehi "fled to the camp of Moroni, and appealed unto him for assistance; for behold they were not in the wrong" (v. 27). This caused the people of Morianton "who were led by a man whose name was Morianton" (v. 28) to fear "lest the army of Moroni should come upon them and destroy them" (v. 28).

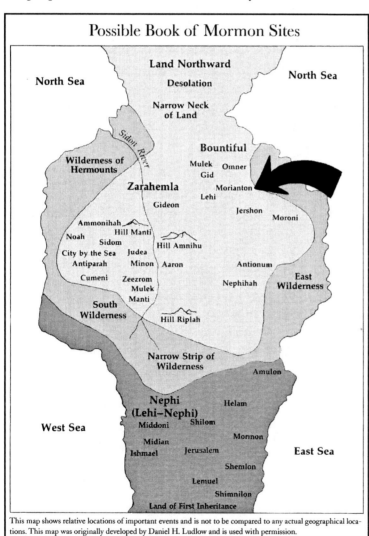

Possible Book of Mormon Sites

This map shows relative locations of important events and is not to be compared to any actual geographical locations. This map was originally developed by Daniel H. Ludlow and is used with permission.

Morianton instructed his people to flee to the land northward (north of the land of Zarahemla), "which was covered with large bodies of water, and take possession of the land" (v. 29). However, in the meantime, "Morianton being a man of much passion ... was angry with one of his maid servants, and he fell upon her and beat her much" (v. 30). She escaped and "came over to the camp of Moroni, and told Moroni ... concerning their intentions to flee into the land northward" (v. 31).

The land northward was a strategic place, obtainable only through a narrow pass in the mountains that separated it from the land of Zarahemla and the former homeland of the Jaredites, who had reduced it to a state of desolation. If the people of Morianton obtained this land, it would "lay a foundation for serious consequences among the people of Nephi, yea, which consequences would lead to the overthrow of their liberty" (v. 32). Therefore, Moroni sent an army to stop them "by the narrow pass which led by the sea into the land northward" (vv. 33–34). The commander of this Nephite army was Teancum, who "did slay Morianton and defeat his army, and took them prisoners, and returned to the camp of Moroni" (v. 35).

Alma 51:2–8 • The Nephites argue among themselves regarding the form of their government. Another group of apostate traitors—the king-men—arose at this time to challenge Pahoran's authority (vv. 2–5). As with so many before them, they wanted to:

▷ Alter "a few points of the law"
▷ Overthrow free government
▷ Establish a king in place of elected judges
▷ Obtain power and authority over the people

These king-men were "those of high birth, and they sought to be kings; and they were supported by those who sought power and authority over the people" (v. 8).

The matter was settled by the voice of the people, who voted for Pahoran and for a group called freemen, who supported him and the system of judges (vv. 6–7).

Alma 51:9, 13–16 • These contentions encourage their Lamanite enemies to attack. The Nephites were more vulnerable now because of the border dispute between the cities of Lehi and Morianton and because of the division between the king-men and freemen. Amalickiah had stirred up the Lamanites and was preparing them for war, having sworn to drink the blood of Moroni (v. 9). When the Lamanites came upon the Nephites, the king-men were glad and refused to take up arms (v. 13).

Angered by their treachery, Moroni "sent a petition, with the voice of the people, unto the governor of the land, desiring that he should read it, and give him (Moroni) power to compel those dissenters to defend their country or to put them to death" (v. 15). His first priority was to "put an end to such contentions and dissensions among the people; for behold, this had been hitherto a cause of all their destruction," and Moroni's petition "was granted according to the voice of the people" (v. 16).

IS MILITARY CONSCRIPTION APPROPRIATE?

Robert L. Simpson said,

> This is a problem stated by a young man who contemplates military call-up. This is what he says: "Didn't the Savior teach peace? To me, peace means no fighting. I am not sure about our present military involvements." I say to this young man, the following facts helped me and they may be helpful to you:
>
> When the Book of Mormon talks about a land choice above all others, I believe it.
>
> When we are taught that our founding forefathers prayed for and received inspiration as they framed our Constitution, I believe it.
>
> When a prophet suggests that the gospel could best be restored in a land of freedom and democracy, I believe it.
>
> When the standard works of the Church instruct me about obeying, honoring, and sustaining the law, I want to do it. I even believe that our elected national leaders are basically honest men and base their decisions upon what they believe to be for the good of the people as they see it.
>
> Last but not least, I also believe that a prophet of God will let me know about any change of policy in the foregoing line of reasoning. Young men, to whatever country your citizenship commitment might be, you honor it, you obey it, you sustain it. To do otherwise would be contrary to law and order; and law and order is the basis of the priesthood, wherever it is established.[19]

Alma 51:17–21 • Moroni slays four thousand dissenters in a civil war that puts an end to the king-men. Moroni "commanded that his army should go against those king-men, to pull down their pride and their nobility and level them with the earth, or they should take up arms and support the cause of liberty" (v. 17). Four thousand of the dissenters were killed in the battle, "and those of their leaders who were not slain in battle were taken and cast into prison, for there was no time for their trials at this period" (v. 19). The rest of them "rather than be smitten down to the earth by the sword, yielded to the standard of liberty, and were compelled to hoist the title of liberty upon their towers, and in their cities, and to take up arms in defence of their countries" (v. 20).

Alma 51:22–28 • Meanwhile the Lamanites attack and capture many Nephite cities along the eastern coast. Among them were the two that had the border contention—the cities of Lehi and Morianton (v. 26). The Nephites "were not sufficiently strong in the city of Moroni" and were therefore driven and slain by Amalickiah's forces (v. 23). The Lamanite army pushed forward, taking possession of many cities, "the city of Nephihah, and the city of Lehi, and the city of Morianton, and the city of Omner, and the city of Gid, and the city of Mulek, all of which were on the east borders by the seashore" (vv. 25–26). All of these cities "were strongly fortified after the manner of the fortifications of Moroni" making it easier for the Lamanites to hold them (v. 27). The Lamanites "marched to the borders of the land Bountiful, driving the Nephites before them and slaying many" (v. 28).

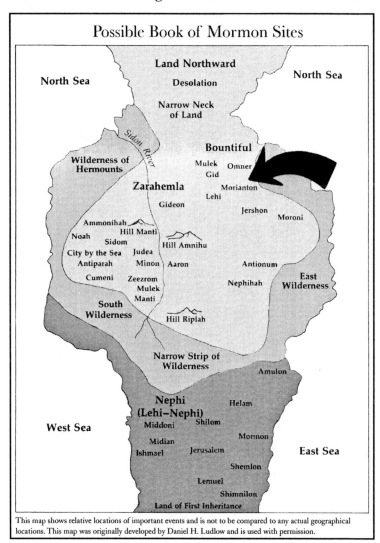

This map shows relative locations of important events and is not to be compared to any actual geographical locations. This map was originally developed by Daniel H. Ludlow and is used with permission.

Alma 51:29–37 • Teancum stops Amalickiah's army and slays him by night. At Bountiful the Lamanite armies were met by Teancum—the same general who had slain Morianton and prevented his people from fleeing northward (v. 29). Teancum and his men were "great warriors; for every man of Teancum did exceed the Lamanites in their strength and in their skill of war, insomuch that they did gain advantage over the Lamanites" (v. 31). When the two armies pitched their tents for the night, "Teancum and his servant stole forth and went out by night, and went into the camp of Amalickiah; and behold, sleep had overpowered them because of their much fatigue, which was caused by the labors and heat of the day" (v. 33). Teancum "stole privily into the tent of the king, and put a javelin to his heart [causing] the death of the king immediately that he did not awake his servants" (v. 34). Teancum then returned to his camp and reported what he had done (v. 35). This was on the New Year's Eve of the Nephites and Lamanites, for the scripture records "thus endeth the twenty and fifth year of the reign of the judges over the people of Nephi" (v. 37).

Alma 52:22–40 • The Nephites outsmart the Lamanites and defeat them. Teancum took a small number of men and marched down near the Lamanite camp on the seashore, while Moroni and his army marched by night through the wilderness to the west side of the city Mulek (v. 22). When he saw Teancum's small army, Jacob—the new leader of the Lamanite army—marched forth against Teancum "supposing by their numbers to overpower Teancum because of the smallness of his numbers" (v. 23). Teancum's army began to retreat northward, by the seashore, causing the Lamanite armies to pursue them "with vigor." Meanwhile, Moroni commanded part of his army to "march forth into the city, and take possession of it" (v. 24), which they did, slaying "all those who had been left to protect the city [and] all those who would not yield up their weapons of war" (v. 25).

The Lamanite army pursued Teancum until they came near the city Bountiful, where they were met by Lehi and a small army, which had been left to protect the city Bountiful (v. 27). When they saw Lehi's army coming against them, the Lamanites "fled in much confusion, lest perhaps they should not obtain the city Mulek before Lehi should overtake them; for they were wearied because of their march, and the men of Lehi were fresh" (v. 28). They did not know that the rest of Moroni's army had been in their rear with his army "and all they feared was Lehi and his men" (v. 29). After fleeing quite a distance, "they were surrounded by the Nephites, by the men of Moroni on one hand, and the men of Lehi on the other, all of whom were fresh and full of strength; but the Lamanites were wearied because of their long march" (v. 31). Moroni commanded his men that they should fall upon them "until they had given up their weapons of war" (v. 32).

Being a Zoramite—an apostate Nephite—and "having an unconquerable spirit, [Jacob] led the Lamanites forth to battle with exceeding fury against Moroni" (v. 33). Many were slain on both sides of the battle, and "Moroni was wounded and Jacob was killed" (v. 35). Lehi "pressed upon their rear with such fury with his strong men, that the Lamanites in the rear delivered up their weapons of war; and the remainder of them, being much confused, knew not whither to go or to strike" (v. 36). Seeing their confusion, and consistent with his compassionate attitude toward his enemies, Moroni said unto them, "If ye will bring forth your weapons of war and deliver them up, behold we will forbear shedding your blood" (v. 37). The chief captains of the Lamanites took him up on this offer and commanded their men to do the same (v. 38). Nevertheless, "there were many that would not; and those who would not deliver up their swords were taken and bound, and their weapons of war were taken from them, and they were compelled to march with their brethren forth into the land Bountiful" (v. 39). The number of these prisoners was greater than the number of men that had been slain on both sides of the battle (v. 40).

WHAT WE LEARN FROM MORONI ABOUT CHRISTIAN WARFARE

Matthew 26:52 • The Savior said, "All they that take the sword shall perish with the sword." This prophecy, given to Peter when he attempted to defend the Savior against the Roman soldiers who had come to take him out of the Garden of Gethsemane, teaches that those who follow Christ must be emissaries of peace, even during times of war.

Alma 52:6 • A nation must prepare to defend itself, but it can go too far in its preparations. Moroni "kept his men round about, as if making preparations for war; yea, and truly he was preparing to defend himself against them, by casting up walls round about and preparing places of resort." But these were defensive preparations, not offensive ones.

The First Presidency said, "We repeat our warnings against the terrifying arms race in which the nations of the earth are presently engaged. We deplore in particular the building of vast arsenals of nuclear weaponry. We are advised that there is already enough such weaponry to destroy in large measure our civilization, with consequent suffering and misery of incalculable extent."[20]

Notes

1. Ezra Taft Benson, *A Witness and a Warning: A Modern-Day Prophet Testifies of the Book of Mormon* (Salt Lake City: Deseret Book, 1988), 20–21.
2. Joseph Smith, "Recollections of the Prophet Joseph Smith," *Juvenile Instructor*, Aug. 15, 1892, 492.
3. Bruce R. McConkie, *Mormon Doctrine*, 2nd ed. (Salt Lake City: Bookcraft, 1966), 826.
4. "Message of the First Presidency," in Conference Report, April 1942, 94.
5. David O. McKay, in Conference Report, Apr. 1955, 24.
6. Charles W. Penrose, in Conference Report, Oct. 1917, 21.
7. David O. McKay, in Conference Report, April 1942, 72–73.
8. Joseph F. Smith, in Conference Report, Oct. 1914; see also *Gospel Doctrine: Selections from the Sermons and Writings of Joseph F. Smith*, John A. Widtsoe, comp. (Salt Lake City: Deseret Book, 1939), 422.
9. *The Teachings of Spencer W. Kimball* (Salt Lake City: Bookcraft, 1982), 414.
10. *Church News*, Dec. 20, 1980, 3.
11. David O. McKay, *Improvement Era*, Oct. 1960, 703.
12. Bruce R. McConkie, *Mormon Doctrine*, 2nd ed. (Salt Lake City: Bookcraft, 1966), 826.
13. Joseph Fielding Smith, *Answers to Gospel Questions*, Joseph Fielding Smith Jr., comp., (Salt Lake City: Deseret Book, 1957–66), 5:38.
14. Bruce R. McConkie, *Mormon Doctrine*, 2nd ed. (Salt Lake City: Bookcraft, 1966), 805.
15. Bruce R. McConkie, *The Millennial Messiah: The Second Coming of the Son of Man* (Salt Lake City: Deseret Book, 1982), 647.
16. Hugh Nibley, *An Approach to the Book of Mormon*, 3rd ed. (Salt Lake City: Deseret Book and the Foundation for Ancient Research and Mormon Studies, 1988), 171–80.
17. Jerry L. Ainsworth, *The Lives and Travels of Mormon and Moroni* (Peacemakers Publishing, 2000), 108–10.
18. John A. Widstoe, in Conference Report, Oct. 1940, 61–62.
19. Robert L. Simpson, in Conference Report, Oct. 1970, 101.
20. Spencer W. Kimball, N. Eldon Tanner, and Marion G. Romney, "First Presidency Statement on Basing of MX Missile," *Ensign*, Jun. 1981, 76.

LESSON 32
"Firm in the Faith of Christ"
ALMA 53–63

Helaman's Stripling Warriors and the Moroni-Pahoran Letters

This lesson contains a great deal of material—far more than can be comprehensively covered in one Gospel Doctrine lesson, or even one CES Institute lesson. The supplementary materials found in this chapter will help you to fill in the blanks historically and geographically for this important period of Nephite history. In this chapter we are introduced to the wonderful stripling warriors who battled for the freedom of the Nephite people, though they themselves were Lamanites—children of the peace-covenanting Ammonites who had buried their weapons with a covenant never to take them up again. We also gain insight into the noble characters of both Captain Moroni and Pahoran, the chief judge and governor of the Nephite people, by reading letters they wrote to each other during some of the Nephites' most perilous times.

Alma 53:8 • "The West Sea, South" Daniel H. Ludlow said,

> When the Nephites first landed in the promised land, they gave names to some of the seas and lands around them. At that time the sea to the west of their landing place was evidently called the "west sea." Later, Nephi left this land, took his followers, and went northward where they settled in the land of Nephi. The descendants of Nephi and his group lived there for several hundred years.
>
> Then Mosiah, under the inspiration of the Lord, led a group of Nephites even farther north to the land of Zarahemla. The major group of the Nephites is now located in the land of Zarahemla, far north of the original landing place. Thus, the original "west sea" is actually far to the south of where they are now living, and they refer to "the west sea, south."[1]

Helaman's 2,000 Stripling Warriors

A "stripling" is a young man. The story of Helaman and the two thousand stripling sons of the people of Ammon, later joined by sixty more of their brethren, is one of the most inspiring stories in sacred literature.

THE IMPORTANCE OF KEEPING COVENANTS

Alma 53:10–15 • The Ammonites (Anti-Nephi-Lehies) made a covenant of peace at the time of their conversion, never again to shed blood (Alma 24:15–19). Since that time, they had been protected by the Nephites at great cost in lives and treasure (v. 13). The Ammonites considered breaking their covenant to aid in their defense rather than just sitting by and watching the Nephites die, but Helaman persuaded them not to break their covenant, lest they should "lose their souls" (vv. 14–15). This teaches us much about the importance of keeping the covenants that we make. People in Book of Mormon times, even sworn enemies, would not make covenants they had no intention of keeping. And once made, they would rather die than break them.

Alma 48:14 • The Book of Mormon approves fighting in defense of oneself, one's family, or one's liberty. But from an eternal perspective, it was more important for the Ammonites to keep their covenant.

D&C 84:40–41 • We are also expected to honor covenants in our own day, including:

▷ Baptismal covenants
▷ Sacrament covenants
▷ The oath and covenant of the priesthood
▷ Temple covenants, including marriage

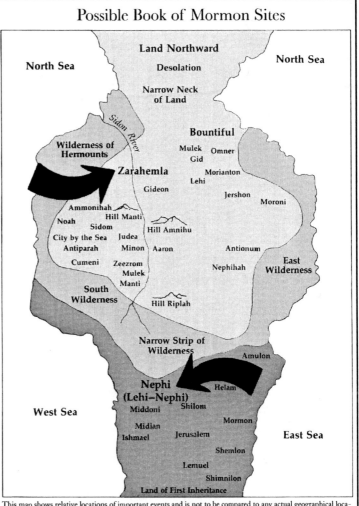

Possible Book of Mormon Sites

This map shows relative locations of important events and is not to be compared to any actual geographical locations. This map was originally developed by Daniel H. Ludlow and is used with permission.

The Prophet Joseph Smith said, "And may God enable us to perform our vows and covenants with each other, in all fidelity and righteousness before Him, that our influence may be felt among the nations of the earth, in mighty power, even to rend the kingdoms of darkness asunder, and triumph over priestcraft and spiritual wickedness in high places, and break in pieces all kingdoms that are opposed to the kingdom of Christ, and spread the light and truth of the everlasting Gospel from the rivers to the ends of the earth."[2]

Joseph Fielding Smith said, "Every covenant, contract, bond, obligation, and commandment we have received by revelation and coming from the Almighty has the one purpose in view, the exaltation and perfection of the individual who will in full faith and obedience accept it. He that 'receiveth a commandment with doubtful heart, and keepeth it with slothfulness, the same is damned,' [D&C 58:29] the Lord has said. Unfortunately there are a great many who receive covenants in that way."[3]

John Taylor said, "We enter into obligations . . . and pledge ourselves in the most solemn manner . . . and if we violate these covenants, and trample under foot the ordinances of God, we ought to be dealt with by the Church and either repent of our sins or be cut off from the Church so that by purging the Church from iniquity, we may be acceptable before God. For the Gods spoken of, are not going to associate with every scallywag in existence; scallywags are not going where they are; and if men do not live according to the laws of a Celestial kingdom, they are not going into a Celestial glory; they cannot pass by the angels and the Gods, who are set to guard the way of life. Straight is the gate and narrow is the way that leads to life, and few there be that find it."[4]

THE AMMONITES' SONS PROVIDE AN ANSWER

Alma 53:16–21 • Two thousand Ammonite young men volunteered to defend their country and were reinforced later by another 60, making a total of 2,060 (Alma 56:3–9). These faithful young men asked a prophet—Helaman—to be their leader, demonstrating the depth of their faith in God and in his designated mouthpiece on earth.

D&C 21:4–6 • We are also commanded to follow our prophet "in all patience and faith." It takes patience and faith to be obedient, especially when the counsel of the prophet contradicts our personal views or ways of life.

Harold B. Lee said,

> The power of Satan will increase; we see it in evidence on every hand. . . . The only safety we have as members of this church is to do exactly what the Lord said to the Church in that day when the Church was organized. We must learn to give heed to the words and commandments that the Lord shall give through his prophet. . . .
>
> There will be some things that take patience and faith. You may not like what comes from the authority of the Church. It may contradict your political views. It may contradict your social views. It may interfere with some of your social life. But if you listen to these things, as if from the mouth of the Lord himself, with patience and faith, the promise is that "the gates of hell shall not prevail against you; yea, and the Lord God will disperse the powers of darkness from before you, and cause the heavens to shake for your good, and his name's glory" (D&C 21:6).[5]

David B. Haight said, "When we sustain the President of the Church by our uplifted hand, it not only signifies that we acknowledge before God that he is the rightful possessor of all the priesthood keys; it means that we covenant with God that we will abide by the direction and the counsel that come through His prophet. It is a solemn covenant."[6]

James E. Faust said,

> We should ask ourselves: What are the Brethren saying? The living prophets can open the visions of eternity; they give counsel on how to overcome the world. We cannot know what that counsel is if we do not listen. We cannot receive the blessings we are promised if we do not follow the counsel given.
>
> As a young stake president, I met many of the General Authorities when they came to speak at our stake conference. . . . President Hugh B. Brown came to one of our stake conferences just a week before he was called and sustained as a member of the Council of the Twelve. We enjoyed his warm spirit and his good humor. As I helped him with his coat and walked out to his car with him, I said, "Elder Brown, do you have any personal advice for me?"
>
> His answer was, "Yes. Stick with the Brethren." He did not choose to elaborate or explain, but he left that indelible message: Have the simple faith to follow the Brethren.[7]

L. Tom Perry said, "Never has there been a time when the written and spoken word can descend upon us from so many different sources. Through the media we find analysts analyzing the analysts, almost overwhelming us with opinions and different views. What a comfort it is to know that the Lord keeps a channel of communication open to His children through the prophet. What a blessing it is to know we have a voice we can trust to declare the will of the Lord. As the prophet Amos taught, 'surely the Lord God will do nothing, but he revealeth his secret unto his servants the prophets' (Amos 3:17)."[8]

Howard W. Hunter said, "As I have pondered the messages of the conference, I have asked myself this question: How can I help others partake of the goodness and blessings of our Heavenly Father? The answer lies in following the direction received from those we sustain as prophets, seers, and revelators, and others of the General Authorities. Let us study their words, spoken under the Spirit of inspiration, and refer to them often. The Lord has revealed his will to the Saints in this conference."[9]

Gordon B. Hinckley said,

How thankful we ought to be, my brethren and sisters, how thankful we are, for a prophet to counsel us in words of divine wisdom as we walk our paths in these complex and difficult times. The solid assurance we carry in our hearts, the conviction that God will make his will known to his children through his recognized servant is the real basis of our faith and activity. We either have a prophet or we have nothing; and having a prophet, we have everything. . . .

As one to whom the Spirit has borne witness, I testify of his prophetic calling, and add my voice to the voices of our people over the earth, "We thank thee, O God, for a prophet to guide us in these latter days." I am grateful. I am satisfied that the peace and the progress and the prosperity of this people lie in doing the will of the Lord as that will is articulated by (the prophet). If we fail to observe his counsel, we repudiate his sacred calling. If we abide his counsel, we shall be blessed of God.[10]

Alma 53:20–22 • Characteristics of the stripling warriors. From these two verses we obtain an excellent word portrait of the character of these marvelous warriors, who marched forth to battle with their prophet Helaman at their head.

- ▷ They were young.
- ▷ They were exceedingly courageous.
- ▷ They were very strong and active.
- ▷ They were true to every trust given to them.
- ▷ They were men of truth.
- ▷ They were sober (serious about their responsibilities).
- ▷ They had been taught to keep the commandments.

Captain Moroni's Motives And Character

A fascinating aspect of Mormon's abridgment of the large plates of Nephi was the inclusion of letters, or epistles, apparently word for word (Alma 54, 56–58, 60–61). Considering the scarceness of space on the plates, Mormon must have considered them very important.

Alma 54:1–4 • Ammoron's letter to Moroni, proposing a prisoner exchange. At the beginning of the twenty-ninth year of the judges (63 BC), Ammoron wrote to Moroni, desiring an exchange of prisoners (v. 1). Moroni was favorably disposed to this proposition because it would permit him to use for the benefit of his own people the provisions he was then giving to his prisoners (v. 2). Unlike the Lamanites, who had captured many women and children, Moroni had kept no women and children as prisoners (v. 3), and he intended to obtain as many prisoners back from the Lamanites as possible (v. 4).

Alma 54:5–14 • Moroni's response to Ammoron. In his response, Moroni wrote to Ammoron referencing the war that Ammoron's brother had begun and that he was now endeavoring to continue against the Nephites (v. 5). He warned, "The justice of God, and the sword of his almighty wrath. . . doth hang over you except ye repent and withdraw your armies into your own lands" (v. 6). He spoke of "that awful hell that awaits to receive such murderers as thou and thy brother have been, except ye repent and withdraw your murderous purposes" (v. 7).

Moroni expected no positive response, saying, "Ye have once rejected these things, and have fought against the people of the Lord, even so I may expect you will do it again. And now behold, we are prepared to receive you; yea, and except you withdraw your purposes, behold, ye will pull down the awrath of that God whom you have rejected upon you, even to your utter destruction" (v. 8–9). He swore, "We will retain our cities and our lands; yea, and we will maintain our religion and the cause of our God" (v. 10). He called Ammoron "a child of hell" and said, "I will not exchange prisoners, save it be on conditions that ye will deliver up a man and his wife and his children, for one prisoner" (v. 11). And if not, then "I will come against you with my armies . . . and I will follow you even into your own land . . . and it shall be blood for blood, yea, life for life; and I will give you battle even until you are destroyed from off the face of the earth" (v. 12). Moroni confessed that he was angry, telling the Lamanites, "Ye have sought to murder us, and we have only sought to defend ourselves. But behold, if ye seek to destroy us more we will seek to destroy you" (v. 13).

Alma 54:15–24 • Ammoron's response to Moroni. Not surprisingly, when Ammoron received Moroni's response he was angry (v. 15). He wrote back to Moroni, accusing him of murdering his brother Amalickiah and swearing to avenge his blood upon Moroni personally, writing, "For I fear not your threatenings" (v. 16). He then offered the age-old criticism of the Lamanites—that Nephi had robbed Laman and Lemuel of their right to govern (v. 17)—even though, as an apostate Nephite, he was not himself a Lamanite.

His counter-offer to Moroni was that his soldiers would lay down their arms only if Moroni and his troops laid down their own arms and agreed to be governed by the Lamanites (v. 18). He also agreed to exchange prisoners on Moroni's terms because it would allow him to preserve his food for his army and allow them to "wage a war which shall be eternal, either to the subjecting the Nephites to [the Lamanites'] authority or to their eternal extinction" (v. 20).

Jacob said concerning "that God whom ye say we have rejected" that neither he (Jacob) nor the Nephites know any such God, but "if it so be that there is such a being, we know not but that he hath made us as well as you" (v. 21). Furthermore, he said, "If it so be that there is a devil and a hell, behold will he not send you there to dwell with my brother whom ye have murdered . . . ? But behold these things matter not" (v. 22). He admitted his lineage as a Zoramite but said, "Behold now, I am a bold Lamanite [and] this war hath been waged to avenge their wrongs" (vv. 23–24).

As is so often the case, this war was a religious war—fought between cultures with totally different ideas about God. The Nephites were believers in the one true God. The Lamanites had an entirely different view of God (if indeed he existed) and his purposes. And our prophets teach us that the final, destructive battle that will usher in the Millennial reign of Christ will also be a religious war.

Bruce R. McConkie said,

> The war they shall wage is a religious war. It will be against the Lord's covenant people, as we shall hereafter see. It will be waged by men who 'worship devils'; they will be in conflict with others whose God is Jehovah. And the blood and carnage and death will not bring the carnal and wicked warriors to repentance. Repentance is a gift of God; it follows faith; and the tares among men, who are being prepared for the burning, are without God in the world and have no faith. . . .

> We repeat: It is a religious war. The forces of antichrist are seeking to destroy freedom and liberty and right; they seek to deny men the right to worship the Lord; they are the enemies of God. The one-third who remain in the land of Israel are the Lord's people. They believe in Christ and accept Joseph Smith as his prophet and revealer for the last days. . . .

> In the coming day—a dire, dread damning day—woes without measure will fall upon men. Pestilence, plagues, and death will stalk the earth. The kings of the earth and of the whole world will gather to fight the battle of that great day of God Almighty. Their command center will be at Armageddon, overlooking the valley of Megiddo. All nations will be gathered against Jerusalem. Two hundred thousand warriors and more—two hundred million men of arms and more—shall come forth to conquer or die on the plains of Esdraelon and in all the nations of the earth. At the height of this war, the Lord Jesus will put his foot on the Mount of Olives and save his ancient covenant people. Of all this we are aware.

> Now it is our purpose to show that this war will be a religious war, a war in which the servants of Satan assail the servants of the Lord and those allied with them. The great and abominable church will wage war against everything that is decent in the world and will then be thrown down by devouring fire.[11]

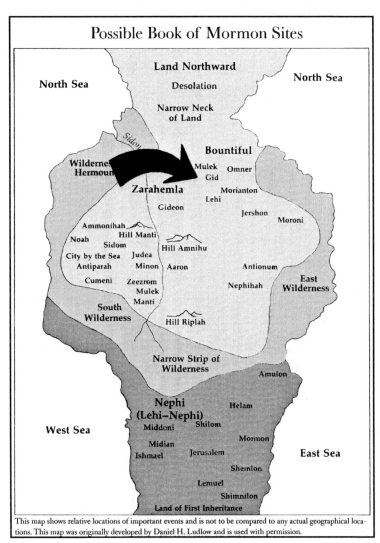

Possible Book of Mormon Sites

This map shows relative locations of important events and is not to be compared to any actual geographical locations. This map was originally developed by Daniel H. Ludlow and is used with permission.

Alma 55:1–3 • Moroni prefers peaceful means but is not afraid to fight. Ammoron's response increased Moroni's anger because he knew for a surety that Ammoron did not believe his cause was just; he simply wanted power (v. 1). He concluded that exchanging prisoners would only give him "more power than what he hath got" (v. 2). He determined that he would "seek death among them until they shall sue for peace" (v. 3).

Alma 55:4–14 • Moroni creates a strategy by which the Lamanite guards of his prisoners are made drunk. Moroni sought a man among his army who was a descendant of Laman (v. 4) and found one, whose name was Laman, who had been "one of the servants of the king who was murdered by Amalickiah" (v. 5). He sent this Laman with a small number of men to speak to the guards who were holding the Nephite prisoners in the city of Gid (vv. 6–7). When Laman approached the guards he hailed them as a Lamanite and told them that he had escaped from the Nephite army and had stolen and brought with them their wine (v. 8). He was received enthusiastically by the guards, who were anxious to drink the wine, claiming, "For we are weary" (vv. 9–11). Laman assented to their wishes, and they drank freely of the wine, which was very strong and made them drunk (vv. 12–14).

Alma 55:15–24 • Moroni does not desire blood and death, only the protection of his people. Seeing that the guards were completely drunk and had fallen into a deep sleep, Laman returned and reported what had happened to Moroni (v. 15). Moroni thereupon sent his men to the city of Gid, where they quietly threw weapons to the captives so that they were all armed—even their women and children (vv. 16–17). Mormon tells us that he could easily have slain the guards but deliberately chose not to because "he did not delight in murder or bloodshed, but he delighted in the saving of his people from destruction" (v. 18). He had achieved his purpose—arming the captives—and that was sufficient to ensure their deliverance (v. 19). He withdrew a bit and surrounded the armies of the Lamanites (vv. 20–21). When the morning came and the Lamanites awoke, they found themselves surrounded and their captives all armed (v. 22). The Nephite captains demanded that they surrender, which they did, pleading for mercy, and were thereafter taken as prisoners, while at the same time the Nephite prisoners were liberated (vv. 23–24).

Helaman's Army Fights With Faith

FACING ADVERSITY WITH COURAGE

When Helaman arrived in the lands of Nephi and Manti, he found the Lamanites had superior strength and the Nephite army had a serious lack of provisions and arms. While this situation was depressing to the Nephite soldiers under Antipus's command, they had decided to conquer or die in that spot. The addition of the provisions and two thousand men under Helaman's command made Antipus' army hopeful and joyous, and it gave them courage.

Alma 56:10 • The army of Antipus nearly falls into the hands of the Lamanites. Antipus' army "had been reduced by the Lamanites because their forces had slain a vast number of . . . men," when Helaman and his two thousand Ammonite "sons" attacked from the rear, defeating the Lamanite army.

Alma 56:19–20 • Helaman's small army is protected from the more numerous Lamanites. He observed, "We [were] favored of the Lord. . .[and] thus were we preserved" (v. 19) when Ammoron, the Lamanite general, commanded his troops not to attack them but to "maintain those cities which they had [already] taken" (v. 20). The year ended (65 BC, the twenty-sixth year of the reign of the judges), with Helaman and Antipus preparing to defend themselves and their city (v. 20).

Alma 56:34–43 • The first army that the young Ammonites face is the Lamanites' strongest and most numerous army. Logically, they had little chance of success, and, knowing this, the Lamanite army marched boldly forth to destroy them (vv. 34–35). Seeing them coming, Helaman and his young men fled northward, leading away this powerful Lamanite army (vv. 35–36). After traveling some distance, Antipus and his army fell in behind the Lamanites but did not deter them from continuing to pursue Helaman and his young men (v. 37). Night fell before the Lamanites could overtake Helaman's army, and before Antipus's army could overtake the Lamanites (v. 38). The next day, the pursuit continued with Helaman and his army fleeing deep into the wilderness with the Lamanites in hot pursuit until night fell again (vv. 39–40). Finally, the next day, when the Lamanites were upon them and might have destroyed them, they halted for some reason, and Helaman feared that perhaps it was a trap and was reluctant to turn and attack them (vv. 41–43).

THE INFLUENCE OF A MOTHER'S FAITH

Alma 56:44–48 • Helaman asks his young soldiers if they want to go against the Lamanites, and because of their faith in God they do not hesitate. In writing to Moroni, Helaman observed, "never had I seen so great courage, nay, not amongst all the Nephites" (v. 45). He lovingly referred to his young army as "my sons" and said to his young men, "God is with us, and he will not suffer that we should fall; then let us go forth; we would not slay our brethren if they would let us alone; therefore let us go, lest they should overpower the army of Antipus" (v. 46). These boys had never fought in a war, but they did not fear death. They cared more about the liberty of their families than their own lives. And perhaps most important, "they had been taught by their mothers, that if they did not doubt, God would deliver them" (v. 47). Because their mothers believed it, they believed it too (v. 48).

From this we can see how vital it is in our own day to teach our children gospel principles in our homes. They need to know that living righteously and heeding the promptings of the Holy Ghost give us power and direction in troubled times. But at the same time, they must not think that they will never have trouble or sorrow.

James E. Faust cites the tender comfort he received from his grandmother one night—with her assurance that Jesus was watching over them—as the "first cornerstone" of a testimony "forged by a lifetime of experiences."[12] And Abraham Lincoln said, "All that I am, or hope to be I owe to my angel mother."[13]

George Albert Smith said,

> [Referring to the stripling warriors and their mothers,] I think that is one of the greatest tributes that has ever been paid to motherhood—that in circumstances such as they were experiencing, when they were surrounded by enemies, they could train their children to have that faith in God that would carry them through and would bring them home without losing their lives. . . . I realize that there is a force in the Latter-day Saint homes where our wives and mothers and daughters are, and when it comes to faith in God and prayer it is equal to any-thing that the men may be able to muster. I fear that sometimes we neglect them. . . .
>
> [Speaking to the Priesthood] I am asking myself the question, "How many of you who are here tonight, before you came here to wait upon the Lord, put your arms around the woman who stood by your side, the mother of your children, and told her that you were grateful that she would keep the home-fires burning when you couldn't be there?" I wonder if we appreciate the daughters of God as He appreciates them. Do we treasure their virtues and their faith and their devotion and their motherhood as our Heavenly Father does?[14]

David O. McKay said, "If I were asked to name the world's greatest need, I should say unhesitatingly wise mothers; and the second greatest, exemplary fathers. . . . The noblest calling in the world is that of mother. True motherhood is the most beautiful of all arts, the greatest of all professions. She who can paint a masterpiece or who can write a book that will influence millions deserves the plaudits and admiration of mankind; but she who rears successfully a family of . . . sons and daughters whose immortal souls will be exerting an influence throughout the ages long after paintings shall have faded, and books and statues shall have been destroyed, deserves the highest honor that man can give."[15]

Ezra Taft Benson offered,

> Suggestions for mothers as they guide their precious children:
> 1. Take time to always be at the crossroads in the lives of your children, whether they be six or sixteen.
> 2. Take time to be a real friend to your children.
> 3. Take time to read to your children. Remember what the poet wrote,
>   > You may have tangible wealth untold:
>   > Caskets of jewels and coffers of gold.
>   > Richer than I you can never be
>   > I had a mother who read to me.
> 4. Take time to pray with your children.
> 5. Take time to have a meaningful weekly home evening. Make this one of your great family traditions.
> 6. Take time to be together at mealtimes as often as possible.
> 7. Take time daily to read the scriptures together as a family.
> 8. Take time to do things together as a family.
> 9. Take time to teach your children.
> 10. Take time to truly love your children. A mother's unqualified love approaches Christlike love.[16]

Spencer W. Kimball said, "To be a righteous woman during the winding-up scenes on this earth, before the Second Coming of our Savior, is an especially noble calling. The righteous woman's strength and influence today can be tenfold what it might be in more tranquil times. She has been placed here to help to enrich, to protect, and to guard the home— which is society's basic and most noble institution. Other institutions in society may falter and even fail, but the righteous woman can help to save the home, which may be the last and only sanctuary some mortals know in the midst of storm and strife."[17]

Alma 56:48 • The importance of punctuation. Originally, the Book of Mormon manuscript had no punctuation. Punctuation was added by the printer John Gilbert of Palmyra, who was neither a prophet nor even a believer in the book. He was however, a skilled typesetter and, for the most part, did an excellent job with punctuation. This verse may be one of the exceptions, since it seems to be punctuated incorrectly. Based on the context of the verse, instead of "We do not doubt our mothers knew it," it should probably be punctuated "We do not doubt, our mothers knew it." In other words, the faith of the stripling warriors that they would be protected was absolute because they knew that their mothers knew it was true.

Alma 56:49–54 • The combined Nephite armies finally defeat the Lamanites. Helaman and his army returned to fight the Lamanites and discovered that Antipus and his army had overtaken the Lamanites and a terrible battle was raging (v. 49). Being weary from the long three-day march, Antipus's army was on the verge of losing the battle, and would have done so had Helaman and his army not returned (v. 50). Antipus and many of his captains had been killed and his army was confused and in disarray (v. 51). The Lamanites pursued them until Helaman's young army appeared at their rear, whereupon they turned around to fight them (v. 52). Antipus's army reorganized themselves and attacked from the rear, and the combined army of Nephites were finally able to defeat the Lamanite army and take many prisoners (vv. 53–54).

Alma 56:55–57 • After the battle, Helaman inspects his warriors and finds that none of them have been lost. The battle had been severe enough that Helaman fully expected to have lost many of his soldiers in the battle (v. 55). But to his great joy, he discovers that "not one soul of them fallen to the earth; yea, and they had fought as if with the strength of God; yea, never were men known to have fought with such miraculous strength; and with such mighty power did they fall upon the Lamanites, that they did frighten them; and for this cause did the Lamanites deliver themselves up as prisoners of war" (v. 56). Their prisoners were sent back to Zarahemla for safe-keeping, and Helaman and his army marched back to the city of Judea (v. 57).

Remaining "Firm and Undaunted"

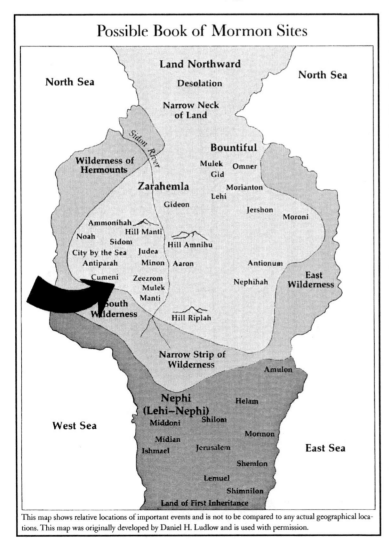

Possible Book of Mormon Sites

This map shows relative locations of important events and is not to be compared to any actual geographical locations. This map was originally developed by Daniel H. Ludlow and is used with permission.

Alma 57:1–18 • The Historical Setting: When Helaman and his army captured the city of Cumeni, they faced a major problem. The Lamanite prisoners of war rebelled, causing them so much difficulty that they decided to send the prisoners to Zarahemla, guarded by part of their Nephite army (Alma 57:16). With reduced numbers to protect themselves, the Nephites were attacked at Cumeni by another Lamanite force sent by Ammoron. The Lamanites were about to overcome the Nephites when the men who had escorted the prisoners returned to help. With their additional strength, the Nephites managed to defeat the Lamanites.

Alma 57:19–21 • The Ammonite soldiers are "firm and undaunted." Helaman attributed the eventual Nephite success

133

at Cumeni to (1) the courage and firmness of his two thousand Ammonite warriors, (2) their obedience to every command with exactness, and (3) their faith in what their mothers had taught them about God.

H. David Burton said, "In latter-day scriptures, the Lord often uses action words in the first sentences of his revelations. Interestingly, 'hearken' is used a number of times in this fashion. We are counseled by the Lord, through the Prophet Joseph Smith, to 'behold,' to 'hearken,' to 'listen,' to 'hear,' in over sixty revelations. . . . Perhaps the greatest obstacle to our ability to 'hearken courageously' to the word of the Lord involves our egos, vain ambitions, and pride. It seems that the proud find it burdensome to hear and accept the instruction of God. We are told in Proverbs that 'pride goeth before destruction' (Prov. 16:18). The proud are more anxious about man's judgment than they are of God's judgment."[18]

Alma 57:22–25 • Not one of them is killed, though every one of them is wounded. This battle had been bitter, and when Helaman inspected his young warriors he found that "not all destroyed by the sword; nevertheless, we had suffered great loss" (v. 23). Two hundred of his 2,060 soldiers "had fainted because of the loss of blood; nevertheless, according to the goodness of God, and to our great astonishment, and also the joy of our whole army, there was not one soul of them who did perish." though it was also true that "neither was there one soul among them who had not received many wounds" (v. 25).

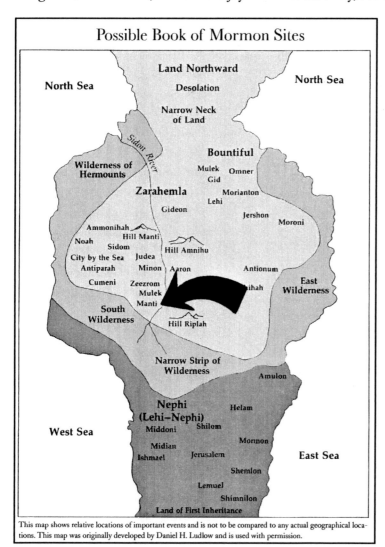

Possible Book of Mormon Sites

This map shows relative locations of important events and is not to be compared to any actual geographical locations. This map was originally developed by Daniel H. Ludlow and is used with permission.

Alma 57:26–27 • The stripling warriors "put their trust in God continually." Moroni wrote, "[The victory of Helaman's army] was astonishing to our whole army, yea, that they should be spared while there was a thousand of our brethren who were slain. And we do justly ascribe it to the miraculous power of God, because of their exceeding faith in that which they had been taught to believe—that there was a just God, and whosoever did not doubt, that they should be preserved by his marvelous power" (v. 26). He says that his young men's "minds are firm, and they do put their trust in God continually" (v. 27).

Alma 57:35–36 • Helaman rejoices over Gid's words because

Gid credits God for their success. Following their success at Cumeni, Helaman, Gid, Teomner, and their respective forces marched to the city of Manti and laid siege to it, eventually gaining the victory. In response, Gid rejoiced, "We are again delivered out of the hands of our enemies. And blessed is the name of our God; for behold, it is he that has delivered us; yea, that has done this great thing for us" (v. 35). Hearing this, Helaman rejoiced again over the goodness of God in protecting them and said, "I trust that the souls of them who have been slain have entered into the rest of their God" (v. 36).

Obtaining Peace Despite Adversity

Alma 58:1–7 • While the Nephite armies led by Helaman, Gid, and Teomner face "an enemy which was innumerable," they receive very little assistance from the land of Zarahemla. The Nephite armies turned next to the liberation of the city of Manti but could not lure the Lamanites out of the city because they remembered what had happened before when they fell for a similar trap (v. 1). They were too numerous to be attacked directly by the Nephite army. Helaman wrote, "It became expedient that we should employ our men to the maintaining those parts of the land which we had regained of our possessions [and] that we should wait, that we might receive more strength from the land of Zarahemla and also a new supply of provisions" (vv. 2–3).

Helaman sent a messenger to the governor of the land in Zarahemla, informing him of the needy condition of his army and requesting "provisions and strength from the land of Zarahemla" (v. 4). It did no good, while at the same time "the Lamanites were . . . receiving great strength from day to day, and also many provisions" (v. 5). The Lamanites used harassing tactics, sneaking out from their strongholds from time to time to try to wear down the Nephites without direct confrontation (v. 6). Meanwhile, the Nephite army waited "many months" for their needed help, until they were finally "about to perish for the want of food" (v. 7).

Alma 58:8–10 • When necessary supplies and men fail to arrive, Helaman's small army grieves and prays. They finally did receive some food, which was brought to them by a small army of about two thousand men. But that was all the assistance they received from Zarahemla while they were trying to "contend with an enemy which was innumerable" (v. 8). They had no idea why they were not receiving more help, and it filled them with both grief and fear for the safety of their nation (v. 9). In response, Helaman wrote, "We did pour out our souls in prayer to God, that he would strengthen us and deliver us out of the hands of our enemies, yea, and also give us strength that we might retain our cities, and our lands, and our possessions, for the support of our people" (v. 10).

Alma 58:11–12 • God answers their prayers by speaking "peace to their souls" and giving them "hope for [their] deliverance." As is often the case when we pray for a solution to our problems, God did not reveal to them precisely how he would deliver them, but he did send forth his Spirit to give them both peace and hope (v. 11). They remained fixed in their "determination to conquer [their] enemies, and to maintain [their] lands, and [their] possessions, and [their] wives, and [their] children, and the cause of [their] liberty" (v. 12). Thus renewed by their faith, they held on and persevered.

Alma 58:31–33, 38 • The Nephites eventually prevail. Miraculously, and with the Lord's help, the Nephites eventually prevailed and regained control of all their cities. Helaman noted,

"Our fathers and our women and our children are returning to their homes, all save it be those who have been taken prisoners and carried off by the Lamanites" (v. 31). He worried, "Our armies are small to maintain so great a number of cities and so great possessions" (v. 32). But he took courage from his "trust in our God who has given us victory over . . . those cities and those lands, which were our own" (v. 33), and he finished by observing, "We are in the possession of our lands; and the Lamanites have fled to the land of Nephi" (v. 38).

Alma 58:39–40 • They "stand fast in that liberty wherewith God has made them free." In all of the young Ammonite's army's battles "the Lord had supported them, yea, and kept them from falling by the sword, insomuch that even one soul has not been slain," exactly as their mothers had taught them to believe (v. 39). Despite receiving many wounds, "they stand fast in that liberty wherewith God has made them free; and they are strict to remember the Lord their God from day to day; yea, they do observe to keep his statutes, and his judgments, and his commandments continually; and their faith is strong in the prophecies concerning that which is to come" (v. 40).

They were brave and effective warriors, but, perhaps more important, they were faithful Christian men who did not forget who they were nor how they should conduct themselves in times of war or peace.

In the midst of World War II, our First Presidency advised Latter-day Saint soldiers to do the same:

> To our young men who go into service, no matter whom they serve or where, we say live clean, keep the commandments of the Lord, pray to Him constantly to preserve you in truth and righteousness, live as you pray, and then whatever betides you the Lord will be with you and nothing will happen to you that will not be to the honor and glory of God and to your salvation and exaltation.
>
> There will come into your hearts from the living of the pure life you pray for, a joy that will pass your powers of expression or understanding. The Lord will be always near you; He will comfort you; you will feel His presence in the hour of your greatest tribulation; He will guard and protect you to the full extent that accords with His all-wise purpose.
>
> Then, when the conflict is over and you return to your homes, having lived the righteous life, how great will be your happiness—whether you be of the victors or of the vanquished—that you have lived as the Lord commanded. You will return so disciplined in righteousness that thereafter all Satan's wiles and stratagems will leave you untouched. Your faith and testimony will be strong beyond breaking. You will be looked up to and revered as having passed through the fiery furnace of trial and temptation and come forth unharmed. Your brethren will look to you for counsel; support, and guidance. You will be the anchors to which thereafter the youth of Zion will moor their faith in man.[19]

The Moroni-Pahoran Letters
(ALMA 59–63)

Mormon's inclusion of Moroni's misunderstanding of what was happening within the Nephite government helps to show the greatness of Moroni's love of liberty, as well as Pahoran's forgiving and gentle spirit. Mormon included the full text of these letters, despite the limited space available on the large plates of Nephi, indicating the importance that he placed on them.

Alma 59:1–4 • When he learns of Helaman's successes, Moroni rejoices greatly and writes to the governor Pahoran, asking him to send reinforcements to Helaman. He shared the good news of Helaman's success with the people in the area where his army was stationed (v. 2) and immediately wrote to Pahoran to ask him to send the needed support to Helaman and his army (v. 3). He then continued his planning to take control of the remainder of the cities that the Lamanites had captured in his part of the land (v. 4).

Alma 59:5–13 • The Nephites lose the city of Nephihah even though Captain Moroni had supposed that reinforcements had been sent and that they could have defended

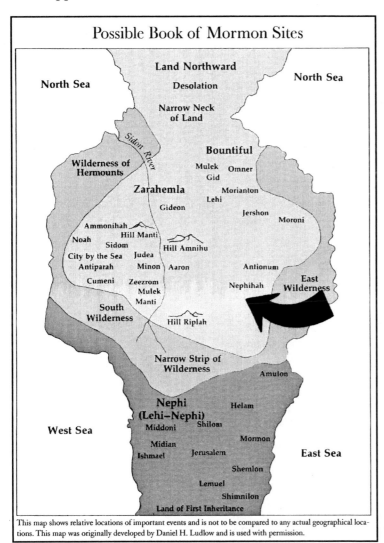

Possible Book of Mormon Sites

This map shows relative locations of important events and is not to be compared to any actual geographical locations. This map was originally developed by Daniel H. Ludlow and is used with permission.

themselves. The inhabitants of Nephihah included those who had gathered there from the cities of Moroni, Lehi, and Morianton, while the Lamanite army had grown with the arrival of those who had been defeated in the battle at Manti (vv. 5–6). This massive Lamanite army attacked the city of Nephihah, slaying many and forcing the rest to flee to the camp of Moroni (vv. 7–8). Moroni had assumed that Nephihah had received sufficient support from the government in Zarahemla to be able to defend themselves, and he was surprised to find that they had not. He had not sent his own troops there because he thought they would be fine and he wanted to hang on to the cities he currently held (vv. 9–10).

The loss of Nephihah caused Moroni and his chief captains to fear that "because of the wickedness of the people . . . they

[might] fall into the hands of their brethren [the Lamanites]" (vv. 11–12). And it also made Moroni angry with the government, "because of their indifference concerning the freedom of their country" (v. 13).

Alma 60:1–5 • Moroni is willing to suffer for his country and his people but feels that Pahoran has neglected them. Moroni wrote again to the governor and chief judge Pahoran (v. 1). He condemned the elected officers of the government for what he considered their neglect in sending reinforcements, weapons, and supplies to the armies who were defending the land against attacking Lamanite enemies (v. 2). He spoke of "exceedingly great sufferings; yea, even hunger, thirst, and fatigue, and all manner of afflictions of every kind" that his army and Helaman's army had suffered (v. 3). Even worse, he reported a great "slaughter among our people; yea, thousands have fallen by the sword, while it might have otherwise been if ye had rendered unto our armies sufficient strength and succor for them" (v. 4).

Alma 60:6–17 • Moroni's summary of Pahoran's lack of support. Moroni demanded to know "the cause of this exceedingly great neglect. . . [and] the cause of [their] thoughtless state" (v. 6). "Can you think to sit upon your thrones in a state of thoughtless stupor, while your enemies are spreading the work of death around you? Yea, while they are murdering thousands of your brethren" (v. 7). He lamented, "Ye might have sent armies unto them, to have strengthened them, and have saved thousands of them from falling by the sword. . . . and many have fought and bled out their lives . . . when they were about to perish with hunger, because of your exceedingly great neglect towards them" (v. 8–9). He accused Pahoran and other leaders of "neglect[ing] them insomuch that the blood of thousands shall come upon [their] heads for vengeance" (v. 10). He wrote, "Behold, could ye suppose that ye could sit upon your thrones, and because of the exceeding goodness of God ye could do nothing and he would deliver you? Behold, if ye have supposed this ye have supposed in vain" (v. 11). Moroni warned Pahoran that "the judgments of God will come upon this people, because of their exceeding slothfulness, yea, even the slothfulness of our government, and their exceedingly great neglect towards their brethren, yea, towards those who have been slain" (v. 14). These are strong words, written by a passionate patriot and general who felt that his army was very much alone in their efforts to defend Nephite freedoms.

While pleading for his valiant and righteous army, Moroni taught important doctrine about why it is that the Lord allows righteous men to die in battle, saying, "The Lord suffereth the righteous to be slain that his justice and judgment may come upon the wicked; therefore ye need not suppose that the righteous are lost because they are slain; but behold, they do enter into the rest of the Lord their God" (v. 13).

Harold B. Lee said,

> Recently I received a letter from parents in California whose son had written home just before last Christmas and then shortly thereafter his life was taken in the war in Vietnam. This is part of what he wrote, "War is an ugly thing, a vicious thing. It makes men do things they would not normally do. It breaks up families, causes immorality, cheating, and much hatred. It is not the glorious John Wayne type thing you see in the movies. It is going a month without a shower and a change of clothing. It is fear creeping up your spine when you hear a mortar tube in the jungle. It is not being able to get close enough to the ground when coming under enemy fire; hearing your buddy cry out because of being ripped with a hot piece of shrapnel. You . . . be proud of your American citizenship, because many brave and valiant men are here preserving your freedom. God has given you the gift of a free nation, and it is the duty of each of you to help in whatever way you can to preserve it. America is the protector of our Church, which is dearer to me than life itself." And then this young man said this very significant thing: "I realize now that I have already

received the greatest gift of all, and that is the opportunity to gain exaltation and eternal life. If you have this gift, nothing else really matters."[20]

Moroni reflected upon the reason the Nephites were suffering under attacks from the Lamanites, saying, "Were it not for the wickedness which first commenced at our head we could have withstood our enemies that they could have gained no power over us" (v. 15). The entire problem, he lamented, originated with Nephite dissension: "Yea, had it not been for the war which broke out among ourselves; yea, were it not for these king–men, who caused so much bloodshed among ourselves; yea, at the time we were contending among ourselves, if we had united our strength as we hitherto have done; yea, had it not been for the desire of power and authority which those king–men had over us; had they been true to the cause of our freedom, and united with us, and gone forth against our enemies, instead of taking up their swords against us . . . we [could have] had gone forth against [the Lamanites] in the strength of the Lord, [and] we should have dispersed our enemies . . . according to the fulfilling of [the Lord's] word" (v. 16).

While the leaders of government sat "on their thrones" and neglected the needs of their army, Moroni wrote, "The Lamanites are coming upon us, taking possession of our lands, and they are murdering our people with the sword, yea, our women and our children, and also carrying them away captive, causing them that they should suffer all manner of afflictions, and this because of the great wickedness of those who are seeking for power and authority" (v. 17).

Alma 60:18–22 • Moroni's strong accusations again Pahoran and the Nephite people. As his frustrations increased while writing to Pahoran, Moroni speculated on what kinds of intrigue might be happening in their capitol city. "For we know not but what ye yourselves are seeking for authority. We know not but what ye are also traitors to your country" (v. 18). Or, could it be "that ye have neglected us because ye are in the heart of our country and ye are surrounded by security" (v. 19). "Have ye forgotten the commandments of the Lord your God? Yea, have ye forgotten the captivity of our fathers? Have ye forgotten the many times we have been delivered out of the hands of our enemies? Or do ye suppose that the Lord will still deliver us, while we sit upon our thrones and do not make use of the means which the Lord has provided for us?" (vv. 20–21). He imagined that the Nephite government was content to "sit in idleness . . . surrounded with . . . tens of thousands, who do also sit in idleness, while there are thousands round about in the borders of the land who are falling by the sword, . . . wounded and bleeding" (v. 22).

Alma 60:23–31 • Moroni threatens to overthrow Pahoran if he doesn't repent and respond to the needs of his armies. Moroni asserted, "Do ye suppose that God will look upon you as guiltless while ye sit still and behold these things?" He observed, "God has said that the inward vessel shall be cleansed first, and then shall the outer vessel be cleansed also. And now, except ye do repent of that which ye have done, and begin to be up and doing, and send forth food and men unto us, and also unto Helaman . . . behold it will be expedient that we contend no more with the Lamanites until we have first cleansed our inward vessel, yea, even the great head of our government" (v. 23–24). Unless the needed support was immediately forthcoming, Moroni threatened, "I will leave a part of my freemen to maintain this part of our land. . . . And I will come unto you, and if there be any among you that has a desire for freedom, yea, if there be even a spark of freedom remaining, behold I will stir up insurrections among you, even until those who have desires to usurp power and authority shall become extinct" (vv. 25–27).

This is a strong threat, that he himself will overthrow the government of the Nephites unless they do their duty toward the people. To the casual reader it might even sound traitorous. As a free people, we abhor the idea of a military coup, yet that is precisely what Moroni is threatening unless Pahoran and his government repent of their neglect. "Yea, behold I do not fear your power nor your authority, but it is my God whom I fear; and it is according to his commandments that I do take my sword to defend the cause of my country, and it is because of your iniquity that we have suffered so much loss" (v. 28), and "except ye do bestir yourselves in the defence of your country and your little ones, the sword of justice doth hang over you; yea, and it shall fall upon you and visit you even to your utter destruction" (v. 29). "For behold, the Lord will not suffer that ye shall live and wax strong in your iniquities to destroy his righteous people" (v. 31).

Alma 60:32–35 • Moroni accuses Pahoran of unrighteousness. Moroni considered his cause to be both just and righteous. He viewed their battles as a fight for freedom but also as a fight for the cause of God against a vicious and godless enemy. He acknowledged that the Lamanites behaved as they did because of "the tradition of their fathers that has caused their hatred, yea, and it has been redoubled by those who have dissented from us," which might explain their unrighteous desires. But the Nephites should have known better, being the people of God. And to fail to support that cause was, in Moroni's eyes, a sin brought on by his government's "love of glory and the vain things of the world" (v. 32). He had apparently prayed much about this problem and claimed to have received inspiration from heaven concerning it: "Behold, the Lord saith unto me: If those whom ye have appointed your governors do not repent of their sins and iniquities, ye shall go up to battle against them" (v. 33). For him, it was a matter of "the covenant which I have made to keep the commandments of my God" (v. 34). This was no ordinary military leader, but one who sought to further the cause of truth, whatever the cost. He concluded with another warning: "And behold, if ye will not do this I come unto you speedily; for behold, God will not suffer that we should perish with hunger; therefore he will give unto us of your food, even if it must be by the sword. Now see that ye fulfil the word of God" (v. 35).

Alma 60:36 • Moroni's motives were pure; he was not seeking worldly power or honors, but was more concerned about the glory of God and the freedom of his people. Although he was a capable military leader, Moroni did not delight in the shedding of blood (Alma 55:19).

Dr. Hugh Nibley said,

> Moroni was bursting with pent-up emotions and the accumulated memories of reverses that could have been avoided and operations that could have ended the war had the necessary support been forthcoming from home. He knows, as Helaman suspects, that someone in high places is working against him, and for his noble and idealistic nature the thought that anyone should make capital of the miseries of others was simply maddening—yet he had seen that sort of thing going on in the capital all his life. . . .
>
> It was, to say the least, not the most tactful letter in the world, but Moroni's patience was worn out. Also it turned out, he was right—on every point but one. And that point was an important one: he had accused the wrong man. Aside from that, he had the situation correctly sized up—his long experience with the king-men had not been for nothing.[21]

PAHORAN'S GENTLE REPLY TO MORONI

Alma 61:1–8 • Pahoran explains the reason he has not sent Moroni reinforcements. At this point in the record, Mormon inserts the text of Pahoran's letter in response to Moroni's. It reveals much about the Christlike character of this noble Nephite chief judge. He began by assuring Moroni, "I do not joy in your great afflictions, yea, it grieves my soul" (v. 2). Nevertheless, Moroni's inspiration concerning unrighteousness among Nephite leaders was true. Pahoran sadly reports, "There are those who do joy in your afflictions, yea, insomuch that they have risen up in rebellion against me, and also those of my people who are freemen" (v. 3). He said, "Those who have risen up are exceedingly numerous" and "have sought to take away the judgment-seat from me" (vv. 3–4). They had "used great flattery, and . . . led away the hearts of many people" (v. 4). Their lust for power had caused them to withhold provisions from the Nephite army and to intimidate any freeman who might seek to come to the aid of the Nephite army (v. 4).

Reading all of this, we might reflect on the similarities between the Nephite situation and the one in our own day, where, while soldiers fight and die in foreign conflicts, politicians (of both parties) debate and maneuver in an effort to either gain or retain power. Meanwhile, the army becomes a pawn in their endless animosity. I, for one, am greatly saddened by what I see, and I must ask myself, could the Book of Mormon be any more relevant to our times? I think not. Mormon has included those events from his day that might to give us the knowledge and perspective in our day. As his Mormon's son Moroni said, "Be more wise than we have been" (Mormon 9:31).

Pahoran had "fled to the land of Gideon, with as many men as it were possible that [he] could get" and "sent a proclamation throughout this part of the land" causing freedom-loving Nephites to flock to his side daily "in the defence of their country and their freedom, and to avenge our wrongs" (vv.5– 6). This army of patriots was large enough that Pahoran said the traitors who had overthrown the government "do fear us and durst not come out against us to battle" (v. 7). Nevertheless, "They have . . . possession of the land [and] city of Zarahemla; they have appointed a king over them, and he hath written unto the king of the Lamanites, in the which he hath joined an alliance with him" (v. 8). They had promised to hold on to the city of Zarahemla while the Lamanite army conquered the remainder of the land, and then their traitorous king would "be placed king over this people . . . under the Lamanites" (v. 8).

Alma 61:9 • Pahoran's reply to Moroni is a classic in scriptural literature. It reveals important things about his character: (1) he was not angered by the false charges and wanted to retain his office only as a means of preserving the freedom of his people; and (2) he wanted to follow the Lord's will.

Neal A. Maxwell said, "There was an exchange of correspondence between Moroni, the chief captain of the armies, and Pahoran, who was chief judge and governor of the land in a time of great turmoil (Alma 60–61). Anxious Moroni did not have all the facts, as is evident in his biting complaint to Pahoran. Pahoran's meek reply is a lesson to us all, as it certainly must have been to Moroni. . . . Where individuals have said too much with too little data, meekness plays a very crucial, correcting role in what follows."[22]

Alma 61:10–14 • The principle of righteous defense of freedom. Pahoran promised Moroni that they would "resist wickedness even unto bloodshed" (v. 10). He made reference to the Lord's commandment that the Nephites should defend their freedoms and their families "even unto bloodshed" when attacked (Alma 43:47). "We would not shed the blood of the Lamanites if they would stay in their own land [and] would not shed the blood of our brethren if they would not rise up in rebellion and take the sword against us. We would subject ourselves to the yoke of bondage if it were requisite with the justice of God, or if he should command us so to do. But behold he doth not command us that we shall subject ourselves to our enemies, but that we should put our trust in him, and he will deliver us" (vv. 10–13). "Therefore, my beloved brother, Moroni, let us resist evil, and whatsoever evil we cannot resist with our words . . . such as rebellions and dissensions, let us resist them with our swords, that we may retain our freedom, that we may rejoice in the great privilege of our church, and in the cause of our Redeemer and our God" (v. 14). Pahoran was clearly a dear friend to Moroni, and the Nephites were greatly blessed to have a chief judge (Pahoran) and a commander in chief (Moroni) who feared God and sought only righteous ends.

Alma 61:15–21 • Moroni and Pahoran do not joy in contending with their own, but will destroy internal evil and rebellion to protect their citizens. Pahoran urged Moroni, "Come unto me speedily with a few of your men, and leave the remainder in the charge of Lehi and Teancum" (v. 15). Pahoran had already sent a few provisions to these other two generals "that they may not perish until ye can come unto me" (v. 16). He asked his noble friend to "gather together whatsoever force ye can upon your march hither, and we will go speedily against those dissenters, in the strength of our God according to the faith which is in us. And we will take possession of the city of Zarahemla, that we may obtain more food to send forth unto Lehi and Teancum; yea, we will go forth against them in the strength of the Lord, and we will put an end to this great iniquity" (vv. 17–18).

Clearly, Pahoran was renewed in his courage and faith by the receipt of Moroni's letter. And being a disciple of Christ himself he had not been angry with the sharpness of his accusations. Instead he said, "I do joy in receiving your epistle, for I was somewhat worried concerning what we should do, whether it should be just in us to go against our brethren" (v. 19). He expressed faith in Moroni's revelation that "except they repent the Lord hath commanded you that ye should go against them" (v. 20). He closed his epistle with an instruction for Moroni to "strengthen Lehi and Teancum in the Lord; tell them to fear not, for God will deliver them, yea, and also all those who stand fast in that liberty wherewith God hath made them free. And now I close mine epistle to my beloved brother, Moroni" (v. 21).

MORONI'S RESPONSE TO PAHORAN'S LETTER

Alma 62:1–8 • Upon receiving Pahoran's letter and request for help, Moroni takes a small part of his army to the governor's aid. When Moroni received Pahoran's epistle, "his heart did take courage, and was filled with exceedingly great joy because of the faithfulness of Pahoran, that he was not also a traitor to the freedom and cause of his country" (v. 1). The iniquity of those traitors who had taken advantage of the nation's weakened condition to seize power caused Moroni to "mourn exceedingly . . . because of those who had rebelled against their country and also their God" (v. 2).

Moroni did exactly as Pahoran requested, taking "a small number of men" and leaving Lehi and Teancum in command over the remainder of his army, taking "his march towards the land of Gideon" (v. 3). Along the way, he raised the standard of liberty in every part of the land through which he marched, gathering thousands to his patriotic cause (vv. 4–5). When he arrived in Gideon, he united his forces with those of Pahoran, creating an army that was "exceedingly strong, even stronger than the men of Pachus, who was the king of those dissenters who had driven the freemen out of the land of Zarahemla" (v. 6). Moroni and Pahoran took their army down into the land of Zarahemla and attacked the forces of Pachus in the capitol city (v. 6). As a result of this battle, "Pachus was slain and his men were taken prisoners, and Pahoran was restored to his judgment-seat" (v. 8).

Alma 62:9–10 • Circumstances under which capital punishment is justified. We are informed that "the men of Pachus received their trial, according to the law, and also those king-men who had been taken and cast into prison" (v. 9). And after having been found guilty of treason, "those men of Pachus and those king-men, whosoever would not take up arms in the defence of their country, but would fight against it, were put to death" (v. 9). All of this was done strictly according to law and "for the safety of their country," with those who would fight against the legitimate Nephite government of Pahoran "speedily executed according to the law" (v. 10).

With regard to capital punishment, the First Presidency (Wilford Woodruff, George Q. Cannon, and Joseph F. Smith) said, "We solemnly make the following declarations, viz: That this Church views the shedding of human blood with the utmost abhorrence. That we regard the killing of human beings, except in conformity with the civil law, as a capital crime which should be punished by shedding the blood of the criminal, after a public trial before a legally constituted court of the land. . . . The revelations of God to this Church make death the penalty for capital crime, and require that offenders against life and property shall be delivered up to and tried by the laws of the land."[23]

This appears to be precisely the procedure followed by Pahoran and Moroni in trying and punishing the traitors among them who had brought much death and destruction upon the Nephite nation.

Alma 62:27–29 • How they treat enemies who surrendered and desired peace. We may compare the swift justice traitors received with the merciful response to those Lamanites whom they took as prisoners during this long and difficult war. Many of these Lamanite prisoners "were desirous to join the people of Ammon and become a free people" and were granted their wish (vv. 27–28). Their conversion to a peaceful lifestyle was genuine, because all of those who joined with the Ammonites "did begin to labor exceedingly, tilling the ground, raising all manner of grain, and flocks and herds of every kind; and thus were the Nephites relieved from a great burden; yea, insomuch that they were relieved from all the prisoners of the Lamanites" (v. 29).

The Connection Between Righteousness and Freedom

Alma 62:39–40 • The correlation between the freedom of a nation and the proper function of the Church. The thirty-first year of the reign of the judges (60 BC) now drew to a close. They had been subjected to "wars, and bloodsheds, and famine, and affliction, for the space of many years. And there had been murders, and contentions, and dissensions, and all manner of iniquity among the people of Nephi" (vv. 39–40). Yet, "for the righteous' sake, yea, because of the prayers of the righteous, they were spared" (v. 40). This shows the effect of the prayers of a righteous minority.

Spencer W. Kimball said, "There are many upright and faithful who live all the commandments and whose lives and prayers keep the world from destruction."[24]

Ezra Taft Benson said,

"Righteousness exalteth a nation" (Proverbs 14:34). This is the key to understanding our heritage and this is the key to maintaining it. The foundations of America are spiritual. That must never be forgotten nor doubted. . . .

There are some in this land, among whom I count myself, whose faith it is that this land is reserved only for a righteous people, and we remain here as tenants only as we remain in the favor of the Lord, for He is the landlord as far as this earth is concerned. If we are to remain under heaven's benign protection and care, we must return to those principles which have brought us our peace, liberty, and prosperity. Our problems today are essentially problems of the Spirit.

The solution is not more wealth, more food, more technology, more government, or instruments of destruction-the solution is personal and national reformation. In short, it is to bring our national character ahead of our technological and material advances. Repentance is the sovereign remedy to our problems.[25]

Mark E. Petersen said,

Another ancient prophet spoke directly to modern America, foretelling the assistance God will give us if we serve him. Said he: ". . . this is a choice land, and whatsoever nation shall possess it shall be free from bondage, and from captivity, and from all other nations under heaven, if they will but serve the God of the land, who is Jesus Christ" (Ether 2:12).

And that prophet also said, even as did Lincoln, that if we in America fail to serve Jesus Christ, we will face certain destruction. This is a divine warning, first from the prophet of old and then from the inspired President of Civil War days.

Oh, America, turn to God. But do not give him mere lip service. Obey him with all your hearts, might, mind, and strength.

Let us save ourselves from the present crisis in the only certain way, remembering that "man shall not live by bread alone, but by every word that proceedeth out of the mouth of God" (Matthew 4:4). [26]

Ezra Taft Benson said, "We must protect the soul of America—we must return to a love and respect for the basic spiritual concepts upon which this nation has been established. . . . God rules this world—It is the duty of nations as well as men to own their dependence upon the overruling power of God, to confess their sins and transgressions in humble sorrow . . . and to recognize the sublime truth that those nations only are blessed whose God is the Lord."[27]

Joseph B. Wirthlin said, "The Lord's law for this land is declared in the Book of Mormon, where we read that this land is a 'land of promise' that 'the Lord God had reserved for a righteous people. . . . And whatsoever nation shall possess it shall serve God, or they shall be swept off.' The only power strong enough to withstand a fulness of iniquity is the fulness of the gospel of Jesus Christ."[28]

J. Reuben Clark Jr. said, "This is a Christian nation. Before the Revolution it was so in accord with law; since the Revolution it has remained so in fact. We, the people of the United States, guarantee full religious freedom to all within our jurisdiction, whether they be non-Christian or Pagan. But the nation itself is a Christian nation. Our standards and principles are Christian. Thus we of America can stand for no cause which would dethrone Christianity here and put in its place any other creed, whether non-Christian or Pagan."[29]

A number of the United States Presidents have acknowledged the same principles that Moroni and Pahoran espoused for the Nephite nation and that these many modern apostles and prophets have repeated in our own time.

George Washington said, "The success, which has hitherto attended our united efforts, we owe to the gracious interposition of Heaven; and to that interposition let us gratefully ascribe the praise of victory, and the blessings of peace."[30]

John Adams said, "Our Constitution was made only for a moral and religious people. It is wholly inadequate to govern any other."[31] Abraham Lincoln said, "It is the duty of nations as well as men to own their dependence upon the over-ruling power of God, to confess their sins and transgressions in humble sorrow, yet with assured hope that genuine repentance will lead to mercy and pardon, and to recognize the sublime truth, announced in the Holy Scriptures and proven by all history, that those nations only are blessed whose God is the Lord."[32]

And Calvin Coolidge said,

> Our government rests upon religion. It is from that source that we derive our reverence for truth and justice, for equality and liberality, and for the rights of mankind. Unless the people believe in these principles they cannot believe in our government. There are only two main theories of government in the world. One rests on righteousness and the other on force. One appeals to reason, and the other appeals to the sword. One is exemplified in the republic, the other is represented by a despotism. The government of a country never gets ahead of the religion of a country. There is no way by which we can substitute the authority of law for the virtue of man. Of course we endeavor to restrain the vicious, and furnish a fair degree of security and protection by legislation and police control, but the real reform which society in these days is seeking will come as a result of our religious convictions, or they will not come at all. Peace, justice, humility, charity—these cannot be legislated into being. They are the result of divine grace.[33]

Alma 62:41 • The effects of war. Like all forms of adversity, war can destroy the faith of a person or increase it. We are told that "because of the exceedingly great length of the war between the Nephites and the Lamanites many had become hardened" while at the same time "many were softened because of their afflictions, insomuch that they did humble themselves before God, even in the depth of humility." Spencer W. Kimball said, "One time or another we all face adversity's chilling wind. One man flees from it, and like an unresisting kite falls to the ground. Another yields no retreating inch, and the wind that would destroy him lifts him as readily to the heights. We are not measured by the trials we meet, only by those we overcome."[34]

Alma 62:42–62 • Following the defeat of the Lamanites, the Nephite nation prospered and began to expand. After fortifying "those parts of the land which were most exposed to the Lamanites," Moroni returned to the city of Zarahemla, Helaman returned to the place of his inheritance, and "there was once more peace established among the people of Nephi" (v. 42). "Moroni yielded up the command of his armies into the hands of his son, whose name was Moronihah; and he retired to his own house that he might spend the remainder of his days in peace" (v. 43). Pahoran returned to his judgment-seat; and "Helaman did take upon him again to preach unto the people the word of God; for because of so many wars and contentions it had become expedient that a regulation should be made again in the church" (v. 44).

The Nephites thereafter enjoyed a season of peace, which came because (1) they repented of their sins, were baptized; (2) they established the Church throughout the land; (3) they strengthened the law and chose new judges; and (4) they remembered God and humbled themselves before him, praying continually (vv. 45–62).

<hr>

Histories and Migrations

NEW CUSTODIANS OF THE SACRED RECORDS

Alma 62:52—63:1–3 • Both Helaman and Moroni pass away. In the thirty-fifth year of the reign of the judges (57 BC), Helaman passed away. His son Corianton had gone to the land northward with a shipload of supplies, for those who had emigrated there, and was therefore not available, as was his heritage, to be made custodian. So his brother Shiblon became custodian of the sacred records. Shiblon was "a just man, and he did walk uprightly before God; and he did observe to do good continually, to keep the commandments of the Lord his God; and also did his brother" (v. 2). Later, the sacred plates passed from Shiblon to his nephew, Helaman II, who was the son of his brother Helaman. The next year (56 BC), Moroni also died, ending the earthly sojourn of one of God's most noble sons.

Can we say too much good about Captain Moroni? It is safe to say that the Nephite nation would not have survived without his protecting care as a righteous leader and general. Mormon himself was called upon at a very young age to defend his nation, and certainly must have felt much in common with Captain Moroni. He so respected the man that he named his own son—Moroni—after him. Consider this compelling tribute paid to him: "[That] the Lord would deliver them. . .was the faith of Moroni, and his heart did glory in it; not in the shedding of blood but in doing good, in preserving his people, yea, in keeping the commandments of God, yea, and resisting iniquity. Yea, verily, verily I say unto you, if all men had been, and were, and ever would be, like unto Moroni, behold, the very powers of hell would have been shaken forever; yea, the devil would never have power over the hearts of the children of men. Behold, he was a man like unto Ammon, the son of Mosiah, yea, and even the other sons of Mosiah, yea, and also Alma and his sons, for they were all men of God" (Alma 48:16–18).

Hagoth and the Polynesians

Alma 63:4–9 • Hagoth: The Book of Mormon records that the Nephite civilization expanded into the land northward. A man named Hagoth constructed a ship to transport men, women, children, and provisions by way of the west sea to the land northward. While this ship was gone, Hagoth built other ships. On a subsequent trip, the first ship was lost. One other ship also sailed and was lost.

The Polynesian People: Latter-day Saints believe that groups such as these became the ancestors of the Polynesian peoples of the Pacific. This belief is substantiated by statements made by several General Authorities.

Mark E. Petersen said, "The Polynesian Saints are characterized by a tremendous faith . . . "Why do they have this great faith? It is because these people are of the blood of Israel. They are heirs to the promises of the Book of Mormon. God is now awakening them to their great destiny. As Latter-day Saints we have always believed that the Polynesians are descendants of Lehi and blood relatives of the American Indians, despite the contrary theories of other men."[35]

Joseph F. Smith said, "Stuart Meha, a Maori, sent a telegram to President Joseph F. Smith asking if his people perhaps were descended from Hagoth's people. President Smith replied, 'I would like to say to you brethren and sisters from New Zealand, you are some of Hagoth's people, and there is NO PERHAPS about it!' "[36]

David O. McKay said in prayer about the Polynesian people, "We express gratitude that to these fertile Islands Thou didst guide descendants of Father Lehi, and hast enabled there to prosper."[37]

Several important conclusions can be drawn from this information. Since Hagoth was sailing on the "west sea" to travel northward, and since the inhabitants of the Polynesian Islands are descendants of Hagoth, then we can assume that the "sea west" was the Pacific Ocean. And we can also assume

Possible Book of Mormon Sites

Land Northward

North Sea

North Sea

Desolation

Narrow Neck of Land

Sidon River

Bountiful

Wilderness of Hermounts

Mulek   Omner
Gid

Zarahemla

Morianton
Lehi

Gideon

Jershon
Moroni

Ammonihah

Hill Manti

Noah   Sidom
City by the Sea   Judea
Antiparah   Minon
Cumeni   Zeezrom
Mulek
Manti

Hill Amnihu

Aaron

Antionum

Nephihah

East Wilderness

South Wilderness

Hill Riplah

Narrow Strip of Wilderness

Amulon

Nephi (Lehi–Nephi)

Helam

Middoni   Shilom

West Sea

Midian

Mormon

Ishmael   Jerusalem

East Sea

Shemlon

Lemuel

Shimnilon

Land of First Inheritance

This map shows relative locations of important events and is not to be compared to any actual geographical locations. This map was originally developed by Daniel H. Ludlow and is used with permission.

that among these migrants who moved northward were the peaceful Ammonites who migrated northward to escape the Nephite-Lamanite wars (Helaman 3:4).

A tradition of never engaging in war existed among certain native tribes in Mexico. Jerry L. Ainsworth observes that "when the Spaniards arrived on this continent and began exploiting the Indians and destroying their culture, they encountered a group of Indians on the west coast of Mexico that would not fight. These Indians claimed a history of never having fought and stated they would not commence at that point. . . . Mexican history records that before AD 1600 the Pacific Ocean was called El Mar del Sur—the 'sea South'; [but] around AD 1600 it was renamed El Oceano de los Pacificos—the 'Ocean of the Peaceful People' (*México a Traves de los Siglos*, 2:459)."[38]

The End of the Book of Alma

Alma 63:10–17 • Shiblon by this time was about to die. Corianton had gone to the land northward in a ship to deliver more provisions to the people who had moved there. Therefore, prior to his death, Shiblon conferred the sacred records upon the son of Helaman, whose name was also Helaman and who is generally referred to by Book of Mormon scholars as Helaman II.

Notes
1. Daniel Ludlow, *A Companion to Your Study of the Book of Mormon* (Salt Lake City: Deseret Book, 1976), 236–37.
2. Joseph Smith Jr., *History of The Church of Jesus Christ of Latter-day Saints*, B. H. Roberts, ed., 2nd ed. (Salt Lake City: The Church of Jesus Christ of Latter-day Saints), 2:375.
3. Joseph Fielding Smith, *Doctrines of Salvation*, Bruce R. McConkie, comp. (Salt Lake City: Deseret Book, 1:155–56.
4. John Taylor, in *Journal of Discourses* (London: Latter-day Saints' Book Depot, 1854), 25:165.

5. Harold B. Lee, in Conference Report, Oct. 1970, 152.

6. David B. Haight, "Solemn Assemblies," *Ensign*, Nov. 1994, 14–15.

7. James E. Faust, "An Untroubled Faith," address, Brigham Young University, Provo, Utah, Sept. 28, 1986; *Ensign*, March 1988, 70).

8. L. Tom Perry, "Heed the Prophet's Voice," *Ensign*, Nov. 1994, 17.

9. Howard W. Hunter, "Follow the Son of God," in conference report, Oct. 1994, 87.

10. Gordon B. Hinckley, in Conference Report, Oct. 1973, 122, 125.

11. Bruce R. McConkie, *The Millennial Messiah: The Second Coming of the Son of Man* (Salt Lake City: Deseret Book, 1982), 387, 465, 476.

12. James E. Faust, "A Growing Testimony," *Ensign*, Nov. 2000, 53.

13. Abraham Lincoln, quotes in Paul Selby, *Lincoln's Life—Stories and Speeches* (Chicago: Thompson & Thomas, 1902), 221.

14. George Albert Smith, in Conference Report, Apr. 1943, 89–90.

15. David O. McKay, *Secrets of a Happy Life*, Llewelyn R. McKay, comp. (Englewood Cliffs, NJ: Prentice Hall, 1960), 2–4.

16. Ezra Taft Benson, *Come, Listen to a Prophet's Voice* (Salt Lake City: Deseret Book, 1990), 32–36.

17. Spencer W. Kimball, *The Teachings of Spencer W. Kimball*, Edward L. Kimball, ed. (Salt Lake City: Bookcraft, 1982), 326–27.

18. H. David Burton, "Courage to Hearken," *Ensign*, May 1994, 67–68.

19. Heber J. Grant, J. Reuben Clark Jr., David O. McKay, in Conference Report, Apr. 1942, 96.

20. Harold B. Lee, "From the Valley of Despair to the Mountain Peaks of Hope" (memorial service address, May 30, 1971, quoted in *New Era*, Aug. 1971, 5–6.

21. Hugh Nibley, *Since Cumorah*, 2nd ed. (Salt Lake City: Deseret Book and Foundation for Ancient Research and Mormon Studies, 1988), 362–63.

22. Neal A. Maxwell, *Meek and Lowly* (Salt Lake City: Deseret Book, 1987), 23–25.

23. *Millennial Star*, Jan. 1890, 33–34.

24. Spencer W. Kimball, *Ensign*, Jun. 1971, 16.

25. Ezra Taft Benson, *The Teachings of Ezra Taft Benson* (Salt Lake City: Bookcraft, 1988), 569, 580.

26. Mark E. Petersen, in Conference Report, April 1968, 62–63.

27. Ezra Taft Benson, *A Nation Asleep* (Salt Lake City: Bookcraft, 1963), 15, 43.

28. Joseph B. Wirthlin, *Ensign*, Nov. 1994, 77.

29. J. Reuben Clark Jr., in Conference Report, Oct. 1939, 10.

30. George Washington, *The Writings of George Washington* (New York: G. P. Putnam's Sons, 1908), 30:453.

31. John Adams to the officers of the First Brigade of the Third Division of the Militia of Massachusetts, Oct. 11, 1798, in *The Works of John Adams* (Boston: Little, Brown and Company, 1853), 9:229.

32. Abraham Lincoln, private paper, Sept. 1862, in John George Nicolay and John Hay, *Abraham Lincoln: A History* (New York: The Century Company, 1890), 6:342.

33. Calvin Coolidge, speech, on October 15, 1924, in *Foundations of the Republic: Speeches and Addresses* (Freeport, NY: Books for Libraries Press, 1926), 153.

34. Spencer W. Kimball, in Conference Report, Oct. 1974.

35. Mark E. Petersen, in Conference Report, Apr. 1962, 112.

36. W. A. Cole and E. W. Jensen, *Israel in the Pacific* (Salt Lake City: Genealogical Society of Utah, 1961), 388.

37. "Dedicatory Prayer Delivered by President McKay at New Zealand Temple," *Church News*, May 10, 1958, 2.

38. Jerry L. Ainsworth, *The Lives and Travels of Mormon and Moroni* (Peacemakers Publishing, 2000), 133.

LESSON 33
"A Sure Foundation"
HELAMAN 1–5

The Rise of the Gadianton Robbers, and the Ministry of Nephi and Lehi

The books of Alma and Helaman cover the history of the Nephites for the first century BC. Each book takes about one half of that century, Alma the first half and Helaman the second half.

THE BOOKS OF ALMA AND HELAMAN

	Alma	**Helaman**
Dates kept	90–51 BC	52–1 BC
Years kept	39	51
Number of chapters	63	16
Number of pages	160	38

The chapters in this lesson cover a twenty-eight-year period of Nephite history from the fortieth to the sixty-eighth year of the reign of the judges (52–24 BC).

Mormon devoted three chapters of Helaman—one-fifth of the book—to just three of the fifty-one years it covered. The reason for this kind of concentration is that during this time of extreme instability, the book of Helaman illustrates the main themes of the entire Nephite history:

The Nephite Pride Cycle: The Nephites wavered from righteousness to unrighteousness and back to righteousness, illustrating the main theme of the Book of Mormon—serve God or perish. We will discuss this phenomenon in greater detail in the following lesson.

Secret Combinations: Because people desired worldly power, they began organizing secret combinations, which eventually took control over Nephite government and society, and proved in the end to be the cause of their utter destruction. This is a theme that we will return to time and again throughout the remainder of the Book of Mormon, but it begins here.

Nephite-Lamanite Role Reversals: The repentant and righteous Lamanites—not the disobedient Nephites—drove the secret combination known as the Gadianton robbers from among them and sent missionaries to the Nephites. As a result, the Spirit of the Lord was poured out on the Lamanites but withdrew from the Nephites because of their increasing wickedness. The preaching of Nephi and Lehi converted large numbers of Lamanites and restored peace to the land for a time. In fact, the Lamanites became more righteous than the Nephites during these years, setting the stage for Lamanite prophets to come among the Nephites and call them to repentance.

Internal Strife among the Nephites
(HELAMAN 1–2)

CONTENTION FOR THE JUDGMENT-SEAT

Helaman 1:1–7 • At the death of Pahoran, the chief judge, a serious contention arises among the Nephites. At the beginning of the fortieth year of the reign of the judges (52 BC), Pahoran the chief judge died, and the Nephites became divided over which of his three sons—Pahoran, Paanchi, or Pacumeni—should succeed him on the judgment-seat (vv. 1–3). Pahoran had more than three sons, but only these three contended for his seat (v. 4).

A vote was taken, and the people elected Pahoran as the chief judge (v. 5). Pacumeni accepted the voice of the people (v. 6), but Paanchi and those who supported him were very angry, and he sought to cause a rebellion against his brothers (v. 7).

Helaman 1:8–12 • The results of Paanchi's rebellion. Capital punishment was the accepted punishment for treason among the Nephites, and after a trial Paanchi was condemned to death for seeking "to destroy the liberty of the people" (v. 8). This only increased the anger of his supporters, and they sent a man named Kishkumen to murder Pahoran "as he sat upon the judgment-seat." Kishkumen completed his task and then escaped (vv. 9–10).

Kishkumen and those who sent him "entered into a covenant . . . swearing by their everlasting Maker, that they would tell no man that Kishkumen had murdered Pahoran" (v. 11). The people had no idea it was Kishkumen who had slain Pahoran because "he was in disguise at the time that he murdered Pahoran" (v. 12). Therefore, Kishkumen and associates could "mingle themselves among the people, in a manner that they all could not be found; but as many as were found were condemned unto death" (v. 12).

Helaman 1:13, 18 • Pacumeni becomes chief judge, and the Lamanites come to battle against the Nephites. The people voted again and Pacumeni was appointed to be chief judge (v. 13). It had now been about one year since his father had died and his brother had assumed the judgment-seat—a year full of internal strife and intrigue. And as had happened so many times before, the Nephites were therefore unprepared to defend themselves against an outside attack from the Lamanites (v. 18).

Helaman 1:13–20 • Coriantumr boldly invades the center of the Nephite lands and the city of Zarahemla. As the next year began (51 BC), "the Lamanites had gathered together an innumerable army of men, and armed them with swords, and with cimeters and with bows, and with arrows, and with head-plates, and with breastplates, and with all manner of shields of every kind" (v. 14). And again, as was so often the case, the Lamanite army was led by a dissenting and traitorous Nephite—Coriantumr, a descendant of Zarahemla and "a large and a mighty man" (v. 15). The Lamanite king—Tubaloth, who was the son of Ammoron—believed that Coriantumr could prevail against the Nephites because of "his strength and also with his great wisdom" (v. 16). The king stirred his people up to anger and sent his army, with Coriantumr at the head, "down to the land of Zarahemla to battle against the Nephites" (v. 17).

The Nephites were taken by surprise, assuming that they were secure in Zarahemla, which was in the "heart of their lands" (v. 18). Before the Nephites were even aware, Coriantumr and his "numerous host" had marched speedily through the land and were falling upon the inhabitants of Zarahemla (v. 19). They quickly cut down the guards at the entrance, marched their entire army into the city, cut down anyone who opposed them, and took possession of the whole city (v. 20).

As with all incidents related in the Book of Mormon, we should ask ourselves, why did Mormon include these events in his abridgement of their history? He left out volumes of information from the original records he was using to compile this book. What is there about this incident that we need to understand?

It is instructive to contrast the motives and methods of Pacumeni with those of Paanchi and his followers (Helaman 1:6–9) in resolving conflicts. Pacumeni, when he realized he had lost the election, united with the voice of the people (Helaman 1:6). But Paanchi and his followers became angry and sought to encourage the populace to reject and rebel against those who had been elected (Helaman 1:7). When he was tried for treason and condemned to death under the laws of the land, his followers assassinated the duly-elected Pahoran (Helaman 1:9).

What kind of society do we live in today? Divided. Seriously divided. There is a cultural and spiritual gap widening between those who choose to be Christlike and those who want nothing to do with religion. There is also a political divide—bitter and rancorous—between people who identify themselves with one party or another. It is not enough to disagree with a president or prime minister or legislative body; warring parties seem to genuinely hate their opposition and will do almost anything to bring down those with whom they disagree.

So far, that has not included assassination, but some have openly wished for the death of those with whom they disagree. The results of elections are disputed in the courts, with losing parties sometimes unwilling to submit to duly elected officers. Established laws are ignored with impunity, with those who disagree with them feeling fully justified in their behavior. Opposition parties, once part of a "loyal opposition," are now bitter and hateful and determined to undermine those who have been elected.

And while we engage in these disputes, our enemies take note of our weakness. Are we vulnerable to an attack from those that would seek to destroy us? Are we perfectly secure within our borders? The Nephites thought so. And then suddenly, they found themselves overrun. I wonder sometimes if we are paying attention to what the Book of Mormon shows us is the result of such divisions and contention.

Bruce R. McConkie said, "Disputation, debates, dissensions, arguments, controversies, quarrels, and strife or contention of any sort have no part in the gospel; they are of the devil. The gospel is one of peace, harmony, unity, and agreement."[1]

Elder Ezra Taft Benson said, "There are some who, for the time being at least, are members of the Church but not in harmony with it. These people have a temporary membership and influence in the Church; but unless they repent, they will be missing when the final membership records are recorded."[2]

Helaman 1:31–33 • Coriantumr finds himself surrounded and is killed. His army is compelled to surrender. Coriantumr was certainly fearless in his attack upon the Nephites, but he was not a great military tactician. They had taken possession of Zarahemla but now found themselves surrounded by the Nephites in the very heart of their nation, unable to retreat— "neither on the north, nor on the south, nor on the east, nor on the west" (v. 31). Coriantumr was slain and his army was forced to "yield themselves into the hands of the Nephites" (v. 32). The commander of the Nephite armies—Moronihah, the son of Captain Moroni—took possession of the city and then, like his father before him, "caused that the Lamanites who had been taken prisoners should depart out of the land in peace" (v. 33).

⚜

Rise of the Gadianton robbers

Helaman 2:1–14 • Rise of the Gadianton robbers. The forty-second year of the reign of the judges (50 BC) found the Nephites at peace but without a chief judge, and with rancorous discord persisting between differing parties (v. 1). Through democratic election, Helaman, the son of Helaman, was appointed to fill the judgment-seat (v. 2). The same Kishkumen who had murdered Pahoran, upheld by his secret and oath-bound supporters, plotted to kill Helaman also (v. 3). A man named Gadianton, "who was exceedingly expert in many words, and also in his craft, to carry on the secret work of murder and of robbery . . . became the leader of the band of Kishkumen" (v. 4). Gadianton entered into a pact with Kishkumen and his murderous band "that if they would place him in the judgment-seat he would grant unto those who belonged to his band that they should be placed in power and authority among the people," providing sufficient motivation for Kishkumen to seek to destroy Helaman (v. 5).

As it turned out, one of Helaman's servants had been out in the streets in disguise and became aware of the plot to kill Helaman (v. 6). He gave Kishkumen some sort of sign which indicated that he was part of the secret band, and Kishkumen "made known unto him the object of his desire, desiring that he would conduct him to the judgment-seat that he might murder Helaman" (v. 7). His object—and that of all secret combinations—was to "get gain" and to obtain power through murder and robbery (v. 8).

The servant of Helaman agreed to take Kishkumen to the judgment-seat, and "this did please Kishkumen exceedingly, for he did suppose that he should accomplish his design" (v. 9). But along the way, the servant of Helaman stabbed Kishkumen in the heart, killing him "without a groan. And he ran and told Helaman all the things which he had seen, and heard, and done" (v. 9). Helaman immediately sent his guards out "to take this band of robbers and secret murderers, that they might be executed according to the law" (v. 10). Meanwhile, when Kishkumen did not return, Gadianton "feared lest that he should be destroyed" and took his band of followers "out of the land, by a secret way, into the wilderness; and thus when Helaman sent forth to take them they could nowhere be found" (v. 11). And with these events the year 50 BC came to an end.

Mormon here interjected the promise that "more of this Gadianton shall be spoken hereafter" (v. 12) and said, "in the end of this book ye shall see that this Gadianton did prove the overthrow, yea, almost the entire destruction of the people of Nephi" (v. 13), making it clear that he means at the end of the entire Book of Mormon and not at the end of the book of Helaman (v. 14). This is verified by Mormon's son Moroni, who said the secret combinations "have caused the destruction of this people of whom I am now speaking [the Jaredites], and also the destruction of the people of Nephi" (Ether 8:21).

Daniel H. Ludlow said, "The introduction to the band of Gadianton (see also known as the 'Gadianton robbers') would indicate that this group was organized by Kishkumen. However, upon the death of Kishkumen, 'Gadianton, who was exceeding expert in many words, and also in his craft, to carry on the secret work of murder and of robbery . . . became the leader of the band of Kishkumen' (Helaman 2:4). Gadianton then led his followers into the wilderness, and they are not mentioned again in the record for several years. But, as Mormon promised, 'more of this Gadianton shall be spoken hereafter' (Helaman 2:12)."[3]

The secret society of the Gadianton robbers has been compared to many modern-day organizations by various teachers and speakers over the years, and all of those comparisons are valid. The mafia, the fascists of Hitler, and the worldwide communist movement have all come to power through violence and have conducted much of their business through secret plots and activities. Yet, we now see an even more apt modern equivalent in the rise of worldwide terrorism.

These secret and murderous bands do indeed tend to hide themselves in the mountains and attack with furious and merciless force when the opportunity arises for them. Sometimes, just as the Gadianton robbers did, they will remain inactive and unnoticed for years before striking. And then, without warning, they will appear and slaughter the innocent as a means of striking fear in the hearts of people and governments, with the end-purpose of seeking cooperation in their plots from those who share their desire for power and from those who wish to "pay them off" to obtain protection. The ancient promise of Satan to Cain that he might kill others in order to "get gain" and do so in secret (Helaman 6:26–27) has arisen in every generation since then, and we are not immune.

Moroni warned us with clarity:

> Wherefore, O ye Gentiles, it is wisdom in God that these things should be shown unto you, that thereby ye may repent of your sins, and suffer not that these murderous combinations shall get above you, which are built up to get power and gain—and the work, yea, even the work of destruction come upon you, yea, even the sword of the justice of the Eternal God shall fall upon you, to your overthrow and destruction if ye shall suffer these things to be.
>
> Wherefore, the Lord commandeth you, when ye shall see these things come among you that ye shall awake to a sense of your awful situation, because of this secret combination which shall be among you; or wo be unto it, because of the blood of them who have been slain; for they cry from the dust for vengeance upon it, and also upon those who built it up.
>
> For it cometh to pass that whoso buildeth it up seeketh to overthrow the freedom of all lands, nations, and countries; and it bringeth to pass the destruction of all people, for it is built up by the devil, who is the father of all lies; even that same liar who beguiled our first parents, yea, even that same liar who hath caused man to commit murder from the beginning; who hath hardened the hearts of men that they have murdered the prophets, and stoned them, and cast them out from the beginning. (Ether 8:23–25)

Ezra Taft Benson said, "Our nation will continue to degenerate unless we read and heed the words of the God of this land, Jesus Christ, and quit building up and upholding the secret combinations which the Book of Mormon tells us proved the downfall of both previous American civilizations."[4]

Converts and Pride
(HELAMAN 3)

Helaman 3 covers about eleven years of Nephite history. During those eleven years, the Nephites again experienced periods of peace and periods of contention.

Helaman 3:1–2 • A brief period of peace. In the forty-third year of the reign of the judges (49 BC), the Nephites began a season of peace, with no contention but "a little pride which was in the church, which did cause some little dissensions among the people, which affairs were settled" (v. 1). The next two years exhibited little or no contention (v. 2).

Helaman 3:3–8 • The migration northward. In the forty-sixth year of the reign of judges (46 BC), "much contention and many dissensions" arose again, causing "an exceedingly great many" people to depart out of the land of Zarahemla and go "unto the land northward to inherit the land" (v. 3). The record indicates that they traveled "an exceedingly great distance, insomuch that they came to large bodies of water and many rivers" (v. 4). Once there, "they . . . spread forth into all parts of the land, into whatever parts it had not been rendered desolate and without timber, because of the many inhabitants who had before inherited the land" (v. 5). This was the land previously inhabited by the Jaredites, who had stripped it of timber. Mormon explains that "no part of the land was desolate, save it were for timber; but because of the greatness of the destruction of the people who had before inhabited the land it was called desolate" (v. 8).

Cement: Because they had no timber to work with, "the people who went forth became exceedingly expert in the working of cement; therefore they did build houses of cement, in the which they did dwell" (v. 7). In this place of relative peace, "they did multiply and spread . . . insomuch that they began to cover the face of the whole earth, from the sea south to the sea north, from the sea west to the sea east" (v. 8).

Dr. Hugh Nibley said,

> The mention of cement in the Book of Mormon . . . has been considered [a] great . . . anachronism. . . . But within the last ten years or so much has been made of the surprising extent to which the ancient Americans used cement, concrete, and gypsum in their building operations. . . . Over-lavish detail . . . extremely high relief, and the tendency to round off all angles in the heavy and serpentine profusion of line . . . is so characteristic of some early American architectural adornment . . . the direct heritage of a time when the builders worked in the yielding and plastic medium of cement (Tatiana Proskouriakoff, *An Album of Maya Architecture*, Norman: University of Oklahoma Press, 1963, xv-xvi).[5]

Helaman 3:9–11 • Conservation of timber and trade with other peoples. The people who migrated northward lived "in tents, and in houses of cement" (v. 9). And if a tree seedling sprung up "they did suffer . . . that it should grow up, that in time they might have timber to build their houses, yea, their cities, and their temples, and their synagogues, and their sanctuaries, and all manner of their buildings" (v. 9). In the meantime, since timber was exceedingly scarce, they engaged in trade (presumably with the people to the south from whom they had migrated) "by the way of shipping" (v. 10). Through this kind of trade, they were able to "build many cities, both of wood and of cement" (v. 11).

This kind of trade through shipping was precisely what Hagoth was doing when he eventually disappeared from among the Nephites (Alma 63:5–8). Presumably, some of Hagoth's people also settled in this "land northward" at that time, while some, we are told, eventually ended up in the Pacific islands. Here, again, we see a description of the Nephites living among others on this continent, not simply isolated on a vast continent without neighboring peoples.

A Period of Spiritual and Temporal Prosperity

Helaman 3:17–21 • For three years (46–44 BC) there are great contentions and wars, but Helaman experiences peace and has two sons—Nephi and Lehi. As mentioned previously, during the forty-sixth year of the reign of the judges (46 BC), there were "great contentions, and disturbances, and wars, and dissensions, among the people of Nephi" (vv. 17–18). These continued for the next two years (v. 19). But their leader, Helaman, filled the judgment-seat "with justice and equity; yea, he did observe to keep the statutes, and the judgments, and the commandments of God; and he did do that which was right in the sight of God continually; and he did walk after the ways of his father, insomuch that he did prosper in the land" (v. 20). And he had two sons born to him—the eldest whom he named Nephi and the youngest whom he named Lehi (v. 21).

Helaman 3:22–26 • For two years (43–42 BC) there is peace and prosperity, despite the presence of Gadianton robbers among them. These robbers had established themselves secretly "in the more settled parts of the land [and] were not known unto those who were at the head of government; therefore they were not destroyed out of the land" (v. 23). Like terrorists in any age, they infiltrated into society, waiting for their opportunity to strike.

One result of this peace was that "there was exceedingly great prosperity in the church, insomuch that there were thousands who did join themselves unto the church and were baptized unto repentance" (v. 24). The work of the Lord went forward with such power and success that "even the high priests and the teachers were themselves astonished beyond measure" (v. 25). Tens of thousands of souls united with the Church (v. 26).

Helaman 3:24–32 • Mormon's conclusions about this peace and prosperity. Mormon saw two great lessons in this increase of prosperity:

   ▷ The Lord is merciful to those who, in sincerity, call on his holy name (v. 27).
   ▷ The gate of heaven is open to all who believe in Jesus Christ (v. 28).

Mormon also noted that the word of God has three effects:

1. It divides asunder the cunning and the wiles of the devil (v. 29).
2. It leads the "man of Christ" in a straight and narrow course across the gulf of misery (v. 29).
3. It helps to land faithful men's immortal souls at the right hand of God (v. 30).

The result, says Mormon, was that there was "continual rejoicing" (v. 31), and there was "peace and exceeding great joy" in the land (v. 32).

Rising Pride and Persecution

Helaman 3:33–34, 36 • In the fifty-first year (41 BC), after two years of peace, some Church members began to persecute others. These contentions arose because of pride among Church members, who were "lifted up in pride, even to the persecution of many of their brethren. Now this was a great evil, which did cause the more humble part of the people to suffer great persecutions, and to wade through much affliction" (vv. 33–34). This pride arose "because of their exceedingly great riches and their prosperity in the land; and it did grow upon them from day to day" (v. 36).

Helaman 3:35 • How the humble Nephite Saints responded to the persecution and affliction, and the result. We are told that their response to persecution included (1) fasting, (2) prayer, (3) increased humility and faith, and (4) yielding their hearts to God. The result was "the filling their souls with joy and consolation, yea, even to the purifying and the sanctification of their hearts."

Elder Neal A. Maxwell said, "It is only by yielding to God that we can begin to realize His will for us. And if we truly trust God, why not yield to His loving omniscience? After all, He knows us and our possibilities much better than do we."[6]

D&C 76:41; D&C 88:74–75 • The principle of sanctification. Understanding Mormon's comments on how enduring persecution had "sanctified the hearts" of these Nephites requires an understanding of what *sanctification* means. Sanctification is the process whereby fallen man is enabled to become pure, holy, and eventually free from sin. This is not possible on our own; we are not capable of it as fallen mortals. But with the assistance of Christ, who "came into the world, even Jesus, to be crucified for the world, and to bear the sins of the world, and to sanctify the world," we can be "cleanse[d] . . . from all unrighteousness" (D&C 76:41).

The Lord has commanded his Saints in the latter days, "Assemble yourselves together, and organize yourselves, and prepare yourselves, and sanctify yourselves; yea, purify your hearts, and cleanse your hands and your feet before me, that I may make you clean" (D&C 88:74) so that he may "testify unto your Father, and your God, and my God, that you are clean from the blood of this wicked generation" (v. 75).

It is comforting to know that perfection is not a *requirement* for sanctification—it is the *result* of sanctification. We do "all we can do" (2 Nephi 25:23) with "full purpose of heart, acting no hypocrisy and no deception before God, but with real intent, repenting of [our] sins" (2 Nephi 31:13), and with full energy of "heart, might, mind, and strength" (D&C 4:2), and then the Lord Jesus Christ does the rest. By this process "just men" are "made perfect through Jesus the mediator of the new covenant, who wrought out this perfect atonement through the shedding of his own blood" (D&C 76:69).

Robert L. Simpson commented on how fasting and prayer aid sanctification:

> The world needs self-discipline. You can find it in fasting and prayer. Our generation is sick for lack of self-control. Fasting and prayer help to instill this virtue. . . . In addition to the occasional fasting experience for a special purpose, each member of the Church is expected to miss two meals on the fast and testimony Sunday. To skip two consecutive meals and partake of the third normally constitutes approximately a 24–hour period. Such is the counsel. Competent medical authorities tell us that our bodies benefit by an occasional fasting period. That is [one] blessing. . . and perhaps the least important. Second, we contribute the money saved from missing the meals as a fast offering to the bishop for the poor and the needy. And third, we reap a particular spiritual benefit that can come to us in no other way. It is a sanctification of the soul for us today just as it was for some choice people who lived 2,000 years ago [Helaman 3:35].[7]

The Holy Ghost is the "sanctifier" of our souls. While the Atonement of the Lord Jesus Christ makes our sanctification possible, the actual process of sanctification is accomplished by the Holy Spirit, which acts as a purifier or cleanser (2 Nephi 31:17; Alma 13:11–12; 3 Nephi 27:20; Moroni 6:4). Since the Holy Spirit cannot and will not dwell in unholy temples, we cannot receive this cleansing experience by deception. Knowing our hearts perfectly, the Holy Ghost can act only when we have truly done "all we can do" and when we humbly and sincerely seek the sanctifying power of the Atonement in our lives.

156

Lamanites and Dissenters Defeat the Nephites
(HELAMAN 4)

TRANSGRESSION LEADS TO TRAGEDY

Helaman 3:37 • Helaman dies in 39 BC, and his son Nephi becomes chief judge. The record indicates that Nephi "did fill the judgment-seat with justice and equity; yea, he did keep the commandments of God, and did walk in the ways of his father." He became one of the greatest prophets in the Book of Mormon. He was also a descendant of many faithful prophets: Alma, Alma the Younger, Helaman, Helaman II, and Nephi.

Helaman 4:1–5 • During the following three years (38–35 BC), the Nephites continue in pride and persecute the righteous. This increasing contention and persecution resulted in (1) further contention and even greater sins, (2) dissenters being driven out from the land, (3) dissenters allying themselves with the Lamanites and inciting them to war against the Nephites, (4) the Lamanites conquering many Nephite lands, including the land of Zarahemla and the land of Bountiful (in 35 BC), and (5) the loss of many lives.

Helaman 4:11–13 • The reason for Nephite losses during this war. Mormon made it clear that the Nephites had brought these tragedies upon themselves because (1) they were proud because they were rich, and (2) they withheld their substance from the poor, mocked sacred things, denied the spirit of revelation, murdered, lied, stole, plundered, and committed adultery (vv. 11–12). And "because of this their great wickedness, and their boastings in their own strength, they were left in their own strength; therefore they did not prosper, but were afflicted and smitten, and driven before the Lamanites, until they had lost possession of almost all their lands" (v. 13).

Helaman 4:14–18 • Moronihah, Nephi, and Lehi preach to the Nephites, who begin to repent and regain half of their lands and possessions. The Nephites' righteous general Moronihah (son of Captain Moroni) understood the reason for Nephite military losses, and he preached "many things unto the people because of their iniquity" (v. 14). Nephi and Lehi (the sons of Helaman) also preached "many things unto the people, yea, and did prophesy many things unto them concerning their iniquities, and what should come unto them if they did not repent of their sins" (v. 14). As a result, the people "did repent, and . . . they did begin to prosper" (v. 15). Encouraged by their repentance, Moronihah set forth to recapture lost Nephite cities, and recovered "one-half of their property and the one-half of all their lands" (v. 16) in 30 BC but "could obtain no more possessions over the Lamanites" during the following year (vv. 17–18).

Helaman 4:19–22 • Motivated by fear, the Nephites repent of their iniquities. The Lamanites had become so numerous that it was pointless to try to evict them, so Moronihah concentrated on "maintaining those parts which he had taken" (v. 19). The Nephites lived in fear "lest they should be overpowered, and trodden down, and slain, and destroyed" (v. 20). And thus humbled, they "began to remember the prophecies of Alma, and also the words of Mosiah; and they saw that they had been a stiffnecked people, and that they had set at naught the commandments of God" (v. 21). They also acknowledged that they had "trampled under their feet the [civil] laws of Mosiah . . . [and] saw that their laws had become corrupted" (v. 22).

Helaman 4:23–24 • Weakened by wickedness. Because of their iniquity, it would have been hard to distinguish a Nephite from a Lamanite during this period. "Because of their iniquity the church had begun to dwindle; and they began to disbelieve in the spirit of prophecy and in the spirit of revelation; and the judgments of God did stare them in the face" (v. 23). They had become "weak, like unto their brethren, the Lamanites" (v. 24).

Helaman 4:24–26 • Left to their own strength. Mormon said, "The Spirit of the Lord did no more preserve them; yea, it had withdrawn from them because the Spirit of the Lord doth not dwell in unholy temples" (v. 24). In this wicked state, "the Lord did cease to preserve them by his miraculous and matchless power" (v. 25). It was only under those circumstances, fearing utter destruction from the Lamanites, that they realized that "except they should cleave unto the Lord their God they must unavoidably perish" (v. 25). And as had happened repeatedly during this period of time, "they become weak, because of their transgression, in the space of not many years" (v. 26).

The Ministry of Nephi and Lehi
(HELAMAN 4–5)

RIGHTEOUSNESS CAN RESCUE A NATION

Helaman 5:1–4 • Nephi gives up the judgment-seat, and he and his brother Lehi devote themselves to preaching. Because the laws established by the voice of the people had become corrupt and most of the people were evil, Nephi decided, as Alma had done before him, that he could better serve the people by preaching the word of God. Those "who chose evil were more numerous than they who chose good, therefore they were ripening for destruction" (v. 2). They "could not be governed by the law nor justice, save it were to their destruction" (v. 3). Nephi devoted himself "all the remainder of his days" to preaching the word of God (v. 4).

This illustrates an important concept—that of "ripening in iniquity." The term is used five times in the scriptures to describe the Jaredites (Ether 2:9) and the Lamanites in the days of Nephi (1 Nephi 17:35), as a warning to those who inhabit the American continents (Ether 9:20), and as a warning to the entire earth as the Lord's Second Coming draws near (2 Nephi 28:16; D&C 18:6). It might also have been applied to the people in the days of Noah, to Sodom and Gomorrah, to the Israelites at the time they were taken captive into Babylon, and to the Nephites in the years prior to the Savior's birth and his visit to them. In every case, these wicked peoples imploded—they brought destruction upon themselves. God patiently waited and worked with them, sending multiple prophets with warnings of destruction if they did not repent and promises of redemption if they would. But at some point, it was "everlastingly too late" (Helaman 13:38), and then they were removed from their circumstances and sometimes from the earth itself.

I remember well one Sunday School class where a student objected to the flood of Noah and the fiery destruction of Sodom and Gomorrah. "How could a loving God do such a thing to his children?" this student asked. I asked him these questions: "How much chance did a child born into those societies have of knowing the difference between good and evil? Was agency possible in such a society?" The answer, of course, is no. So, we might ask ourselves how just it would be to send an innocent child of God into the midst of a completely perverse society, with zero chance of ever being able to choose good over evil. These are the kinds of circumstances that Satan loves and laughs at—times when the agency he sought to deny them in heaven is denied them on earth, and they are in his power.

When a society reaches such a state—fully ripened in iniquity—the only solution is to remove those circumstances and start again. Perhaps the people in Noah's day had a better chance of listening to reason in the spirit world than they ever could have in the midst of their wicked and perverse earthly societies. And those yet to come to earth would not be subjected to such unredeemable circumstances.

We are not immune to this problem in our own day and our own nation. The Lord has clearly warned us that we must be righteous or be swept off this blessed land (Ether 2:9–10). Brigham Young said,

> Assuredly in the preservation of virtue, morality, and intelligence she [a nation] may look for the perpetuity of her free institutions, and the preservation of her liberty. And in the moment of her disregard of these principles, when wickedness and sin can run riot with impunity, and not moral influence and force enough be found in the people to check it, and walk it under foot, then may she reckon on a speedy downfall. . . . In the sincere observances of the principles of true religion and virtue, we recognize the base, the only sure foundation of enlightened society and well-established government. . . . That city, nation, government, or kingdom which serves not God, and gives no heed to the principles of truth and religion, will be utterly wasted away and destroyed.[8]

"REMEMBER, REMEMBER MY SONS"

Helaman 5:5–8 • Names can help us remember who we are. Nephi and Lehi were obedient sons of the prophet Helaman and became prophets themselves. The Book of Mormon records that they "remembered the words which their father Helaman spake unto them" (v. 5). Helaman had said to them, "I have given unto you the names of our first parents who came out of the land of Jerusalem; and this I have done that when you remember your names ye may remember them; and when ye remember them ye may remember their works; and when ye remember their works ye may know how that it is said, and also written, that they were good" (v. 6). His hope, of course, was "that it may [also] be said of you, and also written, even as it has been said and written of them" (v. 7). So what's in a name? Is there any substance to the idea of giving children the names of their righteous ancestors? I believe there is, and I have done so with all of my own sons.

President George Albert Smith was similarly named. His grandfather, known as George A. Smith, was an apostle and a counselor to Brigham Young in the First Presidency of the Church. This fact had a great influence upon young George Albert Smith: "I have thought of this many times, and I want to tell you that I have been trying, more than ever since that time, to take care at that name. I want to say to the boys and girls, to the young men and women, to the youth of the Church and of all the world: Honor your fathers and your mothers. Honor the names that you bear, because some day you will have the privilege and obligation of reporting to them (and to your Father in heaven) what you have done with their name."[9]

Helaman also wished his sons to do the right things for the right reasons—not "that ye may boast, but that ye may do these things to lay up for yourselves a treasure in heaven" (v. 8). They were to seek "that precious gift of eternal life, which we have reason to suppose hath been given to our fathers" (v. 8).

Having the names of our righteous ancestors can help us remember who we are. Helaman was particularly focused on the importance of remembering. In the Book of Mormon there are over 240 instances of the word *remember* or forms of it, and fifteen of these instances are found in this one chapter (Helaman 5).

Helaman 5:9–12 • Remember the Atonement of Jesus Christ. The Atonement of Jesus Christ is the most important thing for all of us to remember. Knowing this, the Lord has given us the ordinance of the sacrament, where we are weekly reminded of the need to remember it. As King Benjamin said, "There is no other way nor means whereby man can be saved, only through the atoning blood of Jesus Christ" (v. 9). But, as Amulek taught, we cannot be redeemed "in our sins" but must repent of them first (v. 10). We need to build upon the rock of Christ so we can withstand the mighty winds and storms that Satan sends upon us (v. 12; 3 Nephi 14:24–27).

Spencer W. Kimball said, "When you look in the dictionary for the most important word, do you know what it is? It could be 'remember.' Because all of [us] have made covenants . . . our greatest need is to remember. That is why everyone goes to sacrament meeting every Sabbath day—to take the sacrament and listen to the priests pray that [we] '. . . may always remember him and keep his commandments which he has given [us].' . . . 'Remember' is the word."[10]

Helaman 5:13 • Righteousness is taught and preserved in the home. We are plainly told that "Helaman taught . . . his sons," not only these things "which are written" but also "many things which are not written." Here is the key to understanding why his sons were so well prepared to serve God in their own lives. They were taught by a righteous father in their youth, presumably in their own home.

The Importance of Following Counsel

Helaman 5:14–16 • Helaman's sons remember their father's counsel and follow it. At this critical juncture in the Nephite history, with their society quickly ripening in iniquity, Nephi and Lehi "went forth, keeping the commandments of God, to teach the word of God among all the people of Nephi" (v. 14). They started at the city Bountiful, then went to Gid, Mulek, and to "all the people of Nephi who were in the land southward; and from thence into the land of Zarahemla, among the Lamanites" (vv. 15–16). It was not sufficient for them to make their own lives righteous; their father had commanded them to teach the people, and they did.

Bruce R. McConkie said, "The great test that confronts us, as in every age when the Lord has a people on earth, is whether we will give heed to the words of his living oracles and follow the counsel and direction they give for our day and time."[11]

Ezra Taft Benson said, "One who rationalizes that he or she has a testimony of Jesus Christ but cannot accept direction and counsel from the leadership of His Church is in a fundamentally unsound position and is in jeopardy of losing exaltation."[12]

Helaman 5:17–19 • They experience great success among the Lamanites. Their preaching was powerful (v. 17). They confounded many of the apostate Nephites who had gone over to the Lamanites, "insomuch that they came forth and did confess their sins and were baptized unto repentance, and immediately returned to the Nephites to endeavor to repair unto them the wrongs which they had done" (v. 17). Eight thousand Lamanites were converted by their preaching in the land of Zarahemla, choosing to reject "the wickedness of the traditions of their fathers" (v. 19; Mosiah 1:5).

Richard G. Scott said, "I testify that you will remove barriers to happiness and find greater peace as you make your first allegiance your membership in the Church of Jesus Christ, and His teachings the foundation of your life. Where family or national traditions or customs conflict with the teachings of God, set them aside. Where traditions and customs are in harmony with His Teachings of the Prophet Joseph Smith, Joseph Fielding Smith, sel. (Salt Lake City: Deseret Book, 1976), they should be cherished and followed to preserve your culture and heritage. There is one heritage that you need never change. It is that heritage that comes from your being a daughter or son of Father in Heaven."[13]

Helaman 5:20–21 • A familiar prison. Having had such great success among the Lamanites who lived in Nephite territory around Zarahemla, they decided to go next to the very heartland of Lamanite society, the land of Nephi (v. 20). The initial reaction of the Lamanites was to arrest them, and they were "cast into prison; yea, even in that same prison in which Ammon and his brethren were cast by the servants of Limhi" (v. 21).

Helaman 5:22–34 • Miracles attend their preaching. They were surrounded by fire, which did not harm them (v. 23). The prison walls shook three times as if they might tumble down (vv. 27, 31, 33). A voice was heard from heaven three times, commanding the people to repent and to cease persecuting Lord's servants (vv. 29, 32–33). And a cloud of darkness overshadowed those assembled near the prison, making it impossible for the Lamanites to flee "because of the fear which did come upon them" (v. 34).

One of the most interesting observations from these events is the description of the voice of the Lord, which the people heard. The voice came "as if it were above the cloud of darkness" (v. 29). The voice they heard "was not a voice of thunder, neither was it a voice of a great tumultuous noise, but behold, it was a still voice of perfect mildness, as if it had been a whisper, and it did pierce even to the very soul" (v. 30). Yet, "notwithstanding the mildness of the voice, behold the earth shook exceedingly, and the walls of the prison trembled again, as if it were about to tumble to the earth" (v. 31). God did not need to shout at them. His voice was perfectly mild. Yet, it penetrated to their very souls and caused both the walls of the prison and the earth to shake.

Harold B. Lee said, "In the Gospel of John is related a parallel experience in the Master's ministry showing how, out of a multitude, only a few—or none—may hear God when he speaks. Only the Master, apparently, knew that God had spoken. So often today, men and women are living so far apart from things spiritual that when the Lord is speaking to their physical hearing, to their minds with no audible sound, or to them through his authorized servants who, when directed by the Spirit, are as his own voice, they hear only a noise as did they at Jerusalem. Likewise, they received no inspired wisdom, nor inward assurance, that the mind of the Lord has spoken through his prophet leaders."[14]

Boyd K. Packer said, "Inspiration comes more easily in peaceful settings. Such words as quiet, still, peaceable, Comforter abound in the scriptures: 'Be still, and know that I am God.' (Ps. 46:10). And the promise, 'You shall receive my Spirit, the Holy Ghost, even the Comforter, which shall teach you the peaceable things of the kingdom' (D&C 36:2). Elijah felt a great wind, an earthquake, a fire. The Lord was not in any of them; then came 'a still small voice' (1 Kgs. 19:12)."[15]

Helaman 5:35–41 • Aminadab's witness. In Zarahemla, Nephi and Lehi had been particularly effective among Nephite dissenters, and now here in the land of Nephi it happened again.

Aminadab, "who was a Nephite by birth, who had once belonged to the church of God but had dissented from them," saw in the midst of the dark cloud that had surrounded everybody that Nephi and Lehi's faces "did shine exceedingly, even as the faces of angels. And he beheld that they did lift their eyes to heaven; and they were in the attitude as if talking or lifting their voices to some being whom they beheld" (v. 36). He told the others around him to look, and they all wondered aloud, "What do all these things mean, and who is it with whom these men do converse?" (v. 38). Aminadab answered, "They do converse with the angels of God" (v. 39) and told the people that if they would repent and have faith in Christ, the dark cloud would be taken from among them (vv. 40–41).

Helaman 5:42–49 • More miracles occur among the converted Lamanites. Crying out loud for relief, the "cloud of darkness was dispersed from overshadowing them [and] they were encircled about, yea every soul, by a pillar of fire" (v. 43). With Nephi and Lehi at the center, "they were as if in the midst of a flaming fire, yet it did harm them not, neither did it take hold upon the walls of the prison; and they were filled with that joy which is unspeakable and full of glory" (v. 44). They were filled with the Holy Spirit and prophesied (v. 45). They heard a "pleasant voice" calling them to peace (vv. 45–46). They saw the heavens open, and angels descended from heaven and ministered unto them (v. 48).

Approximately three hundred people saw and heard these things (v. 49) and were commanded to "go forth and marvel not, neither should they doubt" (v. 49).

Reynolds and Sjohahl said, "The tidings of this glorious appearing were quickly spread near and far in the lands where the Lamanites dwelt. So powerful was the testimony, and so great were the evidences, that the major portion of the people believed, repented and obeyed the Gospel message. Then, like all true Saints, they manifested the sincerity of their repentance by works of restitution; they laid down their weapons of war, they cast aside their false traditions, their hatred gave place to love, and they restored to the Nephites, Zarahemla and the other lands which they had taken from them (30 BC)."[16]

Helaman 5:49–52 • These converts go "throughout all the regions round about," testifying of what they had heard and seen. Many (the "more part") of the Lamanites were convinced by this preaching and gave up their weapons of war and their hatred (vv. 50–51). Even more impressive, "they did yield up unto the Nephites the lands of their possession" (v. 52).

In the end, what was it that brought peace between the Nephites and Lamanites. Nephi had been the political leader of the Nephites but knew that the answer did not lie in weapons nor the acts of government. The answer—as his own father, Helaman, had taught him—lay in the preaching of the word. Alma observed many years earlier, "And now, as the preaching of the word had a great tendency to lead the people to do that which was just—yea, it had had more powerful effect upon the minds of the people than the sword, or anything else, which had happened unto them—therefore Alma thought it was expedient that they should try the virtue of the word of God" (Alma 31:5). And now Nephi and Lehi had found the same to be true in their own time.

Notes
1. Bruce R. McConkie, *Mormon Doctrine*, 2nd ed. (Salt Lake City: Bookcraft, 1966), 160–61.
2. Ezra Taft Benson, in Conference Report, Apr. 1969, 10.
3. Daniel H. Ludlow, *A Companion to Your Study of the Book of Mormon* (Salt Lake City: Deseret Book, 1976), 239.

4. Ezra Taft Benson, *A Witness and a Warning: A Modern-Day Prophet Testifies of the Book of Mormon* (Salt Lake City: Deseret Book, 1988), 6.

5. Hugh Nibley, *Since Cumorah*, 2nd ed. (Salt Lake City: Deseret Book and the Foundation for Ancient Research and Mormon Studies, 1988), 221.

6. Neal A. Maxwell, in Conference Report, Apr. 1985, 91.

7. Robert L. Simpson, in Conference Report, Oct. 1967, 18.

8. Brigham Young, in *Journal of Discourses* (London: Latter-day Saints' Book Depot, 1854), 2:176, 178.

9. George Albert Smith, "Your Good Name," *Improvement Era*, Mar. 1947, 139.

10. Spencer W. Kimball, "Circles of Exaltation" (address to religious educators, Brigham Young University, Provo, Utah, June 28, 1968).

11. Bruce R. McConkie, in Conference Report, Apr. 1974, 100.

12. Ezra Taft Benson, in Conference Report, Apr. 1982, 90.

13. Richard G. Scott, in Conference Report, Apr. 1998, 114.

14. Harold B. Lee, in Conference Report, Oct. 1966, 115–16.

15. Boyd K. Packer, "Reverence Invites Revelation," *Ensign*, Nov. 1991, 21.

16. George Reynolds and Janne M. Sjodahl, *Commentary on the Book of Mormon*, Philip C. Reynolds, ed. (Salt Lake City: Deseret Book, 1955–1961), 3:243–44.

LESSON 34
"How could you have forgotten your God?"
HELAMAN 6–12

The Nephite Pride Cycle

Mormon Illustrates a Repeating Pattern: The Pride Cycle

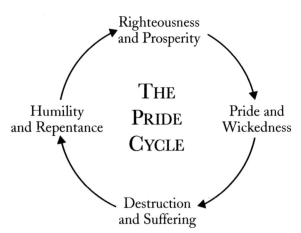

The pattern that Mormon introduced in the first five chapters of Helaman continues in this lesson. Now it becomes even more pronounced.

In Helaman 6–12, the Nephites move rapidly from righteousness, peace, and prosperity, through pride and wickedness, to periods of destruction and suffering. In these circumstances, they are compelled to be humble and to repent, which helps them to achieve again a state of righteousness and prosperity. From there, the cycle repeats itself. All of this happened time and again, so much so that we might be tempted to ask, what is wrong with these people? How can they forget so quickly? I remember distinctly, when I read the Book of Mormon for the first time as a young man, being annoyed with them. Surely, we're not so fickle and forgetful in our own day. Or are we?

PRIDE CYCLE STEP 1
RIGHTEOUSNESS, PEACE, AND PROSPERITY
(HELAMAN 6:1–14)

Helaman 6:1–14 • For three years the people live in peace and security, with growing prosperity. By the sixty-second year of the reign of the judges (29 BC), the majority of the Lamanites had become a righteous people, making them, as a people, more righteous than the Nephites. In a sobering role-reversal, many Lamanite missionaries were sent to preach repentance to the Nephites, as well as to their own Lamanite people.

The Lamanites are described as "firm" and "steady," while the Nephites are described as "hardened and impenitent and grossly wicked, insomuch that they did reject the word of God and all the preaching and prophesying which did come among them" (vv. 2–3). Among the righteous—both Nephite and Lamanite—however, there was "great joy because of the conversion of the Lamanites," and these two former enemies "did fellowship one with another, and did rejoice one with another, and did have great joy" (v. 3).

In 28 BC, Lamanite missionaries came down from their homeland in the land of Nephi and testified among the Nephites at Zarahemla concerning "the manner of their conversion, and did exhort them to faith and repentance" (v. 4). They preached with "exceedingly great power and authority" and brought many Nephites "into the depths of humility, to be the humble followers of God and the Lamb" (v. 5). After this, these Lamanite missionaries continued on to "the land northward" to continue their preaching, as did Nephi and Lehi (v. 6).

As a result of this preaching and repentance, "there was peace in all the land," allowing Nephites and Lamanites to freely mingle and enjoy "free intercourse one with another, to buy and to sell, and to get gain, according to their desire" (v. 8). The natural result of such peace was prosperity, and they all became "exceedingly rich, both the Lamanites and the Nephites; and they did have an exceeding plenty of gold, and of silver, and of all manner of precious metals" (v. 9).

The Book of Mormon here (v. 10) clarifies the names of the geographic regions in which these people lived. The "land south" was called (presumably by the Lamanites) the land of Lehi. The Nephites generally referred to this same area as "the land of Nephi." The land north was called Mulek, which was the name of the son of Zedekiah whom the Lord brought to this land at the time the Israelites were taken into Babylonian captivity. In much of the Book of Mormon record, this same area is referred to as the land of Zarahemla, which was the name of its capitol city.

All of these lands—both north and south—were full of "all manner of gold . . . and of silver, and of precious ore of every kind" (v. 11). In their state of peace, their craftsmen were able to "work all kinds of ore and . . . refine it; and thus they did become rich" (v. 11). Their agriculture also prospered, and they were able to "multiply and wax exceedingly strong in the land," raising "many flocks and herds" and making "all manner of cloth, of fine-twined linen" (vv. 12–13).

These are the fruits of peace—something which we all wish for but which escapes our grasp so long as we remain divided, oppressive to the needy, and war-like. It illustrates beautifully the fact that the answer to world peace and prosperity does not lie in armaments and political negotiations. Peace is the fruit of righteousness, and the preaching of the word of God will bring it about. Only through mankind's acceptance of the gospel of Jesus Christ will men and nations overcome the difficulties that seem to plague them in every age.

Sterling W. Sill said, "War doesn't solve a single human problem, and yet the one place where our generation excels most is in its ability to make war. . . . Our failure has been that while we have perfected weapons, we have failed to perfect the men who may be asked to use them."[1]

David O. McKay said, "No peace, even though temporarily obtained, will be permanent unless it is built upon the solid foundation of eternal principles. The first of these [is] . . . when we sincerely accept God as our Father and make Him the center of our being. . . . Of equal importance is the acceptance of the Son of God as the Savior of mankind. . . . Men may yearn for peace, cry for peace, and work for peace, but there will be no peace until they follow the path pointed out by the living Christ."[2]

President McKay also said, "In these days of uncertainty and unrest, liberty-loving peoples' greatest responsibility and paramount duty is to preserve and proclaim the freedom of the individual, his relationship to Deity, and the necessity of obedience to the principles of the gospel of Jesus Christ. Only thus will mankind find peace and happiness."[3]

That kind of gospel-induced peace was the state of the Nephites and Lamanites in the sixty-fifth year of the reign of the judges (27 BC).

PRIDE CYCLE STEP 2

PRIDE AND WICKEDNESS

(HELAMAN 6–10)

Righteousness and Prosperity

THE PRIDE CYCLE

Pride and Wickedness

Helaman 6:15–19 The Gadianton robbers flourish among the Nephites. After the Nephites became prosperous, many of them began to forget God and seek after riches and other worldly things (v. 17). This is the all-too-common course that people take when the Lord prospers their way. Satan creeps into the hearts of the people and "lulls them into carnal security and leads them carefully down to hell" (2 Nephi 28:20–22).

The Lord himself lamented concerning the Latter-day Saints in Missouri who had forgotten him in the midst of their initial blessings there: "Behold, I say unto you, there were jarrings, and contentions, and envyings, and strifes, and lustful and covetous desires among them; therefore by these things they polluted their inheritances. They were slow to hearken unto the voice of the Lord their God; therefore, the Lord their God is slow to hearken unto their prayers, to answer them in the day of their trouble. In the day of their peace they esteemed lightly my counsel; but, in the day of their trouble, of necessity they feel after me" (D&C 101:6–8).

Ezra Taft Benson said,

> Great civilizations have died by suicide. The first free people, the Greeks, died thus. And why did Greece fall? A slackness and softness finally came over them to their ruin. In the end more than they wanted freedom they wanted security, a comfortable life, and they lost all—security, comfort and freedom. We as a people have never known bondage. Liberty has always been our blessed lot. Few of us have ever seen people who have lost their freedom—their liberty. And when reminded of the danger of losing our liberty and independence our attitude has usually been "it cannot happen here." We must never forget that nations may—and they usually do—sow the seeds of their own destruction while enjoying unprecedented prosperity.[4]

When the Nephites began to "set their hearts upon their riches," the Gadianton robbers began to flourish again among them (vv. 17–18). They accepted these ungodly conspiracies because of their desire for power and riches, hoping to be able to participate in the spoils they might produce. As part of these conspiracies, in the sixty-sixth year of the reign of the judges (26 BC), the Gadianton robbers murdered Cezoram, the chief judge, and also his son who succeeded him on the judgment-seat.

Helaman 6:26–38 • Characteristics of secret combinations. Helaman 6 and Ether 8 provide us with important insights into secret combinations.

1. The devil is the inspiration and source of all such organizations (vv. 26–30). Mormon pointed out that Satan is the grand conspirator, the real organizer of all such organizations.

2. They are a wickedness "above all the wickedness of the whole earth" (3 Nephi 9:9; Ether 8:18). While individuals may rob, steal, plunder, and murder, the truly vast crimes of mankind involve plunder and killing on a national or an international scale involving millions of lives.

3. They flourish and thrive when the majority of the people are wicked and seek to benefit from the spoils of such wickedness (vv. 21, 38).

4. Secrecy is one of the basic operating tenets of such organizations (vv. 22, 25, 26).

5. Their secrecy also involves covenant making—a vow to maintain the secret of the conspiracy (v. 22, 25, 26).

6. Their objectives are power or gain or both (v. 38; Ether 8:22; Moses 5:31–33). Since the government is a source of great power, it is not surprising that often the target of their action is to take over the reins of government (Helaman 1:1–4; 2:4, 5; 3 Nephi 3:6; 6:30; 7:12; Ether 9:1–6; 13:18).

7. They use immorality, money, and violence to achieve their ends (v. 15, 17; Ether 8:10). Assassinations of government leaders to bring their own people to power is common.

8. The only way to stamp them out, once they are established and begin to flourish, is through conversion of the people to righteousness (v. 37; 3 Nephi 5:4–6).

David O. McKay said,

Force and compulsion will never establish the ideal society. This can come only by a transformation within the individual soul—a life redeemed from sin and brought in harmony with the divine will. Instead of selfishness, men must be willing to dedicate their ability, their possessions, their lives, if necessary, their fortunes, and their sacred honor for the alleviation of the ills of mankind. Hate must be supplanted by sympathy and forbearance. Peace and true prosperity can come only by conforming our lives to the law of love, the law of the principles of the gospel of Jesus Christ. A mere appreciation of the social ethics of Jesus is not sufficient—men's hearts must be changed! . . . Only thus will mankind find peace and happiness.[5]

Helaman 6:20–21 • Differences in Lamanite and Nephite responses to the Gadianton robbers. The Lamanites responded to the Gadianton robbers by teaching the gospel to them. The Nephites responded by joining with them in their corruption. Consider the following list of differences between the Nephites and Lamanites in 24 BC.

Nephites (vv. 2, 4–5, 17, 21, 23, 36–37)	Lamanites (vv. 4–5, 20, 38–39)
Hardened	Many converted
Impenitent	Bore testimony
Grossly wicked	Had the spirit of the Lord
Rejected word of God	Hunted down and preached to Gadianton robbers
Rejected God	Drove unrepentant Gadianton robbers from among them
Rejected prophets	
Hearts set on riches	
Secret murders	
Supported robbers	
Robbers controlled government	

Helaman 6:32 • The rapid onset of Nephite corruption. The "more part" of the Nephites' corruption came within "the space of not many years"—indeed, most of it happened in a single year, the sixty-seventh year of the reign of the judges (25 BC).

The Spirit Withdraws from the Nephites

Helaman 6:35–36 • The Spirit withdraws from the Nephites but is "poured out . . . upon the Lamanites." The Nephites lost the spirit "because of the wickedness and the hardness of their hearts" (v. 35). Meanwhile, the Lamanites were blessed with the Spirit "because of their easiness and willingness to believe in his words" (v. 36).

D&C 1:31–35 • Similar conditions in our own day. The Book of Mormon was written for our day. The Nephites never saw it, nor did the Lamanites. Mormon placed these events in the record for our benefit, in our own day. We may therefore expect that he knew we would face a similar situation and need to be warned. And indeed we do. The Lord has withdrawn his Spirit from the earth, and it is again ripening in iniquity.

The Prophet Joseph Smith said in 1833, "The Lord declared to His servants, some eighteen months since, that He was then withdrawing His Spirit from the earth; and we can see that such is the fact, for not only the churches are dwindling away, but there are no conversions, or but very few: and this is not all, the governments of the earth are thrown into confusion and division; and DESTRUCTION, to the eye of the spiritual beholder, seems to be written by the finger of an invisible hand, in large capitals, upon almost every thing we behold."[6]

President Joseph Fielding Smith said, "Now because of the wickedness of the world, that Spirit [of Christ] has been withdrawn, and when the Spirit of the Lord is not striving with men, the spirit of Satan is. . . . The conditions prophesied in D&C 1:35 have been realized."[7]

Helaman 6:39–40 • The Nephites lose control of their government to the Gadianton robbers. Corruption had become so complete that the conspiratorial Gadianton bands "did obtain the sole management of the government" (v. 39). Modern prophets have predicted the same kind of corruption in our own day while Gadianton-like terrorists undermine and then conquer governments all over the world.

Bruce R. McConkie prophesied concerning the coming days before the Second Coming of Christ:

> Bands of Gadianton robbers will infest every nation, immorality and murder and crime will increase, and it will seem as though every man's hand is against his brother. . . .
>
> It is one of the sad heresies of our time that peace will be gained by weary diplomats as they prepare treaties of compromise, or that the Millennium will be ushered in because men will learn to live in peace and to keep the commandments, or that the predicted plagues and promised desolations of latter days can in some way be avoided. We must do all we can to proclaim peace, to avoid war, to heal disease, to prepare for natural disasters—but with it all, that which is to be shall be.
>
> Knowing what we know, and having the light and understanding that has come to us, we must—as individuals and as a Church—use our talents, strengths, energies, abilities, and means to prepare for whatever may befall us and our children. We know that the world will go on in wickedness until the end of the world, which is the destruction of the wicked. We shall continue to

live in the world, but with the Lord's help we shall not be of the world. We shall strive to overcome carnality and worldliness of every sort and shall invite all men to flee from Babylon, join with us, and live as becometh Saints. . . .

We do not know when the calamities and troubles of the last days will fall upon any of us as individuals or upon bodies of the Saints. The Lord deliberately withholds from us the day and hour of his coming and of the tribulations which shall precede it—all as part of the testing and probationary experiences of mortality. He simply tells us to watch and be ready. . . .We do not say that all of the Saints will be spared and saved from the coming day of desolation. But we do say there is no promise of safety and no promise of security except for those who love the Lord and who are seeking to do all that he commands.

It may be, for instance, that nothing except the power of faith and the authority of the priesthood can save individuals and congregations from the *atomic holocausts that surely shall be* (emphasis added).

And so we raise the warning voice and say: Take heed; prepare; watch and be ready. There is no security in any course except the course of obedience and conformity and righteousness.[8]

Godless terrorists care not a whit about the poor and oppressed. The Gadiantons during this period of Book of Mormon history "did trample under their feet and smite and rend and turn their backs upon the poor and the meek" (v. 39). In our own time, we see them slaughtering the poor as well as the mighty. While they bathe themselves in money from their co-conspirators and the power they have obtained by terrorizing the nations, they send forth hopeless youths whom they have convinced to kill themselves for the cause of their anti-Christ conspiracies. Notice, please, that they themselves decline to make any such sacrifice. They reserve that "honor" for the poor and the hopeless.

The Book of Mormon records that the Nephites "were in an awful state, and ripening for an everlasting destruction" under these conditions (v. 40). So, too, are we unless the nations repent of their conspiratorial wickedness.

Nephi Returns from His Mission and Observes the Nephites' Wickedness

Helaman 7:1–3 • The people in the land northward reject the words of Nephi. In the sixty-ninth year of the reign of the judges (23 BC), "Nephi, the son of Helaman, returned to the land of Zarahemla from the land northward" (v. 1). He had been among those people "preach[ing] the word of God unto them, and . . . prophesy[ing] many things" (v. 2). Sadly, "they did reject all his words, insomuch that he could not stay among them, but returned again unto the land of his nativity" (v. 3).

Helaman 7:4–5 • General corruption in government. When he returned, Nephi found that the Gadianton robbers controlled the Nephite government. They had usurped power and set aside the commandments of God. They "condemn[ed] the righteous because of their righteousness; letting the guilty and the wicked go unpunished because of their money" and placed their co-conspirators "at the head of government, to rule and do according to their wills, that they might get gain and glory of the world, and . . . that they might the more easily commit adultery, and steal, and kill, and do according to their own wills" (vv. 4–5).

Helaman 7:6–12 • Nephi sorrows over his people and prays from his tower. The Book of

Mormon records that "when Nephi saw it, his heart was swollen with sorrow . . . and he did exclaim in the agony of his soul: Oh, that I could have had my days in the days when my father Nephi first came out of the land of Jerusalem, that I could have joyed with him in the promised land; then were his people easy to be entreated, firm to keep the commandments of God, and slow to be led to do iniquity; and they were quick to hearken unto the words of the Lord—Yea, if my days could have been in those days, then would my soul have had joy in the righteousness of my brethren" (vv. 6–8).

We see again how Nephi was impacted by the name that his father had given him, and his wish to be like his righteous ancestor. Of course, the original Nephi sorrowed much over the wickedness of many of his father Lehi's family, but he also enjoyed a group of followers who remained righteous. Nephi the son of Helaman longed for a similar people of righteousness and was "filled with sorrow" because of the wickedness of his people (v. 9).

Nephi resorted to a "tower" that was in his garden, which was by the highway that led to the chief market of Zarahemla, and "bowed himself upon the tower" (v. 10). One might wonder why he would pray from the top of a tower, since we do no such thing in our own day. To appreciate the importance of this procedure, we have to understand why Nephite "towers" were built and what they looked like. The image at left is typical of the small, personal worship towers that graced the property of some Mesoamerican peoples. Like the larger pyramids that can be found all over North and South America, these mini-towers were sacred places for people wishing to "stand on holy ground" as they worshipped.

Jerry L. Ainsworth wrote,

Small, personal towers were used by the Maya. King Benjamin and Nephi both made use of such towers

> The book of Moses speaks of the Lord's coming to dwell with his people—who were called Zion—in the days of Enoch. The "glory of the Lord" came upon his people and they were "blessed upon the mountains, and upon the high places" (Moses 7:16–17. The "high places" spoken of may be a reference to pyramid-style places of worship. . . .
>
> In Central America today, the ruins of pyramids are generally crowned with temples or sacred sanctuaries for worship. Evidence of sacrifices made at such sites abounds. . . . A similar trend appears in the Old Testament. At first, Israel's 'high places' were used for offering acceptable sacrifices to God (1 Samuel 9:10–19; 1 Kings 3:2–4). Later, at the corruption of the people's religion, the "high places" became sites for idolatrous practices (1 Kings 12:28–33). . . .
>
> Maya scholars Linda Schele and David Freidel consider the pyramidal temples found in the lowlands of Central America to be "symbolic sacred mountains" that were used for worship (*A Forest of Kings: The Untold Story of the Ancient Maya*, 106).[9]

While Nephi was atop his tower, "certain men passing by . . . saw Nephi as he was pouring out his soul unto God upon the tower; and they ran and told the people what they had seen"

(v. 11). Apparently his mourning was so profound that they wanted to "know the cause of so great mourning for the wickedness of the people" (v. 11). When Nephi arose from his prayer, "he beheld the multitudes of people who had gathered together." He asked them why they had gathered—perhaps "that I may tell you of your iniquities?" (vv. 12–13). He explained, "I have got upon my tower that I might pour out my soul unto my God, because of the exceeding sorrow of my heart, which is because of your iniquities" (v. 14).

Helaman 2:13–14 • The reason for Nephi's deep concern. As discussed earlier in this chapter, secret societies flourished among the Nephites because of the general wickedness of the people. And eventually, secret societies caused the destruction of the Nephite civilization as they had the Jaredites before them. The Nephites were now firmly in the grasp of these godless conspirators and terrorists, and Nephi knew only too well what the eventual outcome would be if they did not repent. It was for that reason they he mourned so heavily and prayed so mightily upon his tower.

Helaman 7:15–17 • Nephi tells the Nephites that God has forsaken them and challenges them to repent. Nephi told his wicked countrymen that instead of marvelling at his mournful prayer, they ought to mourn "because ye are given away that the devil has got so great hold upon your hearts" (v. 15). This people, who only a short time ago had been humble, spiritual, and had prospered greatly, had now succumbed to "the enticing of him who is seeking to hurl away your souls down to everlasting misery and endless wo" (v. 16). "O repent ye, repent ye!" he cried unto them. "Why will ye die? Turn ye, turn ye unto the Lord your God . . . [who] has . . . forsaken you" (v. 17).

Helaman 7:18–21 • Why wicked people allow wicked rulers to govern them. Nephi marveled that the Nephites had "forgotten [their] God in the very day that he has delivered [them]" (v. 20). In a very short period of time, the Nephites had "hardened [their] hearts" and would "not hearken unto the voice of the good shepherd," and had therefore "provoked him to anger against [them]" (v. 18). If they did not repent, Nephi prophesied, "Instead of gathering you . . . he shall scatter you forth that ye shall become meat for dogs and wild beasts" (v. 19). The reason they had succumbed to the corruption of the Gadiantons was their desire "to get again, to be praised of men, . . . and that [they] might get gold and silver" (v. 20). Because they had "set [their] hearts upon the riches and the vain things of this world," they were willing to "murder, and plunder, and steal, and bear false witness, . . . and do all manner of iniquity" (v. 21). Greed and pride had led to a whole list of serious sins.

President Ezra Taft Benson said, "The two groups who have the greatest difficulty in following the prophet are the proud who are learned and the proud who are rich. The learned may feel the prophet is only inspired when he agrees with them; otherwise, the prophet is just giving his opinion—speaking as a man. The rich may feel they have no need to take counsel of a lowly prophet."[10]

Helaman 8:1–10 • Many remain unrepentant. When Nephi called his people to repentance "there were men who were judges, who also belonged to the secret band of Gadianton" that "were angry, and they cried out against him" (v. 1). They called for his arrest for the "crime" of "revil[ing] against this people and against our law" (v. 2). Of course, Nephi had said nothing that wasn't true and nothing that was "contrary to the commandments of God" (v. 3). The corrupt Nephite judges "were angry with him because he spake plainly unto them concerning their secret works of darkness" (v. 4). Corruption hates to be exposed. Those in power will often do anything possible to keep their actions secret. And anyone who challenges their secret works is seen as an enemy who must be eliminated. It was this same spirit that caused the leaders of the Jews to murder their Messiah.

Though they wanted to eliminate Nephi, these corrupt political leaders "durst not lay their own hands upon him, for they feared the people lest they should cry out against them" (v. 4). Instead they called upon the people to do their dirty work, saying, "Why do you suffer this man to revile against us? For behold he doth condemn all this people, even unto destruction; yea, and also that these our great cities shall be taken from us. . . . And now we know that this is impossible, for behold, we are powerful, and our cities great, therefore our enemies can have no power over us" (vv. 5–6).

The people were divided on this matter. Their corrupt leaders "did stir up the people to anger against Nephi, and raised contentions among them," but there were still some who said, "Let this man alone, for he is a good man, and those things which he saith will surely come to pass except we repent" (v. 7). Because of these righteous people among them, "those people who sought to destroy Nephi were compelled because of their fear, that they did not lay their hands on him" (v. 10).

Helaman 8:10–15 • Nephi speaks of Moses and the brazen serpent. Seizing the opportunity to preach while his enemies were powerless to arrest him (v. 10), Nephi cited the example of Moses as a prophet who had power to predict the future and work miracles among his people (v. 11). Nephi reasoned that God had given revelation to his ancient prophets. He asked, "Why should ye dispute . . . that he hath given unto me . . . power whereby I may know concerning the judgments that shall come upon you except ye repent?" (v. 12).

Nephi then cited the example of Moses raising the brazen serpent in the wilderness, which symbolized the saving power of Christ (Numbers 21:6–9; John 3:14–16). He reminded them that Moses "hath spoken concerning the coming of the Messiah" (v. 13). "And as he lifted up the brazen serpent in the wilderness, even so shall he be lifted up who should come. And as many as should look upon that serpent should live, even so as many as should look upon the Son of God with faith, having a contrite spirit, might live, even unto that life which is eternal" (vv. 14–15).

Helaman 8:16–21 • Nephi recalls the prophecies of Abraham, Zenos, Zenock, Ezias, Isaiah, and Jeremiah. Moses was not the only one who prophesied of Christ, "but also all the holy prophets, from his days even to the days of Abraham" (v. 16). In fact, Christ has been preached by every prophet in every age (Mosiah 13:33; Luke 1:69–70; Acts 3:20–24). Nephi said that "Abraham saw of his coming, and was filled with gladness and did rejoice" (v. 17). The prophet Zenos "did testify boldly; for the which he was slain" (v. 19), as did Zenock, Ezias, Isaiah, and Jeremiah who prophesied the destruction of Jerusalem (v. 20). "And now will you dispute that Jerusalem was destroyed?" asked Nephi. "Will ye say that the sons of Zedekiah were not slain, all except it were Mulek? Yea, and do ye not behold that the seed of Zedekiah are with us, and they were driven out of the land of Jerusalem?" (v. 21). These were facts, and Nephi's enemies knew it.

Helaman 8:22–23 • All the Nephite prophets also testified of Christ. "Lehi was driven out of Jerusalem because he testified of these things. Nephi also testified of these things, and also almost all of our fathers, even down to this time; yea, they have testified of the coming of Christ, and have looked forward, and have rejoiced in his day which is to come" (v. 22). Nephi testified that

"[Christ] is God, and he [was] with them, and he did manifest himself unto them, that they were redeemed by him; and they gave unto him glory, because of that which is to come" (v. 23).

Helaman 8:24–27 • The Nephites are now ripening for destruction. Despite all these witnesses, and "notwithstanding so many evidences which ye have received," which included "all things, both things in heaven, and all things which are in the earth, as a witness that they are true" (v. 24), the Nephites were now turning their backs on Christ and his prophets. Said Nephi, "Ye have rejected the truth, and rebelled against your holy God; and even at this time, instead of laying up for yourselves treasures in heaven, where nothing doth corrupt, and where nothing can come which is unclean, ye are heaping up for yourselves wrath against the day of judgment" (v. 25). They were approaching the point where repentance would not be possible—"even at this time ye are ripening, because of your murders and your fornication and wickedness, for everlasting destruction . . . and except ye repent it will come unto you soon . . . behold it is now even at your doors" (vv. 26-27).

Helaman 8:27-28 • By prophecy, Nephi reveals an assassination plot against their chief judge. To their astonishment, Nephi proclaimed, "Go ye in unto the judgment-seat, and search; and behold, your judge is murdered, and he lieth in his blood; and he hath been murdered by his brother, who seeketh to sit in the judgment-seat" (v. 27). Nephi had no way of knowing this except through revelation from God. He observed further that both of these men "belong to your secret band, whose author is Gadianton and the evil one who seeketh to destroy the souls of men" (v. 28).

Helaman 9:1–15 • Five men verify the correctness of Nephi's prophecy and are arrested for murder. Hearing this prophecy, five of those in the crowd ran to the judgment-seat (v. 1). They did not believe that Nephi was a prophet and thought they would prove their point by finding the chief judge alive. If, on the other hand, he was indeed dead then they would believe that Nephi was a prophet (v. 2). When they arrived at the judgment-seat, they found the chief judge dead in a pool of blood, and were so astonished they fell to the earth in fear (vv. 3–4). Knowing now that Nephi was a prophet, they began to quake with fear concerning "all the judgments which Nephi had spoken should come upon the people" (v. 5). When the people in the area gathered at the judgment-seat to see what had happened, they found these five men trembling on the ground (vv. 6–7). These people knew nothing about what had transpired earlier at the garden of Nephi and immediately suspected that these five men had murdered the chief judge, and so the five were cast into prison (vv. 8–9).

On the following day, there was a state funeral for the slain chief judge, and those corrupt judges who had heard Nephi's preaching in his garden attended (vv. 10–11). When they inquired what had happened to the five who had run to the judgment-seat, they were informed that they had been arrested and imprisoned for murder (v. 12). They asked for them to be brought out for questioning and they inquired as to what had happened (v. 13). The five told their story and protested their innocence, saying, "As for the murder of this man, we know not who has done it; and only this much we know, we ran and came according as ye desired, and behold he was dead according to the words of Nephi" (vv. 14–15).

Helaman 9:16–23 • The judges arrest Nephi and accuse him of the murder. Knowing full well that one of their compatriots had committed the murder, the corrupt judges sought to convict Nephi for the crime, saying, "Behold, we know that this Nephi must have agreed with some one to slay the judge, and then he might declare it unto us, that he might convert us unto his faith, that he might raise himself to be a great man, chosen of God, and a prophet. And now behold, we will detect this man, and he shall confess his fault and make known unto us the true murderer of this judge" (vv. 16–17).

The five accused men were immediately released from prison, and "they did rebuke the judges in the words which they had spoken against Nephi" (v. 18). "Nevertheless, they caused that Nephi should be taken and bound and brought before the multitude, and they began to question him in divers ways that they might cross him, that they might accuse him to death" (v. 19). They demanded that Nephi tell them who had committed the murder, and offered him money and a release from bonds if he would acknowledge his role in the crime (v. 20). Instead Nephi condemned them, saying, "O ye fools, ye uncircumcised of heart, ye blind, and ye stiffnecked people, do ye know how long the Lord your God will suffer you that ye shall go on in this your way of sin? O ye ought to begin to howl and mourn, because of the great destruction which at this time doth await you, except ye shall repent" (vv. 21–22). Nephi knew that their anger toward him was "because I have testified unto you that ye might know concerning this thing [as] a witness unto you, that I did know of the wickedness and abominations which are among you" (v. 23).

Helaman 9:24–36 • Nephi provides another prophetic sign by which the real murderer will be identified. Nephi said, "Behold I say unto you: Go to the house of Seantum, who is the brother of Seezoram, and say unto him—Has Nephi, the pretended prophet, who doth prophesy so much evil concerning this people, agreed with thee, in the which ye have murdered Seezoram, who is your brother?" (v. 27). He prophesied unto them that Seantum would say, "Nay" (v. 28). He then told them to ask Seantum directly, "Have ye murdered your brother?" (v. 29) and prophesied that he would "stand with fear," not knowing what to say, denying that he had committed the murder (v. 30). Nevertheless, Nephi said, if they would examine him they would "find blood upon the skirts of his cloak" (v. 31). Then if they will ask, "From whence cometh this blood? Do we not know that it is the blood of your brother?" he will "tremble, and shall look pale, even as if death had come upon him" (vv. 32–33). If they then again accuse him of the murder, Nephi said, "Then shall he confess unto you, and deny no more that he has done this murder" (v. 35) and that Nephi knew nothing concerning the plot (v. 36). "And then shall ye know that I am an honest man, and that I am sent unto you from God" (v. 36).

Helaman 9:37–38 • Seantum confesses to murdering his brother, the chief judge. The judges proceeded to do "even according as Nephi had said unto them. And behold, the words which he had said were true; for according to the words he did deny; and also according to the words he did confess. And he was brought to prove that he himself was the very murderer, insomuch that the five were set at liberty, and also was Nephi" (vv. 37–38).

Helaman 9:39–10:1 • The people debate whether Nephi is a prophet or a god, then leave him standing alone (v. 39). There were some of the Nephites who believed on the words of Nephi and said he was a prophet (v. 40), while others said he was a god, "for except he was a god he could not know of all things" including "the thoughts of our hearts . . . and . . . the true murderer of our chief judge" (v. 41). On this matter the people were divided and went their way, "leaving Nephi alone, as he was standing in the midst of them" (v. 1)

Helaman 10:4–5 • The steadiness of the prophet Nephi. Nephi was blessed and commended by the Lord for his "unwearyingness" and steadfast service to God (v. 4). He had not feared the people, nor sought to protect his own life, but had sought the will of God in all things (v. 4). The Lord promised, "Because thou hast done this . . . I will bless thee forever; and I will make thee mighty in word and in deed, in faith and in works; yea, even that all things shall be done unto thee according to thy word, for thou shalt not ask that which is contrary to my will" (v. 5).

Helaman 10:6–11 • The Lord gives Nephi sealing power. He was empowered to bind and loose on earth and in heaven (vv. 6–7). He was given "power over this people, [to] smite the earth with famine, and with pestilence, and destruction, according to the wickedness of this people" (v. 6). The Lord promised, "And . . . if ye shall say unto this temple it shall be rent in twain, it shall be done. And if ye shall say unto this mountain, Be thou cast down and become smooth, it shall be done. And behold, if ye shall say that God shall smite this people, it shall come to pass" (vv. 7–10). And having thus empowered him, the Lord sent Nephi forth to declare unto the people, "Except ye repent ye shall be smitten, even unto destruction" (v. 11).

Pride Cycle Step 3
Destruction and Buffeting
(Helaman 11:1–9)

The Nephites Experience War and Famine

Helaman 11:1–9 • Nephi calls for natural calamities to humble the people. It was now the seventy-second year of the reign of the judges (20 BC), and contentions increased among the people, producing "wars throughout all the land among all the people of Nephi" (v. 1). These conflicts were the work of the "secret band of robbers" who continued to infest the land (v. 2), and they continued for two years without ceasing.

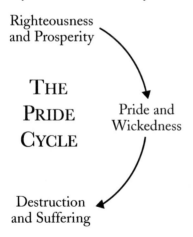

Righteousness and Prosperity

THE PRIDE CYCLE

Pride and Wickedness

Destruction and Suffering

At that point in time, Nephi cried unto the Lord, saying, "O Lord, do not suffer that this people shall be destroyed by the sword; but O Lord, rather let there be a famine in the land, to stir them up in remembrance of the Lord their God, and perhaps they will repent and turn unto thee" (vv. 3–4). "And so it was done, according to the words of Nephi" (v. 5).

A "great famine" engulfed the land "among all the people of Nephi" and in 17 BC caused all warfare to cease (v. 5). "The earth was smitten that it was dry, and did not yield forth grain in the season of grain" (v. 6). The famine affected "the whole earth . . . even among the Lamanites as well as among the Nephites," causing people to perish "by the thousands" in the more wicked parts of the land (v. 6). Suffering and humbled by their circumstances, and as "they were about to perish by famine . . . they began to remember the Lord their God; and they began to remember the words of Nephi" (v. 7). They "began to plead with their chief judges and their leaders" to confess to Nephi that they knew he was a prophet and to beg him to "cry unto the Lord our God that he turn away from us this famine, lest all the words which thou hast spoken concerning our destruction be fulfilled" (v. 8).

D&C 45:29–33 • In these last days, the Lord will also teach the people of the world through disasters, both natural and manmade. The Lord has observed concerning our modern world's rejection of Christ and his gospel, "They receive it not; for they perceive not the light, and they turn their hearts from me because of the precepts of men" (v. 29). As a result, he predicted that "they shall see an overflowing scourge; for a desolating sickness shall cover the land" (v. 31). He promised that if his disciples will "stand in holy places, and shall not be moved," he would protect them, "but among the wicked, men shall lift up their voices and curse God and die" (v. 32). There will also be "earthquakes also in divers places, and many desolations; yet men will harden their hearts against me, and they will take up the sword, one against another, and they will kill one another" (v. 33).

D&C 88:88–91 • These calamities will be sent to cleanse and purify the earth of evil. The Lord said, "After your testimony cometh wrath and indignation upon the people. For after your testimony cometh the testimony of earthquakes . . . [and] the testimony of the voice of thunderings, and the voice of lightnings, and the voice of tempests, and the voice of the waves of the sea heaving themselves beyond their bounds. And all things shall be in commotion; and surely, men's hearts shall fail them; for fear shall come upon all people."

The Prophet Joseph Smith said, "And now I am prepared to say, by the authority of Jesus Christ, that not many years shall pass away before the United States shall present such a scene of bloodshed as has not a parallel in the history of our nation; pestilence, hail, famine, and earthquake will sweep the wicked of this generation from off the face of the land, to open and prepare the way for the return of the lost tribes of Israel from the north country."[11]

Bruce R. McConkie said, "God in his mercy shall pour out destructive plagues upon the wicked and ungodly in the last days. These diseases and calamities shall sweep great hosts of men from the face of the earth, preparatory to that final Millennial cleansing which shall prepare our planet as an abode for the righteous."[12]

Joseph Fielding Smith said, "Satan has control now. No matter where you look, he is in control, even in our own land. He is guiding the governments as far as the Lord will permit him. That is why there is so much strife, turmoil, and confusion all over the earth. One master mind is governing the nations. It is not the president of the United States; it is not Hitler; it is not Mussolini; it is not the king or government of England or any other land; it is Satan himself."[13]

He later observed: "There is more sin and evil in the world now than there has been at any time since the day of Noah, when the Lord felt disposed to destroy the world by a flood so that He could send His spirit children to earth in a better and more righteous environment. . . . There is some degree of worldliness in all of us, and we overcome the world by degrees."[14]

Pride Cycle Step 4
HUMILITY AND REPENTANCE

(HELAMAN 11:10–19)

Helaman 11:9–18 • Nephi prays for the famine to be lifted, and his prayer is answered. We are told that the people repented, but it was not lasting. Their hearts were set on worldly things, and they could only change their lives by first changing their hearts. They never really became righteous

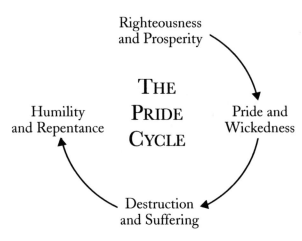

Righteousness
and Prosperity

THE
PRIDE
CYCLE

Humility
and Repentance

Pride and
Wickedness

Destruction
and Suffering

(Helaman 12:3), but they repented sufficiently that he gave them relief from their suffering.

In the seventy-sixth year of the reign of the judges (16 BC), the Lord caused rain to fall, sufficient enough to cause their fruit and their grain to come forth in season (v. 17).

Thus relieved, "the people did rejoice and glorify God, and the whole face of the land was filled with rejoicing; and they did no more seek to destroy Nephi, but they did esteem him as a great prophet, and a man of God, having great power and authority given unto him from God" (v. 18).

Helaman 11:19 • The greatness of Nephi's brother Lehi. While all of these events took place in the life of Nephi, and we hear nothing concerning Lehi during this period, the Book of Mormon assures us that "Lehi, his brother, was not a whit behind him as to things pertaining to righteousness" (v. 19).

Pride Cycle Step 5
THE NEPHITES ARE BLESSED FOR THEIR HUMILITY
(HELAMAN 11:20–21)

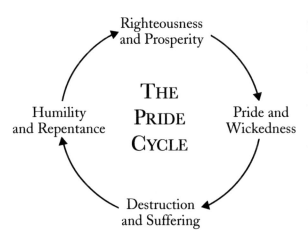

Righteousness
and Prosperity

THE
PRIDE
CYCLE

Humility
and Repentance

Pride and
Wickedness

Destruction
and Suffering

Helaman 11:20–21 • The people are blessed for their faithfulness. As he always does, God rewarded them for their increased faith, as "the people of Nephi began to prosper again in the land, and began to build up their waste places, and began to multiply and spread even until they did cover the whole face of the land, both on the northward and on the southward, from the sea west to the sea east" (v. 20). As a result, the seventy-sixth year of the reign of judges ended in peace, which prevailed through the following year (15 BC).

The Church also prospered and "spread throughout the face of all the land" with "the more part of the people, both the Nephites and the Lamanites" belonging to the church (v. 21). Thus united as a people and a church, "they did have exceedingly great peace in the land" (v. 21).

The Cycle Repeats
(HELAMAN 11:22–12:26)

Helaman 11:22–23 • (13 BC) • After a short-lived period of humility and righteousness, the people begin to contend about doctrine. Nephi, Lehi, and their brethren put an end to this contention by teaching "true points of doctrine," which settled the disputes (v. 23).

Helaman 11:24–27 • (12 BC) • Dissenters among the Lamanites start a terrorist guerilla war against the Nephites. These dissenters had defected to the Lamanites some years before and lived among the Lamanites (v. 24). They managed to stir up some of their Lamanite hosts against the Nephites, and they "commenced a war" with them (v. 24). This was a guerilla war by what we today would call terrorists. They would come out of the mountains and "commit murder and plunder" and then "retreat back into the mountains, and into the wilderness and secret places, hiding themselves that they could not be discovered" (v. 25). They "receiv[ed] daily an addition to their numbers" because of additional dissenters from the Nephites who "went forth unto them" (v. 26). "And thus in time, yea, even in the space of not many years, they became an exceedingly great band of robbers" (v. 26). These terrorists sought out "all the secret plans of Gadianton; and thus they became robbers of Gadianton" (v. 26) and wreaked "great havoc" (terror) and "great destruction among the people of Nephi, and also among the people of the Lamanites" (v. 27).

Helaman 11:28–35 • (12 BC) • The Nephites fight against the terrorists with very little success. It was essential to put a stop to their activities, so they "sent an army of strong men into the wilderness and upon the mountains to search out this band of robbers, and to destroy them" (v. 28). They were not very successful, being "driven back even into their own lands" (v. 29).

The following year (11 BC), they "did go forth again against this band of robbers, and did destroy many; and they were also visited with much destruction" (v. 30). They were "obliged to return out of the wilderness and out of the mountains unto their own lands, because of the exceeding greatness of the numbers of those robbers who infested the mountains and the wilderness" (v. 31).

This was classic terrorism, of the kind that we are all too familiar in our own day. The terrorists "did still increase and wax strong, insomuch that they did defy the whole armies of the Nephites, and also of the Lamanites; and they did cause great fear to come unto the people upon all the face of the land" (v. 32). They caused "great destruction" among them in "many parts of the land," and "did carry away others captive into the wilderness . . . more especially their women and their children" (v. 33).

"Now this great evil, which came unto the people because of their iniquity, did stir them up again in remembrance of the Lord their God" at the end of that troubled year, 11 BC (v. 35). It had taken only three years for the entire cycle of pride to occur among them.

Helaman 11:36–38 • (10–7 BC) • The Nephites begin again "to forget the Lord their God" and this time they do not repent. Only one year after their repentance, "they began again to forget the Lord their God" (v. 36). The next year "they began to wax strong in iniquity" and did not repent either that year or the next (v. 36). By the eighty-fifth year of the reign of the judges (7 BC), "they did wax stronger and stronger in their pride, and in their wickedness; and thus they were ripening again for destruction" (v. 37). Again, it had taken them only three years to fall from grace, but this time they did not repent.

Comparisons to our own day can be found throughout this period of Nephite history. While our earth becomes infested with dangerous and violent terrorists, the proud and increasingly secular governments of the world continue to uphold evil and forget God. Our societies are badly divided between those who would do nothing or even uphold the evils of these terrorists, and those who feel compelled to challenge them.

The prophet Moroni spoke plainly of the seriousness of our situation:

> Wherefore, O ye Gentiles, it is wisdom in God that these things should be shown unto you, that thereby ye may repent of your sins, and suffer not that these murderous combinations shall get above you, which are built up to get power and gain—and the work, yea, even the work of destruction come upon you, yea, even the sword of the justice of the Eternal God shall fall upon you, to your overthrow and destruction if ye shall suffer these things to be.
>
> Wherefore, the Lord commandeth you, when ye shall see these things come among you that ye shall awake to a sense of your awful situation, because of this secret combination which shall be among you; or wo be unto it, because of the blood of them who have been slain; for they cry from the dust for vengeance upon it, and also upon those who built it up.
>
> For it cometh to pass that whoso buildeth it up seeketh to overthrow the freedom of all lands, nations, and countries; and it bringeth to pass the destruction of all people, for it is built up by the devil, who is the father of all lies; even that same liar who beguiled our first parents, yea, even that same liar who hath caused man to commit murder from the beginning; who hath hardened the hearts of men that they have murdered the prophets, and stoned them, and cast them out from the beginning.
>
> Wherefore, I, Moroni, am commanded to write these things that evil may be done away, and that the time may come that Satan may have no power upon the hearts of the children of men, but that they may be persuaded to do good continually, that they may come unto the fountain of all righteousness and be saved. (Ether 8:23–26)

We may also see in our own society how quickly a people can turn from humility and trust in God to a divided and prideful state of complacency. In September 2001, the United States was attacked by terrorists in what turned out to be the worst attack on American soil in history—eclipsing Pearl Harbor in the number of deaths that resulted. It took only three years for the world to forget the way they felt on that terrible day and to begin to argue with each other as to whether we are even "at war" with the terrorists. Members of all political parties engage in political gamesmanship while the threat grows all around us. It will likely not cease until we are again humbled by a violent attack from modern-day Gadiantons.

Can there be any doubt that the Book of Mormon was written for our day?

Conclusions about the Pride Cycle

Helaman 12:1–6 • The unsteadiness of the wicked. Mormon lamented how "false" and "unsteady" people are (v. 1). The Lord blesses and prospers those who trust him with an "increase of their fields, their flocks and their herds, and in gold, and in silver, and in all manner of precious things of every kind . . . sparing their lives, and delivering them out of the hands of their enemies; softening the hearts of their enemies that they should not declare wars against them; yea, and in fine, doing all things for the welfare and happiness of his people" (v. 2). But even while he is in the act of blessing them, "they . . . harden their hearts, and . . . forget the Lord their God, and . . . trample under their feet the Holy One—yea, and this because of their ease, and their exceedingly great prosperity" (v. 2).

"And thus we see," said Mormon, "that except the Lord doth chasten his people with many afflictions, yea, except he doth visit them with death and with terror, and with famine and with all manner of pestilence, they will not remember him" (v. 3).

Mormon called such people "foolish," "vain," "evil," and "devilish," "quick to do iniquity," "slow to do good," "quick to hearken unto the words of the evil one" and "to set their hearts upon the vain things of the world!" (v. 4). He added that we are "quick to be lifted up in pride," "quick to boast" and to "do all manner of that which is iniquity," while we are "slow . . . to remember the Lord . . . and to give ear unto his counsels, yea, how slow to walk in wisdom's paths!" (v. 5). Such people "do not desire that the Lord their God, who hath created them, should rule and reign over them; notwithstanding his great goodness and his mercy towards them," and "they do set at naught his counsels" and "will not that he should be their guide" (v. 6).

Helaman 12:7–17 • The elements obey their creator. "O how great is the nothingness of the children of men," says Mormon. "Yea, even they are less than the dust of the earth" (v. 7), because when the Lord commands, the dust obeys him.

> The dust of the earth moveth hither and thither, to the dividing asunder, at the command of our great and everlasting God. Yea, behold at his voice do the hills and the mountains tremble and quake. And by the power of his voice they are broken up, and become smooth, yea, even like unto a valley. Yea, by the power of his voice doth the whole earth shake; Yea, by the power of his voice, do the foundations rock, even to the very center. Yea, and if he say unto the earth—Move—it is moved. Yea, if he say unto the earth—Thou shalt go back, that it lengthen out the day for many hours—it is done. . . . And behold, also, if he say unto the waters of the great deep—Be thou dried up—it is done. Behold, if he say unto this mountain—Be thou raised up, and come over and fall upon that city, that it be buried up—behold it is done. (vv. 8–17)

What he leaves unsaid, but which is true, is that his children (with their agency) do not obey so readily, but all too often rebel against the God who made them.

Helaman 12:14–15 • Nephite knowledge of the cosmos. There is, buried within this list of physical elements that obey the Lord, an interesting statement that shows that the Nephites knew much more about the cosmos than many of those on the other side of the world, who concluded that the sun rotates around the earth. Mormon said that if the earth is turned back on its axis "it appeareth unto man that the sun standeth still" because "it is the earth that moveth and not the sun."

Helaman 12:23–24 • How to avoid the pride cycle. Mormon observed that those "who will repent and hearken unto the voice of the Lord their God . . . are they that shall be saved" (v. 23). And he prayed that God will "grant, in his great fulness, that men might be brought unto repentance and good works, that they might be restored unto grace for grace, according to their works" (v. 24). It is by this process, and this process only, that we can avoid falling into the same pride cycle that destroyed both the Jaredites and the Nephites.

Alma 62:48–51 • Some people have achieved it. In the days of Captain Moroni, the people of Nephi prospered, began to multiply, and became "exceedingly strong" and rich because of their righteousness and the peace which it produced. again in the land. And they began to grow exceedingly rich (v. 48). Yet, "notwithstanding their riches, or their strength, or their prosperity, they were not lifted up in the pride of their eyes; neither were they slow to remember the Lord their God; but they did humble themselves exceedingly before him" (v. 49). They remember the great things which the Lord had done for them— delivering them from death, from bonds, from prisons, and from "all manner of afflictions," including delivering them from their enemies (v. 50). Despite their great blessings and prosperity, "they did pray unto the Lord their God continually, insomuch that the Lord did bless them, according to his word, so that they did wax strong and prosper in the land" (v. 51). Becoming complacent is not inevitable. We can choose, as this people did, to remember the Lord in the midst of our prosperity.

President Gordon B. Hinckley said, "Seek for the real things, not the artificial. Seek for the everlasting truths, not the passing whim. Seek for the eternal things of God, not for that which is here today and gone tomorrow. Look to God and live."[15]

Helaman 12:25–26 • The fate of those who disobey. Mormon wished "that all men might be saved" but knew that in our day there would be "some who shall be cast out . . . from the presence of the Lord" (v. 25). These will "be consigned to a state of endless misery, fulfilling the words which say: They that have done good shall have everlasting life; and they that have done evil shall have everlasting damnation" (v. 26).

Gordon B. Hinckley said, "No other written testament so clearly illustrates the fact that when men and nations walk in the fear of God and in obedience to his commandments, they prosper and grow, but when they disregard him and his word, there comes a decay that, unless arrested by righteousness, leads to impotence and death."[16]

Notes

1. Sterling W. Sill, in Conference Report, Apr. 1966, 20–21.
2. David O. McKay, *Improvement Era*, Oct. 1960, 703.
3. David O. McKay, *Improvement Era*, Dec. 1962, 903.
4. Ezra Taft Benson, *A Nation Asleep* (Salt Lake City: Bookcraft, 1963), 13, 20.
5. David O. McKay, in Conference Report, Oct. 1962, 7–8.
6. Joseph Smith to N. E. Seaton, esq., Jan. 4, 1833, in Joseph Smith Jr., *History of The Church of Jesus Christ of Latter-day Saints*, B. H. Roberts, ed., 2nd ed. (Salt Lake City: The Church of Jesus Christ of Latter-day Saints), 1:312–16.
7. Joseph Fielding Smith, "The Predicted Judgments," *BYU Speeches of the Year*, Mar. 21, 1967, 5–6.
8. Bruce R. McConkie, in Conference Report, Apr. 1979, 131–33.
9. Jerry L. Ainsworth, *The Lives and Travels of Mormon and Moroni* (Maybank, TX: Peacemakers Publishing, 2000), 51–57, 61.
10. *The Teachings of Ezra Taft Benson* (Salt Lake City: Bookcraft, 1988), 138.
11. Joseph Smith to N. E. Seaton, esq., Jan. 4, 1833, in Joseph Smith Jr., *History of The Church of Jesus Christ of Latter-day Saints*, B. H. Roberts, ed., 2nd ed. (Salt Lake City: The Church of Jesus Christ of Latter-day Saints), 1:312–16.
12. Bruce R. McConkie, *Doctrinal New Testament Commentary* (Salt Lake City: Bookcraft, 1966), 3:359.
13. Joseph Fielding Smith, *Doctrines of Salvation*, Bruce R. McConkie, comp. (Salt Lake City: Deseret Book, 1954–56), 3:315.
14. Joseph Fielding Smith, baccalaureate speech, Ricks College Rexburg, Idaho, May 7, 1971, quoted in *Church News*, May 15, 1971, 3.
15. Gordon B. Hinckley, *Teachings of Gordon B. Hinckley* (Salt Lake City: Deseret Book, 1997), 494.
16. Gordon B. Hinckley, in Conference Report, Oct. 1979, 10.

"Repent and Return unto the Lord"
Helaman 13–16

Samuel the Lamanite

Who Was Samuel the Lamanite and Why Was He Sent?

Samuel was one of the Lamanites who chose to keep the commandments of God. He may have come from among the Ammonites (Anti-Nephi-Lehies), a righteous people who never did, in their entire history, turn away from the Lord or his gospel (Alma 23:6). Or he may have come from among the righteous Lamanites converted by the preaching of Nephi and Lehi, when the Lamanites became more righteous than the Nephites and sent missionaries among them to call them to repentance. Wherever he came from, we know he came to Zarahemla commissioned by an angel to proclaim God's word to the wicked Nephites there (Helaman 13:7).

We might wonder why a Lamanite was sent to preach repentance to the Nephites. The Nephites already had prophets among them—Nephi and Lehi in particular. There is great irony in this—that a Lamanite would be sent to call Nephites to repentance. It demonstrates the roll reversal that these two peoples had experienced.

Samuel the Lamanite's Message

Nephite Choices—Happiness or Misery

Helaman 13:1–3 • Samuel attempts to preach to the Nephites and is rejected. In the eighty-sixth year of the reign of the judges (6 BC) we find the Nephites still living in great wickedness while the Lamanites "did observe strictly to keep the commandments of God, according to the law of Moses" (v. 1). In these circumstances, a Lamanite prophet, whose name was Samuel, appeared among the Nephites (v. 2). He preached "many days" but was rejected, dishonored, and cast out from among them (v. 3).

Richard L. Evans said, "A prophet is seldom popular, and the cost of being a prophet is always great, for he may be called upon to say those things which are not pleasing, . . . and he may find himself fighting against a tide of mass-misconception, and, as history records, be stoned, crucified, banished, ridiculed, shunned, or rejected. For the truth is not pleasing unto all men, and time has proved that majorities are not always right. . . . It is not important that a prophet should say those things with which you and I are in full accord. But it is important that you and I should bring ourselves into full accord with those things which a prophet speaks by virtue of his office and calling."[1]

Helaman 13:3–11 • Samuel returns to prophesy their destruction unless they repent. Thinking his mission to them was finished after his first visit, Samuel the Lamanite "was about to return to his own land" when "the voice of the Lord came unto him, that he should return again, and prophesy unto the people whatsoever things should come into his heart" (v. 3). This time the message was to be of judgment and justice. Heavy destruction awaited the people unless they repented and exercised faith in Christ.

The Nephites would not allow him entrance into the city, so Samuel the Lamanite climbed upon the wall of the city, stretched forth his hands, and "prophesied unto the people whatsoever things the Lord put into his heart" (v. 4). He told them, "The sword of justice hangeth over this people; and four hundred years pass not away save the sword of justice falleth upon this people" (v. 5). This, of course, is a clear reference to the final destruction of the Nephite nation that occurred about four hundred years later.

That was the bad news. The good news was that they might yet be saved by "repentance and faith on the Lord Jesus Christ, who surely shall come into the world, and shall suffer many things and shall be slain for his people" (v. 6). The birth of the Savior into the world was now only six years away. Testifying, "An angel of the Lord hath declared it unto me," he spoke of the "glad tidings to [his] soul" that this news produced. He told them that he had come "to declare it unto you also, that ye might have glad tidings; but behold ye would not receive me" (v. 7).

Then came a series of warnings. If they persisted in wickedness, the Lord would withdraw his "word" (prophets) and the Spirit from among them (v. 8). Within four generations (four hundred years), they would be utterly destroyed (vv. 9–10). Nevertheless, there was still a final opportunity for them to repent at this time (v. 11).

SATAN HAD GREAT HOLD OF THEIR HARD HEARTS

Helaman 6:30–35 • Satan is the author of all sin, including that among the Nephites. Satan is the source of all "works of darkness and secret murder, and doth hand down their plots, and their oaths, and their covenants, and their plans of awful wickedness, from generation to generation according as he can get hold upon the hearts of the children of men" (v. 30). When Gadianton-like bands of terrorists wreak havoc and destruction among the people, they do so under the command of their master, who is Satan.

Satan certainly had hold upon the hearts of the Nephites. They had become "exceedingly wicked," with most of them turning away from righteousness and "trampl[ing] under their feet the commandments of God, . . . turn[ing] unto their own ways, and . . . build[ing] up unto themselves idols of their gold and their silver" (v. 31). As a result, "the Nephites did begin to dwindle in unbelief, and grow in wickedness and abominations, while the Lamanites began to grow exceedingly in the knowledge of their God; . . . to keep his statutes and commandments, and to walk in truth and uprightness before him" (v. 34). In this situation, "the Spirit of the Lord began to withdraw from the Nephites, because of the wickedness and the hardness of their hearts" (v. 35).

This was not the first time, nor the last time, that this happened in Nephite history.

▷ **2 Nephi 33:2 • Nephi described the problem early on in Nephite history.** He said, "There are many that harden their hearts against the Holy Spirit, that it hath no place in them; wherefore, they cast many things away which are written and esteem them as things of naught."

▷ **Alma 12:9–11 • Alma identified it among his people.** He warned his people not to give the "mysteries of God" to the hard of heart and the disobedient, saying, "He that will harden his heart, the same receiveth the lesser portion of the word; and he that will not harden his heart, to him is given the greater portion of the word, until it is given unto him to know the mysteries of God until he know them in full. And they that will harden their hearts, to them is given the lesser portion of the word until they know nothing concerning his mysteries; and then they are taken captive by the devil, and led by his will down to destruction. Now this is what is meant by the chains of hell."

▷ **Helaman 7:15 • Nephi lamented the hardness of hearts in Zarahemla.** He noted that the people had gathered at his garden because of his "mourning and lamentation" for them. He said, "Ye have great need to marvel; yea, ye ought to marvel because ye are given away, that the devil has got so great hold upon your hearts."

▷ **Mormon 3:12; 4:11 • Mormon lamented the hardness of the Nephites' hearts at the time of their destruction.** He had loved his people "with all [his] heart; and [his] soul had been poured out in prayer unto [his] God all the day long for them; nevertheless, it was without faith, because of the hardness of their hearts" (3:12). Eventually, their hearts became so hardened that they produced a "horrible scene of the blood and carnage" and "delighted in the shedding of blood continually" (4:11).

▷ **Mosiah 2:36–37 • Mosiah spoke of the consequences when people harden their hearts.** People who were once righteous, if they "transgress and go contrary to that which has been spoken" and "withdraw [them]selves from the Spirit of the Lord," eventually "cometh out in open rebellion against God [and] listeth to obey the evil spirit, and becometh an enemy to all righteousness." Neither the Spirit nor the Lord can abide with such a person because "the Lord has no place in him, for he dwelleth not in unholy temples."

▷ **D&C 10:10, 20 • Similar conditions exist today in hearts of wicked people.** At the time of the translation of the Book of Mormon, Joseph Smith was warned not to retranslate the lost 116 pages of the Book of Lehi. The Lord said, "Satan hath put it into their hearts to alter the words which you have caused to be written, or which you have translated, which have gone out of your hands" (v. 10). In modern times, we are reminded, "Satan has great hold upon their hearts [and] he stirreth them up to iniquity against that which is good" (v. 20).

Helaman 13:12–16 • The wicked people of Zarahemla are preserved from destruction because of the few righteous among them. Yet "there are many, yea, even the more part of this great city, that will harden their hearts against me," said the Lord (v. 12). He promised to spare those who repented, but said, if it were not for their presence in the city, "I would cause that fire should come down out of heaven and destroy it" (v. 13). It was only "for the righteous' sake" that the city was spared (v. 14).

When the time came that the wicked majority of the city cast out from among them all the righteous, they would be left with no such protection. With no righteousness among them (and therefore no agency to choose between good and evil), the city would be "ripe for destruction . . . because of the wickedness and abominations which are in her" (v. 14). The same warning applied to the city of Gideon and all other Nephite cities in that region because of their similar wickedness and hardness of heart (vv. 15–16).

The Sins of the Nephites

Helaman 13:17–23 • Setting their hearts upon riches. Apparently, the Nephites had a practice of burying their wealth and most treasured possessions in the earth to hide them from others and protect them from the elements. The Lord here pronounces through Samuel the Lamanite a "curse upon the land," with the result that "whoso shall hide up treasures in the earth shall find them again no more" (vv. 18–19), unless he were a righteous man who sought to "hide it up unto the Lord" (as Mormon and Moroni did with the plates). In addition, when they sought to flee from their enemies "in that day shall they be smitten, saith the Lord" (v. 20).

The sin was not the possession of riches. The sin was setting their "hearts upon them" and not "hearken[ing] unto the words of him who gave them unto them" (v. 21). As happens so often when we become, as we suppose, self-made individuals, the Lord lamented of the Nephites, "Ye do not remember the Lord your God in the things with which he hath blessed you, but ye do always remember your riches, not to thank the Lord your God for them; yea, your hearts are not drawn out unto the Lord, but they do swell with great pride, unto boasting, and unto great swelling, envyings, strifes, malice, persecutions, and murders, and all manner of iniquities" (v. 22). It seems there is nothing that an evil man won't do to obtain the riches he desires, no matter how much misery he may cause himself or others in the process.

D&C 59:20–21 • In modern revelation, we are assured that "it pleaseth God that he hath given [earthly blessings of all kinds] unto man; for unto this end were they made to be used, with judgment, not to excess, neither by extortion" (v. 20). The finer things of the earth are not evil, and we need not feel guilty when we obtain them through honest means. In none of this "doth man offend God, or against none is his wrath kindled, save those who confess not his hand in all things, and obey not his commandments" (v. 21).

Helaman 13:24–26 • Rejection of true prophets. The Nephites killed the prophets of their own day but said they would not have the slain the prophets of old, as their fathers did (vv. 24–25; Matthew 23:29–39). But Samuel declared that in fact they were "worse than they." He said, "For as the Lord liveth, if a prophet come among you and declareth unto you the word of the Lord, which testifieth of your sins and iniquities, ye are angry with him, and cast him out and seek all manner of ways to destroy him [saying] that he is a false prophet, and that he is a sinner, and of the devil, because he testifieth that your deeds are evil" (v. 26).

D&C 21:4–6 • In our own day we are commanded to "give heed unto all [the prophet's] words and commandments which he shall give unto you as he receiveth them, walking in all holiness before me; For his word ye shall receive, as if from mine own mouth, in all patience and faith. For by doing these things the gates of hell shall not prevail against you; yea, and the Lord God will disperse the powers of darkness from before you, and cause the heavens to shake for your good, and his name's glory."

Harold B. Lee said,

There will be some things that take patience and faith. You may not like what comes from the authority of the Church. It may contradict your political views. It may contradict your social views. It may interfere with some of your social life. But if you listen to these things, as if from the mouth of the Lord himself, with patience and faith, the promise is that "the gates of hell shall not prevail against you; yea, and the Lord God will disperse the powers of darkness from before you, and cause the heavens to shake for your good, and his name's glory. . . ." Your safety and ours depends upon whether or not we follow the ones whom the Lord has placed to preside over his church. He knows whom he wants to preside over this church, and he will make no mistake. . . . Let's keep our eye on the President of the Church.[2]

Helaman 13:27–29 • Acceptance of false prophets. They allowed themselves to "be led by foolish and blind guides" (v. 29) who came among them, telling them that "there is no iniquity," and "ye shall not suffer," and saying, "Walk after the pride of your own hearts; yea, walk after the pride of your eyes, and do whatsoever your heart desireth" (v. 27). Anybody who said this to them was considered a prophet, who they would "lift up" and "give unto him of [their] substance," and "clothe him with costly apparel" (v. 28). They simply refused to find fault with any man who spoke "flattering words unto [them]" and said "all is well" (v. 28). For this, Nephi called them a "perverse generation," a "hardened and . . . stiffnecked people" who "choose darkness rather than light" (v. 29).

Harold B. Lee said,

> We have some tight places to go before the Lord is through with this church and the world in this dispensation, which is the last dispensation, which shall usher in the coming of the Lord. . . . The power of Satan will increase; we see it in evidence on every hand. There will be inroads within the Church. There will be . . . those who profess membership but secretly are . . . trying to lead people not to follow the leadership that the Lord has set up to preside in this church. Now the only safety we have as members of this church is to do exactly what the Lord said to the Church in that day when the Church was organized. We must learn to give heed to the words and commandments that the Lord shall give through his prophet.[3]

Helaman 13:32 • The Nephites will live to regret their sinfulness. Samuel prophesies, "In the days of your poverty ye shall cry unto the Lord; and in vain shall ye cry, for your desolation is already come upon you, and your destruction is made sure." In that day they would be heard to cry, "O that I had repented, and had not killed the prophets, and stoned them, and cast them out." These words would later be literally fulfilled (3 Nephi 8:25).

Helaman 13:33–36 • They will be unable to hold on to their worldly treasures. They will live to see the fulfillment of Samuel's curse upon their riches and the land. The day would come when they would cry out, "O that we had remembered the Lord our God in the day that he gave us our riches, and then they would not have become slippery that we should lose them; for behold, our riches are gone from us" (v. 33). They would be unable to hold on to anything—tools, swords, treasures, and so forth—"because of the curse of the land" (v. 35). In summary, they would lament that "all things are become slippery, and we cannot hold them" (v. 36).

Helaman 13:37–38 • For the Nephites it would soon become "everlastingly too late." In the midst of their great losses, Samuel predicted that they would say, "We are surrounded by demons," and "we are encircled about by the angels of him who hath sought to destroy our souls," and "our iniquities are great" (v. 37). In this condition they will ask the Lord to turn away his anger from them, but he will say to them, "Your days of probation are past; ye have procrastinated the day of your salvation until it is everlastingly too late, and your destruction is made sure" (v. 38).

Joseph Fielding Smith said, "In relation to the Nephites spoken of by Jacob, Alma, Samuel, and others, we should remember that these were once members of the Church who had turned away and denied the truth and fought to destroy it. They were not like the people in the gentile nations who never received the truth. These Nephites had received the light, rebelled, and then attempted to destroy it. . . . The Lord established his Church in all its fulness among them, and when they began to rebel they did it knowingly. . . . Samuel's castigation of these Nephites was fully justified in his accusation and prophecy of their punishment."[4]

Dr. Hugh Nibley wrote concerning the time when the Nephites finally reached the point of no return: "They [had] reached that point of suicidal defiance which the Greeks called *Ate*, the point of no return, when the sinner with a sort of fatal fascination does everything that is most calculated to hasten his own removal from the scene—he is finished, and now all that remains is to get him out of the way: 'O my beloved son [wrote Mormon], how can a people like this, that are without civilization . . . expect that God will stay his hand . . . ?' (Moroni 9:11, 14). Nephite civilization was thus not extinguished at Cumorah. It had already ceased to exist for some time before the final housecleaning. War had become the order of the day, 'and every heart was hardened' (Mormon 4:11)."[5]

Joseph Fielding McConkie and Robert L. Millet said, "The book of Ether is intended to serve as a second witness of yet another society whose experience parallels that of the Nephites. Both groups were brought to the same promised land by the hand of the Lord. Both were commanded to keep records. Both prospered when righteous, were cursed when wicked, and were destroyed when beyond repentance. Both rejected the prophets and discovered when it was everlastingly too late that those prophets' predictions of destruction were literally being fulfilled. Indeed, the description of the final sages of the destruction of both groups is sickeningly similar."[6]

Helaman 13:38–39 • Wickedness cannot produce happiness. The Nephites had "sought all the days of [their] lives for that which [they] could not obtain; and [had] sought for happiness in doing iniquity, which thing is contrary to the nature of that righteousness which is in our great and Eternal Head" (v. 38).

One of the great and eternal principles of the universe is the law of the Harvest—the economy of judgment whereby we receive the things we value most and forfeit those we don't value. If we marry only for time, we will be together for time, not for eternity. If we worship Christ but do not love and worship the Father as the greater (and separate) being that he is, then in the telestial kingdom we will be blessed to be visited by the Savior whom we loved but not by the Father (D&C 76:77). And in all of these cases, if we want more we shall receive it. For example, if we truly desire exaltation, we will receive it because we will do all in our power to obtain it. But if something else is more important to us, we will receive that thing and forfeit exaltation. In the end, "whatsoever we ask, we receive of him" (1 John 3:22). In this manner, we reap precisely what we have sown. In the economy of judgment, we cannot expect to receive happiness if we sow sorrow. And sorrow is the unalterably-decreed fruit of unrighteousness.

2 Nephi 2:17–18, 27 • Satan has nothing to offer but misery. The original prophet Lehi, while teaching his family, described some of the history of Satan. He says that "an angel of God . . . had fallen from heaven; wherefore, he became a devil, having sought that which was evil before God"

(v. 17). The name Lucifer (which means "light-bearer") indicates that at one time he was a child of light and even perhaps one of God's most chosen sons. Lehi continues by telling us that "because he had fallen from heaven, and had become miserable forever, he sought also the misery of all mankind" (v. 18). It was for this reason that he tempted Eve in the Garden of Eden, and it is for this reason that he tempts you and I. He never seeks to make us happy. Therefore, we can conclude that even though he tries to persuade us that happiness and righteousness are undesirable and that wickedness will bring joy, in fact whatever he entices us to do will, sooner or later, make us miserable. Satan always "seeketh that all men might be miserable like unto himself" (v. 27).

Marion G. Romney said, "Satan is evil: totally and always. He ever seeks to defeat the gospel plan and 'destroy the souls of men' (D&C 10:27). . . . Satan is irrevocably committed to countering and overcoming the influence of the Spirit of Christ upon men."[7]

Alma 41:10–11 • Wickedness never brings happiness. While speaking about the resurrection and how we will all be raised as the kind of being we have become through mortal life, Alma warned his son, "Do not suppose, because it has been spoken concerning restoration, that ye shall be restored from sin to happiness. Behold, I say unto you, wickedness never was happiness" (v. 10). Carnality, bitterness, and iniquity "are . . . contrary to the nature of happiness" (v. 11).

The Prophet Joseph Smith said, "Happiness is the object and design of our existence; and will be the end thereof, if we pursue the path that leads to it; and this path is virtue, uprightness, faithfulness, holiness, and keeping all the commandments of God."[8]

Samuel's Prophecies of Christ's Birth and Death

SIGNS OF THE COMING OF CHRIST

Helaman 14:2–7 • Signs of the birth of Jesus Christ.

Samuel the Lamanite's prophecy	The Fulfillment
Christ to be born in five years (v. 2)	3 Nephi 1:13
No darkness for "one day and a night and a day" (v. 3–4)	3 Nephi 1:15
"A new star [to] arise" (v. 5)	3 Nephi 1:21
"Many signs and wonders in heaven" (v. 6)	No mention
People to "fall to the earth" (v. 7)	No mention

THE IMPORTANCE OF CHRIST'S COMING AND DEATH

Helaman 14:12 • Samuel quotes King Benjamin. This verse is a precise repetition of Benjamin's key words in Mosiah 3:8. This is remarkable because this part of the Book of Mormon was translated much later than the Book of Mosiah, and Joseph Smith had no access to the earlier script at the time he dictated these words. It is yet another internal evidence of the authenticity of the Book of Mormon.

Mosiah 3:8	Helaman 14:12
	And also that ye might
And he shall be called	know of the coming of

Jesus Christ, the Son of God,	Jesus Christ, the Son of God
the Father of heaven and earth,	the Father of heaven and earth,
the Creator of all things	the Creator of all things
from the beginning;	from the beginning;

Helaman 14:13 • We may receive a remission of our sins through the "merits" of Christ. Merits are qualities or actions that entitle a person to claim rewards. This analogy works well to explain the connection between the suffering of Christ and the sanctification that we must obtain in order to dwell with our Father in the Celestial kingdom. We are not capable of living without sin in this fallen world. But if we do "all that we can do" (2 Nephi 25:23), then through repentance and faith, and by virtue of the "merits" of Christ's atonement, we can be "made clean" despite our failings.

2 Nephi 2:7–9 • It is only through the Savior's merits that we can be forgiven of sins. Lehi taught his son Jacob that Christ "offereth himself a sacrifice for sin, to answer the ends of the law, unto all those who have a broken heart and a contrite spirit; and unto none else can the ends of the law be answered" (v. 7).

I once heard a teacher in a high priests group meeting read this scripture and then say that the Savior suffered only for the sins of the righteous, and that the sins of the wicked were never part of it. This was, of course, false doctrine. The Savior suffered for the sins of the *whole* world (1 John 2:2) and made "intercession for *all* the children of men" (emphasis added). But not all of it will be efficacious in the lives of our Father's children. For those who refuse to repent, his suffering was wasted. And it is only to those who humbly repent and have faith in him that the demands of justice can be met by his vicarious suffering.

How important it is, then, for all of God's children to understand this doctrine! As Lehi taught, "there is no flesh that can dwell in the presence of God, save it be through the merits, and mercy, and grace of the Holy Messiah" (v. 8). There is no other behavior, no other good we might do, no other god we might worship that can save us. There is, in fact, no other god. All others are man-made. They do not exist in eternity. We either turn to him and be saved, or our eternal progression will be stopped (damned) forever.

Helaman 14:14–18 • Samuel defines spiritual death. Samuel the Lamanite taught that the Savior must die "to bring to pass the resurrection of the dead that thereby men may be brought into the presence of the Lord" (v. 14). From this we learn that our mortal bodies cannot survive in a celestial world. We must be resurrected beings for that to be possible. Furthermore, he taught that "the resurrection . . . redeemeth all mankind from the first death—that spiritual death" by which "all mankind, by the fall of Adam [were] cut off from the presence of the Lord" (v. 16). And finally, he taught concerning consequence—that "whosoever repenteth the same is not hewn down and cast into the fire" (v. 18). However, "whosoever repenteth not is hewn down and cast into the fire; and there cometh upon them again a spiritual death," which Samuel defines as "a second death" where "they are cut off again as to things pertaining to righteousness" (v. 18).

SIGNS OF THE DEATH OF CHRIST

Samuel continued his preaching by giving unto the wicked Nephites a sign—a sign of the death of the Savior. He offered a number of prophesies, all of which were literally fulfilled.

Helaman 14:20–27 • Signs of the death of Jesus Christ.

Samuel the Lamanite's Prophecy	The Fulfillment
Sun to be darkened, moon and stars to not give light for three days (v. 20, 27)	3 Nephi 8:19–23
"Thunderings and lightnings for . . . many hours" (v. 21)	3 Nephi 8:6–7
Earth to shake and tremble and be broken up (v. 21–22)	3 Nephi 8:12, 17–18
Great tempests, mountains to be laid low, valleys raised (v. 23)	3 Nephi 8:5–6
"Highways [to] be broken up, and many cities [to] become desolate" (v. 24)	3 Nephi 8:8–11, 13
"Many graves [to] be opened, and [people resurrected, who] shall appear unto many" (v. 25)	3 Nephi 23:9–14

Samuel's prophecy that many graves would be opened and would yield up their dead at the time of Christ's resurrection (v. 25) was literally fulfilled. When the Savior visited the Nephites following his resurrection, he expressly commanded that Samuel's prophecy, hitherto overlooked by the record keeper, should be recorded (3 Nephi 23:9–13).

THE CONSEQUENCES OF AGENCY

Helaman 14:29–31 • The consequences of agency. Samuel the Lamanite taught that "[people] bring upon themselves their own condemnation" and that it is essential that we be "permitted to act for [our]selves" so that we will be accountable for our choices. He taught that "whosoever perisheth, perisheth unto himself; and whosoever doeth iniquity, doeth it unto himself; for behold, ye are free; ye are permitted to act for yourselves; for behold, God hath given unto you a knowledge and he hath made you free" (vv. 29–30). The knowledge he refers to here is "that ye might know good from evil," and with that knowledge he has given us agency—"that ye might choose life or death" (v. 31).

By this we can see that our choices determine our future. We are not "victims" or "things to be acted upon" (2 Nephi 2:26), but children of God who came to this earth to learn by our own experience (choices) to distinguish good from evil. God does not excuse us from consequences for our choices because he knows that doing so would strip us of the growth we were supposed to experience in this life. While we can escape suffering for our sins, that can only be done by making an active choice to have faith in Christ, to repent, and to change the course of our lives.

Richard G. Scott said, "Parents, don't make the mistake of purposefully intervening to soften or eliminate the natural consequences of your child's deliberate decisions to violate the commandments. Such acts reinforce false principles, open the door for more serious sin, and lessen the likelihood of repentance."[9]

2 Nephi 2:27 • Satan has nothing to offer but misery. The prophet Lehi assured his son Jacob that God has given unto us "all things . . . which are expedient unto man" and that we are "free to choose liberty and eternal life, through the great Mediator of all men, or to choose captivity and death, according to the captivity and power of the devil" (v. 27). God will force no man to heaven, and Satan cannot force any man to hell. We all choose for ourselves the master to whom we will listen and obey, and we are all, therefore, accountable for whatever choices we make.

Consider what happened in the Garden of Eden to illustrate this principle. After partaking of the forbidden fruit, Adam and Eve were asked to explain themselves to the Lord. In the discourse that followed, we see the three primary excuses that people offer for their sins.

1. **"Somebody else made me do it."** Adam explained, "The woman thou gavest me, and commandest that she should remain with me, she gave me of the fruit of the tree and I did eat" (Moses 4:18). We cannot blame others for the choices we make. Neither our parents, nor our friends, nor our employers, nor our environment are ultimately responsible for the choices we make. *We* are responsible for our choices.

2. **"The devil made me do it."** When Eve was then asked, "What is this thing which thou hast done?" she said, "The serpent beguiled me, and I did eat" (Moses 4:19). It's too easy to say that we couldn't resist, but the truth is that we can. Satan cannot tempt us "above that [we] are able" (1 Corinthians 10:13).

3. **"Everybody else is doing it."** If the whole world should march off briskly down to hell, we ought to be found standing behind (and alone if necessary), unwilling to follow the mob.

None of these explanations will excuse us from the results of our choices. God grants us sufficient understanding to know what's right and wrong and the freedom to choose between them. He does not grant us an unrepentant pathway to avoidance of the consequences.

The Response to Samuel's Message

THE DIFFERING STATES OF THE NEPHITES AND LAMANITES

Helaman 15:1–3 • The cursed state of the Nephites. Because they have been the "chosen people of the Lord" (v. 3) and have chosen to rebel and turn against their Lord, they will soon find themselves "desolate," with no place for pregnant or nursing mothers to hide from the onslaught of destruction (vv. 1–2).

Helaman 15:4–9 • The blessed state of the Lamanites. In contrast to the wickedness of the Nephites, these descendants of Lehi had lived evil lives only "because of the iniquity of the tradition of their fathers. But behold, salvation hath come unto them through the preaching of the Nephites; and for this intent hath the Lord prolonged their days" (v. 4). At this time "the more part of them are in the path of their duty, and they do walk circumspectly before God, and they do observe to keep his commandments and his statutes and his judgments according to the law of Moses" and are "striving with unwearied diligence that they may bring the remainder of their brethren to the knowledge of the truth" (vv. 5–6). Those Lamanites who had been converted were "firm and steadfast in the faith" and had "buried their weapons of war, and they fear[ed] to take them up lest by any means they should sin," suffering themselves to "be trodden down and slain by their enemies [rather than] lift their swords against them, and this because of their faith in Christ" (vv. 7–9).

Helaman 15:10–13 • Samuel prophesies the coming "day of the Lamanite." Samuel prophesied that "because of their steadfastness . . . [and] firmness when they are once enlightened . . . the Lord shall bless them and prolong their days, notwithstanding their iniquity . . . until the time shall come which hath been spoken of by our fathers, and also by the prophet Zenos, and many other prophets, concerning [their] restoration . . . to the knowledge of the truth" (vv. 10–11).

The intervening years would not be easy for them. They will be "driven to and fro upon the face of the earth, and be hunted, and shall be smitten and scattered abroad having no place for refuge" (v. 12). But "the Lord shall be merciful unto them . . . that they shall again be brought to the true knowledge . . . of their Redeemer, and their great and true shepherd, and be numbered among his sheep" (v. 13).

Spencer W. Kimball said,

> The day of the Lamanite is here and the gospel brings opportunity. Millions . . . must have the emancipating gospel. Millions in Ecuador, Chile, and Bolivia serve in menial labor, eking out bare subsistence from soil and toil. They must hear the compelling truths. Millions through North America are deprived, untrained, and achieving less than their potential. They must have the enlightening gospel. It will break their fetters, stir their ambition, increase their vision, and open new worlds of opportunity to them. . . . May the Lord bless us all as we become nursing parents unto our Lamanite brethren and hasten the fulfillment of the great promises made to them.[10]

THE NEPHITES REJECT THE WORDS OF SAMUEL

Helaman 16:1–3 • They try to kill him, but can't. Some believed his words and desired baptism (v. 1). But the majority were angry and sought his life, casting stones and shooting arrows at him as he stood upon the wall (v. 2). Because the Spirit of the Lord was with him, they could not hit him, and when they realized this "many more" of them believed his words (v. 3).

Helaman 16:4–5 • Nephi also teaches and preaches to the Nephites. The prophet Nephi during this same time was "baptizing, and prophesying, and preaching, crying repentance unto the people, showing signs and wonders, working miracles among the people, that they might know that the Christ must shortly come" (v. 4). He taught them of "things which must shortly come" (v. 5). The signs of the Savior's birth that Samuel the Lamanite had predicted were now less than six years away, and most of them would see them fulfilled. Nephi wanted them to "remember at the time of their coming that they had been made known unto them beforehand, to the intent that they might believe" (v. 5).

Helaman 16:6 • Most of the Nephites do not believe. Satan had great hold upon their hearts, and their objections were familiar anti-Christ themes: (1) "he hath a devil"; (2) his claims are not logical; and (3) he is seeking to gain power over the people. In about thirty-eight years, these same people would weep and lament, "O that we had repented" (3 Nephi 8:25).

Richard L. Evans said, "A prophet is seldom popular, and the cost of being a prophet is always great, for he may be called upon to say those things which are not pleasing, . . . and he may find himself fighting against a tide of mass-misconception, and, as history records, be stoned, crucified, banished, ridiculed, shunned, or rejected. For the truth is not pleasing unto all men, and time has proved that majorities are not always right. . . . It is not important that a prophet should say those things with which you and I are in full accord. But it is important that you and I should bring ourselves into full accord with those things which a prophet speaks by virtue of his office and calling."[11]

Helaman 16:7–8 • Samuel the Lamanite flees from them and returns to his own people. As they attempted to lay their hands on him, "he did cast himself down from the wall, and did flee out of their lands, yea, even unto his own country, and began to preach and to prophesy among his own people" (v. 7). And he was never heard from again among the Nephites (v. 8).

Spencer W. Kimball said,

> Has the world ever seen a more classic example of indomitable will, of faith and courage than that displayed by Samuel the Prophet . . . ? Visualize, if you can, this despised Lamanite standing on the walls of Zarahemla and while arrows and stones were shot at him, crying out to his white accusers that the sword of justice hung over them. So righteous was he that God sent an angel to visit him. His predictions were fulfilled in due time relating to the early coming of Christ, his ministry, death and resurrection, and the eventual destruction of these Nephite people. So great faith had he that the multitudes could not harm him until his message was delivered and so important was his message that subsequently the Savior required a revision of the records to include his prophecies concerning the resurrection of the Saints.[12]

Helaman 16:12–14 • (2 BC) • Many signs and wonders begin to appear, as promised. After the departure of Samuel the Lamanite, the majority of the Nephites hardened their hearts and did "more and more of that which was contrary to the commandments of God" (v. 12). In the ninetieth year of the reign of the judges (2 BC), "there were great signs given unto the people, and wonders; and the words of the prophets began to be fulfilled" (v. 13). Angels appeared and declared the glad tidings of the Savior's imminent birth, thus fulfilling the scriptures and the prophecies concerning him (v. 14).

Helaman 16:15–21 • Despite these signs, most of the people disbelieved. Except for the most believing among them, "the people began to harden their hearts . . . among both the Nephites and the Lamanites (v. 15). They were arrogant—depending only upon their own strength and wisdom—and they belittled, complained, denied, criticized, and stirred up fear. They acknowledged that "some things they may have guessed right, among so many; but behold, we know that all these great and marvelous works cannot come to pass, of which has been spoken" (v. 16). They believed that the stories concerning Christ were "a wicked tradition, which has been handed down unto us by our fathers, to cause us that we should believe in some great and marvelous thing which should come to pass, but not among us, but in a land which is far distant, a land which we know not; therefore they can keep us in ignorance, for we cannot witness with our own eyes that they are true" (v. 20). And thus, "by the cunning and the mysterious arts of the evil one, [they will] work some great mystery which we cannot understand, which will keep us down to be servants to their words, and also servants unto them . . . and thus will they keep us in ignorance if we will yield ourselves unto them, all the days of our lives" (v. 21).

Helaman 16:22–25 • Satan "stirred them up to do iniquity continually." Rather than accept the signs that appeared, which clearly fulfilled prophecy, "many more things did the people imagine up in their hearts, which were foolish and vain; and they were much disturbed" (v. 22). Satan stirred them up to do iniquity continually, "spreading rumors and contentions upon all the face of the land, that he might harden the hearts of the people against that which was good and against that which should come" (v. 23).

This reminds me very much of the Prophet Joseph Smith's prophecy concerning what people will say when the sign of the Son of Man appears in the heavens just prior to his Second Coming: "All this must be done before the Son of Man will make His appearance. There will be wars and rumors of wars, signs in the heavens above and on the earth beneath, the sun turned into darkness and the moon to blood, earthquakes in divers places, the seas heaving beyond their bounds; then will appear one grand sign of the Son of Man in heaven. But what will the world do? They will say it is a planet, a comet, etc. But the Son of man will come as the sign of the coming of the Son of Man, which will be as the light of the morning cometh out of the east."[13]

Despite the signs and the wonders which appeared among faithful Nephites and Lamanites "and the many miracles which they did," Satan continued to have "great hold upon the hearts of the people upon all the face of the land" (v. 25). With that observation, the Book of Helaman ends, as did also "the reign of the judges over the people of Nephi" (v. 25).

Notes
1. Richard L. Evans, "Being a Prophet," *Improvement Era*, Nov. 1939, 672.
2. Harold B. Lee, in Conference Report, Oct. 1970, 152–53
3. Ibid., 152.
4. Joseph Fielding Smith, *Answers to Gospel Questions*, Joseph Fielding Smith Jr., comp. (Salt Lake City: Deseret Book, 1957–1966), 1:79.
5. Hugh Nibley, *Since Cumorah*, 2nd ed. (Salt Lake City: Deseret Book and the Foundation for Ancient Research and Mormon Studies, 1988), 436–37.
6. Joseph Fielding Smith, *Doctrinal Commentary on the Book of Mormon* (Salt Lake City: Bookcraft, 1987–1992), 4:260.
7. Marion G. Romney, in Conference Report, Apr. 1971, 24.
8. Joseph Smith, *Teachings of the Prophet Joseph Smith*, Joseph Fielding Smith, sel. (Salt Lake City: Deseret Book, 1976), 255–56.
9. Richard G. Scott, *Ensign*, May 1993, 32–34.
10. Spencer W. Kimball, *Faith Precedes the Miracle* (Salt Lake City: Deseret Book, 1972), 358.
11. Richard L. Evans, "On Being a Prophet," *Improvement Era*, Nov. 1939, 672.
12. Spencer W. Kimball, in Conference Report, Apr. 1949, 109.
13. Joseph Smith, *Teachings of the Prophet Joseph Smith*, Joseph Fielding Smith, sel. (Salt Lake City: Deseret Book, 1976), 287.

LESSON 36
"On the Morrow Come I into the World"
3 NEPHI 1–7

Nephi Departs; Christ Is Born

3 Nephi Is the "Fifth Gospel"

3 Nephi contains the account of the resurrected Savior visiting the Nephites. Its descriptions of the Savior's visit to the Nephites are some of the most powerful in the book. It is often the part of the Book of Mormon that people are invited by the missionaries to read first. It reiterates and reinforces the principles of the gospel Jesus taught his disciples in Jerusalem.

For the prophet Mormon who abridged the record, this is the culmination and central focus of the book. After this, he quickly summarizes the next four hundred years, offers his testimony, and then closes the record.

THE PROPHET NEPHI DEPARTS

3 Nephi 1:1–2 • Nephi departs, and his son Nephi presides over the Church. As the book of 3 Nephi begins, it is the ninety-first year of the reign of the judges, and exactly six hundred years had passed since the time that Lehi left Jerusalem. Lachoneus was the chief judge and the governor over the land (v. 1).

In that year, Nephi, the son of Helaman, departed out of the land of Zarahemla, giving charge of the plates of brass to his eldest son, Nephi. He gave him "the plates of brass, and all the records which had been kept, and all those things which had been kept sacred from the departure of Lehi out of Jerusalem" (v. 2). This would include the Liahona and the sword of Laban, among other things.

3 Nephi 1:3; 2:9 • Nephi is never heard from again and may have been translated, as was Alma. The record states that Nephi the son of Helaman "departed out of the land, and whither he went, no man knoweth" (1:3). We are told ten years later that "Nephi, who was the father of Nephi . . . did not return to the land of Zarahemla, and could nowhere be found in all the land" (2:9). Modern prophets and gospel scholars have suggested that he was translated, just as was Alma the Younger, his great-grandfather. (Alma 45:18)

Joseph Fielding Smith said, "There are several important prophets who were granted the privilege of remaining on the earth. John the Revelator was one of these, and in the Doctrine and Covenants, section seven, is an account of this. Elijah evidently was another, for no living soul could have received the resurrection until after our Redeemer had opened the graves. The scriptural inference is that Moses also was translated as was Alma. . . . It is a very reasonable thought to believe that both Moses and Alma, like Elijah and John, were translated to accomplish some work which the Lord had in store for them at some future day."[1]

Joseph Fielding McConkie and Robert L. Millet said, "It would appear that all persons who were translated before the resurrection of Christ—Enoch and his city, Melchizedek and his city, Elijah, Moses, Alma the Younger, Nephi, and so forth—were resurrected at the time of Christ's resurrection (D&C 133:54–55; Mormon Doctrine, 807–808). Persons who were translated after the time of Christ's resurrection [such as John the Revelator and the Three Nephites] will minister in their terrestrial state until the Second Advent."[2]

The Predicted Signs Appear

THE SIGNS OF CHRIST'S BIRTH APPEAR

3 Nephi 1:4–9 • The time predicted by Samuel for the birth of the Savior (five years in the future) comes without the predicted sign, and the wicked threaten to kill all believers. As the day of the Lord's birth approached "the prophecies of the prophets began to be fulfilled more fully; for there began to be greater signs and greater miracles wrought among the people" (v. 4). But disbelievers said that the time had passed in which the prophecies of Samuel the Lamanite were supposed to be fulfilled (v. 5). This, of course, caused them to rejoice because they assumed that the believers' faith had been in vain (v. 6). They loudly proclaimed their view, to the great sorrow of believers who feared that the prophecies may not be fulfilled (v. 7). Nevertheless, believers continued to watch and pray for the sign—a "day and [a] night and [a] day which should be as one day as if there were no night" (v. 8). Meanwhile, disbelievers set a deadline for the sign to appear, after which they would put to death anybody who continued to believe in the prophecy of Samuel the Lamanite (v. 9).

3 Nephi 1:10–14 • Nephi prays for his people and the Lord declares, "On the morrow come I into the world." Nephi, the son of Nephi, newly ordained to his prophetic office, became "exceedingly sorrowful" over the wickedness of the people (v. 10). He humbly bowed himself to the earth and "cried mightily to his God in behalf of his people," meaning those who "were about to be destroyed because of their faith" (v. 11). After praying mightily all day, the voice of the Lord spoke to him (v. 12), saying, "Lift up your head and be of good cheer; for behold, the time is at hand, and on this night shall the sign be given, and on the morrow come I into the world, to show unto the world that I will fulfil all that which I have caused to be spoken by the mouth of my holy prophets" (v. 13). We can only imagine the joy Nephi must have felt, not only that his people had been spared but that the Son of God would now "come unto [his] own, to fulfil all things which [he] have made known unto the children of men from the foundation of the world" (v. 14).

3 Nephi 1:15–23 • All of the signs of the Savior's birth appear. There was a day and a night and a day without darkness, causing "great astonishment" among the people (v. 15). Many of those who had not believed Samuel's prophecy "fell to the earth and became as if they were dead" because they knew that their plan to destroy the believers had failed (v. 16) and they knew "that the Son of God must shortly appear" (v. 17). In fact, the astonishment was so widespread that the

Book of Mormon declares, "All the people upon the face of the whole earth from the west to the east, both in the land north and in the land south, were so exceedingly astonished that they fell to the earth" (v. 17), fearing "because of their iniquity and their unbelief" (v. 18).

The next morning the sun rose as usual, indicating that a new day had arrived, "and they knew that it was the day that the Lord should be born, because of the sign which had been given" (v. 19). Then, one by one, all of the other predictions came to pass, including the appearance of a "new star" (vv. 20–21). The hard of heart continued to disbelieve, spreading lies about the signs that had appeared, but the "more part of the people" were "converted unto the Lord" (v. 22). Nephi and other priesthood holders "went forth among the people . . . baptizing unto repentance [and] remission of sins" and establishing peace in the land once again (v. 23).

Zechariah 14:7 • These same signs will appear at Christ's Second Coming. The signs that appeared at Christ's birth will be shown again to the world just prior to his Second Coming, including a night in which there will be no darkness (Zechariah 14:7).

3 Nephi 1:24–26 • Some begin to preach false doctrine. Knowing that the Savior was now upon the earth, some well-meaning believers began to teach that the law of Moses had been fulfilled by Jesus' birth—but were corrected and confessed their error (vv. 24–25). The people were taught that the law of Moses had not yet been completely fulfilled and had to be "fulfilled in every whit. . . . yea, that one jot or tittle should not pass away till it should all be fulfilled" (v. 25). That, of course, would not happen until after the Savior's Atonement, death, and resurrection.

Gadianton Robbers Attack the Nephites

WICKEDNESS LEADS TO VULNERABILITY

3 Nephi 1:27–30 • Gadianton robbers, entrenched in the mountains, continue to infest the land and cause much sorrow among the people. Through all of these events, the Gadianton robbers continued to infest the land, attacking and slaughtering the people from their strongholds in the mountains (v. 27). By 4 AD they had many recruits join them from among the dissenters and disbelievers of the Nephites (v. 28). Also, from among the Lamanites, "many children . . . [grew] up and began to wax strong in years" and "became for themselves" (v. 29), which presumably means that they were headstrong and rebellious. These "were led away by some who were Zoramites [apostate Nephites], by their lyings and their flattering words, to join those Gadianton robbers," which caused their parents much sorrow (v. 29). As time passed, the natural result of this rebellion was that the Lamanites "began to decrease as to their faith and righteousness, because of the wickedness of the rising generation" (v. 30).

3 Nephi 2:1–4 • Personal wickedness provides an opportunity for Satan to sow disbelief among the people. By 5 AD "the people began to forget those signs and wonders which they had heard, and began to be less and less astonished at a sign or a wonder from heaven" (v. 1). Satan was succeeding in hardening their hearts and blinding their minds toward "all which they had heard and seen" (v. 1). The rationalization offered by disbelievers was that the signs had been "wrought by men and by the power of the devil, to lead away and deceive the hearts of the people," and that "the doctrine of Christ was a foolish and a vain thing" (v. 2). As is always the case, when they were thus relieved of any constraints on their behavior, they "began to wax strong in wickedness and abominations" (v. 3). This continued for four years (v. 4).

3 Nephi 2:5–8 • The Nephite calendar system changes. Nine years had passed away since the time when the signs were given of the Savior's birth (v. 7). It was now 10 AD, which means that one hundred years had passed since the days of King Mosiah, and 609 years since Lehi left Jerusalem (vv. 5–6). From this time forward, the Nephites began to number their years from the time when the sign was given, or from the coming of Christ (v. 8), and this system was used for the remainder of the Book of Mormon record.

3 Nephi 2:10–13 • The converted followers of Christ—both Nephite and Lamanite—unite for their collective safety. General wickedness continued for three years. By 13 AD "there began to be wars and contentions throughout all the land" precipitated by the Gadianton robbers. These vile terrorists had become "numerous" and continued to "slay so many of the people," lay waste [to] so many cities," and "spread so much death and carnage throughout the land, that it became expedient that all the people, both the Nephites and the Lamanites, should take up arms against them" (v. 11). Believers in Christ, both Nephite and Lamanite, "were compelled, for the safety of their lives and their women and their children, to take up arms against those Gadianton robbers," motivated by a desire to "maintain their rights, and the privileges of their church and of their worship, and their freedom and their liberty" (v. 12). Nevertheless, the war with these terrorists became "exceedingly sore" and threatened to utterly destroy them (v. 13).

3 Nephi 2:14–16 • Righteous Lamanites lose their "curse" and begin to look "fair" like the Nephites. With righteous Nephites and Lamanites gathering together, we are told that the Lamanite "curse was taken from them," and "their skin became white like unto the Nephites" (vv. 14–15). "And their young men and their daughters became exceedingly fair, and they were numbered among the Nephites, and were called Nephites" (v. 16). This all occurred in 13 AD, which came to an end with the war still raging.

We must be careful not to confuse "the curse" that was placed upon the Lamanites and the "dark skin" that came upon them as a mark of their heritage. These verses tell us that both things changed at this time: (1) the "curse" was taken from them, and (2) "their skin became white like unto the Nephites."

Joseph Fielding McConkie and Robert L. Millet said, "Because of their disobedience and their refusal to follow the counsel and direction of the prophets, a curse had come upon the Lamanites. The mark of that curse was a dark skin, whereby they might be known and distinguished so that the Nephites might not mix with them and assume their way of life."[3]

The curse was the withdrawal of the Lord's Spirit. McConkie and Millet said, "The wickedness of this people caused the Spirit of the Lord to be withdrawn, bringing upon themselves a curse, in contrast to the blessings of heaven so freely being poured out upon the heads of the righteous. All who live in a state of rebellion are heirs to such a curse."[4]

The Book of Mormon says about the Lamanites, "they brought upon themselves the curse" (Alma 3:19). McConkie and Millet said, "Essentially we bring the cursings of God upon ourselves whenever we fail to qualify for the blessings—the protecting power of the Almighty and the guidance and direction of his Spirit."[5] Alma said, "Even so doth every man that is cursed bring upon himself his own condemnation" (Alma 3:19).

Bruce R. McConkie said, "Just as obedience and righteousness bring blessings, so wickedness

198

and rebellion result in cursings. . . . Cursings are the opposite of blessings, and the greater the opportunity given a people to earn blessings, the more severe will be the cursings heaped upon them, if they do not measure up and gain the proffered rewards."[6]

Dark skin was not the curse. The purpose of the dark skin that came upon the Lamanites was to set them apart from the Nephites during that early period when all Nephites and Lamanites were closely related and came from the same original parents—Lehi and Sarah. McConkie and Millet said, "Because of their iniquity the Lamanite peoples were cursed with 'a skin of blackness' . . . in order that they would not be enticing to the Nephites (2 Nephi 5:21)."[7]

Dr. Hugh Nibley said, "There is nothing loathsome about dark skin, which most people consider very attractive: the darkness, like the loathsomeness, was part of the general picture (Jacob 3:9); Mormon prays 'that they may once again be a delightsome people' (Words of Mormon 1:8; Mormon 5:17), but then the Jews are also to become 'a delightsome people' (2 Nephi 30:7)."[8]

The differences between Nephites and Lamanites were not racial differences but differences in righteousness. Righteous Lamanites were numbered among the Nephites and intermarried with them freely, which would have made it difficult to tell the difference between them by this time in history.

Dr. Hugh Nibley said,

At the time of the Lord's visit, there were 'neither . . . Lamanites, nor any manner of -ites' (4 Nephi 1:17; 3 Nephi 2:14) so that when the old titles of Lamanite and Nephite were later revived by parties deliberately seeking to stir up old hatreds, they designated religious affiliation rather than race (4 Nephi 1:38-39). From this it would seem that at that time it was impossible to distinguish a person of Nephite blood from one of Lamanite blood by appearance. Moreover, there were no pure-blooded Lamanites or Nephites after the early period, for Nephi, Jacob Joseph, and Sam were all promised that their seed would survive mingled with that of their elder brethren (2 Nephi 3:2, 23; 9:53; 10:10, 19-20; 29:13; 3 Nephi 26:8; Mormon 7:1). Since the Nephites were always aware of that mingling, which they could nearly always perceive in the steady flow of Nephite dissenters to one side and Lamanite converts to the other, it is understandable why they do not think of the terms Nephite and Lamanite as indicating race.[9]

Dean L. Larsen said,

We are informed that only the more righteous part of the people were spared from the devastating destruction that preceded the appearance of the Savior on this continent. Certainly among this number must have been many who had been Lamanites as well as many of those who were Nephites. It is interesting to ponder the language of the verses which describe those who remained. Note the use of the past perfect tense with reference to those who had been Lamanites: ". . . behold, I will show unto you that the people of Nephi who were spared, and also those *who had been called Lamanites*, who had been spared, did have great favors shown unto them" (emphasis added) (3 Nephi 10:18). . . . The curse which had been placed upon those who had been Lamanites had obviously been removed. . . . It is significant that the name "Lamanite" here appears to become a generic term. That is, it refers to a general classification of people—those who revolted from the Church. These people may or may not have been the direct descendants of Laman and Lemuel. Whatever the case, it is evident that these people eventually incurred the same curse which had come upon the seed of Laman and Lemuel in the beginning.[10]

A similar transformation is occurring in our own time with regard to the Lamanites, who will rise in power and righteousness to help prepare the Church for the return of Christ.

Bruce R. McConkie said,

As part of the Lord's covenant people, a part on whom a curse fell because of the iniquity of their fathers, the Lamanites are yet to stand as a sign that the end is near. In March, 1831, the Lord revealed: "Before the great day of the Lord shall come, Jacob shall flourish in the wilderness, and the Lamanites shall blossom as the rose. Zion shall flourish upon the hills and rejoice upon the mountains, and shall be assembled together unto the place which I have appointed" (D&C 49:24–25).

Some Lamanites, gathered into the fold of Christ, have already blossomed forth with all the fruits of righteousness appertaining to the gospel; the scales of darkness have begun to drop from their eyes, according to the promises (2 Ne. 30:6); and they will yet, as a people, become as white, delightsome, and desirable as their Nephite brethren ever were. Already Jacob (with Ephraim at the head) has flourished in the wilderness where Brigham Young led her, a wilderness which has since also begun to blossom as the rose.[11]

Spencer W. Kimball said,

The Lamanites must rise in majesty and power. We must took forward to the day when they will be "white and delightsome" (2 Nephi 30:6), sharing the freedoms and blessings which we enjoy; when they shall have economic security, culture, refinement, and education; when they shall be operating farms and businesses and industries and shall be occupied in the professions and in teaching; when they shall be organized into wards and stakes of Zion, furnishing much of their own leadership; when they shall build and occupy and fill the temples, and serve in them. . . . "And in the day when their prophet shall come, one shall rise . . . mighty among them . . . being an instrument in the hands of God, with exceeding faith, to work mighty wonders. . ." (2 Nephi 3:24). Brothers and sisters, the fluorescence of the Lamanites is in our hands.[12]

3 Nephi 2:17–19 • Nephite society was ripening in iniquity. In 14 AD the Nephites gained some limited success in their war against the Gadianton terrorists, "insomuch that they did drive them back out of their lands into the mountains and into their secret places" (v. 17). However, with the Nephites badly divided and behaving wickedly, the following year the Gadiantons "did gain many advantages over them" (v. 18). By the end of 15 AD the people were "in a state of many afflictions; and the sword of destruction did hang over them, insomuch that they were about to be smitten down by it, and this because of their iniquity" (v. 19).

THREATS MADE BY THE GADIANTON ROBBERS

3 Nephi 3:1–8 • Giddianhi, the leader of the Gadianton robbers, writes to Lachoneus, the governor and chief judge of the Nephites. In 16 AD Lachoneus, the governor of the Nephites, received a letter from Giddianhi, the leader and the governor of the Gadianton terrorists (v. 1). With much phony flattery, he wrote to Lachoneus, "Most noble and chief governor of the land, behold, I write this epistle unto you, and do give unto you exceedingly great praise because of your firmness, and also the firmness of your people, in maintaining that which ye suppose to be your right and liberty; yea, ye do stand well" (v. 2).

Then came sarcasm and bragging. He mocked the Nephites' motives: "As if ye were supported by the hand of a god, in the defence of your liberty, and your property, and your country, or that which ye do call so. And it seemeth a pity unto me, most noble Lachoneus, that ye should be so foolish and vain as to suppose that ye can stand against so many brave men who are at my command" (vv. 2–3). He said his troops were battle-tested and full of hatred toward the Nephites "because of the many wrongs which [they] have done unto them" and would therefore utterly destroy any Nephite they encounter (v. 4).

He insisted he was full of sentiment and concern for the Nephites (v. 5), but his other words belied this. He invited Lachoneus, "Yield up unto this my people, your cities, your lands, and your possessions, rather than that they should visit you with the sword and that destruction should come upon you" (v. 6). He offered the Nephites a partnership if they would give in to his demands (v. 7), and he threatened to destroy them if they did not join with him (v. 8). Spoken like a true terrorist! "You should fear us, and if you don't give in to our demands, we will destroy you." Fear is what all terrorists count on to gain the spoils they desire.

3 Nephi 3:11–24 • Righteous political and military leaders. Lachoneus was astonished by this arrogant letter from Giddianhi, both because of its threats and because of its phony claims that Nephite dissenters had been "wronged" when they "had received no wrong, save it were they had wronged themselves by dissenting away unto those wicked and abominable robbers" (v. 11). Lachoneus was a just man and could not be frightened by the robbers' threats, so he took no heed of Giddianhi's offers. He was also a righteous man, who asked his people to "cry unto the Lord for strength against the time that the robbers should come down against them" (v. 12). He also counseled that they gather together in one place and build fortifications, repent, and "cry unto the Lord" (vv. 13–15). The Lamanites united with the Nephite armies for protection against the robbers, and his people exerted themselves to do as he suggested (v. 16).

Tens of thousands of people gathered themselves and all of their livestock, grain, and substance into "the place which had been appointed that they should gather themselves together, to defend themselves against their enemies" (v. 22). That place was the area "between the land Zarahemla and the land Bountiful," northward "to the line which was between the land Bountiful and the land Desolation" (v. 23). They did not venture beyond that point "because of the great curse which was upon the land northward (v. 24).

Lachoneus chose Gidgiddoni, who was a prophet and a man filled with the spirit of revelation, to be chief captain of the army (vv. 17–18). This was the custom among the Nephites—to appoint righteous men with the spirit of revelation and prophecy to be

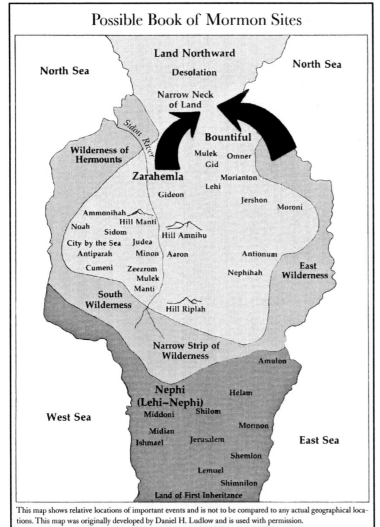

Possible Book of Mormon Sites

North Sea

Land Northward

Desolation

North Sea

Narrow Neck of Land

Sidon River

Wilderness of Hermounts

Bountiful

Mulek Omner
Gid

Zarahemla

Morianton
Lehi

Gideon

Jershon

Moroni

Ammonihah

Hill Manti

Noah
Sidom

Hill Amnihu

City by the Sea
Antiparah

Judea
Minon

Aaron

Antionum

Cumeni

Zeezrom
Mulek
Manti

Nephihah

East Wilderness

South Wilderness

Hill Riplah

Narrow Strip of Wilderness

Amulon

Nephi (Lehi–Nephi)

Helam

West Sea

Middoni

Shilom

Midian

Mornon

Ishmael

Jerusalem

East Sea

Shemlon

Lemuel

Shimnilon

Land of First Inheritance

This map shows relative locations of important events and is not to be compared to any actual geographical locations. This map was originally developed by Daniel H. Ludlow and is used with permission.

their military leaders, "therefore, this Gidgiddoni was a great prophet among them, as also was the chief judge" (v. 19).

The people asked Gidgiddoni to pray unto the Lord and then lead them in an attack on the robbers "upon the mountains and into the wilderness, that [they] may fall upon the robbers and destroy them in their own lands" (v. 20). However, he did not send his armies forth to attack the Gadiantons, but remained "in the center" of Nephite lands and fortified the land against attack, waiting for the Gadiantons to come against them (v. 21).

D&C 98:33 • This policy agrees with the law of God reiterated in our own day: They should not go out unto battle unless the Lord commands them. In other words, we are justified in fighting defensive wars in protection of our lives, our families, and our liberties, but not in attacking others offensively. In the entire history of the Nephites, they never did this until the days of Mormon, when they had become entirely without the Spirit and no better than the Lamanites in any way.

George Q. Cannon said, "Here is a law given that is of the utmost importance to the inhabitants of the earth, as well as to us as a people. It is the law by which the inhabitants of the earth should be governed, and we, as Latter-day Saints especially, should understand this law and be governed by it; and not, as we have been told at this Conference, indulge in warlike demonstrations or manifest a bloodthirsty disposition. We should be a peaceful people seeking peace, and endeavoring to escape all the horrors of war, and to avert them from the nations of the earth, particularly our own nation."[13]

3 Nephi 3:25–26 • The two-fold nature of Nephite preparations for war. First and foremost, they repented of all their sins and offered prayers unto God for their protection when their enemies attacked (v. 25). They also did their part, arming themselves with "weapons of every kind" and making themselves "strong with armor" (v. 26).

3 Nephi 4:11–14 • The Nephites prevail over the Gadianton robbers in the largest battle in Nephite history. The slaughter than ensued was "great and terrible"—worse than any battle in the six hundred years since Lehi and his family came to this land (v. 11). Yet, happily, the Nephites prevailed, driving the Lamanites back to the borders of the wilderness (vv. 12–13). Many of the Gadiantons were slain as they fled, including Giddianhi, "who had stood and fought with boldness, was pursued as he fled; and being weary because of his much fighting he was overtaken and slain" (v. 14).

3 Nephi 4:16–21 • The Gadiantons try to lay siege against the Nephites, but their strategy fails because of the Nephites' wise preparation of storage and supplies. Zemnarihah, their newly appointed leader, had thought to cut the Nephites off from their lands while they were gathered all together (vv. 16–17). The strategy failed because of the substantial resources the Nephites had brought with them, and it was the terrorists themselves who ran out of supplies before the siege was ended (vv. 18–19). The relied on wild game for food, and it "became scarce in the wilderness insomuch that the robbers were about to perish with hunger" (v. 20). In this weakened state, they were susceptible to Nephite attacks "by day and by night," which reduced their numbers "by tens of thousands" (v. 21).

3 Nephi 4:22–33 • The Gadiantons try to march northward but are cut off. • The Gadiantons wanted to abandon their plans and retreat toward the land northward (vv. 22–23). Gidgiddoni took advantage of their weakened condition and cut off their retreat by marching past them in the nighttime, thus surrounding them on the north and the south (vv. 24–26). Under these circumstances, "many thousands . . . did yield themselves up prisoners unto the Nephites, and the remainder of them were slain" (v. 27). Their leader, Zemnarihah, "was taken and hanged upon a tree . . . until he was dead" and then "they did fell the tree to the earth, and did cry with a loud voice" (v. 28). As part of this ceremony, they asked the Lord to "cause to be felled to the earth all who shall seek to slay them because of power and secret combinations," saying, "May the God of Abraham, and the God of Isaac, and the God of Jacob, protect this people in righteousness, so long as they shall call on the name of their God for protection" (vv. 29–30). They also sang, praised God, and shouted, "Hosanna to the Most High God" (vv. 31–32). It was an emotional moment, full of joy and the shedding of tears over "the great goodness of God in delivering them out of the hands of their enemies" (v. 33).

Another Nephite Pride Cycle

A SEASON OF PEACE

Righteousness and Prosperity

THE PRIDE CYCLE

3 Nephi 5:1–2 • For several years after the defeat of the Gadianton robbers, the Nephites enjoyed great peace and prosperity. They forsook their sins and served God "with all diligence" (v. 3). They all believed the words of the prophets, which "they knew . . . must be fulfilled" (v. 1). They also believed in the coming of Christ "because of the many signs which had been given, according to the words of the prophets," which had already been partially fulfilled and which they believed would eventually all be fulfilled (v. 2).

3 Nephi 5:4–6 • The Nephite system of justice. As had been their practice since the days of Captain Moroni, the Nephites' approach to the captured Gadianton members was remarkable in its charity. They preached the gospel to the robbers to see if they would be converted. If converted, the Gadiantons were freed. If the Gadiantons refused to repent, they "were condemned and punished according to the law" (v. 5). And by this means "they did put an end to all those wicked, and secret, and abominable combinations, in the which there was so much wickedness, and so many murders committed" (v. 6).

3 Nephi 5:3, 7 • (AD 21–26) **• The people served God "with all diligence."** The people "did forsake all their sins, and their abominations, and their whoredoms," and they "did serve God with all diligence day and night" (v. 3). This condition of righteousness continued for five years (v. 7).

3 Nephi 6:1–9 • (AD 26–28) **• There is great order, prosperity, and peace.** Thus freed from their Gadianton enemies, the Nephites were now (AD 26) able to return to their own lands, "every man, with his family, his flocks and his herds, his horses and his cattle, and all things whatsoever did belong unto them" (v. 1). They also had many provisions that they had not needed during the siege with the Gadiantons, and "they did take with them all that they had not devoured, of all their grain of every kind, and their gold, and their silver, and all their precious things" (v. 2). They returned to their lands in every direction, and they gave parcels of land to all Gadianton robber who "entered into a covenant to keep the peace of the land" and "who were desirous to remain Lamanites" so that they could subsist in peace among them (v. 3). Under these peaceful conditions "they began again to prosper and to wax great" (v. 4) because "there was nothing in all the land to hinder the people from prospering continually, except they should fall into transgression" (v. 5).

During this period, "there were many cities built anew, and there were many old cities repaired" (v. 7). And an impressive highway system was constructed to aid their commerce (v. 8).

RIGHTEOUSNESS TURNS TO PRIDE

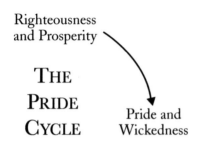

Righteousness and Prosperity

THE PRIDE CYCLE

Pride and Wickedness

3 Nephi 6:10–18 • (AD 29–30) • **Disputing, pride, and boasting create inequality among the Nephites and "a state of awful wickedness."** As is so often the case, prosperity led to pride, and "there began to be some disputings among the people; and some were lifted up unto pride and boastings because of their exceedingly great riches, yea, even unto great persecutions" (v. 10).

The Book of Mormon says that "there were many merchants in the land, and also many lawyers, and many officers. And the people began to be distinguished by ranks, according to their riches and their chances for learning" (vv. 11–12). Some were "ignorant because of their poverty, and others did receive great learning because of their riches," creating yet another class distinction among the people (v. 12). "Some were lifted up in pride, and others were exceedingly humble." Some were contentious, returning "railing for railing, while others would receive railing and persecution and all manner of afflictions, and would not turn and revile again, but were humble and penitent before God" (v. 13).

Thus divided and unwilling to associate with those not of their class, "there became a great inequality in all the land, insomuch that the church began to be broken up." In fact, "the church was broken up in all the land save it were among a few of the Lamanites who were converted unto the true faith; and they would not depart from it." These faithful Lamanites were described as "firm, and steadfast, and immovable, willing with all diligence to keep the commandments of the Lord" (v. 14).

Under these conditions, "Satan had great power, unto the stirring up of the people to do all manner of iniquity, and to the puffing them up with pride, tempting them to seek for power, and authority, and riches, and the vain things of the world" (v. 15). He was also able to "lead away the hearts of the people to do all manner of iniquity" (v. 16).

By 30 AD "the people having been delivered up for the space of a long time to be carried about by the temptations of the devil . . . were in a state of awful wickedness" (v. 17). We are told they did not sin in ignorance, but "wilfully rebelled" against God (v. 18).

Robert L. Simpson said, "Times have not changed. Less than two months ago, most of you read the disturbing article in our newspapers about a group of individuals who have established a so-called Satanic church, with the sole purpose to participate only in the realms of evil and darkness. They are in open defiance of and diametrically opposed to all of His holy purposes that bring us together in this great conference. Without a goodly number of God-fearing men committed to the cause of truth, these societies of evil could well take over our society."[14]

3 Nephi 6:19–23 • (AD 31–33) • Prophets preach repentance; a few people repent, but most of them reject and kill the prophets. These events transpired during the time that Lachoneus, the son of Lachoneus, filled the judgment-seat (v. 19). As he always does before destroying a people, God sent "men inspired from heaven . . . standing among the people in all the land, preaching and testifying boldly of the sins and iniquities of the people" (v. 20). They did not repent, but instead "there were many . . . who were exceedingly angry because of those who testified of these things," mainly "the chief judges, and they who had been high priests and lawyers" (v. 21).

These prophets also testified unto them "concerning the redemption which the Lord would make for his people," meaning the sufferings, death, and resurrection of Christ (v. 20). It is very interesting to note that during these very same years the Savior himself was teaching and blessing the people during his mortal ministry in Israel, with the same results—anger and rejection by the leaders of the people, who felt threatened by his teachings and miracles.

Under Nephite law, "there was no lawyer nor judge nor high priest that could have power to condemn any one to death save their condemnation was signed by the governor of the land" (v. 22), and Lachoneus was certainly not going to allow such wickedness. So, "many of those who testified of the things pertaining to Christ . . . were taken and put to death secretly by the judges, that the knowledge of their death came not unto the governor of the land until after their death" (v. 23).

3 Nephi 6:27–30 • Secret combinations increase and people divide into tribes. Under such lawless conditions, one could not trust anyone except their kin—and sometimes not even them. The chief judges and their families formed tribes that were ruled by these judges, and they were joined by "almost all the lawyers and the high priests" (v. 27).

These tribal groups "did enter into a covenant one with another" (v. 28). This was the same ancient covenants and signs that had begun with Cain and had destroyed so many peoples since that time—including, recently, the Gadianton robbers. Mormon says these secret cults were "administered by the devil, to combine against all righteousness," to "combine against the people of the Lord . . . to destroy them," and to protect those among their cult "who were guilty of murder" from any accountability under the law (v. 28). They "set at defiance the law and the rights of their country," openly defying the law, and they made secret oaths to "destroy the governor, and to establish a king over the land" (vv. 29–30).

3 Nephi 7:1–5 • The central government breaks down entirely. The secret cults were not successful in establishing a king over the land, but they did manage to murder the chief judge Lachoneus (v. 1). Because they were divided into separate family tribes, they could not have a central government and had thus destroyed the system of government that had been in place since the days of Mosiah (vv. 1–2). "And every tribe did appoint a chief or a leader over them; and thus they became tribes and leaders of tribes" (v. 3). These tribes were very large, and to this point they did not engage in wars among them, but we are told that "all this iniquity had come upon the people because they did yield themselves unto the power of Satan" (v. 5).

Daniel H. Ludlow said, "When the central government was destroyed, the people divided 'into tribes, every man according to his family and his kindred and friends' (3 Nephi 7:2). The strong family ties indicated here are reminiscent of the emphasis of the early Hebrews on the family. After the appearance of the resurrected Jesus Christ to these people, they again have a strong central government for over three hundred years. However, after that time, the government begins to disintegrate and by the close of the Book of Mormon almost complete anarchy exists. Apparently after AD 400 the people divide into tribes again, or this is the system of government they had when the white man came almost 1,000 years later."[15]

3 Nephi 7:15–20 • (AD 31–33) • Nephi cries repentance and performs great miracles— healing and raising the dead. During the period of time when the Savior was teaching and performing miracles in the Holy Land, the great prophet Nephi, the son of Nephi, was doing the same thing among the Nephites. He was "visited by angels and also the voice of the Lord," thus becoming an eyewitness to the Lord's ministry, or, as we would call such persons, an apostle. Sadly, he was also an eyewitness to his people's "quick return from righteousness unto their wickedness and abominations" (v. 15).

Being "grieved for the hardness of their hearts and the blindness of their minds," he "went forth among them in that same year, and began to testify, boldly, repentance and remission of sins through faith on the Lord Jesus Christ," just as his father had done before him (v. 16). Mormon tells us that Nephi "did minister many things unto them; and all of them cannot be written, and a part of them would not suffice, therefore they are not written in this book" (v. 17). But we are assured that "Nephi did minister with power and with great authority" (v. 17).

We might expect that such manifestations of miracles and powerful preaching would cause the people to take notice and repent. One might think the same thing about the people among whom the Savior ministered during this same time. But in both cases, many of the people "were angry with him, even because he had greater power than they, for it were not possible that they could disbelieve his words, for so great was his faith on the Lord Jesus Christ that angels did minister unto him daily" (v. 18). In the name of Jesus Christ, Nephi "cast out devils and unclean spirits; and even his brother did he raise from the dead after he had been stoned and suffered death by the people" (v. 19). They saw this miracle for themselves but it only made them "angry with him because of his power" (v. 20). Still, he carried on, doing "many more miracles, in the sight of the people, in the name of Jesus" (v. 20).

3 Nephi 7:21–26 • Nephi and his converts continue to perform miracles and to baptize those who are converted. Sadly, very few people were converted by the miracles and preaching of Nephi, but those who were converted "did truly signify unto the people that they had been visited by the power and Spirit of God" (v. 21). Many of them "had devils cast out from them, and were healed of their sicknesses and their infirmities . . . and they did show forth signs also and did do some miracles among the people" (v. 22). They continued, with limited success, for the next two years, "preaching repentance unto the people and baptizing all who would believe in Jesus Christ . . . as a witness and a testimony before God, and unto the people, that they had repented and received a remission of their sins" (vv. 23–24, 26). All those who joined Nephi in this ministry were "ordained of Nephi" to do so (v. 26) and continued to do so right up to the end of 33 AD—when the Savior was crucified on the other side of the earth, and the destruction of the wicked began among the Nephites.

Delbert L. Stapley said, "This account of wickedness and contentions among the Nephites prior to the Lord's birth in the meridian of time is duplicated in the wickedness, contentions, and deceptions of our day as we approach the second coming of our Lord and Savior Jesus Christ. Prophecies concerning these days are also being fulfilled and Satan is stirring up the hearts of men to do iniquity continually: and to thwart, if possible, faith in the great event of Christ's second coming to earth, which I testify is sure to come to pass. Satan is alert and active. We must be more alert and perceptive of the false and insincere schemes of his agents among us."[16]

The Book of Mormon—A Record for Our Day

3 Nephi 5:8–19 • Mormon describes himself and his record. In the middle of this part of the record, Mormon said, "There had many things transpired which, in the eyes of some, would be great and marvelous; nevertheless, they cannot all be written in this book; yea, this book cannot contain even a hundredth part of what was done among so many people in the space of twenty and five years" (v. 8). He assured us that "there are records which do contain all the proceedings of this people; and a shorter but true account was given by Nephi [the son of Nephi]" (vv. 9–10). It was from these original and more lengthy records that Mormon had condensed the events into the book we have before us today. He added, "I do make the record on plates which I have made with mine own hands" (v. 11).

At this point, Mormon, the abridger of the record that we are reading, offered some personal information, including, "I am called Mormon, being called after the land of Mormon, the land in which Alma did establish the church among the people" (v. 12). He adds, "I am a disciple of Jesus Christ" (v. 13) and "I am . . . a pure descendant of Lehi" (v. 20). He abridged his record from the records of those who came before him (v. 16) and also included the things which he had seen with his own eyes (v. 17). Finally, he testified that his record is true, though it contains only a small part of what took place (v. 18). And then, after this brief personal interlude, he stopped writing "of [him]self" and proceeds to, as he says it, "give my account of the things which have been before me" (v. 19).

3 Nephi 5:20–26 • Mormon prophesies concerning the house of Israel. Mormon tells us, as a direct descendant of Lehi, "I have reason to bless my God and my Savior Jesus Christ, that he brought our fathers out of the land of Jerusalem" (v. 20). He adds the interesting comment that "no one knew it save it were [Lehi] himself and those whom he brought out of that land," and is thankful that Lehi "hath given me and my people so much knowledge unto the salvation of our souls" (v. 20).

Mormon noted that the Lord "hath blessed the house of Jacob," "been merciful unto the seed of Joseph," and "insomuch as the children of Lehi have kept his commandments he hath blessed them and prospered them according to his word" (vv. 21–22). Speaking prophetically, he said that the Lord will, in the future, "bring a remnant of the seed of Joseph to the knowledge of the Lord their God" (v. 23). He was speaking here of latter-day Lamanites.

In addition, the Lord will "gather in from the four quarters of the earth all the remnant of the seed of Jacob, who are scattered abroad upon all the face of the earth" (v. 24). In that manner will "the covenant wherewith he hath covenanted with the house of Jacob be fulfilled in his own due time" (v. 25). "And then shall they know their Redeemer, who is Jesus Christ, the Son of God; and then shall they be gathered in from the four quarters of the earth unto their own lands, from whence they have been dispersed; yea, as the Lord liveth so shall it be. Amen" (v. 26).

Ezra Taft Benson said,

> The record of the Nephite history just prior to the Savior's visit reveals many parallels to our

own day as we anticipate the Savior's second coming. . . . In the Book of Mormon we find a pattern for preparing for the Second Coming. A major portion of the book centers on the few decades just prior to Christ's coming to America. By careful study of that time period, we can determine why some were destroyed in the terrible judgments that preceded His coming and what brought others to stand at the temple in the land of Bountiful and thrust their hands into the wounds of His hands and feet.

From the Book of Mormon we learn how disciples of Christ live in times of war. From the Book of Mormon we see the evils of secret combinations portrayed in graphic and chilling reality. In the Book of Mormon we find lessons for dealing with persecution and apostasy. We learn much about how to do missionary work. And more than anywhere else, we see in the Book of Mormon the dangers of materialism and setting our hearts on the things of the world. Can anyone doubt that this book was meant for us and that in it we find great power, great comfort, and great protection?[17]

Notes

1. Joseph Fielding Smith, *Answers to Gospel Questions*, Joseph Fielding Smith Jr., comp. (Salt Lake City: Deseret Book, 1957–1966), 5:38.
2. Joseph Fielding McConkie and Robert L. Millet, *Doctrinal New Testament Commentary* (Salt Lake City: Bookcraft, 1966–73), 4:190.
3. Joseph Fielding McConkie and Robert L. Millet, *Doctrinal Commentary on the Book of Mormon* (Salt Lake City: Bookcraft, 1987–1992), 3:17; 1 Nephi 2:23; 2 Nephi 5:21–24.
4. Joseph Fielding McConkie and Robert L. Millet, *Doctrinal Commentary on the Book of Mormon* (Salt Lake City: Deseret Book, 1987), 1:224.
5. Ibid., 3:17.
6. Bruce R. McConkie, *Mormon Doctrine*, 2nd ed. (Salt Lake City: Bookcraft, 1966), 175.
7. Joseph Fielding McConkie and Robert L. Millet, *Doctrinal Commentary on the Book of Mormon* (Salt Lake City: Deseret Book, 1987), 1:224.
8. Hugh Nibley, *Since Cumorah*, 2nd ed. (Salt Lake City: Deseret Book and the Foundation for Ancient Research and Mormon Studies, 1988), 216.
9. Hugh Nibley, *Since Cumorah*, 2nd ed. (Salt Lake City: Deseret Book and the Foundation for Ancient Research and Mormon Studies, 1988), 218.
10. Dean L. Lawrence, *You and the Destiny of the Indian* (Salt lake City: Bookcraft, 1966), 21–22.
11. Bruce R. McConkie, *Mormon Doctrine*, 2nd ed. (Salt Lake City: Bookcraft, 1966), 731.
12. Spencer W. Kimball, in Conference Report, Oct. 1947, 22.
13. George Q. Cannon, in Conference Report, Apr. 1898, 35.
14. Robert L. Simpson, in Conference Report, Apr. 1967, 69.
15. Daniel Ludlow, *A Companion to Your Study of the Book of Mormon* (Salt Lake City: Deseret Book, 1976), 238.
16. Delbert L. Stapley, in Conference Report, Oct. 1961, 22.
17. Ezra Taft Benson, in Conference Report, Oct. 1986, 5–6.

About the Author

Randal S. Chase spent his childhood years in Nephi, Utah, where his father was a dry land wheat farmer and a businessman. In 1959 their family moved to Salt Lake City and settled in the Holladay area. He served a full-time mission in the Central British (England Central) Mission from 1968 to 1970. He returned home and married Deborah Johnsen in 1971. They are the parents of six children—two daughters and four sons—and an ever-growing number of grandchildren.

He was called to serve as a bishop at the age of twenty-seven in the Sandy Crescent South Stake area of the Salt Lake Valley. He served six years in that capacity and has since served as a high councilor, a stake executive secretary and clerk, and in many other stake and ward callings. Regardless of whatever other callings he has received over the years, one was nearly constant: he has taught Gospel Doctrine classes in every ward he has ever lived in as an adult—for a total of thirty-five years.

Dr. Chase was a well-known media personality on Salt Lake City radio stations in the 1970s. He left on-air broadcasting in 1978 to develop and market a computer-based management, sales, and music programming system to radio and television stations in the United States, Canada, South America, and Australia. After the business was sold in 1984, he supported his family as a media and business consultant in the Salt Lake City area.

Having a great desire to teach young people of college age, he determined in the late 1980s to pursue his doctorate, and received his Ph.D. in communication from the University of Utah in 1997. He has taught communication courses at that institution as well as at Salt Lake Community College and Dixie State College of Utah for twenty-one years. He is currently a full-time faculty member and Communication Department Chair at Dixie State College in St. George, Utah.

Concurrently with his academic career, brother Chase has served as a volunteer LDS Institute and Adult Education instructor in the CES system since 1974, both in Salt Lake City and St. George, where he currently teaches a weekly Adult Education class for three stakes in the Washington area. He has also conducted multiple Church history tours and seminars. During these years of gospel teaching, he has developed an extensive library of lesson plans and handouts that are the predecessors to these study guides.